JOHN
MULLAN

JOHN
MULLAN

The Tumultuous Life of a Western Road Builder

KEITH C. PETERSEN

WSU
PRESS

Washington State University Press
Pullman, Washington

WASHINGTON STATE
UNIVERSITY

Washington State University Press
PO Box 645910
Pullman, Washington 99164-5910
Phone: 800-354-7360
Fax: 509-335-8568
Email: wsupress@wsu.edu
Website: wsupress.wsu.edu

Library of Congress Cataloging-in-Publication Data

Petersen, Keith C.
  John Mullan : the tumultuous life of a western road builder / by Keith C.
  Petersen.
    pages cm
  Includes bibliographical references and index.
  ISBN 978-0-87422-321-7 (alk. paper)
  1. Northwest, Pacific—Biography. 2. Mullan, John, 1830-1909. 3. Mullan
  Road—History. 4. Military engineers—United States—Biography. 5. United
  States. Army. Corps of Engineers—Officers—Biography. 6. Explorers—West
  (U.S.)—Biography. 7. Surveyors—West (U.S.)—Biography. 8. Lawyers—United
  States—Biography. 9. Washington (D.C.)—Biography. I. Title.
  F852.P38 2014
  623'.62092—dc23
  [B]

                                                              2014001207

On the cover: John Mullan took a rare day off from road building in 1861 to visit Palouse
Falls. His longtime assistant and friend Gustavus Sohon made this sketch. "A beautiful and
interesting falls," Mullan wrote. "The whole river...here leaps in a single sheet over a rocky
ledge...a picturesque scene well worth a visit." *Washington State University Libraries, Manuscripts, Archives, and Special Collections.*

This project was supported by a Research Fellowship from the Idaho Humanities Council,
the state-based affiliate of the National Endowment for the Humanities

To my cousin, Ted Craig

Thanks for the companionship while
on the trail of John Mullan

Contents

John Mullan posed for few photographs. This one, taken in Washington, D.C., in the early 1860s, is the most recognized image of the road builder. *John Mullan Papers, Georgetown University Library, Special Collections Research Center, Washington, D.C.*

Prologue

Twenty-five-year-old Rebecca Mullan found herself in Manhattan on May 7, 1863, Cyrus Field at her elbow. Field, the "world-renowned parent" of the first transatlantic telegraph cable, guided Rebecca through the grand Clinton Hall at Astor Place, selecting two seats from which to observe the evening's lectures at the American Geographical and Statistical Society. Captain John Mullan, her husband of ten days, would deliver the night's first oration—on the Pacific Northwest—a region he knew as well as any man; a place Rebecca would soon call home.[1]

Rebecca sat anxiously as Henry Grinnell, the society's president and founder, advanced to the podium to introduce her husband. Grinnell, retired from the family transatlantic shipping business for thirteen years, now focused on financing polar expeditions. Grinnell Land, a peninsula deep in the Canadian arctic, bore his name, testimony to exploration philanthropy. The thirty-two-year-old Mullan, well educated, self-assured, and the focus of considerable press attention himself as "The Northwest Road Builder," confidently commenced his address "in compliance with your polite invitation to lay before the Society such geographical facts as my explorations in the Rocky Mountains have developed."[2]

Mullan described his time with Isaac Stevens's Pacific Railroad Survey when he explored five possible rail routes through the Rocky Mountains. He detailed his multi-year effort to construct a military road connecting the Missouri and Columbia Rivers, finally fulfilling Thomas Jefferson's vision when he had sent Lewis and Clark west fifty years earlier. He narrated tales of the region's Indians.

Mostly, he lauded the land and its potential. "All the elements of happy homes are here to be found," he said. "Let those who have never traveled through this…region make once…the journey and see for

1

themselves…grand mountains and useful rivers, forests of orchards and oceans of grain, miles of sluice boxes and tons of gold." To an audience two years into a bloody, protracted civil war, Mullan offered hope. In the Northwest, "the Chinaman…dines side by side with the French voyager…or the burly Englishman…and hence…political homogeneity shall result."

In all this land of aspiration and beauty, no place held greater potential than Walla Walla in eastern Washington Territory, where John and Rebecca would soon reside. "Wheat, oats, barley, and corn are here produced in rich abundance," he enthused. "Apples, pears and peaches here grow well….Potatoes yield 400 to 600 bushels to the acre."

As Mullan spoke that night, he might have reflected on the recent exploits of his West Point classmate Phil Sheridan, promoted to Major General just days earlier following heroic action in the Civil War. But Mullan likely had no regrets about his own recent resignation from the army; he foresaw his main chance as a civilian entrepreneur, capitalizing on his reputation as builder of the first engineered highway in the Northwest, the one already gaining notoriety as the chief supply course for booming western El Dorados.

Mullan spoke on—and on: thirty minutes, sixty, ninety. Always meticulously well prepared for any task, Mullan's zeal served him poorly on this evening. Henry Grinnell must have grown restless, for the main attraction remained to come, a report on the Arctic explorations of Captain C.F. Hall, now deterred well into the night. Mullan's discourse underwhelmed *The New York Times*, which charitably termed his presentation "a lengthy but still interesting paper," before devoting the bulk of its story to the ongoing Arctic excitement.[3]

As Mullan accompanied Rebecca out of Clinton Hall late that evening, it would not have occurred to either that Mullan's career might have peaked a few hours earlier as he prepared to give his invited presentation to the nation's most prestigious geographical organization. Until then, Mullan's life had been an ascending arc: presidential appointee to West Point, explorer extraordinaire, aspirant to become Idaho's first territorial governor, recently-appointed commissioner of a western railroad. Rebecca and John, still relishing this honeymoon evening spent with luminaries, had no way of knowing that their future held considerably less predictability.

Prelude

OUT WEST, 1841

I N MAY 1841 JOHN MULLAN could look upon his surroundings at the Preparatory School of St. John's College in Annapolis, Maryland, and observe the following: a brick boardinghouse and classroom; wood-frame stable, barn, woodshed, and meat house; and two privies. Some trees provided a hint of landscaped order to the rustic scene.[1]

Probably the ten-year-old Mullan did not contemplate the West as he walked these grounds. But the West would one day beckon, and in that May of 1841, two men who would wield considerable influence over Mullan—a future California businessman and a priest—serendipitously met in the small town of Westport, Missouri, as they prepared to venture into a land virtually unknown to whites. Fewer than six thousand non-Indians resided in California, and probably less than two hundred in all of what became Montana, Idaho, Washington, and Oregon. Of the multitude of wagon trains that would cross the nineteenth-century West, it could be argued that this one was the most significant.

Teacher John Bidwell had come under the influence of French fur trader Antoine Robidoux, who spoke so highly of California that the twenty-one-year-old Bidwell joined the Western Emigration Society, an assemblage of five hundred people determined to claim new lives on the Pacific Coast. By the time the group gathered in Missouri for the excursion west, its numbers had shrunk to sixty diehards, the rest frightened away by reports of dangers confronting Americans venturing into Mexican-controlled California. None of the exiles knew the route; the Oregon and California trails did not yet exist. They postponed their departure until Jesuit priest Pierre-Jean DeSmet and his guide could arrive.[2]

Heeding numerous pleas from Flathead Indians over the course of a decade, DeSmet had finally convinced his superiors in 1840 to authorize his travel west to investigate potential mission sites. In that year, he

3

journeyed as far as what became eastern Idaho before returning to St. Louis, convinced of the practicality of providing missionary services in the Northwest. In May 1841 he, along with six other Jesuits and their guide, fur trader Thomas "Broken Hand" Fitzpatrick, prepared to head west to establish missions. They agreed to travel with the Western Emigration Society. As the only ones familiar with the country, Fitzpatrick and DeSmet led the way, followed by the twenty wagons of the Emigration Society—an expedition "composed of a curious collection of individuals," in DeSmet's estimation.[3]

Fitzpatrick knew the region well. He had been trapping in the West since 1823. He brooked no stragglers. Some in the 1841 caravan turned back, unable to keep up with Fitzpatrick's unyielding pace. Those who remained crossed the Rockies at South Pass and proceeded to Soda Springs, in what would become Idaho. There the expedition split into three parties. Twenty-two emigrants made their way across southern Idaho on a route pioneered the year before when some mountain men took the first wagons overland to the Columbia River. These 1841 voyagers continued to the Willamette Valley, the vanguard of thousands over what became the Oregon Trail.[4]

Flathead Indians led DeSmet and his Jesuits north to the Bitterroot Valley, becoming the first to take wagons across the continental divide at Monida Pass into what became Montana—a route John Mullan would retrace a dozen years later. Once in Montana, DeSmet established the first Catholic mission in the interior Northwest near where Mullan would construct winter quarters in 1853–54.[5]

The third party of those 1841 emigrants, under the leadership of John Bartleson and John Bidwell, veered south to the Great Salt Lake, headed into the Great Basin, and, near starvation, reached San Francisco at the end of October, the first American party to cross the Sierra Nevada into California, pioneers of what became—with numerous alterations—the California Trail. Bidwell sent the diary of his 1841 trip to the East where, a year later, it became the first of dozens of published overland emigrant guides that enticed ever more settlers west; Mullan would add to that body of literature with his own manual in 1865. Bidwell eventually moved north to found the town of Chico, where he would form a business partnership with John Mullan in the 1860s.

In that same spring of 1841, a man twelve years Mullan's senior resided up the coast from Annapolis, in Newport, Rhode Island. He was as unconversant with the West as Mullan, but, like Mullan, was destined to be forever linked to that country. Second Lieutenant Isaac Stevens graduated from West Point at the head of his class in 1839 and, now assigned to duties at Fort Adams, found ample time to enjoy Newport's robust social life. He appeared with increasing frequency that spring with Margaret Hazard, descendant of two prominent Newport families. Married in September, they honeymooned at West Point—as would John and Rebecca Mullan in 1863. Mullan and Stevens did not yet know each other, but no person would have a greater influence on Mullan's life.[6]

Just twelve years after the wagon train headed west out of Missouri into virtually uncharted land, twelve years after DeSmet "set up a large cross in the middle of camp" in the Bitterroot Valley, Isaac Stevens and John Mullan would make their own passage west to search routes for a possible transcontinental railroad into the rapidly growing region. Pierre-Jean DeSmet could hardly have imagined such rapid transformation of the country as he accompanied the wagons out of Missouri in 1841 into a land few whites then knew.[7]

CHAPTER 1

ᛦ

Annapolis

THE STREETS OF ANNAPOLIS spread from the state capitol and St.
Anne's Church in perplexing diagonals, sectioning the city into
oddly shaped blocks. Annapolis exhibits none of the symmetry one
might imagine if contemplating the spokes of a wheel. This city's plat
is more haphazard, as asymmetrical streets dissect gridded avenues at
bewildering angles. All this is set upon a peninsula jaggedly indented
by Chesapeake Bay and cut through by the meandering Severn River.

The second Royal Governor of Maryland, Francis Nicholson, probably had a more orderly vision when he moved Maryland's capital here
in the late seventeenth century, named the place in honor of Princess
Anne (soon to become England's queen) and directed that the city be
built on the model of great European capitals, with streets emanating
from the centers of political and religious authority. Annapolis became
the political, social, cultural, and economic hub of Maryland.[1]

To this peninsular community migrated families of wealth and
influence. It was here, at Maryland's capital in the center of Nicholson's
most prominent hub, that George Washington tendered his resignation from the Continental Army, Congress ratified the treaty ending the
Revolutionary War, and Thomas Jefferson spent a pleasant afternoon in
the capitol dome's soaring balcony, relishing the spectacular views.

Young John Mullan could be excused if he failed to recognize
Nicholson's planned elegance as he weaved his way through his home-
town's jumble of intersecting streets and pedestrian pathways. John
Mullan Sr. and his wife, Mary Bright Mullan, moved to Annapolis
from Norfolk, Virginia, in 1833, along with three-year-old John Jr. and
his two-year-old sister Mary—the first two of eleven Mullan children.
By then, Baltimore had long eclipsed Annapolis as a commercial and
cultural center, and elegance did not now always come to the minds of

Annapolis residents and visitors. Pedestrians like young John Mullan had to navigate carefully through streets that billowed with dust in the dry season and stuck like gumbo in the wet, avoiding gutters streaming foul wastes to the waterfront. Residents dumped garbage directly in the streets. John Mullan Sr. once complained that the street in front of his house "during the rain is always in terrible condition," and the Mullan property in spring flooded with effluent "bringing with it filth of all kind." Mullan requested the flow, "provocative of disease," be routed directly into the Bay.[2]

But Annapolis still had trappings of grandeur, and these helped form the world view of John Mullan Jr. The modest Mullan house, jammed with children, sat on the pie-shaped southwestern corner of the block formed by East, Maryland, King George, and Prince George streets. Three of Annapolis's most stately mansions lined the periphery, reminders of the city's prime.[3]

Exiting the Mullan house at 30 East Street and walking north, John would have first come to the Brice house, an eighteenth-century plantation manor that dominated the neighborhood. Turning east onto Prince George Street would have brought Mullan to an even more imposing mansion, constructed by former governor William Paca, its two-acre garden nearly abutting the Mullan house. And turning again onto Maryland Avenue brought into view the home constructed by Matthias Hammond, an inspiration for Thomas Jefferson's Monticello.

The juxtaposition between these stately mansions and John Mullan's own modest frame house could not have been more stark. Mullan's lifelong aspiration to emulate these childhood neighbors, to attain wealth—sometimes skirting ethical and legal boundaries—began here.

Perhaps equally influential upon his future endeavors was the view up East Street. Stepping out of his house, Mullan's eyes would have been attracted to the dignified, wooden octagonal statehouse dome. Here a young man, incubating a lifelong interest in politics, could sit in the ballustraded spectators' galleries to view spirited debates in the same building that had witnessed some of the nation's most dramatic political events.

If he journeyed past the capitol he might have ended at nearby St. John's College, where John enrolled in the preparatory department as a nine-year-old. Once he began classes at St. John's, Mullan—like the seventy or so other students at the male-only school—had little exposure to the community. St. John's faculty feared the town's wicked influence. The faculty forbade students from leaving the college grounds except to attend Sunday services.[4]

Students lived in "The Boardinghouse," second-oldest building on campus, constructed in 1835. McDowell Hall stood as the only other substantial structure. In this cupola-topped, three-story building, John Mullan took his classes, just as had St. John's students for half a century.

Those students learned the classics, in their original Greek and Latin. They studied history, algebra, geometry, logic, and philosophy. They learned to debate, criticize the fine arts, and appreciate civics. But St. John's also taught the sciences, courses made to order for a student like Mullan, destined to become an engineer. To receive his degree, Mullan also took classes in weights, distances, navigation, surveying, chemistry, mineralogy, and geology—all useful subjects in his later western explorations.

Mullan grew up in a crowded home headed by an army sergeant. Orderliness and discipline came as second nature, attributes that characterized Mullan his entire life. While some St. John's students chafed under the school's austere rules, there is no indication that these displeased Mullan. Strict bedtime curfews, combined with decrees so draconian they led to expulsion for playing cards or sneaking off campus, led some St. John's students to rebel, but Mullan contentedly remained on campus for eight years, completing his prep schooling and receiving his AB degree in 1847.[5]

Although Annapolis at this time retained some remnants of the city's glorious past, essentially it was a poor community. Wealthy families elsewhere in Maryland seldom sent their sons to St. John's, which suffered financially along with the city. The student body became "completely local and in-bred," according to the school's historian. But for the Mullans, it served as an only hope for a family that valued education but could afford to pay little. All of John's brothers—James, Charles, Horace, Louis, Dennis, and Ferdinand—followed him to St. John's.[6]

A native of Ireland and passionately Catholic, John Mullan Sr. might have preferred it had St. John's mandated attendance at Catholic services. But despite its name, St. John's had no religious affiliation, welcoming students of all faiths. While the campus maintained a small chapel, it did not require attendance. But on Sundays the school relaxed its rules obligating students to remain on campus so those who desired could attend services in town. Given his strong religious background, young John Mullan no doubt took full advantage of the privilege.

Along with the capitol, St. Anne's Episcopal Church dominated Annapolis. But Catholics worshipped at a more modest facility. In the words of one city historian, "the handful of Catholics feebly held their own in the little chapel that [Charles] Carroll's...beneficence had built." Carroll, born in Annapolis in 1737 and educated by Jesuits in Europe, returned to America at the outbreak of the Revolutionary War, eventually becoming one of America's richest men. Despite suffering disenfranchisement in Maryland, as did all Catholics, Carroll supported the revolutionary cause, becoming the only Catholic signer of the Declaration of Independence.[7]

In the 1820s, Annapolis Catholics erected St. Mary's Church on ground provided by Carroll. On those Sundays when he left campus to attend services, John Mullan entered the small church through double doors under a stepped gable facade topped by a cross and a stone panel with the inscription "D.O.M."—*Deo Optimo Maximo*, "To God, Great and Good." On most Sundays, lay ministers served the congregants. Jesuit priest Mathew Sanders visited Annapolis once a month at best. But Mullan would have known him; it was here that Mullan's lifelong appreciation for Jesuits originated.[8]

Although St. Mary's parishioners included some people of influence—a former mayor, a physician, a lawyer, and proprietors of various businesses—the congregation had modest means. St. Mary's could not afford a resident priest. While most African American churchgoers belonged to Protestant congregations, a number were Catholics. And the poor African Americans attending the church, like their white counterparts, could afford to contribute little. By 1850, 40 percent of Annapolis residents were black, a little less than half of them enslaved. The Mullans lived in a neighborhood with free black residents. It is unclear if his early association with African Americans had any impact on Mullan's adult inclinations. He would express many of the racial views that characterized his generation. On the other hand, his opinions of Indians could at times be quite enlightened. Regardless, Mullan's association with African Americans while coming of age in Annapolis differed from many white Americans of the time, for their free black neighbors were the economic equals of the Mullans.[9]

Annapolis's fortunes began to improve in 1845 when Secretary of War William Marcy transferred Fort Severn, on Windmill Point, to the jurisdiction of the Secretary of the Navy, George Bancroft. Bancroft, attracted by "the healthy and secluded" location of Annapolis, believed the fort would provide an isolated campus for his proposed United States Naval School, where midshipmen would be free from "the temptations and distractions that necessarily connect with a large and populous city." Annapolis did not rise phoenix-like after the transfer. But its decline in the first half of the nineteenth century ironically led to its ascent in the latter half, as the small community provided just the quietude that George Bancroft sought, and his Naval School brought economic growth. Between 1840 and 1880, Annapolis's population doubled and economic opportunity improved, the Mullans among the beneficiaries.[10]

In addition to transferring the 1808 fort and surrounding ten acres to the Navy, Marcy also requested that Ordinance Sergeant John Mullan Sr., a twenty-two-year army veteran then serving at Severn, be permitted to remain at the new school to perform "such light duties as might be assigned him as a servant for long and faithful service." And there, on naval grounds, the professional army man spent the rest of his career.[11]

In the thinly staffed school, Mullan undertook multiple tasks, including "the cleaning of all the Students' Quarters, pavements, cellars, &c, &c." And he performed well. Despite being "quite advanced in years," Naval Academy Superintendent L.M. Goldsborough requested that the fifty-four-year-old Mullan be retained as a Seaman when the army refused to reenlist him. The army and navy agreed to the unusual request for a transfer among services, for it seemed a hardship to discharge this man of few resources who had "spent the best years of his life in the service." On June 9, 1855, Goldsborough received permission to change Sergeant Mullan's title to Seaman Mullan, and, albeit with a change in employers, the elder Mullan remained at the same place of employment.[12]

The Naval Academy provided an isolated haven for midshipmen and a paycheck for John Mullan Sr. But at the time John Mullan Jr. sought a free education beyond St. John's, the naval school received no congressional funding, and its fifty students took classes in dilapidated wooden buildings. While Mullan had brothers who attended the Naval Academy, John sought a more established and better-funded institution. He wanted to attend West Point.

Despite its modest means, the staunchly Democratic Mullan family had connections in Democratic Annapolis; John Mullan Sr. briefly served as a city alderman. Not surprisingly, John Jr. found influential support for his appointment to West Point.[13]

Annapolis cabinetmaker Thomas Franklin wrote that Mullan was "a young man of much promise" who will "at a future day, be an accomplished officer in the army." St. John's College President Hector Humphreys testified that "John Mullan...is a young Gentleman of excellent moral character and assiduous habits of study," adding, "I have...never known him to do anything wrong." And the entire Democratic delegation of the Maryland legislature petitioned fellow Democrat James K. Polk—President of the United States—to recommend his "favourable consideration" of the West Point appointment of Mullan, whose "general deportment has allways been such as to receive the best wishes of the community where he resides."[14]

Mullan's life would be marked by bulldogged determination, and he demonstrated this trait in his effort to become a West Point cadet. He audaciously journeyed to Washington, D.C., letters and petition in hand, to speak directly to the president. In the scant biographical literature about Mullan, one story is often repeated, frequently embellished. It got its start in 1892 when his wife Rebecca wrote her reminiscences:

> He got influential friends to give him letters....Armed with these he proceeded to Washington, to present his letters and desires before James K. Polk....He often tells us how he, a poor boy without influence, rather shy yet with high ambitions and an unswerving will, entered the presence of the Chief Magistrate of the Nation....
>
> Polk was reclining in an arm-chair, his feet resting on the mantel place, smoking an ordinary clay pipe. Extending his hand to John, he said,
>
> "Well, my little man, what can I do for you?"
>
> John told him of his desire to enter the army by graduating at West Point. After questioning him for some time the President said:
>
> "Well, my young friend, leave your address, and I will see what I can do for you."[15]

Despite all the trappings of an apocryphal tale, the story is essentially true. Mullan did travel to Washington, D.C., in 1848 to seek an appointment. While Polk's papers do not verify that he gained an audience with the president, they do not disprove it either: Access to presidents proved easy in the nineteenth century, and Polk saw many visitors who remain anonymous today, unlisted in official records. Polk took a more active interest in West Point than any pre-Civil War president, and fully used his authority to appoint cadets; he made John Mullan one of ten at-large selections to the class of 1852. "I was taken by the hand by President Polk," Mullan later wrote, "and by him educated at West Point."[16]

Mullan's father died in 1863, his mother Mary in 1888. John Jr., late in life, proposed that his daughters erect a "Memorial Building" at the site of his childhood home to honor his family. Anticipating a generous payment from the State of California for long overdue—but disputed— legal fees, Mullan instructed his daughters to set aside $6,000 for the project. But as happened so often in his life, monetary aspirations far exceeded his financial reality. The expected legal fees never materialized. Annapolis would never host a memorial to this modest family that produced a son honored by dozens of monuments in the West.[17]

CHAPTER 2

🌿

West Point

JOHN MULLAN DISEMBARKED THE STEAMER at the small wharf along
the Hudson River on June 3, 1848. Loading his sparse belongings
onto a waiting wagon, he followed the horse-drawn cart up the steep
hill to his home for the next four years—the campus of the U.S. Military Academy at West Point, New York. Making his way to the school's
treasury, he handed over all of his pocket cash, $35. West Point safeguarded the sums in a "Treasurer's Account," providing cadets with
credit for purchasing such things as cakes, cookies, and other snacks
from the barracks soda shop; administrators allowed no cash on campus. Mullan's life as a civilian—at least for the foreseeable future—had
ended. "I will serve in the army of the United States for eight years" he
pledged, a return on the government's investment in a free education.[1]

Even by Mullan's past experience with modest accommodations,
his barracks room was Spartan: furniture consisted of two metal beds
and two metal desks with chairs. Like other cadets of this era, Mullan
probably walked that first day to the commissary, picked up a slate,
bucket, tin washbasin, candlestick, and sundry items, tied them in a
blanket, inserted the academy-issued broom handle through the knot,
and shouldered the load back to his new quarters. Among the articles
he unpacked were a dozen sheets of West Point stationery. "If there is
in the world a faithful correspondent, it is a new cadet during his first
weeks at the Military Academy," reminisced one student of the time.
Though his West Point letters no longer exist, John Mullan—always
bonded to Annapolis and family—no doubt wrote home frequently.
Surely he noted his meager quarters, for during his tenure at the academy his mother shipped him a four-drawer, mirrored chiffonier as well
as an ornate crystal-prismed candlestick to add refinement to his barren
chambers.[2]

Mullan arrived on campus with the lean build of an athlete, a handsome young man with deep-set blue eyes, the high forehead of one prematurely balding, square chin, and dark hair prone to curling. At 5'4", he stood slightly shorter than average, but several inches taller than the minimum height standards for cadets. He entered a forty-six-year-old post situated on a high plain overlooking the splendid Hudson River Valley. "Sublimity and beauty...spread out before us," recalled one cadet.[3]

On that first day, Mullan probably marched on the parade grounds in civilian clothes—a comical sight much anticipated by locals and upperclassmen with the arrival of each summer's class of plebes. "As we marched, or tried to march, there was a constant losing of step, occasioning the most ludicrous and...vexatious shuffling, stumbling, and kicking of heels," noted one cadet. But they would improve; much marching lay in their future, particularly during annual summer encampments, when cadets practiced soldiering. But this was a school that mostly produced engineers.[4]

By the time Mullan arrived West Point stood as the preeminent civil engineering college in the United States, a response to the needs of a rapidly expanding nation and its thirst for internal improvements. The school's graduates furnished "science for exploring the hidden treasures of our mountains and ameliorating the agriculture of our valleys."[5]

Although the academy had emphasized science since its founding by President Thomas Jefferson, its reputation as an engineering school came with Superintendent Sylvanus Thayer, who transformed the curriculum during his tenure between 1817 and 1833. Thayer and superintendents who followed viewed their mission "as being the production of engineers who could function as soldiers rather than the reverse." It was a most suitable environment for a future road builder.[6]

Mullan and his classmates spent about 70 percent of classroom time on mathematics, science, and engineering. All other subjects—tactics, French, philosophy, grammar—competed for the remainder. Virtually all classroom instruction emphasized recitation. For hours each day, cadets memorized answers to lessons they replicated the next day in class. Success at West Point depended more upon rote learning than innovative thinking. At week's end, instructors reported grades to the superintendent; monthly summaries went to parents. John Mullan's father, for one, eagerly awaited those reports. "I have not got my sons standing for October 1850," he once wrote. "If you would be so kind as to send it to me." Twice a year, cadets completed general examinations. These established a cadet's ranking in his class, with some subjects—notably math, science, and engineering—weighted more heavily than others. A cadet's final class standing proved all important in determining the branch of service a graduate would enter, as well as his placement on the promotion list.[7]

West Point cadets awoke to reveille at dawn. Having cleaned their rooms and passed inspection, they headed to breakfast. Lights went out with evening tattoo at 10:00 p.m. Between those times, they spent about ten hours studying or in class, three in military exercises, two recreating, and two hours at meals. On Saturday nights they could attend plays, concerts, or debates.[8]

Despite the engineering emphasis, West Pointers did drill, receiving training in infantry, artillery, cavalry tactics, fencing, and equitation. Summer encampments provided the best occasion to augment soldiering skills.[9]

Over the course of a long life, beginning with the personal audience with President Polk leading to his West Point appointment, John Mullan met some of the most intriguing characters of nineteenth century America. The first summer's encampment in 1848 introduced him to two classmates—Phil Sheridan and George Crook—destined to become among the country's most decorated generals. Mullan also met another future general—and presidential candidate—that first summer, Captain George B. McClellan. McClellan had graduated from West Point in 1846 and returned as an instructor the same month as Mullan arrived. He endured three rocky years at the academy, exhibiting the traits that made him "one of the most difficult subordinate officers with whom any commander at the time had to deal." The paths of McClellan and Mullan would cross a few years later in the West, when Mullan learned first-hand of McClellan's intransigence—the same that would so exasperate President Lincoln during the Civil War.[10]

During his time at the academy, Mullan would have known America's preeminent civil engineering theoretician, Dennis Hart Mahan, the engineering department head who, more than anyone else, guided West Point to its position as the nation's outstanding engineering school. Mullan studied natural and experimental philosophy from William H.C.

Bartlett, one of the country's distinguished scholars of astronomy and mechanics. Mullan's class was among the first to ascertain how to plot routes with a compass and odometer—a skill he would practice extensively in the West. In mineralogy and geology he learned to accurately describe geological formations and mineral deposits. Mullan later complained of his "many and frequent annoyances" while studying French, but he took his requisite two years, which proved fortunate in his later dealings with Western tribes, some of which also had acquaintance with the language, gained from trappers and Jesuit missionaries. What will seem astonishing to anyone who has attempted to decipher his handwriting, Mullan, like all cadets, passed a penmanship exam. Despite finishing in the middle of his class in all-important engineering, he did better in most other disciplines, enabling him to rank fifteenth out of forty-three at graduation.[11]

Mullan's required studies served him well during his time in the West. And his extracurricular reading reflected his fascination with that region. The academy provided all required textbooks; cadets did not need to use the library to succeed in class. The library's fifteen thousand volumes, geared to support the faculty, skewed heavily toward science, mathematics, engineering, and military affairs. Some cadets used the library extensively; others not at all. Throughout his tenure at West Point, Mullan regularly checked out books.[12]

The Class of 1852 attended the academy at a time of burgeoning interest in the West. The young nation had just completed the process of expanding its boundaries to the Pacific. Even more on people's minds was California and gold. Mullan's reading had a Western bent. He perused everything by Washington Irving, including works on Oregon, Astoria, and Benjamin Bonneville; several books on Mexico and the Mexican war; and he tackled George Kendall's multivolume *Santa Fe Expedition*.[13]

Visions of Western fortune might have inspired Mullan, who always dreamed of improving his lot beyond his modest Annapolis childhood. But on Saturday night, January 19, 1850, he nearly relinquished all chance at a West Point degree and the opportunities it promised. He played cards, and for that authorities arrested him, along with classmates John Forney, Hugh Fleming, and Alfred Latimer. Rule 114 of the academy's *Regulations* clearly pronounced the consequences: Get caught playing cards and risk "being dismissed [from] the service of the United States."[14]

For four agonizing days Mullan and his cohorts endured confinement, awaiting court martial and possible dismissal. Then Superintendent Henry Brewerton abruptly released them. The rational is a bit complex. Cadets faced dismissal for both drinking and card playing, vices that plagued the academy and its reputation. But the school retained an alternative to automatic expulsion: the superintendent could pardon cadets if their entire class pledged to abstain from the offense in question during their length of stay at West Point. With their classmates' promise "not to violate in any manner" Rule 114, Superintendent Brewerton, "in view of the high standing and previous exemplary conduct of some of the delinquent Cadets," reprieved them all. No doubt the superintendent had Mullan particularly in mind when considering "high standing and…exemplary conduct," for at the time Mullan stood eighth in the class—far higher than the other offenders—and had far fewer demerits than his card-playing associates.[15]

This leniency aside, Mullan attended West Point at a time of heightened discipline. Superintendent Brewerton proved unwilling to replicate the "reprehensible course" of previous administrations "in allowing flagrant violations of the regulations of the Academy to go unpunished." Brewerton's decision to retain Mullan displayed tolerance not always forthcoming. Mullan entered West Point with Thomas Wright, another of the ten presidential appointees to the Class of 1852. Mullan would later serve under Wright's father, Colonel George Wright, in Washington Territory. During summer encampment in 1849, Thomas Wright absented himself "from his tent at night between tattoo and revile [reveille] for a longer period than half an hour," engendering a letter from Brewerton to Wright's distinguished father informing him that, with "sincere regret" he had dismissed his son from service.[16]

West Point enforced discipline with a demerit system that had peculiarities: Though he faced expulsion for playing cards, Mullan received no demerits for that serious offense. In fact, he received no demerits at all during that year, one of only three members of his class with perfect records for 1849–50. During the length of their time at the academy, Mullan's classmates averaged 295 demerits; Mullan made it through with 43.[17]

Mullan's temperament meshed well with West Point's demerit system. Demerits came in eight categories. First-grade offenses, such as unauthorized absences, received ten demerits; eighth-grade offenses, for things such as having improperly polished shoes, received two. A cadet receiving 200 demerits in a year faced discharge. Mullan's offenses were trivial. As a plebe learning the system he received demerits for "gazing about in ranks" and arriving tardy for dinner. Grooming proved his undoing for most demerits, as he preferred long hair and a mustache. His most serious offenses came for "visiting" during quiet time (five demerits), leaving his hair uncut for a month (five), and "neglect of duty [for] not delivering an official paper to the commandant promptly when asked for it" (four).[18]

The demerit system rewarded compliance, compensating "docility and punctilious obedience to a set of minutely detailed rules." Most times the system rewarded the Mullans of the academy and punished others not so drawn to conformity. Phil Sheridan—later known for his spontaneous initiative on battlefields—amassed 161 demerits through three years before being suspended; a few years later, George Armstrong Custer infamously led his class with 726. Mullan, on the other hand, proved over his lifetime an affinity for organization, discipline, and acquiescence—traits he attained at home, reinforced during his time at West Point.[19]

Cadets had to bathe once a week; those "desiring to bathe more than once a week" could "petition the superintendent." They had to attend chapel every Sunday, squeezed together on hard, backless benches for two-hour services. They were subject to inspection several times a day, privacy being "the rarest of luxuries at antebellum West Point." For Mullan, son of an Army ordnance sergeant used to discipline, from an overflowing house that provided little opportunity for privacy, the system worked. For the most part, he followed orders and adhered to rules.[20]

But even Mullan surely anticipated relief from all this structure and orderliness when he received his furlough in the summer of 1850. Summer furloughs following their second year at the post provided cadets with their only opportunity for extended leave, opportunities to reacquaint with family and homes; for some it would be their only time away during their entire tenure.

Mullan boarded a steamer for New York at noon on June 18, 1850, the first leg of his trip to Annapolis. He would return to the academy on August 28. Officers who accompanied Mullan and his classmates were instructed to ensure that the cadets left New York "without unnecessary delay" lest they come under the unhealthy influence of the city. The officers were to "immediately place in arrest, and order back to this Post, any Cadet who may be guilty of any irregularity, or impropriety of conduct."[21]

Not surprisingly, no irregularities occurred on the outbound journey; summer furloughs were too precious for a cadet to risk by acting recklessly. Pined one student: "Furlough…had been our daydream…in every leisure hour." Cadets returning to campus did not feel so compelled toward good conduct. A professor who accompanied cadets on the steamer returning to West Point a year after Mullan's leave complained of their "ungentlemanly conduct…from the use of spirits and tobacco…puffing their smoke among the ladies and using the most boisterous and profane language."[22]

It would have been within the realm of possibility for Mullan to have smoked, drank, and spoken profanely, but no serious scandal surrounded Mullan, his card-playing incident the only grave behavioral blemish during his West Point years. He had entered with seventy other classmates in 1848. These were not the children of America's elite. The academy listed one cadet from that class as from an affluent family. West Point, suffering from accusations as a "breeding ground for an aristocratic officer corps," diligently sought a broad representation of white males, and succeeded with the Class of 1852. Most, like Mullan, came from families of "moderate means." But while the academy's modest admittance standards enabled many to attend, in actuality those—like Mullan—with a preparatory school background were more prone to complete their studies. Only forty-three members of Mullan's class graduated on time.[23]

In June 1852 Mullan received instructions to proceed home and "await further orders." Those came on July 1 when he was promoted to brevet second lieutenant in the First Artillery and directed to nearby Fort Columbus, New York, a familiar first posting for academy graduates. Within a year, he would be ordered much farther afield—and begin to make his reputation as one of the West's preeminent explorers.[24]

CHAPTER 3

Railroad Survey

I N THE SPRING OF 1853 people swarmed to Isaac Stevens's roomy,
brick home on Third Street in Washington, D.C. Secretary of War
Jefferson Davis had just appointed Stevens to head the northernmost of
several surveys to determine the best route for a long-envisioned transcontinental railway. As Stevens's son remembered, "The fitting out of
the expedition attracted much attention in Washington, and the parlors
were filled every evening with gentlemen connected with or interested
in it."[1]

Stevens's residence in the nation's capital furnished him access to
the most able representatives of the scientific and military communities
from which to staff his survey party. From these ranks he selected young
Lieutenant John Mullan, not yet a year out of West Point, to serve as
one of seven army officers. That decision provided Mullan with access
to the man who would become his mentor, as well as an opportunity to
make a reputation in the West. Had it not been for Stevens's guidance,
Mullan would in all likelihood be unremembered today.[2]

A frail baby at his birth in 1818, Isaac Stevens never gained much physical stature: at maturity he stood slightly over five feet. But his size belied
a boundless energy. One member of the railway expedition described
Stevens as "a smart, active, ubiquitous little man…[who] wears a red
shirt and helps pull on the rope when we get stuck in a mud hole."[3]

Though small, no one questioned Stevens's intelligence and drive.
He graduated first in the Class of 1839 at West Point. When the Chief of
the Army Corps of Engineers requested the service of four or five "eminently qualified" cadets from that 1839 class, Stevens won an assignment.
Later, seriously wounded in the Mexican War, he received two brevets
for gallantry and a personal commendation from the commander of

American forces, General Winfield Scott. More pertinent to his future aspirations, Stevens became acquainted with General Franklin Pierce.

Following the war Stevens returned to the Corps. In 1849 he accepted a coveted position as chief assistant to the director of the United States Coastal Survey. The new job took him to Washington, D.C., where he thrived on the city's politics.

A lifelong Democrat, on the surface it might have seemed unsurprising that Stevens supported fellow Democrat and army officer Franklin Pierce for president in 1852. But doing so meant bucking a powerful military tide, for national hero Winfield Scott opposed Pierce, and most military officers remained loyal to the man they called "Old Fuss and Feathers."

Scott had no one to blame but himself for Stevens's decision to back Pierce. In 1851 Stevens had published a pamphlet defending Scott's Mexican campaign, which had come under criticism. The amply praiseworthy piece nonetheless irritated the notoriously vain Scott because it also included mild criticism. Scott harshly dismissed Stevens's effort. Not only did the rebuff anger Stevens, he also foresaw little future in the army after unwittingly irritating Scott.

Stevens became one of the few military officers supporting Pierce. The Democratic nominee gratefully accepted the help and put Stevens on the stump. When Pierce won, Stevens sensed an opportunity for political recompense.[4]

Shortly after Pierce defeated Scott, forty-four men met in a former Catholic Church in Monticello, a tiny community near the mouth of the Cowlitz River in Oregon Territory. Disenchanted with the great distances and the time it took Oregonians living north of the Columbia River to travel to the capital at Salem, they petitioned Congress for a new territory. Congress approved, naming the huge region Washington, and two days before Pierce's inauguration, President Millard Fillmore signed the act creating the new territory. He left for Pierce the task of selecting Washington's first governor. One day after Fillmore's signature on the territorial act, March 3, 1853, Congress passed a measure calling for the survey of several potential routes for a transcontinental railway. And on March 4 Franklin Pierce roused the crowd gathered for his inaugural address by proclaiming that he would vigorously support the nation's westward expansion.[5]

To Stevens the serendipitous convergence of these March events presented an unparalleled opportunity. First he called in political favors from the new president. Stevens's patronage request surprised some by its modesty: he sought the governorship of Washington. Few considered territorial governorships to be significant rewards. Stevens's friends believed Pierce owed him more. But Stevens saw an opportunity to consolidate power in a region he believed held great promise. In addition to the governorship he also received appointment as superintendent of Indian affairs for the territory. But he eyed an even bigger prize.[6]

When Stevens first moved to Washington, D.C., he lived in the same boarding house as Commodore Matthew Perry, who influenced Stevens's views about the potential of the Pacific Northwest. During the frenzied three days in March 1853 when the future for Stevens opened so dramatically, Perry was steaming to Japan, the first of two voyages to open that country to western trade. Stevens believed that a transcontinental railroad, terminating at Puget Sound, would catapult the Washington Territory he was about to head into the premier port of entry for Asia.

While working with Congress during the Coastal Survey, Stevens earned the trust and friendship of Mississippi Senator Jefferson Davis. Now Secretary of War under Pierce, Davis would assign personnel to the transcontinental railroad surveys. After much lobbying by Stevens, Davis assigned him to lead the northernmost expedition. Stevens resigned from the military, recognizing his future no longer lay there. Thirty-five-year-old Isaac Stevens suddenly found himself not only a governor and superintendent of Indian affairs, but also the leader of an expedition with national transformational potential.[7]

From the time workers laid the first track in the United States, visionaries dreamed of connecting the Atlantic to the Pacific via rail. But it remained for Asa Whitney to stir masses. Like Matthew Perry, Whitney foresaw a lucrative Asian trade enriching western territories. He spent years giving speeches, organizing conventions, writing articles, and bombarding Congress, advocating a transcontinental line.[8]

Whitney supported a route beginning at Lake Michigan, a nonstarter in the hopelessly divided America of the mid-nineteenth century.

Southerners foresaw economic advantage accruing to the North with a transcontinental road leading out of Chicago. Northerners feared a southern route would facilitate expansion of slavery to the West. By 1852 no less than six potential routes, ranging from the Canadian to the Mexican borders, had their powerful advocates. The thirty-second Congress devoted most of its session to discussing the railroad issue, leading to the March 3, 1853, act calling for the survey of several routes.

Hopelessly embroiled in sectional gridlock, congressmen believed the disinterested judgment of science might lead them out of the morass: let the natural landscape, as verified by some of the nation's leading scholars and explorers, dictate the route. There was nothing new about western exploration incorporating scientific components. Thomas Jefferson's goals for Lewis and Clark emphasized science as much as politics and commerce. But the Pacific Railroad Surveys brought a heightened emphasis to the concept that science could influence public policy. Geologists, botanists, and zoologists flooded the mails to whomever they believed might best help them secure a position with a western command; once Jefferson Davis appointed Stevens to head one of the expeditions, the Stevens home became a bustling point of call.[9]

As directed by Congress, Davis had only until January 1854 to submit a report on the most practical transcontinental route. The deadline lent earnestness to the project. The lack of sufficient time to lay out detailed courses meant these would be reconnaissance missions to glean general information about the proposed routes. Expedition leaders "brought back specimens that made the Smithsonian one of the world's great museums." And they published the results of their surveys in twelve massive volumes, a monumental compilation of data and art describing the West.[10]

But as aids to determining the best transcontinental railroad route, the surveys were virtually worthless—at least in the short term. Intended to find the "most practicable and economical route" to the Pacific, the surveys instead showed there were many potential avenues, failing to solve sectional divides. Expedition leaders described the terrain they traversed in the broadest of terms. To politicians attempting to ascertain the optimum course and to the businessmen who would construct the line, such general information had dubious value.[11]

❧

The earliest of the Pacific Railroad Surveys got underway in May 1853, led by Isaac Stevens, who tracked the basic route long advocated by Asa Whitney. With little time to complete the enterprise, Stevens split his 240-man expedition into four parties.

He sent two groups west via the Isthmus of Panama. Under the leadership of Captain George McClellan, one of these would explore routes across the Cascade Mountains, working its way east to meet Stevens, who would lead the largest contingent overland to the Northwest. Stevens had considerable—as it turned out, misplaced—confidence in McClellan, a friend from their time together in Mexico. "I have in the strongest terms pressed your case" for inclusion on the expedition, Stevens wrote McClellan, adding, prophetically, "We must not be frightened with long tunnels or enormous snows." Perhaps Stevens had premonitions of McClellans's forthcoming dalliance in the face of Cascadian weather.[12]

Stevens also sent Lieutenant Rufus Saxton to the West with a smaller contingent to transport supplies from Fort Vancouver to Fort Owen in the Bitterroot Valley. Saxton, a West Point graduate who would earn a Medal of Honor during the Civil War, proved a wise choice for the task. Accompanying Saxton was another whose talents first surfaced during the expedition, Private Gustavus Sohon.

Often dressed in a red flannel shirt and slouch hat, Stevens led the largest party of 120 west from St. Paul. Though casually attired, Stevens had scrupulously prepared. Convinced his would be the greatest scientific and topographic expedition since Lewis and Clark, Stevens pored over the writings of those earlier explorers, as well as everything else he could—from Washington Irving to Father Pierre-Jean DeSmet—in the scant literature on the Northwest.[13]

The final group, headed by Lieutenant Andrew Jackson Donelson, would travel by steamer up the Missouri River to Fort Union. While accompanying the prodigious quantities of supplies needed to provision Stevens's main body, Donelson would also survey the river and the country near Fort Union. Lieutenant John Mullan found himself one of nine assigned to Donelson's group. He would begin his first western adventure from St. Louis.

❦

High above the Mississippi's bank sat the St. Louis courthouse with its round cupola, the first sight to emerge as the steamer churned along the city's boat-clogged wharf, the greatest inland port in America. Exiting the steamship he had traveled to this river town, John Mullan made his way over the gangway, past porters, through towering stacks of freight, around carriages and hacks awaiting passengers, and up the steep steps to town. As he topped the bluff, the honey scent of locust filled the air as the animated bustle of the wharf gave way to a city reemerging from a devastating fire four years earlier. Brick commercial buildings spread to the west, church spires rose skyward, and dozens of hotels lined the streets, for this was St. Louis, gateway to the West, the embarkation point for virtually all travel north and west. Mullan, who for years had read and dreamed about the West and this very city, might have indulged "in a fit of extatic delight at beholding the wonders which he [had] heard of in his youth…gaping at St. Louis, in all its magnitude and glory," as had another passerby the previous year.[14]

Isaac Stevens probably experienced the same reaction a few days later. He arrived in St. Louis on May 15 to oversee Donelson's provisioning. Here he met John Mullan for the first time. Stevens laconically reported only that "I met Lieutenant…Mullan, who had proceeded me." Mullan left no record of his first encounter with the man who would change his life.[15]

Stevens remained in St. Louis long enough to see Donelson and Mullan off on May 21, then left for St. Paul to join his contingent of the survey party. But the steamboat *Robert Campbell*, with Donelson and Mullan on board, backed away from the wharf only after Stevens had stirred a controversy sparked by his concern that some of the boat's passengers were a threat to the scientific supremacy of his expedition.

The *Robert Campbell*—fitted with a huge banner emblazoned with the name of Pierre Chouteau Jr. of the American Fur Company, who had leased the steamer—carried three hundred tons of freight and more than one hundred passengers. These included Alexander Culbertson, a fur trapper with twenty years' experience with the American Fur Company, founder of Fort Benton, and married to a Blackfoot Indian. Stevens anticipated difficulties with the proud Blackfeet, and hired Culbertson to serve as his special intermediary to the tribe. John Sarpy, a wealthy financier and partner with Chouteau in the American Fur Company, accompanied Culbertson.[16]

Scientists Fielding Bradford Meek and Ferdinand Vandeveer Hayden also climbed aboard. Their presence exasperated Stevens, for also on the boat were his own scientists, John Evans and Benjamin Shumard, traveling with Donelson. Stevens's insistence upon the scientific hegemony of his expedition prompted his efforts to prevent Hayden and Meek from making the trip. Mullan probably observed all this with great interest. One day he would supervise his own scientific collectors.

The feud involved some of America's eminent geologists and paleontologists. John Hall, at different times state geologist for New York, Iowa, and Wisconsin, had trained Meek and Hayden and sent them on their journey of western exploration. The thirty-six-year-old Meek had already established a reputation for fossil collecting before joining twenty-four-year-old Hayden, who would become the most acclaimed scientific explorer of the West. Hayden's studies of Yellowstone brought him international fame and helped convince Congress to establish it as America's first national park. His pioneering work on this 1853 expedition provided the model for future endeavors undertaken by the United States Geological Survey, which he would one day head.[17]

But Hall would have had little inclination to send Meek and Hayden west had it not been for the earlier exploits of Shumard and Evans, the leading Western geologists of their time. Evans and Shumard had been as far as Oregon, traversing some of the very courses Stevens envisioned for a possible railroad. No one in his expedition knew the country better. They had returned from those investigations with tales that fueled geologists' yearnings. At the White River Bad Lands in what became South Dakota, Evans had come upon a virtual emporium of fossils unique to science. "At every step objects of the highest interest present themselves," he wrote. His discoveries won him international renown. The work of Evans and Shumard laid the foundation for the many other western scientific explorations to follow in the nineteenth century. No wonder Meek and Hayden hoped to share a boat with them.[18]

One of the first people Meek and Hayden met in St. Louis had been Culbertson, who had a keen scientific bent himself, having already sent several specimens to the Smithsonian. The fur trader befriended the two young scientists and encouraged them to join him on the *Robert*

Campbell. But Evans and Shumard resented sharing their rich western finds with the upstarts and complained to Stevens. Hayden wrote to Hall that Stevens "violently opposed...our going to the Bad Lands," behaved "in an overbearing...way," and threatened to recruit more men for his own Bad Lands exploration, which would destroy the opportunities for Hayden and Meek.

Still, Stevens had no authority to prevent passage on the boat, and Meek and Hayden made it aboard. But the controversy left a bitter taste. "I was deeply pained to witness the spirit of rapacity, envy and sickly emulation evinced by most of the persons of interest," wrote George Englemann, a naturalist living in St. Louis. "There is a want of the true spirit of science...in all of this." As it turned out, the four scientists got along quite well and eventually—at the suggestion of Evans—explored the Bad Lands together while Evans and Shumard awaited Stevens's arrival at Fort Union.[19]

Sparks of a different kind ignited the steamer four days into its journey. On May 24 fire broke out in the bow, threatening to reach kegs of powder stored below. Passengers and crew scurried to the stern, ready to abandon ship, but cool-headed John Sarpy calmly doused the flames.

The boat tied up each night to avoid snags and sand bars; during the day it stopped frequently to gather wood for fuel. At each stop the scientists collected specimens, while Mullan recorded weather observations. The *Robert Campbell* moved slowly, making about four miles an hour. The scenery proved monotonous to some. "Nothing is to be seen but low alluvial bottoms, and islands clothed with a dense growth of gigantic sycamores, cottonwoods, oaks, maples," wrote a bored Meek. But the pace provided Mullan opportunity to take notes and sketch maps. Donelson and Mullan observed "all the features of the river and adjacent country," and gleaned what they could in conversations with Culbertson, Sarpy, and others knowledgeable with the region.

For forty-two days the boat steamed up river. Monotonous to some, it must have been grand adventure for Lieutenant Mullan, on his first excursion beyond the eastern seaboard states. And surely nothing impressed him more than Sioux Indians—his first encounters with Native Americans.[20]

The boat passed fields of Indian-cultivated vegetables and steamed by villages where these local residents offered friendly salute. One time

Sarpy invited nearly two hundred Indians on board, where they feasted on dog. The *Robert Campbell* also carried Indian agent Alfred Vaughn, heading to his new post at Fort Pierre. On occasion the boat stopped so Vaughn could distribute gifts, and at least once he held council, an event Mullan likely attended, first-hand experience with the "really fine looking" Indians who, "mounted on good horses...cut quite a figure" as they swept across the prairies "with their long hair...flying in the wind."

In July the Donelson party exited the boat at Fort Union. Adhering to Stevens's instructions, Donelson led his group to the north and west, exploring "a vast plain, destitute of timber." After recording the region's topography and minerals, the men returned to Fort Union to await Stevens.

On August 1, 1853, John Mullan and others inside Fort Union heard a rifle volley from the plain below, and responded with a thirteen-gun salute. Approaching the fort on "its beautiful bluff banks" was a most impressive, if incongruous, sight. At the head of a large column rode Isaac Stevens, accompanied by a member of his expedition carrying an American flag crafted from red flannel. Engineers came next carrying their own logo-festooned banner featuring a locomotive chasing a buffalo, emblazoned with the words, "Westward Ho!" Meteorologists had fashioned a pennant with an image of the Rocky Mountains and a barometer, over the inscription "Excelsior." The astronomical party's flag featured stars, a half moon, and telescope. On came the parade—teamsters, packers, hunters—all carrying their own insignia. What a sight, even for a place sometimes referred to as the "Times Square of the Plains." Stevens had traveled 715 miles in two months, and the residents of Fort Union had never seen anything quite like this showy extravagance.[21]

The American Fur Company had constructed Fort Union, upstream of the junction of the Missouri and Yellowstone Rivers, in 1830, and it quickly became a commerce center. A grassy plain surrounded the outpost, where Assiniboines, Gros Ventres, Crows, and other Indians exchanged furs for commodities. The lively fort would be the last oasis of western culture Stevens would encounter for some time, and the party spent ten days here, resting, repairing equipment, mending clothes, and replenishing supplies.[22]

On the evening Stevens arrived at the fort, Mullan and other members of the expedition met in front of the governor's tent to receive his congratulations—toasted by champagne—for the work completed so far. Stevens gave each man an opportunity to return east, noting the challenges that lay ahead. The men unanimously agreed to continue. But during the next several days the voyageurs of the fur company "thought it a good practical joke to spread bugbear stories about the immense snows to be expected" in the West. Some men now had reservations about continuing, but Stevens read to them pertinent sections of Father DeSmet's *The Oregon Missions and Travels Over the Rocky Mountains*, calming nerves. As it turned out, not a man quit.[23]

On August 10 Stevens led his men, accompanied by sixty Blackfeet Indians, out of Fort Union. For three weeks the Stevens expedition traveled through the Great Plains to Fort Benton. The route proved relatively easy, a jaunt "made with the ease and comfort as if at home." But the trip must have astonished those unacquainted with such a landscape.

Imagine John Mullan's reaction. From the forested East, he now came full upon America's grasslands: short brush, big sky, windswept grass, crags and coulees, sheer-cliffed valleys. Expedition members walked a good part of the way to Fort Benton, conserving their animals' strength for the upcoming mountain crossing; the easy pace encouraged inspection of the strange steppe scenery for those like Mullan disposed to observation.[24]

Stevens ordered each expedition member to check his firearms twice a day, for he anticipated possible problems with Indians. Indeed, tempers rose to near violence among the Blackfeet accompanying the party. The tribe had been suspicious of white intrusions into their homeland since the time Meriwether Lewis had killed two Blackfeet in an 1806 encounter. Luckily, Stevens had Alexander Culbertson and his Indian wife Natawista along, and they tactfully restored calm. The party's encounter with Gros Ventre Indians on August 25 proved more convivial. Stevens distributed one ton of gifts to two thousand people. On several nights, a comet appeared, "shining most brilliantly in the northwestern portion of the heavens." Once the northern lights shone, a spectacular display that so energized Stevens that he ordered the howitzer fired. But no doubt the most memorable event had to be first sighting of the Rocky Mountains—for most, like Mullan, an unprecedented experience. At the first range encountered, the Bear's Paw, Stevens dispatched expedition artist John Mix Stanley to climb one of the highest peaks and sketch the surrounding country. "Bear's paw...presents a rugged, grotesque appearance," wrote Stevens. Mullan had read about these mountains, no doubt imagined them—but nothing can prepare a person for that initial glimpse of the Rocky Mountains stretched across a vast horizon. Mullan would spend much of the next decade exploring, working, and living in these mountains.[25]

On September 1 the chorus of a fifteen-gun salute welcomed the Stevens party to Fort Benton, on the banks of the Missouri, 377 miles from Fort Union. At Benton, home to about a dozen men and their families who provided merchandise to the Blackfeet in exchange for furs, Stevens would remain for nine days, contemplating the best means of attacking the imposing Rocky Mountains.[26]

Stevens gathered information from employees and Indians about the best mountain passes. But he received conflicting reports and decided to explore the territory thoroughly. He split his party to investigate as many tracks as possible, for, other than Lewis and Clark, no effort had been made to systematically survey passages in this region, and even Lewis and Clark agreed the one they chose, over Lolo Pass, was abysmal.[27]

Stevens sent Donelson to explore Cadotte's Pass. Frederick Lander, a civilian engineer, headed north to Marias Pass. Abiel Tinkham went as far north as the forty-ninth parallel. To Cuvier Grover and George Suckley went the most daunting challenges. Grover made a winter trip to Puget Sound, crossing the mountains with a dog team, measuring snow depths as he went, while Suckley traveled by canoe down the Clark Fork and Columbia Rivers to Fort Vancouver, collecting scientific specimens.

Since leaving Fort Union, Stevens had gained confidence in John Mullan and now gave the young lieutenant his first independent assignment. Mullan was to make an extensive survey of the country south of Fort Benton, meet with Indians to determine best routes through the mountains, and encourage them to attend a council. He would end up at the Bitterroot Valley, where Stevens would meet him.

Even more impressed with Mullan following this reconnaissance survey, Stevens would direct the lieutenant to set up winter quarters in the valley and survey a vast area. It proved to be the most significant assignment of Mullan's life, establishing his reputation as one of the eminent explorers of the West, and leading to his future as a road builder.

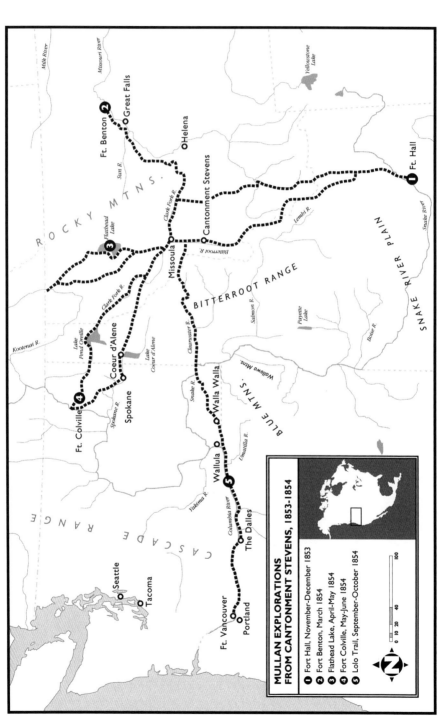

MULLAN EXPLORATIONS FROM CANTONMENT STEVENS, 1853-1854

1. Fort Hall, November-December 1853
2. Fort Benton, March 1854
3. Flathead Lake, April-May 1854
4. Fort Colville, May-June 1854
5. Lolo Trail, September-October 1854

Courtesy David C. Hoyt; with thanks to Paul D. McDermott, Ronald E. Grim, and Philip Mobley.

CHAPTER 4

✥

Explorer

Two Indians paddled ashore at Council Bluffs, Iowa Territory, on September 18, 1839, landing their canoe near the log home of Father Pierre-Jean DeSmet. It was hardly an unusual sight, for DeSmet lived at St. Joseph's, a Catholic mission among the Potawatamis. But these Indians—Pierre Gauche and Young Ignace—had traveled far, from the Bitterroot Valley of today's southwestern Montana, intent on their own mission: to convince Black Robes to serve among Flathead Indians. Pierre and Ignace, however, were not Flatheads but Iroquois, among the last of two dozen who had settled with the Flatheads decades earlier. DeSmet on that day realized his future lay in the West among Indians uncorrupted by white vices.[1]

The Flathead way of life had changed dramatically in the early nineteenth century. Canadian fur traders bartered guns with the neighboring Blackfeet, a threat to the poorly armed Flatheads. At the same time, white diseases crept their way east to the Bitterroot Valley after wasting coastal tribes. In this climate Ignace Partui, or Big Ignace, had found a receptive audience, having led a group of Iroquois fur traders to live among the Flatheads prior to 1820. A noted storyteller, his references to black-robed teachers validated Flathead oral tradition that had long anticipated the arrival of these conveyors of knowledge and prosperity. But the teachers were slow in arriving. In 1831 the Flatheads began efforts to recruit the Black Robes, believing their powerful teachings could protect them from both the Blackfeet and disease.

A combined delegation of Flatheads and Nez Perces made the first arduous journey from the Bitterroot Valley to St. Louis to seek the counsel of William Clark, who they remembered from his famous expedition years earlier. This 1831 trip transformed the Northwest, though not in a way the Indians could have imagined. Misinterpreted as a plea for Christian conversion, news of pagans seeking the white man's "book of Heaven" sparked an outpouring of evangelical fervor. Missionaries rushed to serve, and the Northwest would never be the same. But none of these earliest missionaries toiled among the Flatheads, which was just as well with Ignace and his adopted people. The missionaries all were Protestants, not the desired Catholic Black Robes. But the Jesuits of St. Louis were too poor to respond.

Big Ignace personally led two additional voyages to entice Black Robes. Sioux killed him on his second attempt. Finally, in 1839 Pierre Gauche and Young Ignace induced the Jesuits to dispatch a missionary. The superior of the Missouri Mission in St. Louis initially planned to send someone other than DeSmet, but that young priest so aggressively sought the position that it seemed judicious to assign him. Or, in the words of his superior, "He manifested such eagerness and ardent zeal for the work." Indeed, he would manifest ardent zeal for that work the rest of his life.

In 1840 DeSmet traveled with fur traders to the Green River rendezvous in present-day western Wyoming. He did not get to the Bitterroot Valley, but learned enough from the Flatheads who met him to recognize it as their preferred location for a mission. The following year, along with Thomas Fitzpatrick, John Bidwell, and members of the Western Emigration Society, he journeyed on that famous wagon train that would divide into three parts in eastern Idaho. DeSmet headed north to the Bitterroot.

In September 1841 DeSmet halted at a resplendent meadow. He erected a cross, and anointed this—the first Jesuit mission in the Inland Northwest—as St. Mary's. Here the Jesuits built Montana's first sawmill and flour mill and constructed a church of cottonwood logs. They cultivated fields and enclosed their community of cottages and farm buildings with a palisade of three thousand lodgepoles. This would always be Father DeSmet's favorite mission. But as one of the indefatigable wanderers of the nineteenth century, he spent little time in one place, even here among his beloved Flatheads. Still, St. Mary's abandonment less than a decade after its founding depressed him.[2]

As the influence of the Christian Iroquois waned, the Flatheads proved less enthusiastic about the Jesuits in their midst. They had sought teachers, but did not expect the Jesuits to stay. More significantly, threats by menacing Blackfeet forced the priests to abandon the valley. In November 1850 the Jesuits sold their mission to Major John Owen, the first recorded transfer of real estate in Montana. He renamed the place Fort Owen.[3]

In the tradition of many trading posts of the nineteenth century West, Fort Owen was not a fort, nor was its owner a major, though he fancied the courtesy title. A heavy man with dark hair, loud voice, a Shoshone Indian wife named Nancy, and, according to John Mullan, owner of "the finest library…on the north Pacific coast," Owen arrived in the West in 1849 as a sutler with a regiment of army troops. The next year he traveled to the Bitterroot Valley and acquired the mission, mills, buildings, and cultivated fields from the weary Jesuits. Here John and Nancy established a store.[4]

By 1853 Owen had moved his fort—now consisting of a couple of buildings enclosed by a stockade—to higher ground a short distance from the mission site. To this post, Isaac Stevens, while on the East Coast, had dispatched Lieutenant Rufus Saxton to deliver a pack train of supplies in advance of the arrival of Stevens's party traveling overland from the east. On his way to the Bitterroot, Saxton met John Owen, who had, unbeknownst to Saxton, abandoned his trading post for the same reason as had the Jesuits: Blackfeet had killed one of his employees and frightened away potential customers. Taking heart that the army's arrival might turn his fortunes, Owen returned with Saxton, and continued to sell goods from his store for almost two more decades.

When Isaac Stevens arrived at Fort Owen in late September 1853, he found nearly two thousand rations transported by Saxton—supplies that a contingent of men under the command of Lieutenant John Mullan would consume during the coming winter. Impressed with Mullan's performance during the expedition west, Stevens had assigned him the most critical exploration of his railroad survey. John Mullan would be John Owen's neighbor for the coming year.[5]

By the time the large grizzly charged his camp at 8:00 p.m. on September 12, John Mullan knew he was in for an adventure. This would be his first trip around, into, and across the Rockies. From this time forward he would cast his lot with the West, where opportunity beckoned. During this particular sally, he described the West's potential almost rapturously: "I hesitate not in saying that this section may yet prove the great key to unlock…our country's rich and hidden treasures."[6]

This, Mullan's first independent assignment, had begun three days earlier, when he led eight men out of Fort Benton to invite Flathead Indians to a council with Governor Stevens. He lyrically described the country, riding through valleys alternatively "rich and luxuriant," "beautiful and charming," or "large and beautiful," with trees "in abundance, and growing to a large size." The party slept under stars "as comfortably, rolled up in our blankets, as if we had been resting under some hospitable roof in more civilized climes." Nights of rain only temporarily dampened his spirits. And of course, he marveled at "snow-capped peaks" that "towered high above the surrounding country," mountains unlike anything he had seen before, "the object of all our hopes and ambition." "Far to our left lay a high ridge of the Rocky range," he wrote, astonished at seemingly endless columns of mountains. "And in the rear of it a snow-clad range, which in the bright sunshine glistened like a mountain of silver. Far to our right lay another rough and ragged ridge of the Rocky range, while to our front lay a third."

They caught trout two feet long. They dined on ducks, deer, elk, antelope, and the "excellent dish" of prairie dogs. Once they saw a hill "as far as the eye could reach…perfectly alive and black with buffalo." He beheld badgers, mountain goats, wolves, and of course that rampaging grizzly, which the men somehow managed to turn before it stampeded their horses.

Magnificent scenery and grand adventure aside, Mullan traveled with a purpose: to invite Flatheads to council with Stevens. On September 14 his party finally came upon a Flathead camp, vacated about three days earlier. Mullan realized he would never catch the Indians while encumbered with pack animals. Early the next morning, accompanied only by his Indian guide and mounted on their best horses, he followed on the trail of the Flatheads, covering an extraordinary eighty miles over "rugged country" until, at 7:00 p.m., they finally came upon a camp of 120 lodges. Immediately Mullan recognized the influence of more than a decade of Jesuit teachings at St. Mary's: "The chief offered up a prayer. This astonished me. It was something for which I had not been prepared. Every one was upon his knees, and in the most solemn and reverential manner offered up a prayer to God. For a moment I asked myself, was I among Indians? Was I among those termed by every one savages?"

The meeting turned more worldly when Mullan, who left camp that morning without his interpreter, realized that none of the Flatheads spoke English. But West Point training came to good use as he discovered one of them could speak French. "Imagine my feelings of joy at this," he wrote. "It fully and amply repaid me for the many and frequent annoyances I had met with studying the language" at the Military Academy. Mullan requested the Flatheads follow him to Fort Owen to meet with Stevens. The Indians, on their way to hunt, explained they could not turn back, for they needed meat for the winter. But they did assign a party of four men to accompany Mullan, a group he characterized as "noble…pious, aged, firm, upright, and reliable."

Now leading a party of thirteen, Mullan continued toward Fort Owen. On September 25 he came upon a pile of stones concealing a note left by another member of the Stevens expedition, Frederick Lander, who had passed through two days earlier on his own exploration for Stevens—considerably off course. For just such reasons Stevens lost confidence in Lander, and assigned ever more responsibility to Mullan, forging a rivalry between Mullan and Lander, the two most famous road builders of the mid-nineteenth century West.

Mullan arrived at Fort Owen on September 30, after an excursion of twenty-two days. Stevens awaited. He faced several critical deadlines simultaneously. As territorial governor he desired to get to Olympia. As Indian superintendent he needed to plan for upcoming councils. And as head of the railroad survey, already behind schedule and over budget, he had to determine the best route over the Rocky Mountains. Well pleased with Mullan's first independent reconnaissance, Stevens delegated the latter task to him. For the next year Mullan would conduct surveys from a post near Fort Owen.

Stevens left Mullan a complex assignment. He was to explore and map mountain passes, trace the headwaters of the Missouri River, measure snow depths in winter and stream velocities in spring, gather geographical, meteorological, and statistical data, and most importantly, recommend the best route for a future railroad. He was to accomplish all of this with a contingent of fifteen men, exploring a vast area that stretched from the Oregon Trail to the south, nearly to the Canadian border in the north.

On October 8 Mullan escorted his men about twelve miles from Fort Owen to a spot of excellent grass and ample wood where he constructed winter quarters. He called the place Cantonment Stevens. Mullan and his men built two barns and a corral and threw up a rectangle of four log cabins. In the center they planted a flag pole, and connected the cabins with a rail fence. Soon a number of Flatheads erected teepees nearby. Mullan made this modest post his base camp for some of the most significant explorations ever undertaken in the West.[7]

Mullan's first excursion from Cantonment Stevens hardly prophesied an explorer with a promising future. He retreated to camp far short of his goal—Fort Hall on the Oregon Trail. Mullan blamed John Owen for the misadventure.

Mullan and Owen had left camp on October 15. Owen seemed a natural choice for guide; he had traveled to the Bitterroot Valley via Fort Hall and told Mullan "he knew the route full well." But a few days into the trip Owen "totally mistook his road." Mullan made the best of the situation by carefully noting the country.[8]

In November Mullan left again, determined to complete a trip "of greater extent and of greater interest." Along with fifteen horses and ten mules, he took five men, including two of his best, Thomas Adams and Gabriel Prudhomme.[9]

Adams had served so well as a civil engineer under Stevens that the governor appointed him a non-commissioned officer; Mullan would come to rely upon him. Gabriel Prudhomme provided a direct link between DeSmet and Mullan. A mixed-blood voyageur, Prudhomme had lived for years among the Flatheads. Throughout DeSmet's time at St. Mary's, Prudhomme served as his most reliable interpreter. As one of the few natives knowledgeable of requirements for wagon travel, Prudhomme would guide Mullan over routes that wagons could negotiate. Indeed, no one proved more influential than Prudhomme in determining Mullan's course for the eastern portion of his eventual wagon road.[10]

Prudhomme led the party on a vast loop that covered seven hundred miles in an effort to determine the feasibility of connecting a wagon road with the best-known interstate highway of its day, the Oregon Trail. To comprehend why Stevens, head of the northernmost Pacific Railroad Survey, dispatched Mullan so far south in search of a wagon route, one must understand the peculiar politics surrounding government-financed road building in the mid-nineteenth century.

Almost invariably, the federal government surveyed and constructed the routes. The myth of rugged individuals taming the West is mostly that: myth. Certainly there were rugged individuals involved, and in the case of the Oregon Trail, emigrants pounded out a significant highway without government assistance. But to understand most road building in the West, one must understand the rule, not the exception.

For generations members of Congress debated the constitutionality of federal internal improvements undertaken for any reason other than military necessity. Those who believed in restricted powers for the central government resisted federally funded internal improvements in states. But all agreed Congress possessed nearly unlimited power in territories, and, with little opposition, sent expeditions into territorial lands to scout and construct roads. Until the mid-1850s, these projects almost invariably came under army supervision, and at least superficially, army officers explored and constructed roads under the guise of military necessity. In a country with a small army and vast frontiers, American security hinged on the ability of troops to move quickly on good roads, or so the argument went. In actuality, once settlers arrived, they nearly always clamored for federal road construction to ease civilian transportation; military necessity usually took a back seat.

Congress not only responded to these settlers' needs, but also added to western road-building demands when it authorized the Pacific Railroad Surveys. Railroad construction crews would need roads to transport supplies. So survey expeditions searched for wagon routes as ardently as they did for railroad lines. Often, they were one and the same, with railroads eventually running alongside or over the wagon roads.[11]

So it was, at the onset of winter 1853, that John Mullan found himself traipsing far from the proposed northern railroad route to examine a possible supply line with the Oregon Trail. On December 13 his party reached Cantonment Loring, five miles from Fort Hall, and here they rested for five days.

Colonel William Loring's mounted rifle regiment, with John Owen as sutler, had constructed the camp in 1849 to help shield Oregon Trail emigrants from Indians growing increasingly resentful about trespassers destroying their forage and wild foods. Because the cantonment lay too far from the Oregon Trail to offer effective protection, the army soon abandoned it. Richard Grant, retired chief trader at the Hudson's Bay Company's nearby Fort Hall, moved into the camp with his family in 1852.[12]

Grant—fat, jovial, with a long grey beard "as rough as a grizzly bear"—had a half-Kalispel wife named Helene. The two enjoyed preparing enormous feasts for guests, and they did not disappoint Mullan's party, which was miserable, exhausted, wet, and cold after sixteen days on the trail, many of them "exceedingly disagreeable." Grant "spread before us all the comforts and many of the luxuries of life, and gave us a comfortable bed under his hospitable roof—all of which none more than ourselves could appreciate."[13]

Mullan left the comfort of Grant's home on December 15 to visit Fort Hall, established as a trading post in 1834, one of the Oregon Trail's principal supply points. Four days later, he left Cantonment Loring, leading his men north, retracing the 1841 route of DeSmet. Traveling in winter allowed Mullan to check snow depths on passes. But it had its challenges. Consider Christmas 1853. Snow fell all Christmas Eve, whipped by strong winds that sent the chill factor plummeting; it was a tough night for camping. Christmas began "cold and gloomy," the thermometer registering fourteen below. The group shivered over Monida Pass, though they did note its easy grade. Bundled the best they could, they managed only eleven miles before stopping to build a fire. All in all, Mullan observed, "this was by far our most disagreeable day."

Forty-five days after commencing the trip, the group returned to Cantonment Stevens. They had crossed the continental divide four times in the middle of winter, often as pitiable as humans can be, cold wind and wet clothes chilling joints to throbbing—or as Mullan wrote, "there was no one in the party whose limbs were not thoroughly benumbed." Sometimes the ground was so frozen they could not drive stakes; one evening their tents blew down, "compelling us to spend a long, dreary, and uncomfortable night" with no shelter. River and stream crossings, often with lead horses crashing through ice, brought excruciating cold.

Traveling with minimal rations and expecting to find more game than they did, they were often hungry as well as frigid.

But they identified two workable wagon routes between the Bitterroot Valley and the Oregon Trail. Mullan met Nez Perce Indians for the first time. He gathered mineral specimens for Dr. John Evans's Smithsonian collection. He observed Western landmarks he previously knew only from books: the Teton Mountains; the Three Buttes near Fort Hall, milestones to generations of Oregon Trail emigrants; the camp where Blackfoot Indians had raided Captain Benjamin Bonneville in 1835; and Beaverhead Rock, Sacajawea's touchstone with her home during Lewis and Clark's 1805 journey.

Gustavus Sohon executed some of the earliest landscape paintings of the Pacific Northwest. His drawings of Indian chiefs—the only known likenesses of several significant leaders—have provided illustrative material for generations of historians. A gifted linguist, he quickly learned Indian idioms and became a valued interpreter. His ability to scout routes and his cartographic skills helped lay the course for the first engineered highway in the Northwest. No one appreciated Sohon's talents more than John Mullan. The two met in 1853 and became lifelong friends. Yet that initial meeting apparently made little impression, for neither recorded the event.[14]

Sohon emigrated from Germany at age seventeen in 1842. He joined the army in 1852. Listed as 5'7" with dark hair and dark complexion, he received assignment the following year to Stevens's railroad expedition, serving as a private under Lieutenant Rufus Saxton. Probably in September 1853 Sohon met John Mix Stanley, Stevens's expedition artist. Their initial encounter also went unrecorded. But whenever they met, Sohon and Stanley also struck a friendship, and Stanley deserves credit for discovering Sohon's artistic abilities.

At some point in fall of 1853 Sohon made his way to Cantonment Stevens, where he served under Mullan. Sohon ably served Mullan both in 1853–54 and again as they returned to the Northwest to construct the military road a few years later. Shortly before he died in 1909, Mullan offered this tribute to his friend: "Sohon was a good engineer, a skilled mapmaker, could speak English, French and several Indian languages, and was not afraid to go fifty or a hundred miles in advance looking for the best route. He had a way of making friends with Indians. Sohon was my right-hand man."[15]

Mullan left Cantonment Stevens again on March 1, 1854, taking with him five unnamed men, though we know Sohon went along, for Mullan included several Sohon sketches in his field report to Stevens. For two weeks Mullan, Sohon, and the four others slogged north along the Missouri River, grappling through a region of deep coulees and high bluffs, "in a word, one immense bed of mountains...for one hundred and fifty miles." The haggard men reached Fort Benton on March 14, having followed a route "impracticable for anything save a pack train."[16]

But Mullan had learned from Prudhomme of a potential alternate return route suitable for wagons. After resting three days he and his crew hitched four mules to a wagon and rolled easily to the Little Prickly Pear River. Continuing on, they crossed a mountain with a descent "so exceedingly gradual" that the men left the wheels unlocked as the mules trotted down. Mullan had just traversed the pass that would permanently bear his name. The group arrived at Fort Owen on March 30.

An ecstatic Mullan immediately sent an expressman to Stevens. "The route I passed over on my return," he wrote, "I can...report as perfectly practicable for a railroad route, and for a wagon road." Mullan had reason to exult. He had piloted the first wagon over the northern Rockies, "in a season heretofore deemed impracticable for travelling." He would later construct a road over this same route. And here one day the Northern Pacific would lay a railroad. Others immediately recognized the significance of Mullan's discovery. "Lieutenant Mullan... is confident of being able to come with teams to Fort Walla Walla," gushed the *Oregon Statesman*. "Emigrant trains from Minnesota will doubtless pass over the Northern Route to Oregon and Washington territories next year." That prediction proved premature, but Mullan and Sohon had made one of the notable discoveries of western exploration.[17]

On his next trip out of Cantonment Stevens, Mullan took his best men—Gustavus Sohon, Gabriel Prudhomme, Thomas Adams, and W. Gates. They were lucky to return alive.[18]

The party left on April 14, 1854, hoping to find a practicable wagon route from the Flathead Valley west to the Spokane Plains. Northwest rivers surged with spring snowmelt, but Mullan, with limited time to explore, decided to push north despite the hazards. As a consequence, his men endured a five-hundred-mile cold, wet slog.

The party constructed rafts to portage across the swollen Jocko River, before emerging onto a large prairie on April 17. Here they camped among a group of Pend Oreille—or Kalispel—Indians. The Pend Oreilles treated them well. The women pitched the explorers' tents, carried wood, built fires, "and would probably have extended the limit of their kindness much farther had we not requested them to desist." The men provided fresh buffalo tongue—"the epicurean dish of the plains or mountains." The Pend Oreilles had a number of cows, a welcome if unexpected sight in the Northwest wilderness of 1854. "They brought us milk in such abundance that our lodge might have been taken for a dairy," Mullan remembered.

Leaving the prairie, Mullan's crew continued north and, on the night of April 19, camped again among Indians. Here Mullan met the Yakama chief Owhi, "the great friend of the white man." Mullan proclaimed Owhi "a noble and generous Indian," who deserved "humane and kind treatment at the hands of every white man." A few years later, under different circumstances, Mullan would ride with an army force that apprehended and killed the proud warrior. It was at this camp that Sohon sketched the first of his many portraits of Northwest Indians.

Continuing on, the party reached Flathead Lake, a glaciated defile 370 feet deep, the greatest body of fresh water west of the Mississippi, a spectacular pool that occupies more than 190 square miles. But Mullan hardly noticed its beauty. His spirits dampened under "exceedingly gloomy and disagreeable weather," and "exceedingly heavy" rain. The terrain did not help. "Our trail to-day lay through an immense pine forest, in the greater part of which the light of day is ever excluded," Mullan wrote. "We found the travelling more difficult than on any day out; the great number of fallen logs and large trees impeded our progress."

After reaching the northern tip of the lake, Mullan trudged on for another forty miles toward the forty-ninth parallel, until the trail—such as it was—faded. He harbored no fond memories of this country, either. "The greatest difficulty that we found was to travel without bruising or breaking every limb, from the standing and fallen timber," he wrote.

"Truly, I considered this one of the worst roads, if not *the* worst, ever travelled by whites or Indians."

With both horses and men debilitated from the journey, Mullan turned back to the Bitterroot Valley on April 27, striking a different course. On the bank of the swollen Tobacco River they felled trees to construct a bridge. Later, on another fork of the Tobacco, they swam its frigid waters. And if the party had optimistically hoped for an easier march than the one north, they were grievously disappointed. If anything it was worse: "Our road…was indescribably horrid—fallen timber piled up for many feet, over which our animals had to jump, innumerable mud-holes and quagmires, rocks, under-brush—in a word, everything to make our road miserable in the extreme, and endangering the lives of both men and animals."

On April 29 they came to the camp of a Kootenai Indian who prepared a welcome dinner. Now, having looped back to the trail they had previously followed north, the next day they met up with Michael Ogden—who they had first encountered on their way to Flathead Lake. Ogden, the Hudson's Bay Company's chief factor at nearby Fort Connah and son of legendary fur trader Peter Skeene Ogden, had established a temporary trading post. "Fortunately for us," Mullan wrote, "he had, a few days previous to our arrival, received a supply of goods and provisions from Fort Vancouver, for we arrived at his camp without an iota of provisions. He willingly supplied us with a sufficiency to last us to the Bitter Root valley. We had here the luxury of a cup of coffee and a piece of bread."[19]

Well fed and rested after spending an extra day enjoying Ogden's hospitality, the group continued south, and on May 4 survived the most perilous incident in Mullan's many western adventures.

Near present-day Missoula the party came to the Hellgate River (today's Clark Fork)—swollen, deep, rapid. The lieutenant ordered his men to construct two rafts. Prudhomme and Gates boarded one, along with an Indian woman and her children, who had accompanied the party from Ogden's post. Mullan, Adams, and Sohon departed on the other, hoping to strike a point of land across the river.

Prudhomme, swimming with his horses, managed to pilot his raft close to the desired spot. Mullan's craft never got started in the right direction. The current swept it downriver, crashing into rocks, snags, islands, "in fact everything that formed an obstruction in the stream." Thrown to the opposite bank, the tiny raft smashed into a fallen tree. The men desperately seized its limbs in a fruitless effort to slow their descent. As the raft hurtled by the snag, a branch swept Mullan into the torrent. Sohon sketched a dramatic image of the event showing Mullan on his back in fast water, desperately clinging to one of the tree's branches, with heavy, potentially deadly flotsam dangerously jettisoning downstream nearby. His men managed to drag him back onto the raft. But in their collision with the tree they had lost their poles and "were thus left to the chances of fortune."[20]

Mullan ordered his men to strip so they could better swim. As they hurtled past a rocky island two miles downstream, all three jumped into the "impetuous current," each with a rope attached to the raft. Gaining the island, they drug the craft against fallen timber. Here they somehow managed to lay down some logs, creating a crude bridge to yet another island, and began a frenzied effort to save their supplies, rescuing most before the current propelled the craft downstream, where it broke to pieces as they watched.

They had landed "on a desolate island, naked, with a broad stream still between us and our shore of destination." Somehow Thomas Adams—who Mullan praised profusely—found the energy to swim the remaining channel, and, naked and barefooted, made his way through "bushes, briars, and fallen timber" to Prudhomme, who returned to the rescue with horses.

Anti-climatically the group arrived at Cantonment Stevens the next day, completing, as Mullan laconically reported, "a short but eventful trip," one that eliminated this route as the course of a possible wagon road.

Mullan had two more explorations to undertake before reporting to Stevens on the best route over the mountains.

Ironically Mullan recorded little about his excursion in May and June 1854, the trip that most influenced the route he recommended to Stevens, and the one that incurred lingering controversy over whether he chose the best course. Returning from his arduous trip to Flathead Lake, Mullan realized there were only two wagon routes realistically capable of connecting the plains of the Missouri with those of the Columbia. One split through the Bitterroots east of the Coeur d'Alene Mission, and the other traveled along the Clark Fork River north of Lake Pend Oreille. Mullan inspected them both on this trip and made a decision that even he came to question. "Had I known in 1854 what I did not learn until 1859," Mullan later wrote, "I should have recommended that the…road…should have followed the Clark's route."[21]

In the spring, as Mullan had guided a wagon from Fort Benton to the Bitterroot Valley, he had also dispatched Thomas Adams on a separate expedition to explore the route over the Bitterroot Mountains—the course Stevens had followed in October 1853 on his way to Olympia. Adams found the path deep with snow. That should have been an omen, but Mullan failed to recognize it.

Mullan had spent much time in the Bitterroot Valley asking Indians about the best route over the mountains. Most refused to discuss the matter, showing no "friendly signs to have their country explored." Some deliberately lied. But among those who would talk, most professed the best course lay through the Bitterroots. These Indians, of course, had no knowledge of the requirements necessary for wagon travel. On May 21, 1854, Mullan set out to determine for himself between the two routes.[22]

Mullan traveled along the Clark Fork to Lake Pend Oreille, finding spring runoff had flooded the route. He abandoned his horses and canoed across the lake and down the Pend Oreille River to St. Ignatius Mission. From there he dispatched a messenger to John Owen, then in the Spokane Valley: deliver government horses to the mission so Mullan's party could continue.[23]

The group then traveled to the Hudson's Bay Company's Fort Colville above Kettle Falls on the Columbia, where he purchased supplies before continuing to the Coeur d'Alene Mission. Mullan had arrived at the metropolis of the Inland Northwest, another Jesuit outpost. He would come to know the place well. Set on a grassy knoll overlooking the Coeur d'Alene River, the mission consisted of eight log houses, a barn, stable, flour mill, and several small buildings, all dominated by a stunning church completed the year before Mullan arrived, the grandest structure for hundreds of miles. Father Antonio Ravalli had overseen the three-year construction project, hoping to evoke the eloquence of European cathedrals. He succeeded in a rustic way, Indian laborers erecting a church of hand-hewn logs topped with a dome. They cut trees five feet in diameter to support the alter. No nails being available, they held the building together with wooden pegs. Ravalli proved equally ingenious when decorating the interior. He papered the walls with hand-painted newspaper and fashioned chandeliers from tin cans. Below the mission, on the flat near the river, a small community of teepees and lodges housed about forty permanent Indian residents who raised cattle, pigs, wheat, and an assortment of vegetables.[24]

Here Mullan followed his usual pattern of querying locals, asking both Indians and missionaries about the best route over the mountains. Taking their advice, he headed east over the Bitterroots, the path Stevens had traveled eight months earlier. Returning to Cantonment Stevens, he wrote his assessment of the two routes.

Mullan told Stevens about the swollen rivers around Lake Pend Oreille, "rendering their crossings exceedingly dangerous," concluding it would be economically infeasible to construct a wagon road there, where workers would need to blast a trail through rocky outcrops above the flood zone. Instead, he recommended the route through the Bitterroots, east of the mission. Despite Adams's report on the snow-covered pass, Mullan reasoned that, since this route lay south of the Pend Oreille trail, in most years it would receive less snow. Further, the mountain route was shorter. He therefore pronounced this "the most feasible and practicable" course.

Yet as early as that same year, even some members of Stevens's expedition disagreed. John Suckley wrote, "A road *might* be built over the tops of the Himalayeh mountains—but no reasonable man would undertake it." Nor would a reasonable man, he averred, construct a road through the Bitterroots with its steep grades and deep gullies.[25]

Stevens believed either the Bitterroot or Pend Oreille route workable, with costs about the same. But he had confidence in Mullan and favored his advice. Stevens noted the mountain route's shorter distance, a significant advantage. When wagon road authorization eventually came, it would be over Mullan's preferred route.[26]

There remained only one possible route to explore—the one over Lolo Pass taken forty-nine years earlier by Lewis and Clark. That most resourceful group of explorers nearly starved on that crossing, subsisting on colt meat, bear grease, candle wax, and a disgusting concoction they called "portable soup." Here William Clark, this nation's epitome of an adventurer, wrote that he had "been wet and as cold in every part as I ever was in my life." Travel here was not for the timid.[27]

Mullan, who knew well the Lewis and Clark journals, harbored no illusions about the daunting task ahead, nor about the likelihood of finding a suitable wagon path. But Stevens had ordered him to explore all possible routes over the mountains, so he would travel the Lolo, at the same time of year as had Lewis and Clark. Mullan left the Bitterroot Valley on September 19, 1854. "We parted from our late home with feelings of true and heartfelt regret," Mullan wrote. "Our comforts had been few and crude, it is true, but sufficiently great to endear us to a place and a people we shall not soon forget."[28]

Within a few days Mullan fully empathized with that earlier army expedition. His crew clambered over "steep mountains, obstructed by much fallen timber, which proved very fatiguing to our animals." The further they went, the harsher the travel. "We could see in every direction, and nothing met our view but one immense bed of pine-clad mountains."[29]

The Stevens Pacific Railroad Survey effectively ended when, after eleven days of mountainous struggle, the Mullan party emerged onto the Weippe Prairie, a welcome place of "grass two feet high." Even the obsessive Mullan could now officially eliminate Lolo Pass as a wagon or railroad route. "I have never met with a more uninviting or rugged bed of mountains," he wrote Stevens. "It cannot be converted to any useful purpose." What a welcome relief it must have been when, a few days later, Mullan came upon the residence of William Craig.

Although an Idaho town and a mountain bear his name, Craig remains an under-recognized figure in Northwest history. He entered the Oregon Country in 1829 as a fur trader. Ten years later he married Isabel, a Nez Perce woman, and the two settled among the tribe. Craig provided safe haven for Presbyterian missionary Henry Harmon Spalding following the massacre of Spalding's associates at the Whitman mission in 1847; served as long-time Nez Perce Indian agent; and interpreted for Stevens during his treaty councils in 1855. The Nez Perce thought so highly of Craig that they enjoined Stevens to write a clause into their treaty allowing him to retain his farm—on a reservation otherwise off limits to whites.[30]

As Mullan came out of the mountains, he found William and Isabel Craig living comfortably in a log house surrounded by a picket fence on prime farm land in the Lapwai Valley. They raised chickens, goats, pigs, corn, onions, melons, pumpkins, and tomatoes "in great abundance." The Craigs invited Mullan to dine, while local Nez Perce farmers sold his men fresh vegetables, "the first we had seen for twenty-one months; they proved truly refreshing."[31]

Mullan continued on the next day, arriving at Fort Walla Walla on October 9 and The Dalles five days later. There he discharged his party and turned over government property to the quartermaster. No other member of Stevens's expedition had traveled so extensively. "In winter and summer," wrote one historian, "struggling with his pack animals in deep snows and fording swollen streams, this indomitable, coura-geous, dynamic trail-blazer had halted at no hazard, however perilous, had never turned back before gaining his objective." No wonder Isaac Stevens championed his selection to construct the Walla Walla to Fort Benton wagon road. "Should Congress make an appropriation for a military road," Stevens wrote Secretary of War Jefferson Davis, "it could not be placed in better hands than Lieut. Mullan's."[32]

Isaac Stevens commanded best when subordinates shared his vision and unquestioningly obeyed his instructions. It helped, too, if, like John Mullan, they possessed similar energy and courage. As Stevens com-menced his expedition, he hoped it would culminate in a congressional appropriation for a military wagon road; he intended to find not only the best route for that road, but also the best man to build it. At the onset of his excursion, even a seer could not have predicted that Mullan, one of the party's most junior officers, would become Stevens's choice to undertake that important task. But Mullan's stock rose as Stevens spurned a number of his potential rivals.

Lieutenant Andrew Jackson Donelson served as Mullan's command-ing officer as they ferried supplies upriver from St. Louis. That work so impressed Stevens, then suffering poor health, that he appointed Donel-son to supervise daily activities of the expedition on the march west to

Fort Benton. But the meticulous Stevens became disenchanted with Donelson. Donelson protested the reprimand he received from Stevens, "under whom I have served for so long a time, and under such peculiar circumstances." But Donelson's complaints did not alter Stevens's opinion: he would not trust Donelson with road construction.[33]

At least Stevens did not threaten to shoot Donelson "like a dog," as he did Frederick Lander; nor did Donelson contemplate challenging Stevens to a duel, as did Lander. Lander would not receive Stevens's road-building endorsement, either. But he certainly began the expedition with an impressive resume.[34]

At the time he formed his party, Stevens knew of Lander's stellar reputation as a railroad engineer. President Franklin Pierce probably sealed Lander's selection to the Stevens party when he appointed Lander's brother as a federal judge in Washington Territory. The new governor would need allies once he got to Olympia; it would not hurt to ingratiate himself to a judge by asking his brother to join his party.[35]

Any chance Lander had of gaining Stevens's favor evaporated when the expedition reached Fort Benton. Stevens sent Lander on an exploration north of the fort, but called him back as "there was not...harmony in Mr. Lander's party." On another exploration Lander got lost. Finally, Lander enraged Stevens by failing to follow his instructions to explore the Cascade Mountains. The success of Stevens's survey rested on his ability to ascertain that trains could cross the Cascades. Stevens fumed when Lander, complaining of a winter crossing in heavy snow, opted instead to travel to Puget Sound via the milder Columbia River.[36]

Lander chafed under Stevens's exacting supervision—and his increasing favoritism toward Mullan. He did all he could to undermine their northern railroad dreams, in the process torching a rivalry between two of the West's best known road builders, Mullan and himself.

Having reached Puget Sound, Lander extricated himself from Stevens and convinced his brother to finance an expedition to explore what Lander considered a more viable railroad route than Stevens's northern passage. It turned out Lander was correct—the first transcontinental railroad would more closely follow his central course than that of any of the official Pacific surveys. But Lander nearly killed himself making that point.[37]

Lander set out to explore a line south of Stevens's course, a forced march to reach Washington, D.C., in time to influence Congress before it designated an official transcontinental route. Accompanied by three others—two of whom wisely quit midway through—Lander explored the Rockies and the Great Basin, nearly freezing in the mountains and almost starving on the plains. On a sweltering day in July 1854 the two emaciated travelers stumbled upon a log cabin isolated in the vast Nebraska Territory. It turned out to be one of those serendipitous moments that happen rarely, but end up changing history.

The farmer they met turned out to be Grenville Dodge—whom Lander had previously tutored. While Lander convalesced, he and Dodge talked railroads. Both agreed the most viable transcontinental route lay near Dodge's farm, along the Platte River. In Lander, Dodge had access to perhaps the most knowledgeable man in America regarding possible railroad courses; he knew two prospective routes personally. And Lander's passion for the course he had just passed inspired Dodge. In 1859 Dodge would meet Abraham Lincoln, convincing the future president of the superiority of a central transcontinental railroad, and Dodge would become chief engineer of that route.[38]

Despite Dodge's hospitality, Lander's companion died from exposure to the harsh elements of their trip. Lander, nursed to health by Dodge, continued on to Washington. There he privately printed his report advocating a central transcontinental route. Remarkably, Jefferson Davis presented it to Congress with the same stature as the meticulously planned and documented official Pacific Railroad Surveys. But when Davis eventually deemed a southern route as best for America's first transcontinental, Lander—along with many others—realized any hope of constructing a transcontinental had, for the time being, dissipated into a mire of sectional politics. Only after the South seceded would Lincoln guide through Congress the act authorizing Lander's route.

Lander knew that wagon roads would precede transcontinental railroads. Though he knew Davis's decision had delayed transcontinental railroad construction, Lander sought approval to construct a wagon road. Lander's course—technically the Fort Kearney, South Pass, and Honey Lake Wagon Road—essentially traced the route that Dodge and Lander had schemed. It took Lander three years, but he completed the road well before Mullan finished his road further north, and enjoyed mocking his rival, who he termed an "old explorer" unable to complete a task on time—though Lander was eight years Mullan's senior. Mullan returned fire by noting Lander's substandard work under Stevens, complete with "erroneous judgments, opinions and reports." Both men had considerable egos, neither abided criticism, and both believed their reputations hinged on the perceived supremacy of their particular road. It is little wonder they did not get along. Lander died in 1862. Their rivalry might have simmered for years had Lander lived longer.[39]

Lander had received support for his independent survey from Captain George McClellan who, at the onset of the Stevens survey, clearly seemed the obvious choice to construct a northern wagon road. Stevens recruited no person more aggressively; none of his personal relationships soured more bitterly.[40]

Stevens assigned McClellan to explore the Cascade Mountains in search of the best pass for a railroad. McClellan abysmally failed.[41]

Showing none of the urgency that characterized Stevens's approach to the railroad survey, McClellan dallied once he reached the Northwest. He spent inordinate time provisioning and organizing his party—a procrastinating characteristic that would so dishearten Abraham Lincoln a few years later. He took time to fish and sail. Compared to the dangers Mullan faced, McClellan's efforts seemed a pleasure excursion.

When McClellan and Stevens met at Fort Colville in the fall of 1853, a frustrated Stevens learned that McClellan had not yet explored the Cascades. Stevens again ordered him to do so. McClellan continued to stall. Though he had not even been in the mountains, he claimed them too snow-clogged to permit passage. Then he said he would need more time to provision before even contemplating such a venture. Exasperated, Stevens ordered Lander to undertake the Cascades exploration. When Lander also refused, Stevens lambasted both men. McClellan petulantly responded, "I have done my last service under civilians and politicians." That same disdain for civilian authority would later lead to McClellan's downfall when President Lincoln relieved him of duty as General-in-Chief of the Union Army during the Civil War.[42]

Civilian engineer Abiel Tinkham eventually crossed the Cascades through Snoqualmie Pass and must have wondered about all the angst of Lander and McClellan; he found the route comparatively easy. Much pleased to finally find someone willing to venture into the mountains, Stevens emphasized Tinkham's description of Snoqualmie Pass in his report to Jefferson Davis. But Davis, who would become president of the Confederacy, was predisposed to a southern railroad and sought every reason to criticize northern routes. Not surprisingly, he emphasized McClellan's uninformed critique of the Cascades over Tinkham's first-person observation.[43]

Stevens never forgave McClellan. In reality, Davis would not have approved any railroad benefitting the north. But Stevens optimistically hoped otherwise, and believed McClellan's insubordination had killed his route's chances.

Stevens did have confidence in some members of his expedition who performed to his exacting standards, particularly Lieutenant Rufus Saxton and civilian Abiel Tinkham. But no one had accomplished more than John Mullan. "In the establishment of his quarters," Stevens wrote, "the management of his command, and in his intercourse with the Indians, he evinced the soundest judgment, and the whole sphere of duty was filled by him in a manner entitling him to the warmest commendation." Mullan would be Stevens's handpicked choice to construct the wagon road.[44]

On February 28, 1854, Isaac Stevens gave his first address to the territorial legislature in Olympia. He laced the speech with references to the need for a variety of wagon roads in the new territory, most particularly one from Fort Benton to Walla Walla. He found a receptive audience. The legislature petitioned Congress to fund the road.[45]

Stevens knew his way around Washington, D.C. He realized territorial resolutions accomplished little unless accompanied by someone to advocate on their behalf. So Stevens sailed south, crossed the Isthmus of Panama, and then shipped north to Washington, D.C.

Stevens did not succeed in obtaining congressional appropriations, but he made allies and returned to Washington Territory optimistic about the future. He arrived back at Olympia in December 1854—the same month John Mullan made his way to the territorial capital. Mullan joined other members of the survey team working out of offices in two small Main Street buildings, their desks littered with maps and papers, preparing reports for Stevens. Over that winter Stevens and Mullan formed a close friendship and refined plans to again seek congressional authorization of the Fort Benton to Walla Walla wagon road. This time, John Mullan would go to the nation's capital as advocate.[46]

In January 1855 Mullan left the Northwest with letters for the War Department from Stevens, along with additional legislative resolutions requesting construction of the Fort Benton road. As he made his way east, President Franklin Pierce, acting on Stevens's earlier request, signed a bill providing $30,000 for construction of the military road. But Secretary of War Jefferson Davis refused to spend the money. He had valid reasons. The appropriated amount "was entirely inadequate to effect the object" of completing the road through rugged terrain. There would be no road building in the immediate future.[47]

Despite that setback, the previous two years had been good for Mullan. He had left St. Louis in May 1853 as an unknown second lieutenant. He had become a seasoned western explorer held in the highest regard not only by a territorial governor, but also by those who served with him. He had demonstrated the tenacity that would characterize his every undertaking. But it would be three years before Lieutenant Mullan returned to the Northwest.

CHAPTER 5

Killing Time

T HE "SAFFRON SCOURGE" SOME CALLED IT; others, "black vomit."
Some said "Bronze John" or "yellow jack." By any name, it killed.
When 230 New Orleanians died from yellow fever on August 20, 1853,
the newspapers labeled it "Black Day." But it was just one of many. That
year 7,849 Louisianans succumbed to the disease, 2,425 more in 1854,
and 2,670 in 1855. Another name for the affliction: "stranger's disease."
Louisiana residents understood little about yellow fever, but they did
know it mainly wracked newcomers. The army sent Lieutenant John
Mullan into the heart of this pestilence. It might explain his absence
without leave while on his way there. Certainly, he was in no hurry. The
man who had survived sub-zero nights on mountain passes and near-
death encounters with engorged western rivers now faced a much more
intimidating challenge—service in Louisiana in the summer of 1855, the
season when yellow fever struck hardest. Indeed, he received the transfer orders to Louisiana precisely because the officer corps there, gutted
by yellow fever deaths, required replenishing.[1]

Mullan had arrived on the East Coast in 1855 after an absence of nearly
two years. He unsuccessfully lobbied the War Department to release the
congressionally approved $30,000 for his road so he could immediately
return west and start construction. Instead, he would be away for three
years, his first assignment being the most dreaded of his army life.

Mullan received orders to join Company H, Second Regiment of
Artillery, in Baton Rouge, Louisiana. Yellow fever had killed two lieu-
tenants and a sergeant there in 1854. The post needed replacements, but
Baton Rouge was hardly the place a twenty-four-year-old officer with
aspirations—for living, not to mention advancement—hoped to locate.
Mullan tarried; Company H reported him absent without leave.[2]

Even for an officer who disdained stuffy army conventions, a serious breach of military etiquette by going AWOL was out of character for the disciplined Mullan. Perhaps he encountered travel obstacles. We have no explanation, but Mullan could be excused if he deliberately prolonged his trip. Things were particularly bleak in Baton Rouge. His entire company had to move fourteen miles away "on account of the prevalence of epidemic." While we do not know what caused his tardiness, we do know he wanted out of Louisiana. Almost immediately upon arrival he applied for a transfer to the Corps of Topographical Engineers.[3]

Congress appropriated large sums of money to the War Department in the 1850s for extensive public works projects. Topographical Engineers usually headed the surveys and road-building efforts, and young officers could make reputations with the "Topos." Mullan hoped to get back West to construct the road; he believed assignment to the Topographical Bureau provided his best opportunity. But the army refused. Mullan would spend the next three years in frustrating assignments, biding his time, far away from Washington Territory.[4]

Mullan's Company H returned to Baton Rouge in November 1855. Winter temperatures had calmed the previous summer's epidemic. A few weeks later his company received word of a deadly Florida encounter involving one of Mullan's West Point classmates, touching off the third, and final, Seminole War.

Lieutenant George Hartsuff graduated five places below Mullan in 1852. On the morning of November 20, 1855, he was camped with ten men in Florida. One member of his party cooked breakfast, a couple saddled horses, and some warmed themselves by the fire while Hartsuff combed his hair preparing for another day's survey for a military road. A party of Seminoles surreptitiously approached the tents and opened fire. In minutes they had killed four of Hartsuff's men and wounded four others. Hartsuff struggled away, hid in a pond, then spent two nights concealed in a palmetto grove—bleeding from three wounds, hungry, and thirsty. Remarkably, he survived the ordeal.[5]

Florida's Seminole Wars, the longest and most expensive of America's Indian wars, stretched over forty years in three major conflicts. The army had been repeatedly humiliated, particularly in the Second War in the 1830s, when a ragtag group of Seminoles outclassed America's finest military leaders. Army officials had no desire to return, but, especially after the Hartsuff attack, white residents demanded protection from the four hundred and fifty or so Seminoles who remained in Florida, perhaps one hundred of whom could be classified as warriors.[6]

The hopelessly outnumbered Seminoles fought with outdated weapons, at times reduced to digging bullet lead from trees that had been used by army troops for target practice. Finally, in 1858 they surrendered and moved to Indian Territory in what would become Oklahoma. The last of the Seminole Wars had ended.[7]

And where was John Mullan? In 1891 George Cullum, in his *Biographical Register* of West Point graduates, stated Mullan spent part of 1855 "in Florida hostilities against the Seminole Indians." Mullan's wife Rebecca, in her 1892 reminiscences, wrote that "hostilities breaking out in Florida among the Seminole Indians, he was ordered to join his regiment" there in early 1855. Both sources are at least partially wrong, since hostilities did not begin until late in 1855—and John's location throughout that year is documented; never did he appear in Florida.[8]

When it came time to compile the *Encyclopedia of Frontier Biography* nearly a century after Cullum's report, Mullan's service in the Seminole conflict had undergone a dramatically expanded—and often repeated—exaggeration. Now it seemed he had engaged in "two years of fighting the Seminole Indians." But if Mullan set foot in Florida at all, it would have been for a few weeks at most.[9]

Records of Mullan's activities account for all but two short periods of time when he could have been in Florida, the first coming in January and February 1856. Mullan received a transfer to Company A in January 1856. Notations in company records state he remained on detached service with Company H until March. But Company H did not go to Florida—it remained in Louisiana. It is possible Mullan was detached from both companies and served in Florida, but if so his time was brief. By March 5 he appeared with his new Company A in Maryland. Mullan was once again detached from Company A in May and June, but virtually all of that time he served again at Baton Rouge. A detour to Florida would have been virtually impossible. If John Mullan did service in Florida, it was short, and it is doubtful he engaged in hostilities. The often-cited story of Mullan's service in the Seminole War is mostly—if not totally—myth.[10]

This much we do know. After Mullan received transfer to Company A of the Second Regiment of Artillery in January 1856, he spent sixteen of the next twenty months at Baltimore's historic Fort McHenry. It must have been during this period that he met the Williamson family of that city—and his future wife, Rebecca. While at McHenry he received his commission as a first lieutenant. In September 1857 Company A transferred to Kansas, and Mullan spent a couple of months at Fort Leavenworth.[11]

In December 1857 Mullan received instructions to return to Washington, D.C. There he again worked with Isaac Stevens. While Mullan had bided his time for nearly three years, much had transpired in the Northwest that would directly impact his future. And Stevens emerged during this period in an even more powerful political position to influence decision-makers about who would head construction of the Walla Walla to Fort Benton road. Of course, he would recommend Lieutenant John Mullan.

The enthusiasm with which much of America greeted the Pacific Railroad Surveys held no such allure for the indigenous residents of the Inland Northwest. The Yakamas, Spokanes, Palouse, Nez Perce, Coeur d'Alenes, and other Inland tribes understood that wagon roads cutting through their lands would usher a rush of unwelcome intruders. Little wonder that in 1853 Captain George McClellan, on duty with Isaac Stevens's railroad survey expedition, reported that Yakama Chief Kamiakin bristled at the idea of a military road crossing Yakama lands. Tensions had risen to such a level that Jesuit priest Charles Pandosy feared for his life, despite his longtime friendship with the tribe: "The clouds are gathering on all lands. The winds begin to lower, the tempest is pent up. Ready to burst."[12]

Isaac Stevens also recognized the significance of roads, but for him they held great promise. In order to build them, the government first had to secure title to Indian land via treaties. In late 1854 and early 1855 Stevens conducted a flurry of treaty councils with Puget Sound tribes. But his major interest lay east of the Cascade Mountains, with Indians through whose lands a wagon road—and eventually a railroad—would traverse. In March 1855 he dispatched emissaries to meet with interior tribes and establish "some point favorable for holding treaties." His envoy selected Walla Walla.[13]

On May 24, 1855, Gustavus Sohon climbed a slight rise of land, withdrew his sketch pad, and started drawing. He would be busy over the next several minutes, capturing the grand entrance of more than five hundred Nez Perce warriors arriving at the Walla Walla treaty council, resplendently painted and decorated. "Their plumes fluttered about them," wrote one observer. Eventually Sohon would turn his pencil sketch into the most dramatic color image of all the many he painted during his lifetime. In the middle of that treaty council painting, one can see diminutive Isaac Stevens clustered with his aides beneath an American flag. Facing Stevens is a group of Nez Perce warriors. One tall white man dominates the scene. William Craig, choosing the side of his Nez Perce relatives as they prepared to shake the governor's hand, had traveled from his home in Lapwai to assist in the proceedings, and would ably serve both the tribe and the governor as interpreter over the ensuing days.[14]

The council commenced under cloudy skies five days later. For two weeks Stevens and Indian chiefs negotiated treaties, a stormy meeting of two cultures. Most of the Indian leaders eventually signed the document, but only after Stevens bullied them by alleging, probably accurately, that whites would enter tribal lands with or without treaties, so the Indians should make their best deal. The three separate agreements with various tribes that Stevens negotiated in Walla Walla carried similar terms. Tribes would move to reservations, ceding thousands of square miles to the federal government. The government would provide improvements at the reservations and guarantee Indians the right to fish, hunt, and gather food at their usual and accustomed places. And, in the section dearest to Stevens, the various bands agreed that "whenever in the opinion of the President of the United States the public interest may require it, that all roads highways and railroads shall have the right of way through the reservation." Stevens specifically had the Fort Benton to Walla Walla wagon road in mind. Of all the provisions in these flawed treaties, none more aroused the tribes than this one.[15]

With the exception of some Nez Perce, tribal leaders who affixed their Xs on the treaty documents did so grudgingly. Kamiakin, the last to sign, agreed only after personally meeting with Stevens, at which time Stevens allegedly told the chief that Kamiakin would "walk in blood knee deep" if he refused. Kamiakin particularly objected to the treaty's road provisions, sarcastically commenting at the council that he hoped Americans would "settle on the wagon route…so the Indians may go and see them."[16]

Stevens departed Walla Walla satisfied. He believed he had done estimable service to the federal government, settlers, Indians, and, ironically, the cause of peace. He made his way east to treaty councils with the Flatheads and Blackfeet. He had been absent from Walla Walla less than three months when his fragile amity collapsed. It seems obvious in hindsight why Stevens's forced settlements failed. But news that Yakamas had started a war shocked the governor.

Stevens should not have been surprised. While negotiating the Walla Walla treaties, a different messenger brought the governor disturbing information: miners had discovered gold in Colville. Stevens hurried the Walla Walla proceedings before Indians learned the news. It proved a short-term solution. By autumn 1855 the rush to the "Eldorado of the North" was on, and the Inland tribes witnessed their fears of uncurbed trespass.[17]

"Suddenly all eyes turned to Colville," the Olympia newspaper trumpeted. Tensions grew. In August 1855, several Yakamas, led by Qualchan, son of Chief Owhi, killed six miners as they traveled to Colville. Qualchan epitomized a younger generation of warriors who brooked no compromise when it came to transgressions on Indian land. Several other deaths followed. Stevens sent Indian agent Andrew Bolon to investigate. "I place great confidence in his energy and determination of character to keep things straight," Stevens wrote. He should not have been so confident.[18]

As Bolon rode into the Yakima Valley, Kamiakin's younger brother encouraged him to return to The Dalles. No whites were safe from Qualchan's band. Bolon took the sound advice. While on the trail back he met three young Yakamas, including Moshell, Kamiakin's nephew, whom he knew and trusted. But Moshel was jealous of Qualchan; killing an important white man would bring him prestige among younger tribal members. As the party stopped to rest on September 23, one warrior jerked Bolon to the ground, another pinned him, and a third slashed his throat.[19]

White residents largely ignored the deaths of miners: small parties traveling through Indian country faced hazards, and if miners decided to gamble their lives for gold, that was their choice. But the murder of Bolon—Indian agent, member of Washington's first territorial legislature—brought outrage. There is only one recourse, blared the Olympia newspaper—"the extreme measure." Bolon's death became "a watershed moment in Pacific Northwest history." It incited the Inland wars fought between 1855 and 1858.[20]

The initial army confrontation with Indians, commonly known as the Yakama War, proved as inconclusive as it was discomfiting. Brevet Major Granville Haller led a force of one hundred out of Fort Dalles on October 3, 1854, to atone for Bolon's death. Three days later he engaged Yakamas under Kamiakin. Fighting continued for two days. Facing an enemy he embellished at being fifteen hundred strong, Haller retreated, arriving at The Dalles having lost five men, his cattle, his howitzer, many of his provisions, and his pride.[21]

Haller's defeat set off a clamor for revenge. Both Washington and Oregon territories formed militias; the Olympia newspaper implored them to blot the Yakamas "from existence." In late October, Major Gabriel Rains led another force out of Fort Dalles: three hundred and fifty army regulars accompanied by an equal number of Oregon volunteers. They briefly engaged the Yakamas, but Kamiakin ordered a tactical retreat, and the frustrated troops accomplished little other than destroying a Catholic mission, erroneously blaming Jesuits for providing arms to the Indians. Rains petulantly left a note for Kamiakin at the plundered mission: "We will…war forever until not a Yakima breathes in the land he calls his own—the river only we will let retain this name, to show to all people, that here the Yakimas once lived."[22]

Considerable bluster, but when boiled down, Rains's mission accomplished little more than killing two Indians and sacking a defenseless mission. The army having dismally disappointed locals, the Oregon militia decided to tend to matters itself. In December, militia volunteers appeared in the Walla Walla Valley to confront Walla Walla and Cayuse tribes that, until then, had remained peaceful. When Chief Peopeomoxmox rode into their camp under a white flag, the volunteers imprisoned him. Later, after a harrowing running battle that killed several whites, frustrated militia members scalped the great chief, skinned him, and pickled his ears in alcohol, which they took to Portland. There they reportedly drank a toast to their great success from the same alcohol in which his ears had been preserved. Until then the Yakamas had fought alone. But with the desecration of Peopeomoxmox, a man who had countenanced peaceful relationships between whites and Indians, the interior war took on complexity. Now the army would face combined tribes fighting in a unified effort, heretofore unheard of in the Inland Northwest.[23]

The army called on a new commander to meet the increasingly explosive situation. Colonel George Wright—West Point graduate of 1822 and decorated veteran of the Seminole and Mexican wars—took control of the newly reorganized Ninth Infantry. Wright and his field officers, including Major Edward Steptoe, led the troops through rigorous training at Fort Monroe, Virginia, before heading west. The arrival of the seven-hundred-fifty-man Ninth Infantry brought the number of military personnel in the Northwest to two thousand—nearly one-fifth of the entire United States Army. The smartly turned out Ninth Infantry, complete with regimental band, had no better luck engaging interior Indians than had Haller and Rains.[24]

Army tactics involved luring an elusive guerilla force to open battle, a game of hide and seek in which the Indians not only knew the hiding places, but could also travel faster than the army. Wright's ponderous force moved at a snail's pace and could sneak up on no one.

Wright, recognizing the difficulties in finding and fighting Indians, was more inclined to negotiate. He also sympathized with the interior tribes. He believed the Stevens treaties of 1855 responsible for the uprising, and felt the interior of the Northwest—land he believed to be of little utility to whites—should be reserved for Indians. That concept infuriated Stevens, a threat to his plans for interior roads. On his expedition to Yakama country, Wright parleyed with Indians, something Haller and Rains had never attempted, gaining promises from Yakama leaders that they would return stock taken from the army and cease hostilities. In an effort to provide the army better future access to the interior, Wright also ordered Steptoe to construct a fort at Walla Walla.

Little changed in the Northwest as a result of the 1855–56 war—except that Inland Indians grew emboldened. When Stevens held a second council at Walla Walla in 1856, he found the four thousand gathered Indians disinclined to negotiate. The governor escaped with his life only because Steptoe and troops intervened.[25]

Still, a period of calm settled over the Inland Northwest. The army's policy of prohibiting white incursion into the interior ushered a precarious peace, but incensed Stevens. He railed against army actions he believed coddled Indians and denied whites access. Most Northwest army officers believed Stevens's treaties had stirred discontent. Indeed, Congress did not ratify Stevens's treaties until 1859, primarily because of army opposition.

Stevens determined he would be more effective countering army policies if operating from Washington, D.C., rather than Olympia, Washington. In 1857 he easily won election as Washington's congressional delegate. He spent most of his time seeking ratification of his treaties and funding for roads—particularly the Walla Walla to Fort Benton wagon road.[26]

Determined to convince the War Department to begin construction of the Fort Benton wagon road, and to gain additional congressional funding for the project, Stevens probably proposed that Lieutenant Mullan be transferred from Leavenworth, Kansas, to the District of Columbia to assist him in lobbying efforts. In any event, Mullan received those orders in late 1857.[27]

As Mullan made his way to Washington, he stopped by St. Louis University to meet and pay respects to a man he had long admired—Father Pierre-Jean DeSmet. DeSmet must have expressed concern over the lack of ratification of the Stevens treaties, for a few months later Mullan wrote DeSmet: "I have seen the chairman of the Indian Committee and he says that all the Indian treaties made by Governor Stevens are to be confirmed, and that in the treaties the most ample provision has been made for schools, farms, utensils, etc. All of which, in the mountains, will be under the eye of the Jesuits." Mullan's response proved far too optimistic.[28]

Once he reached the District of Columbia, Mullan quickly renewed his friendship with Stevens. One night Mullan accompanied Stevens and his wife to a reception at the residence of Senator Stephen Douglas. Returning to the Stevens home, the two stayed up until 3:00 a.m. discussing the wagon road. Mullan worked throughout that winter with Stevens to gain support for the project.[29]

Despite opposition from the Topographical Engineers, who wanted all western road building supervised by their officers, Stevens and Mullan succeeded in convincing the War Department both to construct the road and to place regular army officer Mullan in charge. Mullan's 1855 request while stationed in Baton Rouge to transfer to the Topographical Engineers had been denied; now he would be leading a project the Topos believed should be theirs. Mullan would report to the Topographical Bureau, but an outsider would be in charge of road construction. The tense relations between Mullan and the Topographical Engineers would escalate in coming years.[30]

In March 1858 Mullan received orders to proceed again to the Northwest. He and Stevens had not yet won additional congressional funding for the road, but a new Secretary of War, John Floyd, believed the $30,000 appropriation already in hand enough to get started. Road construction, Mullan thought, would begin soon. Kamiakin and other Inland tribal leaders had different ideas. The war of 1855–56 had settled nothing. A new war was about to begin. Mullan's construction would be postponed again.[31]

Prelude

LATAH CREEK, WASHINGTON TERRITORY, 1858

O N WEDNESDAY, SEPTEMBER 22, after a march of twenty miles, Colonel George Wright halted his army of seven hundred men along the banks of Nedwhauld Creek, also called Latah Creek. The army spread out on wooded bottom lands. Lieutenant John Mullan probably camped near the thirty Nez Perce allies he had recently led in two battles against warring Inland Northwest tribes. In those encounters, Wright had prevailed in one-sided triumphs, and here he camped near representatives from several of the vanquished groups, called to this ancient crossing by Jesuit priest Joseph Joset to appeal for peace.[1]

Wright's success would enable Mullan to once again commence road building in 1859. Mullan's 1858 efforts had abruptly halted four months earlier when Inland tribes handed the army one of its most ignominious defeats, already called the Steptoe Disaster. But now the Indians had been quelled, clearing Mullan's way to complete the road that had been largely responsible for igniting that conflict.

The next day, aged Yakama Chief Owhi—father of Qualchan; uncle of Kamiakin—sadly approached Wright's camp to parley for peace. A short time earlier he had bid a mournful farewell to his family, fearing he would never see them again. His premonition proved accurate. Wright accosted the old man for reneging on promises to surrender tribal members accused of killing whites in 1856. He ordered Owhi shackled.

As Mullan watched, he no doubt recalled his first meeting with Owhi in 1854 near Flathead Lake. Then he had called him a "great friend of the white man." Now he observed this "noble and generous Indian" shuffle away in chains, an imprisonment from which he would never escape.[2]

Wright's blood was up. Still, this old Yakama warrior posed little threat. Wright fettered Owhi as bait to lure into camp the much more dangerous Qualchan. The colonel commanded Owhi to send a message to his son: unless Qualchan capitulated, Wright would hang Owhi.

Over the next few days the Nedwhauld would acquire yet another name: Hangman Creek.

CHAPTER 6

"Lieutenant Mullan's Party Has Been Saved From Destruction"

IN THE SPRING OF 1858 JOHN MULLAN's reputation as a road builder was about to be delayed. Edward Steptoe's as a soldier was about to be destroyed. And Isaac Stevens found, to his gratification, that John Floyd disagreed with Jefferson Davis. New Secretary of War Floyd disdained his predecessor's reticence about constructing underfunded military roads. Davis had thought the congressional appropriation of $30,000 too meager to justify beginning the highway between Walla Walla and Fort Benton. Floyd disagreed, and after lobbying by Stevens, on March 12, 1858 the secretary sent Lieutenant John Mullan these orders: "Proceeding to Fort Walla Walla...you will collect the tools, materials, & animals, and employ the men necessary for the successful accomplishment... [of rendering] the road practicable for the passage...of wagon trains." While Floyd disagreed with Davis about the advisability of beginning the road, he understood the necessity for additional money to complete it, instructing Mullan to "make a detailed estimate of the amount required to build a more permanent road."[1]

An eager Mullan wasted no time. On the day he received his instructions, he drew up a budget. He would, he claimed, complete his duty by December 1858 using a modest force of thirty men. While the "clearing of timber" and "bridging of streams" would present some difficulties, Indians would pose no problem: "My impressions now are that no apprehension of danger need be feared from the Indians...for their temper and disposition is...towards peace."[2]

Mullan's assessment proved wrong on every count.

Mullan bid his family farewell in Annapolis, traveled to New York, and on April 5 boarded a boat bound for Panama. After crossing the Isthmus, he disembarked from the side-wheel steamer *Sonora* in San Francisco on May 1. In both New York and San Francisco he told reporters of "the importance of [the] road," precursor of a lifelong affinity for self-promotion. He then traveled by steamer up the coast to Vancouver, "the most flourishing of the towns on the Columbia." On May 15, he reached The Dalles.[3]

"In the month of May, 1858, the little town of the Dalles was all that a frontiersman would desire—a regular 'hurrah camp,'" wrote an eyewitness. Here, the Columbia River compressed to a narrow, roaring chasm pinched between perpendicular stone walls. A recently refurbished army post occupied high ground a half mile from the river, overlooking a community of stores, saloons, and stables. The town bustled as several parties simultaneously provisioned for excursions into the interior—including Mullan's acquaintance from his previous trip to the West, John Owen, purchasing supplies for his trading post in the Bitterroot Valley.[4]

Despite the competition for men and material, Mullan and his chief assistants, Gustavus Sohon and Theodore Kolecki, skillfully organized their party. Yet, despite their obvious talents, neither Kolecki nor Sohon had been Mullan's first choice for their positions.

Mullan initially suggested as his aides lieutenants Augustus Kautz, his West Point classmate, and A.C. Gillem, who graduated in 1851. The army rejected the request, apparently believing one officer sufficient for the road task. Mullan then suggested civilian Theodore Kolecki, who would become one of his most trusted associates. Mullan considered his brother, Louis, for the other key position, but instead recommended James King, an experienced civilian surveyor. But King did not make it to New York in time to travel west with Mullan. "I wrote him twice before leaving Washington," Mullan informed Captain A.A. Humphreys of the Topographical Engineers, "and also called to see his uncle [in New York]....If he arrives not tonight, I will sail without him." And Mullan did. That staff vacancy provided the opportunity to hire his friend, the man who became Mullan's most able assistant, Gustavus Sohon.[5]

After completing his duty with Isaac Stevens at various treaty councils in 1855, Sohon had transferred to the army post at Benicia, California, receiving his honorable discharge in July 1857. Mullan enlisted

Sohon in place of the mysteriously absent King. He never made a wiser choice.[6]

Mullan, Kolecki, Sohon, and the rest of the road crew were about to take up a "line of march for Fort Walla Walla" when an expressman on a hard-ridden horse brought shocking news of a deadly encounter between Colonel Edward Steptoe and Inland tribes. Anxious to get on with his road project, and disbelieving the initial horrific report that Steptoe had lost dozens of men in the confrontation, Mullan sent a return rider to Walla Walla to determine if the colonel was prepared to furnish Mullan with a sixty-five man military escort "as directed by the Secretary of War." The request flummoxed Steptoe, who had no troops to lend. His losses were not as dramatic as initially reported, but he had been lucky to survive.[7]

While awaiting a response from Steptoe, Mullan set his men to work—the initial construction of his military road. In a country with "not a tree growing or to be seen," the crew smoothed over an existing trail and started constructing a bridge five miles east of The Dalles when, on May 31, another express rider brought more news from Steptoe: he could not possibly provide an escort, and any road building north of the Snake would meet deadly resistance from a huge confederation of Northwest tribes.[8]

Finding silver linings is difficult if you have just suffered one of the most inglorious defeats in America's Indian wars. But Steptoe tried. Things could have been worse, he wrote his superiors. While his force suffered losses, the Indians had really hoped to annihilate a poorly armed Mullan road crew, and no doubt would have succeeded. It was this road that inflamed the Northwest tribes. Wrote Steptoe:

> The fight with my command only committed the Indians to hostilities a little earlier, and probably under more fortunate circumstances to us.... The Coeur d'Alenes [and] Spokanes…had bound themselves to massacre any party that should attempt to make a survey. I…make no question that Lieutenant Mullan's party has been saved from destruction.[9]

An obvious attempt to salvage what remained of his reputation, Steptoe's account nonetheless bore truth, as Mullan admitted. "Your encounter with the Indians has saved my party from disaster," Mullan wrote Steptoe, "probably from a complete massacre."[10]

Mullan retreated to The Dalles and, with the exception of Kolecki, Sohon, and a skeleton crew retained to care for his stock, disbanded his company. He had no choice, but did so grudgingly, and only after firing off an angry complaint lamenting that "a superior race" had allowed a band of Indians to disrupt the progress of such a momentous project as his road.[11]

✿

Ascending reputations have a way, sometimes, of plummeting. Edward Steptoe's certainly did in 1858.

A West Point graduate of 1837, Steptoe rose to brevet lieutenant colonel after meritorious service in the Mexico-American War where, like Isaac Stevens, he befriended future president Franklin Pierce. Their association grew close and President Pierce sent Steptoe to Utah to investigate an Indian attack that killed members of a railroad survey party, as well as to supervise construction of a wagon road. Steptoe soon found himself embroiled in that territory's peculiar politics.[12]

Pierce also intended to appoint Steptoe territorial governor, replacing Brigham Young, president of the Church of Jesus Christ of Latter-day Saints. Supplanting the religious leader of the Mormon church would be contentious, and Steptoe declined, choosing instead to remain in the army.

It seemed he had made a wise choice when he became Colonel George Wright's second-in-command of the Ninth Infantry in the Pacific Northwest. Wright recognized that the lack of interior fortifications had limited the army's ability during the 1856 Yakama War. So he ordered Steptoe to construct a new compound. It became Fort Walla Walla, and the ragtag town that soon surrounded it took the name Steptoeville—eventually changed to Walla Walla.[13]

Military hero, presidential comrade, prospective territorial governor, namesake of a Northwest town—Steptoe could be excused if, in the spring of 1858, he foresaw an illustrious future. Yet he would soon become a disgraced and ruined man. Shortly after his ignominious retreat in 1858 he received a furlough and never returned to active duty. He resigned in 1861, and died in 1865 at the age of forty-nine. The inscription on his gravestone perhaps attests to the realization that he had made the wrong decision in Utah: "A grateful Government testified its sense of the value of his services....crowning all with the graceful tender, through an Executive who had been his companion in arms...of exalted civil position, which he declined."[14]

The army forbade settlement in the Inland Northwest following the 1856 war, but had excepted miners. Meeting in a log store near Fort Colville in November 1857, some miners petitioned the army to send soldiers to the valley to protect them from increasingly agitated Indians. Steptoe had also received reports that Palouse Indians had killed two miners on their way to Colville. Indians had raided his own commissary and stolen cattle from settlers near Steptoeville. He believed it time for a show of force.[15]

On May 6 he led 158 men north out of Fort Walla Walla through bunchgrass plains "enameled with flowers [of] various forms and colors." This, he anticipated, would be a peaceful mission to allay fears of whites and to impress Indians.[16]

The Palouse, Spokane, and Coeur d'Alene Indians viewed the situation differently. Theirs was not just a land of pretty flowers. As a Coeur d'Alene tribal elder observed years later, "We didn't want to go to war, but what do you do when someone breaks into your home?" In 1858 Indians witnessed increasing numbers of miners breaking into their home, chasing gold in the Colville Valley and on Canada's Fraser River.[17]

The Inland tribes might have forgiven this civilian trespass. But as early as 1855 they had warned Stevens that any military presence north of the Snake River would meet resistance. As Father Joseph Joset admonished, "The very sight of an armed force would be enough to make all the Indians of the country take up arms." When Steptoe marched out of Walla Walla, particularly when he chose to suspiciously meander through Indian territory rather than take the well-established Colville Road to the mines, he set off an uprising.[18]

But the Indians might even have forgiven Steptoe's encroachment had they not been so enraged over the army's plan to build a road across their lands. They knew Lieutenant John Mullan would soon begin such construction. They actually wished it had been Mullan's poorly guarded road crew that had exited Fort Walla Walla. But Steptoe would do. They would stop his march, destroy his army—and send an incontestable message about the fate of Mullan and his road builders should they dare to follow.

On May 17, 1858, an exhausted Father Joset, having ridden the previous day from the Coeur d'Alene Mission, caught Colonel Steptoe as he rode unwittingly into a deadly confrontation. Joset hoped to avert a battle, but Steptoe kept marching. During their horseback conversation, Joset informed Steptoe of the Indians' anger over the road: "Most of the excitement among the tribes was due to mischievous reports that the government intended to seize their lands, in proof of which they were invited to observe whether a party would not soon be surveying a road through it." Colonel George Wright was also well aware of the cause of the Indians' rage. Congress had not yet ratified Stevens's treaties. Mullan's road would be an egregious trespass. "This proposal opening a road through Indian country," he wrote a few days after Steptoe's battle, "was a primary cause of the attack on Colonel Steptoe, and had Lieutenant Mullan preceded Colonel Steptoe his whole party would have been sacrificed." Instead, Steptoe paid the price.[19]

Steptoe led his troops into a country that seemed a cavalryman's dream: Vast expanses of open ground and ample visibility, covered with abundant bunchgrass. With Nez Perce guides leading the way, the troops advanced at a leisurely pace, unconcerned about the guns and ammunition they carried. They should have been concerned.

Just why Steptoe moved into Indian country so poorly armed has been a matter of conjecture for more than 150 years. Some claim he had no intention of engaging Indians, aiming instead to merely intimidate them with the army's presence. Others have stated that Steptoe did not realize how little ammunition his troops carried. However it happened, Steptoe's forces were about to encounter a rarity: the army would confront an Indian enemy better armed than were they.

Most of Steptoe's men carried musketoons that had an almost useless range of less than fifty yards. "Couldn't kill a rooster across the barnyard," stated one authority. Some of the men had long rifles, difficult to carry on horseback. A few took pistols, and a handful had breechloading carbines. And for all of this miscellany of weaponry, the force carried only forty rounds of ammunition per man, an amount quickly spent in the frenzied fighting that ensued. "In their excitement, the soldiers could not be restrained from firing…in the wildest manner," Steptoe later reported. The Indians, on the other hand, were well-armed with Hudson's Bay Company trade muskets of long-range capability. Those without firearms used bows and arrows that carried farther than most of Steptoe's guns.[20]

On the morning of May 17 a band of Palouse warriors ambushed the soldiers, igniting a ten-hour running battle. Warriors mortally wounded two company commanders—Captain Oliver Taylor and Lieutenant William Gaston—unleashing a panic among the troops. Steptoe moved to a hill and awaited an all-out assault that never occurred—no doubt because the Indians did not know his men were nearly out of bullets.

Steptoe lost three enlisted men and three Nez Perce scouts in addition to the two officers. His remaining troops grew increasingly dispirited, "not to be relied upon." So he laid plans for a nighttime retreat. Keeping fires burning to deceive the Indians, his men muffled their horses' hoofs and lashed wounded soldiers to their saddles. Leaving behind two howitzers, one hundred pack animals, and a herd of cattle, Steptoe's troops quietly exited the hilltop at ten that night.[21]

Once out of earshot of the Indians, Steptoe ordered a forced march that brought his men to the Snake River the following evening, a hard retreat of seventy-five miles, with two of his wounded, unable to keep pace, left behind to die. Assisted by friendly Nez Perce in crossing the Snake, the beleaguered troops there met Ulysses Grant's brother-in-law, Captain Frederick Dent, leading sixty soldiers. Dent escorted the vanquished troops to Fort Walla Walla.

On the depressing ride back to Walla Walla Steptoe had time to ponder ways to salvage his reputation. Reporting a few days later, he gave his account the most optimistic spin plausible. And he sought an opportunity at redemption. "I hope the general will send us as strong a force as possible, and with all the dispatch possible," he wrote to departmental commander General Newman Clarke in San Francisco. Clarke would dispatch a strong force, but Steptoe would never again engage in battle. The next time the army confronted Indians in the Northwest, Steptoe would remain behind at Fort Walla Walla, a humiliating censure for the second-in-command of Northwest forces.[22]

Old Fuss and Feathers doomed any future Steptoe might have had in the military. In a terse response to Steptoe's report, the commanding general of the army, Winfield Scott, noted, "This is a candid report of a disastrous affair. The small supply of ammunition is surprising and unaccounted for." Steptoe also found himself in a journalistic maelstrom as newspapers demanded an explanation for what the army would officially label "one of the most sad events that ever befell our cavalry."[23]

But in Washington, D.C., Isaac Stevens gloated. As his son later recalled, the Steptoe disaster "was looked upon as a complete vindication of Governor Stevens's views and policy in regard to the management of Indians, and a convincing proof of the folly and failure of the... military peace policy." Stevens, then territorial delegate to Congress, jumped on the opportunity presented by his surge in respectability. He sought more troops for the Inland Northwest. He demanded the region be opened to settlement. And he pressed for ratification of his 1855 treaties—with their provisions legitimizing the Fort Walla Walla to Fort Benton military road so the Inland tribes could no longer call this intrusion a trespass. Congress granted his every request.[24]

Out in the Northwest, General Newman Clarke sailed to Fort Vancouver to formalize retaliatory plans. Colonel Wright would move against the Indians with a large, well-provisioned force, punishing those who had attacked Steptoe. But first Clarke offered one last chance at peace. Conflict could still be averted if the tribes agreed to return their Steptoe plunder, surrender those guilty of masterminding the attack, and acknowledge "the right of the United States to construct a road to the Missouri River on which troops and travelers could move unmolested." The Inland tribes, buoyed by their triumph, had no intention of complying.[25]

The confederated tribes grew overconfident after their victories in 1856 and 1858. Their warriors seemed braver, their arms better, their guardian spirits stronger, their numbers larger. At Fort Colville, warriors returning from the Steptoe battle triumphantly and gruesomely paraded Captain Taylor's bloody saddle and pronounced themselves ready for further battle. John Owen, having provisioned at The Dalles at the same time as Mullan, found himself deep in hostile Indian country, caught between Colville and the Bitterroot Valley, confronted by warriors who threatened his life. He narrowly escaped, and then only after fervent negotiating. "The war whoop is heard from one end of the valley to the other," he wrote.[26]

In that summer of 1858 war seemed inevitable. Unable to build his road, unwilling to sit idle, John Mullan volunteered to serve under Colonel George Wright.

CHAPTER 7

❦

Wright's Revenge

NEVER HAD THE NORTHWEST seen anything like this. General
Newman Clarke, commander of the Pacific Department, flooded
the region with troops, virtually draining every post west of the Mississippi in a show of force as conspicuous as the antebellum American
army could muster. "Companies were converging to the hostile country
from every part of the Pacific coast," reported Lieutenant Lawrence Kip,
"even from Fort Yuma on the far distant banks of the Colorado, and
from San Diego on the border of Mexico." Newport Barracks in Kentucky dispatched four hundred men. The Sixth Regiment out of Utah
marched for sixty-one days to San Francisco before catching a steamer
to Washington Territory—one of the longest infantry advances in the
history of the American West. Clarke proposed to confront Inland
tribes with overwhelming numbers.[1]

Many of the soldiers converged on The Dalles, where John Mullan
witnessed the teeming bustle of couriers, packers, teamsters, and troops
in frenetic preparation to avenge Edward Steptoe's embarrassment.
General Clarke placed Colonel George Wright in command. "You will
attack all the hostile Indians you may meet, with vigor," Clarke ordered.
"Make their punishment severe." And should "any of the chiefs…visit
you for the purpose of offering the submission of their people," Wright
was to accept such peace offerings only on the condition that tribes
allowed Mullan to build his road through the heart of their homelands.
"The government of the United States has this right, and will make the
road," Clarke charged. "Parties working on it must not be disturbed."[2]

Clarke had lost all confidence in Steptoe. He would sit out the campaign at Fort Walla Walla. Clarke assigned Captain Erasmus Keyes as
Wright's new second-in-command. Keyes, a West Point graduate, had
served as instructor of field artillery and cavalry tactics at the academy;

Mullan had taken his courses. Keyes arrived at The Dalles from California on June 21, 1858, and began training his men.[3]

On the day Keyes arrived at The Dalles, John Mullan, confident of eventually being allowed to construct the road, sent a letter urging the Topographical Bureau to request additional congressional funding for that task. He now realized what Jefferson Davis had suspected years earlier: given the Northwest's expensive labor and supplies, his $30,000 appropriation made it "impossible to resume operation" even should Wright pacify the Indians.[4]

Five days later Mullan volunteered to serve as Wright's topographical engineer. Mullan knew much of the route of his proposed road. But territory north of Walla Walla—where Wright would venture— remained largely a mystery. He wanted "to become cognizant of such topographical facts as would give me a correct idea of the western section of the road." Wright gladly accepted the offer. It would be good for them both: Wright gaining the services of an exemplary topographical engineer, and Mullan learning the lay of the land. "I doubt not that the reconnaissance of the country through which I shall march will be highly important...with reference to the military road to be constructed by you," Wright replied.[5]

Mullan—along with Gustavus Sohon, Theodore Kolecki, an "Indian boy," and three employees Mullan had retained from his road crew— soon left The Dalles for Fort Walla Walla through a "perfectly lifeless... sun-burnt plain." Keyes's wool-uniformed soldiers had earlier sweated for twelve dusty days and 177 miles on this route, enduring sun as "hot as the tropics." Mullan's smaller party made the journey in nine days. Mullan even took time one evening to fish at a "cool, shady & pleasant place along the bank of the river." But he knew this section would provide a key link with his road. So he took along his odometer, carefully measured distances, and noted locations where future travelers could find wood and water.[6]

Mullan's crew occasionally caught glimpses of "hostile Indians... hovering along the line of our route." They came upon the grave of a man "brutally butchered" by Indians a few days earlier. Mullan, always conflicted when it came to Indians, at one point in his trip journal made note of the "vile and relentless savages." But he also noted how the country was rapidly changing: his party had sipped eggnog at one settler's cabin; enjoyed the serenading of two young girls at another. So he also lamented that few Indians remained in this region where "the white man and his civilization" intruded: "The streams that were once their haunts from whence they drew…their yearly supply of salmon and their berries along its banks…now…flow noiselessly on, their rich and abundant supplies…undisturbed."[7]

On July 25, the Mullan party reached Walla Walla, and one can already sense that here is where John Mullan hoped one day to stake his claim. The valley afforded "one of the most beautiful pictures that could break upon the view," he wrote. Here was a land capable of supporting "a population of 30,000 people," a place where an enterprising business-man could prosper.[8]

Mullan, always anxious to gain information about the country through which his road would travel, probably took this opportunity to visit an old acquaintance who knew the region as well as anyone—William Craig. Craig, as Nez Perce Indian agent, had moved to Walla Walla from his Lapwai home where Mullan had visited when leaving the Bitterroot Valley in 1854. Mullan, and no doubt Craig, too, appeared at Colonel Wright's camp on August 6 when Wright signed an alliance with the Nez Perce. Nez Perce warriors would fight alongside the army in Wright's upcoming campaign; John Mullan would lead them.[9]

Since the time of Lewis and Clark the Nez Perce had accommodated whites. But this was no monolithic tribe. A number of Nez Perce had attacked Isaac Stevens after his 1856 Walla Walla council, necessitating Colonel Steptoe's rescue of the governor. Yet when Steptoe had required assistance crossing the Snake River during his 1858 retreat, a different group of Nez Perce came to his aid. Some Nez Perce would fight against Wright. Wright realized he had to exploit the Nez Perce schism to, as Kip stated, abrogate "some seventeen hundred Hudson Bay muskets from the ranks of hostile Indians." Clarke authorized Wright to "employ as many of the friendly Nez Perce as you think judicious." So Wright negotiated a treaty. The Nez Perce would provide warriors "to the extent of their ability," and the army would furnish them arms, ammunition, and provisions.[10]

Nez Perce leaders selected thirty mounted warriors to serve as guides, scouts, and interpreters for Wright. They would wear army uniforms. Wright placed Lieutenant Mullan in charge of this "eagle-eyed" corps that would stealthily and bravely make its way in advance of the troops through country Mullan described as "affording dangerous, murderous ambushes for a lurking enemy."[11]

Mullan was a logical choice to lead the Nez Perce. He knew Indians better than any other officer in Wright's command, having lived among the Flatheads. "To know an Indian you must be with him," Mullan believed. Of course none of Wright's officers, including Mullan, really knew Indians. But Mullan's experiences led him to distinguish between "good" and "bad." The Flatheads topped his hierarchy. From the time of Mullan's first encounter with Flatheads in 1853—when he questioned, "Am I among people whom all the world call savages?"—he tested other Indians against their standard. Nez Perce were among the few to measure up, "far advanced already in civilization—much farther than any tribe west of the Rocky Mountains, except the Flatheads."[12]

Mullan would spend much of his life working on behalf of "good" Indians. But now, in the August heat of 1858, he had to lead a handful of these good Indians against a united front of "bad"—Indians who threatened the completion of his cherished road.

On August 7, at 9:00 a.m., Captain Keyes led an advance column out of Fort Walla Walla to establish camp along the Snake River and await the arrival of Colonel Wright and the bulk of the troops. John Mullan, dressed in buckskin—exhibiting his disdain for the army's preferred attire—rode along, heading the group of Nez Perce, who did not share their lieutenant's wardrobe haughtiness: they proudly wore their army-issued blue uniforms. For four hot days they marched over burned prairies, Coeur d'Alene, Spokane, Palouse, and Yakama Indians having scorched the earth to deprive the army of forage. On their first day out, a party of Indians captured thirty-six oxen from the rear of Keyes's train.[13]

On August 10 the force arrived near the mouth of the Tucannon River. Here, bordering an Indian burial ground, the army constructed Fort Taylor, dominated by tall basalt outcroppings nearby that the troops named Points Taylor and Gaston—commemorating the two officers killed during Steptoe's fight. As Keyes's men cleared ground, Lieutenant John Mullan nearly became a war casualty.[14]

On August 11 sentries captured two Indians. But the hostages broke free and ran into the Snake River. Mullan, standing nearby, plunged in after one, who Kip described as "exceedingly athletic...the sight of whose proportions would have tempered most persons' valor with discretion." But Mullan, "not one to calculate odds," chose to fight anyhow, firing his pistol at the Indian, who dove under the water, arising with a handful of rocks he hurled at the lieutenant. He then grabbed the distracted Mullan, and the two fought hand-to-hand. Luckily for Mullan, getting the worst of it and being repeatedly "soused," the Indian stumbled into a hole, losing his grip. Surfacing downstream, he swam to the other shore and escaped. Mullan's unconventional attire might have saved him—at least from embarrassment. Had his pants "not been very strong in the seat (being of buckskin) he would have had to have gotten another pair. As it was he came very near being killed."[15]

The troops had no further confrontations as they constructed Fort Taylor, a parallelogram of low-walled protection flanked by basalt cliffs. Workers fashioned alder posts for two bastions, piled rock embankments, mounted two six-pound howitzers, and awaited the arrival of Colonel Wright's main force.[16]

Wright appeared on August 18, dismayed by the view across the Snake River. "We have a lake of fire before us," he wrote headquarters. "Possibly we may find sufficient grass left to subsist our animals. Should it prove otherwise, it would be worse than madness to plunge into that barren waste, the inevitable result of which must be the sacrifice of men and animals."[17]

The army had few officers as seasoned as George Wright. He had entered West Point at age fourteen, and by the time he reached Fort Taylor on that "intensely hot...suffocating" August day, he had been in uniform for more than forty years. But the Steptoe fiasco had humbled army officers. Wright recalled his difficulties in the 1855 conflict against Inland tribes when he could hardly find his adversary. Indian warfare in the vast expanse of Washington Territory seldom favored the army. Even with Mullan's eagle-eyed scouts, Wright would have difficulty keeping track of his foe, while his own approach would always be "known to the hostiles." Merely conquering territory meant nothing, for the Indians gladly relinquished land in exchange for outlasting invaders. Wright had to survive in a country with scarce forage, against a more mobile enemy, while enticing that enemy to engage in decisive battle—before his rations ran out.[18]

Things started ominously when, three days after Wright's arrival, a severe wind swept the canyon, leveling tents and stirring up dust so thick the men could scarcely see their own hands. Then came four days of rain. Despite his misgivings about the upcoming fight, Wright welcomed the clear skies of August 25. At 5:00 a.m., his massive column began ferrying across the Snake River.[19]

In hindsight Wright's trepidation seems preposterous. His regiment was so extensive it took two days to cross the Snake. And no wonder. Accompanying him were six hundred army regulars, one hundred civilian packers and herders, thirty Nez Perce warriors, sixteen hundred "animals of all kinds," and subsistence for more than a month. Heading that vast assemblage were twenty-four officers, some of the best talent available to the army: seventeen would become Civil War generals. "Altogether the Indians can have plenty of fighting to do if they want it," noted one observer.[20]

And Wright would not repeat Steptoe's mistake of being outgunned. He outfitted his troops with percussion cap rifles having a range of a thousand yards—more than five times the distance of the Indians' muskets. Others carried Sharps rifles, noted for accuracy. The Indians, many still fighting with bows and arrows, learned to keep a distance; charging Wright's force was suicidal. Wright could march wherever he pleased.[21]

As Wright's men made their way north of the Snake River canyon, they entered some of America's most forlorn landscape—the dun-colored Channeled Scablands—an area the size of Connecticut ripped free of topsoil during the Missoula Floods, the greatest inundations in geological history. John Mullan described it as, "one immense bed of broken basalt," a land "of most perfect desolation." They would travel this country for three days.[22]

Mullan and the Nez Perce scouts traveled in advance or on the flanks of Wright's vanguard, sometimes appearing "perched upon…hill tops overlooking the country," but usually out of contact. Mullan's warriors often went out again on evening reconnaissance, while the troops rested in camp. Still, the Nez Perce failed to spot a single adversary.[23]

During most days Mullan traveled with the Nez Perce, leaving scientific analysis to Sohon and Kolecki. But at times he remained with the main body, taking measurements. Whether reading the landscape or reading his instruments, at all times, even during periods of danger, Mullan made careful notes, for this was country he had not before encountered, through which his road would one day pass. For his army colleagues, avenging Steptoe's defeat was paramount. For Mullan, such revenge provided a means to a different end—learning the lay of the land.

His most critical instrument was also his simplest—an odometer. The odometers of Mullan's time were uncomplicated, but indispensible for road builders. Mullan never appeared in the field without one. Years later, as he planned a stage route from California to Idaho, the Chico, California, newspaper announced that he had been seen leaving town, an odometer attached to his coach wheel. "That's Mullan sure," responded Idaho's *Owyhee Avalanche*, awaiting his arrival. "He's the only man that travels with 'an odometer attached.'" Odometers measured the number of rotations of a wheel. After calculating the revolutions and wheel circumference, distance could be figured. Mullan probably had his attached to a two-wheeled cart, pulled by one horse. Readings were quite accurate, given the technology. Mullan, Kolecki, and Sohon made daily recordings throughout the campaign—undeterred even during times of fighting—until September 12, when Mullan abandoned his wagon near Lake Coeur d'Alene in timber so thick it could not pass. A party of Indians gleefully burned it.[24]

On August 30, the odometer safely in camp, Mullan helped inaugurate the long-anticipated fighting. Wright had made it through the scablands into a partially forested country. At 5:00 that afternoon, having marched eighteen miles, the colonel halted his troops and set out pickets. A band of Indians, riding undetected, fired on the sentries. Wright sent Mullan and his Nez Perce in chase. They gained fast on the enemy, and were "on the heels of the Indians" when a bugler called them back. The warriors, unchastened, "remained still in the hills bantering for…a fight."[25]

The next day Mullan led his group on a scouting mission, becoming separated from the main command, deep in enemy territory. "It was only after great difficulty" that they made it back to Wright. "Our absence had [been] somewhat missed," Mullan wrote. By now, with "the enemy appearing in number along the hills during the day," it became apparent that a major fight would soon ensue. The Battle of Four Lakes loomed.[26]

✿

Wright's men awoke on September 1 to find above them a hillside lined with Indians, "inviting an attack," according to Lieutenant Kip. Wright accommodated. Advancing to the base of the ridge, he ordered Mullan and his Nez Perce to sweep the right side, Major William Grier and his cavalry to secure the left, while he marched the main force up the middle. The movement easily chased away the Indians—which was the warriors' plan. Most of their allies had gathered on flat land beyond the hill at a carefully chosen site. By the time Kip crested the hill, he gazed onto an unforgettable scene:

> Below us lay 'four lakes'....On the plain...we saw the enemy. Every spot seemed alive with the wild warriors....They were in the pines on the edge of the lakes, in the ravines and gullies, on the opposite hillsides, and swarming over the plain. They seemed to cover the country for some two miles.[27]

Chief Kamiakin's Palouse and Yakamas occupied the center, flanked by Qualchan with additional Yakamas, and Stellam and the Coeur d'Alenes. Spokanes under Polatkin and other chiefs backed up the main force. The Indians had especially picked this spot, far removed from army reinforcements. They thought Wright would attack with his cavalry. Believing themselves superior horsemen (which they were) and having faster horses (which they did), they planned to dispatch the cavalry, leaving Wright's infantry isolated in Indian country. Then they would simply prevent retreat and wait for the army's ammunition to run out. It was a reasonable tactic. But they had not reckoned that this time the army came with fire power they could not possibly match.[28]

Instead of cavalry, Wright ordered his infantry down the hill "with all the precision of a parade." They stopped when six hundred yards away, a distance at which the Indians assumed they were safe, and opened fire with a deadly barrage. The Indians approached the troops on horseback, firing and rapidly retreating, but the battle proved no contest as the infantry rifles had a range that dwarfed that of Indian muskets and bows. Suddenly the cavalry burst onto the field at "headlong speed," chasing the warriors into surrounding woods. Despite the one-sided nature of the armament, the battle, remarkably, lasted several hours, and the Indians' basic concept proved accurate. The heavily weighted army horses proved no match for the Indians' sleek ponies, and the cavalry soon gave up pursuit, their horses "too much worn out" to continue.[29]

In military terms the Battle of Four Lakes inflicted minimal damage. Wright's forces killed seventeen to twenty Indians. Significantly, however, the victory Kamiakin hoped to achieve, thus enticing more Indians into his alliance, never materialized. One non-combatant observing the battle reported back to his tribe that he "had seen the soldiers, but never wished to see them" or their long-range rifles again. Kamiakin would receive no reinforcements.[30]

Mullan and his Nez Perce engaged in the battle effectively, coming under fire while clearing the hill from which Wright launched his attack. Some of the Nez Perce then charged into the woods flanking the battle site, driving enemy warriors from the field. Others fended off attacks to Wright's rear. Of course, just how Mullan's small band of thirty could simultaneously fight at the front and rear indicates Mullan's overall lack of control over his warriors. The Nez Perce fought like Indians. They were brave, but engaged in battle independently, not as a cohesive unit, paying little heed to Mullan's orders. When Wright called his troops back to camp, most of the Nez Perce continued their pursuit of the enemy, in search of spoils.[31]

Even so, Wright devoted more space in his official report to praising Mullan, who "moved gallantly" with his Nez Perce, than any other officer. Tellingly, despite the adrenaline rush of the combat, when Mullan penned his own official report, he spent most of his space noting his success in gathering information about the future site of his road: "My party of assistants [and I] have been able to collect material for a complete map of the country from Ft. Dalles to this point." Only after detailing this survey did he mention meeting "the enemy" and driving "him from the ground." Even for an engineer, it is a peculiar personality that would first report on the previous week's scientific measurements before the previous day's battle. But Mullan recognized his reputation depended upon his success as a road builder, not as an Indian fighter. He performed his fighting responsibilities courageously. But the road remained uppermost in his thoughts.[32]

Wright rested for three days at Four Lakes. Only the Nez Perce remained active, making daily reconnoiters, but returning with no information on the enemy's whereabouts. Kamiakin had managed to find a place in which to hide five hundred warriors.[33]

The remarkable effort of Kamiakin to unite multiple tribes in defense of Indian homelands has gone underappreciated. Even more underappreciated is the fact that he could once again rally forces to confront an overpowering enemy after his defeat at Four Lakes. When Wright finally moved his troops on September 5, he found the united tribes waiting.

For fourteen miles and seven hours, Indians and whites engaged in a running battle. For a time it appeared, against all odds, that the Indians might win. As Wright's cumbersome force lumbered along, Indians set fire to the tinder-dry prairie grass around them. With the wind "blowing high and against us," Lieutenant Kip described great billowing clouds of smoke nearly enveloping the troops, while the Indians, in Mullan's words, attempted to "destroy our train and put us at their mercy." Mounted warriors, partially hidden behind the smokescreen, engaged in "feats of horsemanship which we have never seen equaled," according to Kip. "The Indians would dash down a hill...at the most headlong speed" and then fire into the troops. Kamiakin had found a way to negate the long-distance superiority of army guns. "The enemy fired from every point," recalled Mullan, who left the most vivid description of what became known as the Battle of Spokane Plains. "The balls whistled and moved over our heads much too close for our personal comfort." But that proved the high point of the Indian attack. In the end, not a single soldier died. And Wright came upon a tactic that turned the battle.[34]

In a remarkable battlefield sketch, Gustavus Sohon captured the strategy. Wright, sitting on his horse surrounded by a half dozen officers, directs the action. Through great billows of smoke, he sends out skirmishers, his "best marksmen." The cavalry readies at Wright's rear to charge once the shooters have softened the Indian's ranks. Occasionally, Wright would order up a howitzer to rake the hillsides, forcing the Indians to retreat.[35]

In this inchworm fashion Wright made his way to the Spokane River: infantry skirmishers and howitzers clearing the way, cavalry giving chase, supply train pulling up for protection. And in front of all, Mullan's "trusty Nez Perces" leading the way, "pointing the direction... [for] our now wearied columns."[36]

The battle inflicted few casualties on the Indians. One historian claimed that Wright accomplished nothing: "Almost no one had been hurt by his battles, though the bullets fell thick as rain. It had been all flags and sabers, foam-flecked horses and a confusion of musketry: the game of war with an illusion of danger."[37]

But Wright had actually made an indelible impression. He demonstrated that the army could move through Indian country with impunity. And the Indians would soon see how willing Wright was to thoroughly destroy his enemy's resolve and fighting ability.

After resting two days Wright moved his troops east on September 8. In a few miles they noticed "a cloud of dust" in the distance. Wright sent Mullan, the Nez Perce, and some cavalry to investigate. They soon came upon the dust-maker: a herd of eight hundred horses, with a few Indian escorts attempting to lead them to safety. The pursuers fired a few shots, sending the Indians fleeing, then herded the horses back to Wright's camp. That night Wright hanged an Indian prisoner without trial or hearing, the first of many. He agonized far longer over the disposition of the horses.[38]

Wright convened a panel of officers to decide the horses' fate. The group determined that these, the "most prized of all the possessions of the Indians," could not return to enemy hands. The officers and Nez Perce selected some to replace their own wasted animals. Wright then had his men shoot the remainder. It took two days. The bleached bones of the 700 horses killed at what became known as Horse Slaughter Camp remained visible for generations. "It was a cruel sight to see so many noble beasts shot down," wrote Keyes. "I fancied I saw in their beautiful faces an appeal for mercy." Mullan noted, "I know not when I have witnessed a more distressing sight."[39]

"The slaughter added not a little to the fright of the Indians," wrote Father Joset. A military force that could systematically destroy such a valuable resource was a different type of enemy, as Wright proved in other ways, foreshadowing Civil War tactics the Union army would soon employ. He ordered his men to burn storehouses filled with vegetables, wheat, and oats; destroy caches of dried camas and berries; torch fields; kill cattle. It would be a long winter of suffering for the Indians. "We have spread death and desolation in our path wherever we [have] gone," wrote Mullan. Reported Wright: "I have treated these Indians severely.…They will remember it."[40]

Wright's troops continued to the Coeur d'Alene Mission, where Father Joset had gathered Coeur d'Alene tribal members who listened as Wright threatened them. "You see that you fight against us hopelessly," he said. "I have a great many soldiers.…I can place my soldiers in your plains, by your fishing-grounds, and in the mountains where you catch game." The Coeur d'Alenes recognized bravado. They knew enough of the army to understand that placing troops for any length of time on plains, in mountains, and along rivers was highly unlikely. On the other hand, they understood the destructive power of a column of troops destroying their homes. They agreed to peace terms Wright dictated, including the "promise that all white persons shall [be allowed to] travel through their country unmolested." This applied to white men constructing a wagon road—a road the Indians now recognized as inevitable.[41]

Wright then moved to Latah Creek on Wednesday, September 22, where some of the campaign's most dramatic moments occurred. Chief Owhi rode into camp the following evening. Captured and shackled, Wright ordered him to send a message to his son: Qualchan must appear before Wright or Owhi would hang.

The next morning, John Mullan and Gustavus Sohon left camp, joining troops under Major William Grier on a mission to recover the remains of soldiers killed the previous spring in Steptoe's battle. After twelve miles they arrived at "the memorable spot of Steptoe's battle-ground." Here at this "scene of desolation and sadness," as Mullan recorded, the detail "silently and mournfully…disinterred" the bones of those killed when Colonel Steptoe barely escaped a Custer-like demise.[42]

Owhi's message never reached Qualchan. Yet, inexplicably, that Yakama warrior boldly rode his bay horse into Wright's camp at 9:00 a.m. on the morning Mullan had left for the Steptoe battlefield. He casually dismounted and began a conversation with Wright, unaware he had ridden into a trap. If Qualchan hoped to talk peace, Wright would have none of it. He informed Qualchan that he had imprisoned his father, news clearly startling the son. "He seemed to be paralyzed," wrote Lieutenant Kip, a witness. "His whole expression changed as though he had been stunned." Wright ordered Qualchan disarmed, an act requiring six soldiers, for Qualchan, a powerful man "finely shaped with a broad chest and muscular limbs," had "the strength of a Hercules." He resisted furiously. The soldiers finally shackled him and shoved him into the guard tent.[43]

Colonel Wright called for packmaster Thomas Beall. Beall had, a few days earlier, volunteered that he knew how to fashion a hangman's knot. He would be a busy man serving under Wright that fall. On this day, Wright ordered him to slip a noose around Qualchan—no easy task. Though bound, Qualchan fought mightily. Soldiers had to throw him to the ground before Beall could affix the loop. He then threw the rope's end over a stout tree limb. A handful of soldiers slowly hoisted the muscular Qualchan into the air. No snap of the neck to bring a quick demise this day; Qualchan excruciatingly choked to death.[44]

Some say Qualchan rode into Wright's camp under a flag of truce. If so, Wright ignored this universal signal of mediation. What is certainly true is that, without trial, Wright executed Qualchan. Later that day he ordered several other Indians hung. Altogether, Wright would oversee sixteen similar deaths that fall.[45]

On a cold, rainy day on September 26, Mullan and the salvage mission returned from Steptoe's battlefield. There they had, with all the decorum army troops could muster at that isolated site, gathered the remains of Steptoe's fallen men. Wright would eventually transport these to Fort Walla Walla and order their reburial with full military honors. This was a stark contrast to the events that occurred at Wright's Latah Creek camp. Upon returning to the camp, Lieutenant Mullan not only learned of Qualchan's hanging, but also that soldiers had disinterred his body when a rumor spread that Qualchan had concealed money under his clothes. Troops found "nothing of value…upon him," the exhumation accomplishing nothing but further indignity.[46]

While encamped on Latah Creek, Wright signed a treaty with the Spokanes similar to the one he concluded with the Coeur d'Alenes a few days earlier. He then continued to the Palouse River, where he refused to enter into a treaty with the Palouse tribe—the group he considered most responsible for miners' deaths, cattle thefts, and Steptoe's defeat. On September 30 he hanged four Palouse and told the shocked spectators he would be doing "no wrong" were he to "hang them all."[47]

A few days later, near Fort Taylor, Chief Owhi, approximately seventy years old, attempted an escape, having been held prisoner since his capture at Latah Creek where Wright had hanged his son. "I often visited him," reported Erasmus Keyes. "I never saw him smile, and frequently deep sadness would mantle his countenance." But Owhi still had pride. Bashing the head of his much younger guard, he spurred his horse, and despite "a chain and strap attached to his ankles," made a race of it, until pursuing troops shot him multiple times. Two hours later he died. In 1854, on his expedition to Flathead Lake, Mullan had asserted that Owhi deserved "humane and kind treatment at the hands of every white man." The whites had not treated him kindly on this day. Mullan's Nez Perce warriors added further indignity when they stripped his body of valuables.[48]

Mullan might have prevented that Nez Perce looting out of deference to the Yakama leader. But he was not present at Owhi's death. Mullan had written to the Topographical Bureau seeking permission to travel to Washington, D.C., to "confer personally" about his road-building plans. On September 30 he received authorization to proceed to Fort Vancouver and await further orders. On October 2—the day before Owhi's death—he left Wright. He arrived at Vancouver a week later, and managed to incur the indignation of the publisher of the Salem *Oregon Statesman* after he publicly bragged about his accomplishments during Wright's campaign. Calling him a "bombastic little lieutenant," the paper chided him for his "painful exhibition of mingled egotism and toadyism....The indelicacy and impropriety of a soldier celebrating the glory and renown of his own accomplishments is apparent to everybody." Mullan ever sought publicity. Some of it proved flattering; some not.[49]

Wright's main force continued to Fort Walla Walla through hard rains and bitter cold, entering that small outpost on October 5. There he called Walla Walla Indians to a council—and hanged four. By this time his men were inured to hangings. They exhibited more emotion on October 7 when they buried the soldiers' remains that Mullan had helped retrieve from Steptoe's battlefield. Troops had unceremoniously carried the bones to Walla Walla in parfleshes. But when it came time for interment, Wright insisted upon pomp. All the post's men stood at attention as black-draped horses carried coffins to the cemetery, where the remains were laid away amid volleys of rifle fire.[50]

The Wright campaign had ended. He lost two men by food poisoning; one was mildly wounded in combat. His troops had marched for sixty days on thirty-eight days' rations, marking their way with "slaughter and destruction," an Indian campaign one military historian called "the decade's most spectacular." Noted Kip, "That immense tract of splendid country over which we marched is now opened to the white man, and the time is not far distant when settlers will begin to occupy it." Many of those settlers would travel to new homes on the road John Mullan could now safely construct.[51]

George Wright benefitted little from his campaign's success. As the Civil War commenced, he was isolated in the West, far removed from the action. He took little solace in receiving command of the Department of the Pacific in 1861, but performed his task loyally and eventually became a brevet brigadier general, a rank far below that achieved during the war by many men he once commanded. The subject of a newspaper smear campaign, the army replaced him in 1864 with Major General Irwin McDowell, who had been routed in the First Battle of Manassas. Despite that opprobrium, Wright continued to faithfully serve the army until July 28, 1865, when he and his wife, traveling from Fort Vancouver to California, drowned when the steamship *Brother Jonathan* sank.[52]

Despite his triumphal campaign, Wright never captured the Indian leader he most sought, Chief Kamiakin, who escaped into the Bitterroots. A few months after the Wright campaign, Father Pierre-Jean DeSmet found Kamiakin and his family living in "poverty and misery" and interceded with the army to allow the "once powerful chieftain" to return home. The army agreed and Kamiakin, escorted by Indian agent John Owen, arrived in Walla Walla on May 13, 1859. Uneasy in that virtually lawless community, Kamiakin escaped. Finally in 1860 he returned to Rock Lake in Palouse country, where he remained until he died in 1877.[53]

Although he incurred the disdain of the Salem newspaper for his braggadocio, John Mullan exited the Wright campaign mostly to accolades. "The distinguished and gallant conduct of Lieut. Mullan... justly entitle him to the warmest praises," noted Colonel Wright. "The vast amount of reliable information he has obtained...will prove...of

paramount importance in connection with the great military road."
Enthused Wright's second in command, Captain Erasmus Keyes: "He
possessed uncommon mental and physical activity; he knew all the trails
and fords, and in the crossing of streams which were not fordable his
ingenuity was…remarkable.'"[54]

Mullan also emerged with a greater respect for the country through
which his road would pass. He now knew that he would need more
men, supplies, and money than he had originally planned. He would
go to the nation's capital to personally lobby the War Department for
increased funding.

CHAPTER 8

Mullan's Road, 1859–1860

MOST JUNIOR OFFICERS WOULD AWAIT orders before embarking on a transcontinental trip at government expense, but not John Mullan. In the fall of 1858 his request to travel to the nation's capital had not been approved. He could, as virtually all lieutenants would, remain in the Northwest, patiently awaiting instructions. Or he could, as John Mullan frequently did, flaunt military protocol and act independently. He chose the latter. Mullan boarded a ship from Fort Vancouver, crossed the Isthmus of Panama, steamed to New York, and traveled to his parents' home in Annapolis.[1]

From Mullan's perspective the unauthorized leave made sense, the action of a man refusing to leave the fate of his road to chance. "Should I…remain idle during the winter, and, laying the facts in official reports before the [topographical] bureau, await in hopes that they would be favorably acted upon?" he questioned. "Or should I go in person and solicit the aid…of those friends of the project who were in a position to give strength to their views by legislative action?"[2]

Mullan went "in person," and in an audacious letter to a superior officer, explained his peculiar behavior. Then, rather than awaiting further orders, he boldly told his superior what he would do next. He felt "unwell" he wrote Captain Andrew Humphreys of the Topographical Bureau, but when better, he would travel to Washington, D.C., and meet with the captain. He then proposed that Humphreys sanction his unusual behavior, for he had acted in the best interest of everyone: "Having in view the special interest of the Bureau, in which *time* is an essential element, I have deemed it proper and prudent to act as I have done, and can only hope that my course may meet with the approval of the Dept."[3]

Remarkably, Mullan received no censure, the beneficiary of seren-dipitous timing. Isaac Stevens, the recognized expert on Northwest affairs, was then in the capital as territorial congressional delegate and welcomed his young friend's assistance. Mullan could help Stevens gar-ner an appropriation for the road. Stevens's enthusiasm deflected crit-icism from Mullan, as did Northwest residents who clamored for the road's funding. And even the army recognized the need for improved transportation; nearly three-fourths of its entire force served in the West. Colonel George Wright had experienced the fragility of provi-sioning a command in the interior Northwest while tethered to a thin supply chain of steamships, pack trains, and wagons that stretched to San Francisco. A road linking the Missouri and Columbia Rivers would open a route that "can be made by Troops with easy marches," noted Mullan. All this boosterism protected Mullan from reprimand. So he spent the winter of 1858–59 in the capital, his third time in five years, learning the ways of the federal bureaucracy—lessons for his future.[4]

Mullan, like Stevens, recognized that the money remaining in his original $30,000 appropriation was "not sufficient to construct the road." Stevens had worked hard but unsuccessfully in 1858 for an additional $200,000. But in 1859 he found new allies, particularly his long-time friend Jefferson Davis, now chair of the Senate Military Affairs Com-mittee. As secretary of war, Davis had realized the inadequacy of the original appropriation and had prevented the commencing of road work. Now, with the support of his successor in that cabinet post, John Floyd, Davis introduced a bill to furnish an additional $100,000. Disap-pointed the bill provided only half of what he believed necessary, Ste-vens nonetheless supported Davis's effort. He could fight another day for the remaining sum. Though most southern members of Congress fought Davis's request to construct a northern wagon road—a potential precursor to a transcontinental railroad—the bill passed, and President James Buchanan signed it on March 3, 1859. John Mullan would soon return to road building.[5]

Just how John Mullan made the acquaintance of Theodore Kolecki is unclear. But he hired him as an engineer on his initial road crew in 1858 and never regretted the decision. Next to Gustavus Sohon, no person would serve him longer or more ably. When Mullan traveled to the nation's capital, he took Kolecki along, and the two worked side by side that winter, finalizing maps and drafting the topographical memoir that George Wright attached to his official report of the 1858 campaign. Their time in the capital sealed Mullan's opinion that he had wisely chosen his assistant. In seeking a raise for him Mullan wrote, "Mr. Kolecki is…working day and night with me…to get our work completed….He has labored most faithfully and assiduously and well merits…this compensation." Mullan had found a man to match his own hard-driving passion for the road.[6]

In addition to working on the Wright report, Mullan spent that winter gathering information, sometimes from people he appreciated far less than Kolecki, including his rival, Frederick Lander. Lander was in the capital completing an emigrant guide to his own western road. Mullan would later emulate Lander's meticulous style of noting landscape details when he wrote a guide to his own road. But for now he interviewed Lander about the supplies, equipment, and manpower required for successful road building.[7]

Once Congress had appropriated additional money, Captain Humphreys ordered Mullan to "immediately…report the nature and extent of the outfit necessary." Armed with his own 1858 experiences and his interview with Lander, Mullan sent a volley of responses. He now recognized the need for a far larger expedition than he had originally anticipated. He would need about one hundred men and a military escort. He would require key assistants to work with Kolecki and Sohon. He had to have odometers, compasses, chronometers, thermometers, and sextants in addition to rations, tools, horses, wagons, and livestock. And he would appreciate additional money to purchase gifts for Indians.[8]

Mullan was ready to proceed. He would be on his way in a few weeks. But before departing he had a final obligation—in Baltimore.

Rebecca Williamson Mullan floats to us through time on the most fragile tendrils of historical evidence. From an 1885 passport application we learn she had hazel eyes, brown hair, a fair complexion—and stood an inch taller than John at 5'5". From a ten-page, 1892 typescript we learn how fiercely she protected the fading memory of her husband's western exploits. And from a diary she kept over the course of six months in 1859 we learn of a deeply religious, well-educated, shy, introspective young woman of twenty-three, deeply in love with Lieutenant John Mullan, who, before departing for the West in 1859, visited Rebecca in Baltimore. "When I parted from you my best beloved friend on the evening of the 31st of March," she wrote, "you can form but a slight idea of... emotions that stirred my very soul....The knowledge that I was beloved, for of that I no longer felt a doubt, took much from the pain of parting. I durst not trust myself to look back as I ascended the stairs, yet I had no sooner entered my room than I would have given worlds to have returned to you."[9]

John had served at Baltimore's Fort McHenry in 1856. It must have been then that he met hazel-eyed Rebecca. It is all speculation, of course, how they became acquainted. It would be natural for a Baltimore debutante to meet one of the fort's young officers at a dance or party. Perhaps these two devout Catholics introduced themselves at church. Whatever the circumstances, they began a courtship that would continue each time John's travels brought him east.

Rebecca, born June 18, 1836, might have retained a few memories of her maternal grandfather, Luke Tiernan, who died late in 1839. He passed along to his family his Baltimore social status, but none of the considerable fortune he once enjoyed. Tiernan partnered in several businesses. Prominent politically—Henry Clay frequently came calling—he persuaded the Maryland legislature to incorporate the Baltimore and Ohio Railroad, the nation's first common carrier. A few months before his death, he conveyed six thousand acres of land valued at $120,000 to a trust to pay his creditors. It did not come close to eradicating his nearly half-million-dollar debt.[10]

John Mullan coveted wealth, but also the affinity of family. Though Rebecca's family inherited none of the Tiernan money, it was a close-knit group, which Mullan appreciated. He befriended the lot, sometimes to the exasperation of a jealous Rebecca: "Oh, my loved friend, how hard was my trial the other day when [sister] Pink received your letter."

But it was Rebecca who had set the rules: John was not to write to her personally. She insisted on hearing from him only through missives to her family. Intensely shy, she sought a quiet romance. "You know my dislike to having my name before the public in any way," she commented in a diary written as though addressed to John, but one she never intended for him to read. John had hoped they would become publicly engaged before he headed west that spring, but Rebecca loathed the attention: "The ring you placed on my finger" she hid in her bedroom so as not to "excite suspicion," although she "would have loved to have kept it on my finger, to have it constantly before me."

But the secretive arrangement also anguished Rebecca, who denied herself the pleasure of writing to John. "When questioned as to whether I correspond with you, I answer in the negative, so that prevents further interrogation." But there is no mistaking her love: "Oh, if only I had you by to look at me, to feel, to know your affection, that would have been the sun that would have dispelled the clouds and warmed me into love with yourself and all the world."

Still, John's actions at times irritated her. Ever the egotist, he kept newspapers appraised of his progress once he started road construction, but proved less diligent in sending notes to the Williamsons. "I've read several statements in the papers of the progress of your expedition," she chided. "I hoped that the same mails that brought the communication for the paper would have brought us letters from you, but several times I've been disappointed."

Rebecca's diary records an unnamed, but severe, illness she suffered in 1859. She was feverish and under a doctor's care. She suffered such pain that she admitted "at times I have felt...a preference for death." She lost her hair "and became so accustomed to my wig, that I scarcely mind at all."

Her diary, with frequent references to poets and authors, reveals a cultured and well-educated young woman. Before boarding his ship for Panama, John visited a New York gallery and sent an exhibit catalog to the Williamson household. "It refreshed my memory in what I had taken such a peculiar pleasure in visiting and gazing at when in New York two years ago," Rebecca noted.

The journal reflects a deeply religious person who wonders if she meets God's expectations. "God is very good, and how much better I ought to be," she wrote one day. And on another: "If I could only be all that my religion expects of me, how much happier I would be."

She looked forward to her future with John, a life she believed promised civility: "I am glad to find you don't seem wedded to the life you are leading—to some it has great fascination. But I am glad you appreciate more the refinements of a civilized life. Oh, there is so much more peace, more comfort, more happiness in it."

Mullan left New York on April 5, 1859—exactly one year after he had departed that city on his initial aborted road construction effort. He arrived at The Dalles on May 15, also exactly one year later. But there the similarities ceased. Colonel George Wright had calmed the interior. Mullan could proceed with road building—to the exultation of Northwest journalists.

The road, predicted the *Oregon Union*, "will open up a direct communication between the valley of the Mississippi and Oregon," bringing "an immense immigration." The Olympia *Pioneer and Democrat* pronounced Mullan the consummate choice for the task. "His knowledge of the country is perhaps greater than that of any other man" the paper glowed in one article. In another: "His characteristic energy and intelligence, as displayed in past duties, furnish an ample guarantee that his future labors will be performed in a manner highly credible to himself and eminently satisfactory to the Government."[11]

Always focused on family, on this expedition Mullan worked closely with three brothers—and a future brother-in-law. Louis Mullan went west in 1858. He guarded government stock while John joined Colonel Wright's campaign, and he remained with the animals while John lobbied in Washington, D.C. Charles apparently first went west in 1859, assisting John from a post in Walla Walla, arranging for mail deliveries to the work crew. And James accompanied the road crew as physician, at a salary of $125 per month, one of its best-paid men.[12]

While at The Dalles John inquired about Rebecca's brother David, who had journeyed west sometime earlier, perhaps estranged from his family. Remarkably, Mullan not only found David, but also hired him. "Oh, John, do good to my brother, he was made for something better than the life he has been leading," Rebecca lamented in her diary. "There is no knowing the good that may accrue, then I'll thank you every night in my prayers." Good did accrue from that hire; Williamson became one of Mullan's most valued assistants.[13]

Mullan hired more than eighty additional civilians—topographers, teamsters, cooks, laborers, carpenters, herders—a "healthy and robust set of men," in the opinion of one newspaper. Mullan detected no extravagance in his hiring: "I do not deem that I have one man too many. The work to be done is heavy, and the means must be appropriate." But he was rapidly burning through his appropriation—and attempting to rationalize the expenditures in frequent letters to the Topographical Bureau.[14]

At army expense the government also provided an escort of 140 under the command of Lieutenant James White—about forty being civilian packers and teamsters. Mullan had permission to engage the enlisted men in road construction, if they volunteered for such duty. Most did, extra pay providing incentive. But road work also combated boredom, for the military escort encountered no troublesome Indians.[15]

Mullan had a knack for logistics. He knew that the success of his endeavor—the survival of his crew—depended upon his organizational acumen. He was about to send 220 men, 180 yoke of oxen, and dozens of mules, horses, and cattle into a land of sagebrush and rock, forests, rivers, and mountains: a country bereft of stores. Hard-laboring men and hard-hauling animals consume massive quantities of food. His crew would work at the nether end of a fragile supply artery. Imagine the complexity of his provisioning assignment.

At The Dalles, Mullan amassed heaping stacks of flour, beans, sugar, coffee, and soap; tons of pork, gallons of molasses, bushels of salt. He laid in vinegar, candles, rice, desiccated vegetables, pickles, whiskey, tents, clothes, blankets, boots, medicine, and beef on the hoof. His men needed rope, chains, picks, shovels, augers, nails, spikes, and crowbars.

Assembling a mountain of supplies is one thing. Now Mullan needed someone to transport it. For that he turned to a wagon master already respected for conquering difficult terrain. John Creighton earned his reputation in 1858 by leading a wagon train from Fort Leavenworth, Kansas, to Benicia Barracks, California—a two-thousand-mile, five-month journey, with the first wagons to cross Bridger's Pass.[16]

Following that successful endeavor, the army hired Creighton to accompany 140 mules on a month-long, seasick-ridden voyage up the Pacific to Fort Vancouver, and then overland to Fort Walla Walla to be delivered to John Mullan. Creighton arrived on time; the mules in good shape. Mullan recognized talent. He hired Creighton at $100 a month to manage his complicated transportation network. Creighton oversaw an ever-lengthening supply line as the road crew worked its way east.

Mullan knew the basic contours of his route. But nuances mattered. His road could never stray far from water—the fuel of nineteenth century travel. He had to avoid swamps and, when possible, steer clear of rocky ledges requiring time-consuming blasting. Mullan needed experienced advance men feeding him details about the best path. As he accumulated provisions, Mullan sent out parties of his best scouts.

On May 16, Conway Howard left The Dalles, accompanied by Walter W. DeLacy. A few miles into the trek, Howard developed a painful swelling in his legs and returned to Fort Walla Walla. DeLacy took charge and served in advance of the crew until it reached winter quarters in December.[17]

In the forty-year-old DeLacy, Mullan reaped the expertise of one of the West's most experienced engineers. A family friend of West Point's Alfred Thayer Mahan, DeLacy studied engineering, mathematics, and topography at the academy without appointment, a rare occurrence of a non-cadet receiving training at America's preeminent engineering school. DeLacy conducted railroad surveys in Illinois and Missouri. In 1848 he nearly starved, living on boiled mule broth while plotting the course of a wagon road between San Antonio and Chihuahua, Mexico. He laid out an infantry route across Texas, surviving five days without water. In 1854 he mapped a course from Texas to California. Then he headed to Puget Sound, where Isaac Stevens commissioned him as an adjutant with Washington volunteers during the 1856 Yakama War.[18]

In 1858, DeLacy charted a trail from western Washington to booming Canadian gold camps, a one-man endeavor completed in three months. Stevens probably recommended DeLacy to Mullan, but Mullan had no doubt heard of his exploits. Following his work with Mullan, DeLacy would lay out the townsites of Fort Benton and Deer Lodge and create the first map of Montana. He became one of Mullan's most trusted assistants, serving for all four years of road building.[19]

Mullan also sent P.M. Engle and Theodore Kolecki on reconnaissances. Engle mapped the country to Fort Colville, and Kolecki explored the Palouse region surrounding the stark landmark of Pyramid Peak, later known as Steptoe Butte. Like thousands of tourists who followed, Kolecki irresistibly climbed to the top, leaving the first recorded description of the breathtaking view.

> We were much fatigued by the long march, and, therefore, rather disposed to delay the ascent until morning. But the delicious coolness of the atmosphere…inspired us with new energy, and we climbed up this steep and rocky cone that stretches its crown more than one thousand feet above its dingy neighbors.
>
> From the top we had a view of the whole country for eighty miles around us….The Blue Mountains, the high table-land stretching from…Fort Walla Walla to the Columbia…the mountains from the Coeur d'Alene mission and lake, and the Bitter Root mountains, were distinctly visible.

Kolecki did not find a shortcut across the Palouse country. But, entranced by this spectacular vista, he lingered here. After camping half-way up the butte, the next morning he and his two companions arose early to once again climb to the top, "enjoying the sunrise, which beyond doubt offers one of the most interesting spectacles."[20]

Of course, Mullan reserved the most difficult reconnaissance for Gustavus Sohon. Jesuit priests had requested that Mullan's road bypass the Coeur d'Alene Mission; they feared increased traffic would disrupt their work among the Indians. Mullan also wondered if he might have missed a shorter route over the Bitterroots when he had scouted for Stevens. Sohon would take a look.

Sohon attempted to hire Nez Perce guides, but when they discovered he would explore routes south of the mission they did their best to dissuade him from traveling through their country. "They represented to me that the whole region was one immense bed of rugged mountains… over which they never heard of any persons having travelled, and therefore they declined to join my party," he reported. But rugged mountains never deterred Sohon, who made the survey anyway, along with Frank Hall.[21]

A week out of Walla Walla, in a camas field on the banks of Latah Creek, Sohon and Hall came across an encampment of Coeur d'Alenes. "During the day the chiefs and principal men, who had been my old friends, visited me in camp and exchanged news," Sohon wrote. But they also refused to assist him. Though defeated in battle, they would do all they could to passively resist the road. "Their disposition was to retard my movements, obstruct my passage…and have me consume a large portion of the summer in fruitless efforts at an examination," Sohon wrote.

But Sohon proved hard to deter. He finally secured the service of a Coeur d'Alene named Augustine as guide, though it seems Augustine might have had ulterior motives.

Augustine, Sohon, and Hall set off on a trip that would take them "over steep sidehills where the ground was obstructed by dense forests and fallen timber, and even now covered with snow." On the third day they stopped to rest their animals, "weary and fatigued," and here an "evil genius seemed to have attended us in the person of Damass, the brother of my guide Augustine, whom we met hunting in the mountains."

Augustine dissuaded Sohon from going farther, perhaps because he and Damass planned to trap Sohon and Hall. "If all the Americans would work here a thousand years they could never make a road," Augustine told Sohon. But by now Sohon detected a diversionary pattern. Northern Indians encouraged road construction to their south. Nez Perce said the road should lie to the north. All recognized they could not halt the road, but all seemed determined to prevent it from crossing their own backyards. By now Sohon questioned whether he could get accurate information from any Indians, and thought Augustine's just one of many efforts to thwart his exploration.

But Augustine refused to go farther. Sohon contemplated his options. His horses were "jaded," his provisions "scanty." But he had seldom encountered an obstacle he did not attempt to overcome. "Even in this extremity I should have tried to continue the exploration," Sohon explained to Mullan, "had I not perceived…some mischief from [Damass] who desired to detain me until other Indians should join them."

Reluctantly, recognizing that Damass might be setting an ambush, Sohon and Hall left the mountains. Sohon sent Hall to Mullan for further instructions. Sohon was willing to continue despite the danger, if Mullan requested. But Mullan recognized a fruitless endeavor. "The Indians have not only thrown every obstacle in his way," Mullan wrote, "but his life has become much endangered." Mullan sent an expressman to Sohon instructing him to give up the search and rejoin the main party. Mullan's road would enter the Bitterroots near the Coeur d'Alene Mission. If his most trusted assistant could not find a better route, there was no alternative.[22]

Mullan dispatched his frustrations to East Coast newspapers, prompting Rebecca to ironically note in her diary, "The Indians have not been so peaceful as you imagined. They were not so intimidated…by Col. Wright's victories, they are an illustration of the proverb—'he that fights and runs away may live to fight another day.'" Northwest Indians would not carry a fight to John Mullan. But the depth of their animosity toward a road bisecting their land remained. They could not prevent its construction. But they were not about to sanction it, either.[23]

Walla Walla, in that summer of 1859, flourished, mushrooming around Fort Walla Walla—the gateway to the interior. The town's residents had dropped the name Steptoeville, and Walla Walla became the most populous city in Washington, a title it held for two decades. Mullan recognized that his road would further swell the community, and in 1858, prior to Wright's campaign, he purchased businesses he planned to operate with his brothers. Mullan would build his road and then settle in Walla Walla, growing wealthy with the boom. At least that was the design as he left Walla Walla on a hot, dusty July 1, 1859. Mullan had finally begun construction of his long-anticipated road.[24]

The first miles out of Walla Walla presented little challenge. The road crew followed a well-established route. The men did some grading and constructed three short bridges—all so hastily that the supply train seldom stopped.[25]

After a couple of days they came to Fort Taylor, that bastion of the previous year; it seemed but a memory now. No howitzers. No armed guard. The collapsed walls of the basalt fortress resembled the littered remnants of "ancient ruins."[26]

Past the fort, the construction crew and army escort—strung out over the march from Walla Walla—accordioned as it reached the Snake and waited to cross. Here they set up a large camp. Conical-shaped Sibley tents, patterned after Plains teepees, rose a dozen feet high. Ingenious devices, these circular shelters slept up to twenty men—feet facing the center like wheel spokes—and required only a single central pole and a few stakes for support. Surrounding the Sibleys were six-man A-tents, long sheets of canvas supported by a central stringer. When staked they resembled a capital A. Soldiers occupied high ground above the camp. Civilians on horseback, "guns capped and loaded," guarded the stock. Here in the early days of the expedition the road crew established the basic rhythms of a camp life they would mimic nightly in the coming months.[27]

Placid at this place much of the year, the Snake now roiled, gorged with spring runoff. Working sixteen hours a day, it took five days for the outfit to cross, mainly because of panicked cattle and horses. "In swimming our stock," recorded crew member John Strachan, "they would get about half way across and lose sight of shore and most of them turned back again after being carried down several miles." Mullan had to devise a better means of crossing. Among all those supplies he carried, Mullan had packed pontoon boats, and the crew now brought them out. Several animals had already drowned, and the survivors were so frightened they would not cross without being led. Men on the pontoons guided them across. John Creighton even ferried wagons on the pontoons. On one crossing he fell in and "had to swim to save my life."[28]

Private Henry Zunowester, with Lieutenant White's escort, was not so lucky. Zunowester walked upstream to gather firewood. Bundling his sticks into a makeshift raft, he "foolishly" rode downstream and got caught in "a most dangerous current." With the raft out of control, the terrified Zunowester leaped off and splashed wildly in the torrent. But the river sucked him under, "and no trace of him has since been found." Lieutenant White's bugler became the only fatality of Mullan's road-building project.[29]

"I have been much delayed and annoyed at this point in crossing the Snake river," reported Mullan, who gave Zunowester's death little notice; just one more aggravating setback in a frustratingly slow start to his project. Mullan reported the drowning as an afterthought: We crossed "the Snake river without accident, save the drowning of one of my men who…was…swept out of sight before aid could reach him." Mullan made no mention at all that another private, Anthony Brown, stabbed himself in the stomach in a suicide attempt, or that a "fearful fight" had broken out when Thomas Lowza, a Jamaican cook and the expedition's only African American, "was laid senseless on the ground by an awful blow with an ax," according to a witness.[30]

Until the Army Corps of Engineers constructed dams that turned the Snake and Columbia rivers into a series of slackwater reservoirs in the twentieth century, stretches of these streams had never been navigable. To circumvent the Columbia River's Cascades and Celilo Falls required painstakingly removing everything from a boat, portaging, and replacing materials in another boat. Despite the challenges, river transportation moved goods faster and cheaper than pack mules or wagons. In the 1850s the army contracted with R.R. Thompson and E.F. Coe to transport supplies in a bateau from Celilo Falls to Fort Walla Walla at Steptoeville.[31]

Shrewd businessmen, Thompson and Coe recognized an even greater opportunity with Mullan's road building. Sustaining 220 men and hundreds of animals constructing a 624-mile road would require a lot of provisions. They devised a way to haul those supplies part way up the Snake River by boat. In 1858 they laid the flat hull of what would become the first steamboat to run the middle Columbia and lower Snake. They named her after the Northwest's hero of the day. The stern-wheeled *Colonel Wright*, 110 feet long, 21 feet wide, could navigate the shallowest, most turbulent waters. In April 1859, she took her maiden voyage under the intrepid captaincy of Leonard White. Thompson and Coe, monopolists, could afford to pay well, and they did; White earned the astronomical salary of $500 a month, a sound investment for a captain willing to accept any challenge. A couple of months after that initial voyage, the *Colonel Wright* became the first steamboat to travel on the Snake River. By the time Mullan's expedition members coalesced along the Snake, they saw evidence of White's pioneering success—stacks of provisions at the mouth of the Palouse River, under the watchful protection of Lieutenant Hylan Lyon of the army escort.[32]

No one appreciated the efforts of steamboat captains more than John Mullan. In the summer of 1859, as his crew worked its way eastward, an express rider delivered word that "the staunch little steamer Chippewa" had delivered 24,000 rations for his crew from St. Louis to a point a few miles downstream of Fort Benton. From the time of earliest European exploration of North America, visionaries had sought a Northwest Passage. Mullan, by connecting the routes pioneered by the *Chippewa* and *Colonel Wright*, would finally accomplish that dream, connecting the headwaters of navigation on the Missouri and Columbia Rivers. He recognized the enormity of the project. "It needs no special proof to show what bearing our present labors are having in connecting these two…great arteries of the country," he immodestly wrote Humphreys. Once completed, his road would provide a "saving of 50 per cent to the Treasury Dept." every time it shipped materials and troops from east to west. Mullan anticipated ample praise as the man who finally engineered the Northwest Passage.[33]

❧

As Mullan pushed his road builders forward, the *Colonel Wright* continued ferrying supplies up the Snake. Creighton's wagons moved back and forth on the line, empty wagons to the Snake to re-provision, full wagons to the crew, a continuous supply thread, growing ever longer.[34]

When Mullan's wagons strained up from the Snake River canyon to the plateau, they traversed a land "destitute of timber." Mullan found here "one of the best natural wagon roads I have ever seen," and his crew again made "rapid & very successful" progress. Road building consisted of little more than keeping the wagons moving, creating a track. The crew had ample time to fabricate mileage markers.[35]

Mullan later explained how he came upon the idea of placing markers along the route, giving distances from Fort Walla Walla. "I happened to think of the way the old Roman roads of Europe are marked," he reminisced. "We had an old branding-iron with us containing the letters M and R. So I had a young tree cut down, the bark stripped off, then the wood was branded and there was our first milepost." The branding crew remained busy all the way to Fort Benton. Technically, the initials stood for "Military Road," but for most people the shorthand became "Mullan Road." If they had time, crew members carved additional information onto the posts: The number of miles to a creek, how far to a good campsite. Sometimes they noted special events. One marker commemorated the road crew's celebration of Independence Day, 1861. Blazed into a giant pine on the top of what has since been known as Fourth of July Pass in Idaho, the tree stood until 1988—the last of hundreds of markers that once dotted the road.[36]

When Mullan heard that Palouse Indians had destroyed some markers in an act of defiance against the road, he reacted entirely out of proportion to the crime. He wrote Captain Alfred Pleasonton, assistant adjutant general for the Department of Oregon, that he would "unhesitantly hang them up" if he captured the culprits, and threatened that "good Indians" would "suffer the same fate" if they did not report their offending tribesmen. Tough punishment for damaging a stake. Mullan calmed a bit when he received word that only "a few [had been]…. defaced but none of them entirely destroyed."[37]

Mullan believed the mile markers would help ensure his road's success, useful to military personnel as well as civilian emigrants. Beyond this, they symbolized a scientific approach to road building. His crew carefully calibrated each mile. But Mullan demanded more. He wanted to "leave nothing undone…to…determine every point that will be necessary to refer to at any time in the future." To accomplish that required more than mileage markers. Thanks largely to the skills of astronomer John Wiessner and topographer Theodore Kolecki, Mullan's expedition did achieve much more. It compiled "the first series of longitude observations ever made across the continent north of 42 [degrees]," and created sophisticated maps that would remain unimproved for half a century.[38]

Prior to the Stevens expedition, geographic knowledge of the interior Northwest had been virtually non-existent. "The…basis that formed our…understanding of the country was the map left us by Lewis and Clark," wrote Mullan. Stevens added to that body of information, but Mullan brought refinement.[39]

Accurate readings of latitude—locations north or south of the equator—and longitude—locations east or west of a designated imaginary line known as the Prime Meridian through Greenwich, England, and expressed in degrees or time—are essential to locating geographic features. Assessing latitude could be done relatively easily in the nineteenth century by measuring the elevation of the sun or North Star above a flat horizon. Determining longitude is trickier, requiring comparing the local time of an event, such as when the sun is due south, with the time the same event occurs at the Prime Meridian. Timing is the key. Get off by a second a day, and calculations are thrown off by a fifth of a mile. Multiply that by all the days Mullan worked in the field, and what starts as an effort at precise measurement soon cascades into geographic chaos. Mullan's astronomical party used four chronometers, extremely accurate timepieces.[40]

Mullan's team determined elevations by using barometers—he had five, and noted that his astronomical crew took barometrical observations "almost hourly." Barometers measure pressure in the atmosphere—the weight of air bearing down on the earth's surface. Air pressure decreases the higher one is above sea level. A one-inch decrease in barometric pressure corresponds to a thousand-foot increase in elevation. But precision is not as easy as simply reading a barometer. Air pressure changes as high and low pressure systems intermingle, and as temperatures vary. Thus, Mullan's astronomical team also employed a variety of other instruments to bolster accuracy. Thermometers helped them make barometric adjustments, odometers measured distances between camps. The combined regular readings of all these implements enabled Mullan's group to assign contour elevation lines to maps decades before these appeared on other government charts.[41]

Before Mullan sent topographer Kolecki on his exploration of Pyramid Peak, he first assigned him to a month working with Wiessner and two other men who made up the astronomical team. They established a series of base latitude, longitude, and barometric readings at Walla Walla, necessary for all the measurements that would follow. The party then made multiple barometric readings at several places to ensure accuracy—60 at Fort Taylor, 416 at the Coeur d'Alene Mission, 225 on the mountain pass named for Gus Sohon.

The party remained at the Coeur d'Alene Mission an entire lunar month to determine latitude and longitude. They established astronomical stations in the Bitterroot Valley, at Hellgate, and at Fort Benton. They accumulated an astonishing amount of information. Given the sophistication of the equipment, their measurements were remarkably accurate, the baseline of all subsequent scientific elevational and longitudinal studies in the interior Pacific Northwest. The expedition, in short, accomplished much more than the mere grading of a road.[42]

Mullan's road builders moved rapidly across the prairie above the Snake River—thirteen miles on July 11, sixteen on July 12, nine on July 13, sixteen on July 14. Oxen pulling wagons travel at about two miles an hour. In places, "road building" consisted of little more than keeping the train moving. On July 14 they passed Steptoe's battlefield. Noting Indians on the hills, Mullan ordered his men to inspect their arms, issued extra cartridges, and urged "great precaution." But the Indians only observed. That night the crew camped at the site of Qualchan's death, and Mullan lamented the "poor creatures" whose impending "doom...is...pitiable."[43]

Approaching Lake Coeur d'Alene, Mullan made a serious blunder that would later need correction. The Topographical Bureau instructed him to construct his road "skirting the southern shore of the Coeur d'Alene Lake to the Coeur d'Alene Mission." But the orders also gave Mullan flexibility to find the "proper location of the road." Mullan sent out reconnaissance teams to determine the best route. He knew the rugged country around Lake Coeur d'Alene; he had traveled there with Colonel Wright. But, obsessed with taking the shortest route to Fort Benton, he chose to retrace Wright's course along the south edge of the lake. He would regret the decision. "He will have to cut his way through a heavily timbered region," reported the Olympia newspaper. "And of course his progress will be slow."[44]

But he did at least enjoy the area's beauty. Trained as a military engineer, Mullan usually reported with impersonal objectivity. This was a man who recorded the death of a crew member without emotion. But at times the West's grace brought him to lyricism, and he now headed into such country. "The valley of the St. Joseph's is a beautiful gem embedded in a noble range of mountains," he wrote. "Viewed from an elevation, on a summer's day, the scenery and effect is grand and picturesque—the river winding from side to side in graceful curves, while copses of willow, cottonwood, and alder fringe its banks, and silvery lakes dot here and there the green sward in which it is clothed." Beautiful to perceive;

not so nice when building a road. Mullan soon found "the work [to be]…more severe than I had any idea of."[45]

Mullan later referred to this shortcut south and east of the lake as "a cut in truth," for the crew not only "cut," but also blasted, dragged, hacked, shoveled, raked, and scraped its way through an old-growth forest stacked high with fallen timber. "It seemed as if every foot was covered with trees or underbrush," Mullan recalled.[46]

Tough going even on level ground. But Mullan encountered precious little flat earth. "Our first…difficulty was to make the descent of seven hundred feet from the table land to the valley of the St. Joseph's," he wrote. Difficult indeed, through a jungle of monster trees with diameters of three, four, five feet—fir, pine, and larch, some two hundred feet high, their interlacing branches forming a canopy so dense "the rays of the sun cannot penetrate." Below lay decaying mounds of downed trees and branches. Tangled masses of willow, alder, buckbrush, honeysuckle, elderberry, current, and thimbleberry clogged what few natural openings the men encountered. And, of course, there was rock. Partially submerged boulders anchored the maze of roots in this fertile landscape, stones that could trip horses or tip wagons if left in a roadway. They had to be removed.[47]

Arrayed against this nearly impregnable barrier: a few horses, and men armed with shovels, picks, saws, axes, sledgehammers, wheelbarrows, sleds, scrapers, and, their one great equalizer, black powder. We "pushed ahead to cut out, inch by inch…the timber marked by the engineers, who were crawling through the undergrowth, unable to see more than a few feet before them," recalled crew member Charles Schafft.[48]

The engineers marked the most efficient route they could find. The crew achingly followed, felling huge trees, grubbing boulders, hacking brush. And that earned them a clearing—but hardly a road. John Mullan would have recoiled at his highway being called a "trail." Deer, Indians, and explorers took trails. He had been sent west to construct a road—where practical, twenty-five-feet wide. In densely forested, rocky regions like this the crew mostly adhered to a construction width of fifteen to twenty feet. Even so, it was much more than a trail, and Mullan would have been sorely disappointed that, 150 years later, so many people referred to his thoroughfare as "The Mullan Trail."

Having cut their way down the mountainside to the St. Joe River valley, they next had to construct a sixty-foot bridge over a pool of water. Mullan purchased this short piece of progress from plateau to river bottom at the cost of eight days of hard-won progress. Then came the swamps.[49]

Mullan was approaching the site Father DeSmet had originally selected for a mission to the Coeur d'Alene Indians, a beautiful spot "where fine springs gushed from the slopes." Here the Jesuits "maintained themselves" until "finding the overflow of the lower portion of the valley entered as an impediment…to pleasant travel." Or, put differently, they built a mission in a marsh. Mullan knew the cause of the Jesuits' problems and why they had moved their mission to higher ground. But once he had committed to building his road south and east of Lake Coeur d'Alene, he inevitably faced the same boggy hazards. To cross the worst of the wetlands took valuable time. Mullan's crew cut logs that they laid down side-by-side, giving them a "covering [of] loose stone" to make "a very good road." The resulting ribbed pathway resembled the wide wales of coarse corduroy fabric—and hence the name, corduroy road.[50]

At the point where they needed to cross the St. Joe River, they found it ran 240 feet wide. Mullan did not have time to bridge this expanse, so he set his men whipsawing lumber for two flatboats, each capable of ferrying a loaded wagon and four yoke of oxen. While most of the crew ferried across the St. Joe in one, a group of men rowed the second up the lake to the Coeur d'Alene River, where it awaited the crew's crossing there. Mullan's men built the boats well. Two decades later, travelers still used them.[51]

Mullan "did not hesitate to put his shoulder to the wheel," as one worker recalled. He expected the same diligence from his crew, and for the most part was satisfied. His men even worked on Sundays. Still, progress went more slowly and expensively than expected. Captain Humphreys reprimanded him for over-expending the amount appropriated for this section of the road. "I am directed by the Secretary of War to state that there appears to have been no sufficient reason to have justified you in drawing upon the appropriation beyond the amount which had been designated by the Department," Humphreys sternly wrote Mullan. It would not be the only time Humphreys chastised him.

But criticism came easy from a desk in Washington. The Topographical Bureau had no experience with this type of terrain.[52]

On August 16 the crew arrived at the Coeur d'Alene Mission, where they "received the welcome of the fathers." Mullan, as was his custom when at this oasis of Christian civilization, attended mass. He probably prayed for his crew; maybe for understanding from Humphreys for the expenses he was about to incur. For Mullan knew the previous work had been a warm-up. They had laid a road 198½ miles to this point. But the excruciating part lay east of the mission—in the Bitterroot Mountains.[53]

❧

Mullan gave his scouts little time to enjoy the mission's civilized pleasures, "for we knew we must cross two if not more mountain ranges before we came to the Plains." He sent Kolecki west to determine the feasibility of connecting his road to the army post at Fort Colville. Engle explored a path to the northeast. And Sohon again embarked on the most adventurous exploration, into the Bitterroots, to ascertain "the best point of passage over the...mountains."[54]

Sohon, taking with him "the best Indian guides we could procure," did not disappoint. A couple of weeks out he reached the summit of a pass; noting that he had found their route, he sent a rider to Mullan with detailed sketches and a map. Mullan rewarded the effort by naming the pass "in honor of Mr. Sohon, my long and faithful companion."[55]

Sohon also confirmed what Mullan already knew. The "principal difficulties" of his entire road-building effort lay ahead. To reach Fort Benton by the next summer, Mullan had to conquer the mountains before winter struck, a narrow window of opportunity. He split his crew into smaller groups to cover more ground. Twenty-three men moved forward eleven miles and then cut their way back west; Mullan headed a second group working east toward the advance party. When the two met, he divided his force again, working simultaneously east and west, meeting, splitting. It became his "plan of operations."[56]

"The forest was so dense that we scarcely saw the sun for six weeks," recalled John Strachan. They worked in "timber...heavy to cut and equally so to clear." Axemen hacked through the tangle of downed timber. Cutters sawed standing trees to ground level. Laborers rolled logs off the road, retaining smaller ones for corduroyed sections. Then came "grading in thousands of places, made necessary by the physical nature of the country." In October, Lieutenant White wrote, "our progress has been very slow." Mullan "pushed forward with all the energy and will at our disposal....Every teamster, cook, laborer—in fact my every man is daily, with pick, shovel, and axe, on the road." His experienced crew knew how to fell trees, remove timber, corduroy marshes, and grade a forested road. They had encountered all these obstacles earlier. But now they confronted something more daunting. Lieutenant White assessed the situation accurately, noting a stream "on our maps" called the Coeur d'Alene River. But he had a more descriptive appellation. He called it, simply, "Crooked River." Mullan's timbermen would become expert bridge builders.[57]

Counting the bridges along Mullan's road is baffling. Even the meticulous Mullan surrendered to the infeasibility of enumeration: "Suffice it to say that every point has been bridged or corduroyed that required it." Did his men construct forty, fifty, sixty bridges along the Coeur d'Alene River? One thing is sure: they did not build as many as advance scout Walter Johnson advised. "Nearly 100 crossings have been made...which must be bridged in order to render the road passable at all seasons," he wrote. "The average length of these bridges will be fifty feet each." Mullan recognized he did not have the time or money to accomplish such a prodigious bridge-building feat, so in many places he simply forded the exasperatingly "crooked river."[58]

His men worked this stretch of road in the fall. Already the days grew so short that the sun hardly glanced the road's surface, buried deep in the steep-walled, tree-blanketed canyon. Mullan knew that this stretch of highway would primarily provide seasonal passage for travelers. Winter snows would remain on the path for months before surrendering to the sun's melt. No need to bridge every crossing, for travelers would journey here only in summer, when the stream could be waded in many spots. "All crossings are now fordable...from 1st June," he explained to Humphreys. "Owing to the number...of these, I have deemed it, with my present time and appropriation, a matter of complete impossibility...to bridge them." Still, there were places where only bridges would do.[59]

To build a bridge required strong backs, sharp saws, and ample nearby timber—the latter not a problem along the Coeur d'Alene River. Mullan provided few details about his bridges, but did note one as being seventeen feet wide, probably a standard. The simplest bridges were single spans of stringers decked with logs. Most consisted of at least two spans, and some had three or four. To create supports for the spans, Mullan's crew constructed triangular cribs of logs or hewn timber, then sank them "by means of rock placed in the bottom…until they rested on the river bed." They then filled the boxes with stones. Next they connected these piers with a framework of hewn lumber and covered it with decking—logs on shorter spans, planks "three inches thick" on longer. To hew all that lumber required exhausting work, for the crew turned logs to boards with two-man whipsaws. The men lifted each log to the top of a six-foot-tall platform, one man straddling the log on top while another stood below. They then worked a two-handled saw, through an opening in the platform, pulling up and down. A whipsaw's teeth are angled to cut only on the downward stroke, making it easier on the man above to raise the saw. The man below had gravity working in his favor, but contended with sawdust and the constant threat that a falling log might crush him.[60]

Given the rudimentary equipment of the time, the task of building seemingly endless bridges would daunt spirits under the best of conditions. But Mullan could only wistfully hope for such conditions; the fall of 1859 did not cooperate.

October brought "four weeks [of] incessant rain, which rendered our road very…muddy." By the end of the month "the road had been rendered very nearly impassable." One member of the crew wrote to a newspaper in mid-October, "The weather is cold and disagreeable. There is already snow. We are still living in tents."[61]

Soon matters grew even graver. Lieutenant White reported on November 3, "The snow again visited us, falling to the depth of fifteen or eighteen inches." Mullan characterized it as "a perfect storm…with great fury." After seven consecutive days of snow "with slight intermission," a cold front hit. The temperature fell below zero. Supplies grew short. In November the army escort began furnishing food to the crew. A pack train with winter clothes for Mullan's civilians got "cut off by the snow," and the army escort also lent the crew warm garments.[62]

The difficult work, hurried pace, severe weather, and substandard clothing took a toll. As early as November, White reported one member of his escort "severely frost bitten." Two of Mullan's civilians cut themselves with axes, a falling tree injured another, and one accidentally shot himself in the knee. Mullan discharged another four "as they did not come up to the…requisites for laboring men on this expedition." Fortunately, Mullan had the option of hiring members of the army escort. For the extra pay, thirty to forty regularly engaged in road construction. It had become clear by then that the escort was not really required for protection from Indians. But the expedition had had its times of concern.[63]

"About midnight the cries of an Indian was heard, approaching," recalled John Strachan of a camp the crew made east of the Coeur d'Alene Mission. "He…came nearer.…Every man got ready, as an attack was… almost certain.…The Indian approached and still kept talking. Some of our men had a little knowledge of the Indian language.…They…made out that he had come…in advance to inform us that a large party of Indians were on their way to attack us."[64]

Turns out the men did not know enough Indian language. Their interpreter had camped that night with another work party. He arrived the next morning to set the would-be linguists straight. The wayfaring Indian had come on quite a different task: to seek medical help for his wife.

For the most part, John Mullan held a progressive attitude toward Indians. But he would harbor no interference with his road. If Indians threatened construction, his scorn could be as harsh as anyone of his generation. "Indians…are not to be trusted," Mullan wrote as his crew made its way east. And should one "dare to depredate upon our road," Mullan threatened the direst of consequences: his friend Colonel Wright would return to complete his business with the tribes.[65]

Mullan seemingly had some cause for worry. Though Wright had won a decisive victory, army troops did not control the country. The major cause of the Indians' original discontent—the military road—remained. "We found them very…much opposed to our passing through their country," professed Strachan. Receiving erroneous reports about obstreperous Indians from an unidentified road crew member, the

Olympia *Pioneer and Democrat*, a race-baiting trumpet, stirred the froth. Recalling the "well-merited whipping Colonel Wright gave them," the editor opined that "if a few more had the rope around their necks it might be well."[66]

Mullan took the Indians' discontent seriously, though he believed it would likely manifest itself in vandalism, not overt attacks. Still, with his force strung thinly on a long line, "the temptation to them is great." After reaching Lake Coeur d'Alene, the crew met nearly daily with Spokanes or Coeur d'Alenes. Mullan permitted his men to trade only in the presence of an interpreter, so there would be no misunderstandings. When Indians came into camp, Mullan gathered them in the center, where "they are surrounded."[67]

But Mullan was more inclined toward diplomacy than confrontation. "Be assured I have left and shall leave nothing undone that shall create any but the most friendly relations with them," he reported to Humphreys. He made friends with Coeur d'Alenes by allowing them free use of his flatboats, enabling them to "cross and recross with their bands of animals without being compelled to unpack." At other places he invited tribal members to use the road "instead of their Indian trails."[68]

In reality the Indians became reconciled to the road. And some no doubt perceived advantages from its use. Thomas Hughes probably exaggerated when he reported after a visit to Mullan's camp that "the Indians have given him the name of 'Little Man with a big heart.'" But, employing a combination of tough talk and peace accords, Mullan constructed his road with no significant Indian interference.[69]

Winter descended fast and hard, catching Mullan's crew in the mountains and producing a wasteland of animal carcasses. John Strachan chronicled the carnage:

> Cattle, horses and mules lay dead in every direction. All the open space resembled the precincts of a slaughter house, giving an exceedingly desolate aspect to the scene. Near the river it was a perfect mass of corruption. Hundreds of carcasses dotted the banks where they had gathered for water and dropped down from fatigue and starvation. Hundreds of buzzards gathered...from all parts to the great carnival of flesh...bears, wolves and panthers were here in great numbers, feeding

on the foul masses of carrion. They scarcely deigned to move as we passed them.[70]

Mullan had hoped to winter in the Bitterroot Valley, that "land of eternal spring." But the snows came too fast, the livestock died too suddenly. When the temperature plummeted below negative forty degrees on December 5—freezing the mercury, or the "thermometer would have shown a lower temperature"—Mullan called a halt. Mullan's balmy experience during the Bitterroot Valley winter of 1853-54 left him emotionally unprepared for this harsh onslaught. A few months earlier he had optimistically predicted his crew could ride out the season in their Sibley tents "unless the character of the winter should be more severe than I now anticipate." Mullan anticipated wrong. Caught on the banks of the frozen St. Regis River, overtaken by rapidly accumulating snow, he now realized the survival of his crew depended upon shelter more substantial than tents. He set his men constructing a winter quarters. He named it Cantonment Jordan after Captain Thomas Jordan, quartermaster at The Dalles and Walla Walla, for whom Mullan felt "indebted for all co-operation that was in his power to accord" as he outfitted his expedition.[71]

Mullan stopped his advance at a small flat sheltered by mountains, surrounded by timber, twenty-five yards from the river, with good spring water, near the current community of DeBorgia, Montana. Here his men constructed a storehouse, office, and collection of primitive huts. To insulate the log huts they shoveled dirt embankments along their sides, earthworks visible well into the twentieth century. Mullan enclosed it all with a stockade and four blockhouses. He termed Cantonment Jordan "a curious little town," and his former West Point classmate Augustus Kautz, passing by the site ten months later, called it "quite a village." But as Mullan admitted, his men were about to pass a severe winter "as much out of the world as though we were on an island at sea."[72]

Mullan slaughtered his remaining cattle, the meat freezing solid shortly after butchering. It would last until spring. He herded most of his horses and mules—those that somehow managed to survive—toward the Bitterroot Valley. It became a hundred-mile death march. The emaciated animals drowned crossing ice-clogged rivers, slipped to their deaths on snowy mountain trails, starved as they futilely pawed for grass.[73]

John Creighton's wagons managed to move most of the winter supplies to Cantonment Jordan. But he had to leave ten tons piled behind on the east side of Sohon Pass, his animals too weak to carry it farther. Mullan ordered some of his men off construction detail and had them fabricate twenty hand-pulled sleds, each capable of hauling six hundred pounds. In these, his crew hauled the remaining freight. Who was the unluckiest? The men with frostbit feet working in temperatures that seldom reached zero building log cabins? Or those with equally frostbit feet harnessed belly and chest to crude sleds, straining along the torturous, winding road, pulling six hundred pounds of cargo? And yet, Mullan's men accomplished all this "with cheerfulness and zeal." In the accolades Mullan has received as an engineer, none have mentioned what might have been his greatest accomplishment—keeping his crew "cheerfully" working in life-threatening conditions.[74]

Mullan's brother James, the expedition's physician, busied himself treating frostbite. All "yielded readily to medical treatment," except escort member Edward Murray. Disregarding orders, Murray hiked into the forest alone, got lost, wandered four days without food or blankets, but somehow managed to crawl back to camp, his feet solidly frozen. James Mullan "cut off one leg," and, to save Murray's life, a few days later amputated the other.[75]

Neither frostbite, the gloom of winter, nor rapidly accumulating snows stayed Mullan's couriers from their appointed rounds of delivering mail. And thus, on April 1, 1860, readers of St. Louis newspapers read about the sad plight of Edward Murray. News of the outside world also reached the isolated camp. "The mails were distributed," wrote John Strachan after receiving a package from his brother, "and…the Rockford [Missouri] *Register*…was read by all our camp with great interest."[76]

Mullan established an elaborate express system. "I regard the interests of our work such that I feel warranted in pursuing the plan indicated, both at the risk of expenses, difficulty, and danger," he informed Humphreys. Cantonment Jordan sat 267 miles from Walla Walla. In good weather, Mullan's expressmen carried mail twice a month. When storms hit in November, he determined to keep the route open for once-a-month service. He provisioned grain depots at four places and enlisted P. E. Toohill and George Young at $100 a month each to carry the mail, hiring Indians to assist them.[77]

After the snows set in, the expressmen negotiated the mountains on snowshoes. In December, Toohill measured five feet of snow on Sohon Pass; six weeks later, seven feet. After one trip, Toohill gave Mullan the discouraging news that he had to clamor over 165 trees that had toppled over the road. Toohill's record of a trip begun from Cantonment Jordan on April 7 gives an indication of the journey's challenges. He still found seven feet of snow at the pass. But now the river had thawed, washing out virtually all of Mullan's bridges, forcing Toohill to wade through every icy crossing. At the Coeur d'Alene Mission he borrowed a canoe and paddled until the river clogged with ice. He then hiked to a depot where he had left horses on his previous trip, and made it to Walla Walla on April 16. Two days later he began his return, reaching Cantonment Jordan on May 4. The system actually worked surprisingly well. A letter sent September 10 from Washington, D.C., reached Mullan on January 16.[78]

Toohill's experiences paled compared to Ed Williamson's. Williamson knew his way around mountains; on one winter expedition in 1858 he survived by eating his horse. He was spending the winter at Fort Owen when Mullan hired him to purchase mules at Salt Lake to replace those lost to starvation. Mules cost $150 in the Bitterroot Valley; a tenth that in Utah. Williamson had gone only a short way when he lost both his horses in deep snow. Undaunted, he fashioned snowshoes from their saddle riggings and, snowblind, trudged several hundred miles on foot to Utah. He returned to Fort Owen fifty days later. "He proved himself a hardy fellow," Mullan understated.[79]

Overwrought stories of Mullan's plight began appearing in Northwest newspapers in December 1859. "Lieutenant Mullan's command have met with a serious misfortune," lamented the *Weekly Oregonian*. There is "great danger that a large number of them [will] perish in the mountains." The Dalles *Journal* reported a week later on the men's "deplorable conditions....It is feared the most disastrous anticipations imaginable may be realized and that the expedition will be a failure."[80]

Mullan's reputation depended as much on the illusion of success as its actuality. "We have noticed from time to time the many exaggerated accounts of our suffering & privation &tc.," he wrote. "These at times have vexed us." So much so that in early January he dispatched civilian engineer Walter Johnson to Washington, D.C., on a mission of multiple goals, one of which was to dispel such rumors. In February, Johnson left a message with the San Francisco *Herald* to counter the "many exaggerated accounts of the situation." Mullan himself sent word directly to Humphreys. "The department may rely on one thing," he resolutely wrote. "As I was sent out to build and construct the road, it *shall* be constructed."[81]

🌱

Garry, the western-educated, English-speaking chief of the Spokane Tribe, rode his horse to Cantonment Jordan in the middle of that harsh winter. His simple act of delivering mail forced the ever-confident Mullan to question the hard-won miles his crew had so laboriously attained on the road. While Mullan's well-paid expressmen snowshoed over Sohon Pass, Garry crossed the mountains astride a horse. It perplexed Mullan. "Spokane Garry brought the mail by the way of the Clark's Fork," he wrote, and though he "lost one horse en route, yet he nevertheless made the trips mostly on horseback." A lone man on horse had ridden the shore of Lake Pend Oreille on a route Mullan had rejected as infeasible. The headstrong Mullan rarely second-guessed himself. But Garry's appearance so flummoxed him that he made a comment that has been repeated often by those who proclaim Mullan's road a failure, blaming his choice of routes. "Had I known in 1854 what I did not know until 1859," Mullan wrote in his road report, "I should have recommended that the...road...[follow] the Clark's [Fork] route."[82]

But Mullan was too hard on himself. That same season of Garry's ride, George Clinton Gardner, with the party marking the border between Canada and the United States, took Garry's trail. He swam mules in icy rivers, built rafts, and even after that effort, admitted he had traveled the course at the only feasible time. Come spring—the same season Mullan had traveled this way in 1854—the course would be impossible. "The route thus far has been along the water's edge over boggy ground in many places," he reported, "and will be impassable at high water."[83]

Of course it took more than Spokane Garry on horseback to convince the scientifically trained Mullan that he had erred. He studied the situation. He had Garry measure snow depths on future trips while his expressmen continued their snow readings on Sohon Pass. And when all this evidence confirmed greater snowfall on his route than Garry's, he theorized an isocheimal line zig-zagging its way across America. An isocheimal line is a mapmaker's term used to connect places with similar mean temperature. Mullan's theoretical line would have baffled any road builder attempting to follow the warmest route across the country. Starting in Missouri, it curved west, then zigged north to the Black Hills, zagged south to the geysers of Yellowstone, twisted west to his Bitterroot "valley of Eden," north to Lake Pend Oreille, then plunged dramatically south to Walla Walla. "Thus we find the same climate along the Clark's Fork…that we find in St. Joseph's, Missouri," he noted. Mullan could have dispensed with the theorizing had the local inhabitants been more cooperative. He always asked Indians for advice on best routes, but they often demurred, having no affinity for his road. Only when trapped in the mountains did Mullan discover that "no Indians had ever been known to cross the mountains in winter, via the Coeur d'Alene route, while it was quite a usual thing for them to do via the Clark's Fork."[84]

Recognizing he had chosen the more difficult passage, Mullan recommended that, should a transcontinental railroad traverse the north, it follow the Clark's Fork, and the Northern Pacific eventually did. But Mullan acted on the best information he had available and engineered a viable course—albeit generations ahead of its time. A century later America's longest interstate, I-90, proved the wisdom of Mullan's choice when it took the same route as his road, a passage then made feasible with snow-clearing advancements. Given the size of his appropriation, Mullan had accurately assessed the impracticability of building through the quagmire of Lake Pend Oreille. The Northern Pacific opened that route only when much larger work crews could excavate side hills and build permanent bridges. Mullan could indulge in neither extravagance.

Mullan scientifically theorized again when scurvy set in. By February the disease had struck twenty-five escort troops, but no civilians. Mullan blamed the outbreak on Lieutenant White's adherence to new army regulations dictating meals of salted meat five days a week. Mullan, typically, ignored those directions. Not until the 1930s would scientists discover scurvy's cause. But Mullan was on the right track when he speculated that heavier doses of vegetables and a preference for frozen over salted meat stilled the disorder among his civilians.

Mullan acquired vegetables from the Pend Oreille Mission for White's troops. Dr. James Mullan administered the fresh food and replaced salted meat with frozen. "The dreaded malady…disappeared," and all the men were soon "cheerful and strong." Mullan made sure his superiors knew of his success in curing the disease and suggested a change in army regulations. "I enclose the report of the physician," he immodestly wrote Humphreys, "as I deem it one worthy to be brought to the special attention of the war department." The write-up apparently went no farther than Humphreys. Fifty years later Mullan still rankled at that lack of respect, ridiculing the military bureaucracy while praising his own actions: "When the scurvy threatened to kill off the soldiers, I took matters into my own hands and assumed control [of the escort]…. By cutting off the [army] red tape, we probably saved many lives."[85]

Mullan had an even more serious concern that winter: finances. He had been running over budget since fall. He paid a high price for labor; had to replace virtually all his stock; spent a premium for supplies. "I shall push forward with all the energy possible…to a successful completion, whether it involves a deficiency or not," he asserted to Humphreys. But not all his crew felt the same way. When Mullan informed his men that he could not guarantee their wages unless Congress appropriated more money, five left camp. They chose a tough way to demonstrate discontent. As John Strachan oversimplified, they had "a severe undertaking" as they tramped their way to Walla Walla through bone-numbing cold and high-piled snow. At least one suffered severe frostbite. Remarkably, most of Mullan's crew remained on the job.[86]

The area's few settlers provided what animals they could spare, and Flathead Indians loaned Mullan horses and men to transport supplies from Fort Benton. But Mullan recognized his effort teetered on the verge of collapse unless Congress appropriated more money. So he dispatched Walter Johnson to Washington, D.C., "a young man…whose thorough knowledge of the work pointed him out as a suitable person to perform what I desired." Johnson would meet with Isaac Stevens, who Mullan hoped could convince Congress to allocate more funds. And that is how Walter Johnson saved Mullan's road-building expedition.[87]

❦

Nancy Johnson saw that her adopted son received training as a civil engineer. That served the twenty-three-year-old, Michigan-raised, Walter Whipple Johnson well when he signed on with Mullan's road crew. Entranced with the West, Johnson remained after the road's completion. He settled in the Bitterroot Valley and won election to the territorial legislature where, in 1866, he introduced a resolution to Congress requesting funds to improve the road he had helped build. But had Mullan not dispatched Johnson to Washington, there might not have been a road to fret about. Walter Johnson made his way out of Cantonment Jordan in January, snow-shoed over Sohon Pass, rode to Walla Walla, and steamed to San Francisco, where he wrote his letter to the editor dispelling myths about the demise of Mullan's crew. He then crossed Panama and got to the capital just as Captain Andrew Humphreys, weary of Mullan's continuing budget overruns, had determined to cancel the road project.[88]

Mullan continually groused to Humphreys about insufficient funds. "To build a line of six hundred miles…in a country where the lowest price of labor is $50 per month, and transportation at the rate from $200 to $300 per ton…and the difficulties and length of the route, and the manner of overcoming them, have been so often…set before the department in my previous reports that it would hardly seem necessary to call attention to them again," Mullan wrote in September. Necessary or not, Mullan maintained the incessant grumbling.[89]

Officers at the Topographical Bureau remained unmoved. Mullan's overspending had to stop. "I am…directed by the Secretary of War to inform you," wrote Lieutenant J.C. Ives of the bureau, "that the accounts, which you have submitted to the department…show that by the time you will have reached Fort Benton, your liabilities will have exceeded your appropriation by a considerable amount, which is contrary to law, and to the express instructions of the Department." As a consequence, the department would administer a crushing punishment: "The [road] expedition is disbanded."[90]

For once Mullan could be thankful for slow mail. Before he received Ives's letter, Walter Johnson arrived in Washington, but he found Humphreys in no mood to negotiate. Mullan, never one to abide criticism, had exploded at an earlier letter from Humphreys containing a minor admonition, and sent a remarkable letter to a superior officer. "If...I have violated either a rule or a custom of the Department I can only say that I did it innocently and for the best interests of the Expedition," he wrote. He then petulantly continued:

> And feeling as I do an interest and an identity in opening this route... with which I have been connected for the last seven years, I cannot but regret and am pained to feel that though now nine months actively engaged in the field that the only letter in connection with my course and operations that I have received from the Dept. has been this, that contains an apparent reprimand.[91]

Mullan's letter had no impact, other than perhaps irritating Humphreys and confirming his opinion of Mullan as an apologist. But Johnson worked effectively with Isaac Stevens, who rekindled efforts to convince Congress to appropriate an additional $100,000. Unlike Humphreys, Mullan and Stevens knew the Northwest and recognized the expense involved in building a road. Stevens had originally sought $200,000 for the job, and was not surprised that the $100,000 so far appropriated proved insufficient. But Johnson and Stevens might have failed except for gold.

In a letter to Humphreys in September 1859, Mullan had nonchalantly revealed that his crew had found gold. Recognizing the difficulty of retaining a work force should news of a gold discovery leak, Mullan downplayed the episode, and swore its discoverers to secrecy. But his report intrigued Secretary of War Floyd, who became a powerful advocate for an additional appropriation. After noting in his annual report to the president the potential value of Mullan's road in keeping Indians under control and aiding emigration, Floyd came to the point: "A further appropriation for its completion is now necessary. Reliable information has been recently furnished to the department of great mineral wealth in the mountains through which a portion of the road passes."[92]

Congress granted the additional $100,000. John Mullan's expedition had been reprieved. The Topographical Bureau dispatched Walter Johnson to deliver the good news. He took with him one additional piece of satisfying information: the War Department would send an army expedition over the road, fulfilling one of Mullan's aspirations.

Mullan realized that to attain validity as a military highway, his road required army use. He had given Johnson two primary missions: convince the "callous and apathetic persons" of Washington, D.C., that he needed more money, and persuade the War Department to dispatch troops over his new road. Johnson succeeded on both counts.[93]

Mullan had lobbied for troop usage of his road as early as 1858. While serving under Colonel Wright, he wrote Humphreys a letter advocating military use of the soon-to-be-built road as a means of assuring peace. "An important question with me is suppose the Indians are whipped this season, will they remain whipped—It is more than doubtful," he wrote. To remind them of the army's ongoing strength and presence, any "regiment or large body of troops" crossing the continent in the near future should do so on the Fort Benton to Walla Walla road.[94]

After he began road work, he incessantly appealed to Humphreys. In the pack of correspondence carried east by Johnson, Mullan summed up his rationale:

> We shall reach Fort Benton with our road, say in August, with a large and empty train, which has cost much. We shall then be compelled either to take this train back empty to Walla Walla…or abandon it at Fort Benton. Strict economy, and a desire to see the route practically opened by a new line for military operations, therefore, prompt me to recommend…that a detachment of three hundred recruits…be sent… from St. Louis to Fort Benton…[where they should be] turned over to my command…and I will guarantee to guide and take them to Walla Walla in security and with success.

Mullan predicted the route would save the army 50 percent of its normal expense of diverting troops across the Isthmus of Panama.[95]

The army agreed to try. It commanded Major George Blake to transport three hundred troops by steamer to Fort Benton, then continue overland on Mullan's road. But Blake commenced his trip with the outdated information that Humphreys had disbanded Mullan's road crew. It would cause awkward tension when Mullan and Blake met at Fort Benton. But first Mullan had to reach that post.

Tenaciousness and determination characterized John Mullan, traits exemplified in the months he awaited news from Johnson. Though out of money and not yet aware of Congress's decision to appropriate more, Mullan rejected inertia. In January, with Cantonment Jordan socked in with snow, Mullan sent a contingent of men under David Williamson to the Clark Fork to construct a ferry and six small boats. The men snow-shoed all their clothing, blankets, provisions, and tools fifteen miles, "the greatest undertaking I had yet encountered," according to John Strachan, who had encountered quite a few. As they struggled out of the mountains they arrived at a "fine valley" where the St. Regis River emptied into the Clark Fork. Here they constructed a small cabin, set up a whipsaw frame, built a forty-five-foot-long flatboat to haul Mullan's crew across the river, and six smaller craft to move supplies up the Clark Fork as Mullan's men worked near its banks.[96]

In late February Mullan sent the bulk of his party to Williamson's camp, taking advantage of its more hospitable climate to jump-start road building. Each man shouldered a fifty-pound pack. Experiencing "much difficulty…with these heavy burdens," they reached the valley "much fatigued." Once there, Mullan again split his crew into "sub-parties." As spring thaw gradually arrived in the mountains, Mullan had Lieutenant White's military escort work its way east, meeting a party under Walter DeLacy laboring west. By June they had cut that fifteen-mile segment of road "through some of the most dense timber we have had in the line." Thankfully, on June 4, the last of the crew abandoned Cantonment Jordan, their "dreary" winter camp.[97]

❧

John Mullan had briefly left the dismal confines of Cantonment Jordan on February 26. Imagine his pleasure as he arrived at the home of his old friend John Owen, he who plied guests with "sundry nips" of brandy while his wife Nancy provided "Mince Pies and Cakes that would have done Credit to a table in a More Civilized part of the World." Fort Owen had changed considerably since Mullan had departed from the valley in 1854. Owen had replaced the timber palisade surrounding the post with twelve-foot-high adobe walls. He had constructed a barracks, two bastions, shops, and a school for employees' children. John and Nancy's private quarters held the library Mullan so admired—floor-to-ceiling bookshelves spanning two walls. And they had added a private guest room for traveling dignitaries, complete with a fireplace and closet. No doubt Mullan stayed there, luxuriating for two weeks.[98]

Mullan discovered that a few head of his stock had survived the winter in the valley. He also found P.M. Engle at Fort Owen. He had spent part of the winter there, unable to make it through the snows to Cantonment Jordan following a harrowing trip to Fort Benton to purchase cattle and supplies. But Mullan needed many more animals and provisions. From John Owen he purchased 1,159 pounds of flour, 1,193 pounds of beef, 98 pounds of sugar, and 47 pounds of coffee. Mullan's purchases brought a boon to Owen. Never had business been so brisk. Ironically, once Mullan completed his road—bypassing Fort Owen by thirty-five miles—the post steadily declined. But in March 1860, it bustled. Even so, Mullan required vastly more provisioning than Major Owen could supply. To bridge that gap he turned for aid to his favored Indians—the Flatheads.[99]

"There were many Indian lodges" around Fort Owen, reported John Strachan. From these Flatheads, who possessed a "nobleness of character...seldom seen among Indians," Mullan asked for one hundred twenty horses and seventeen Indians to accompany Gus Sohon to Fort Benton. The Flatheads agreed, leaving Fort Owen on March 16 and returning a month later with rations that had been shipped from St. Louis. Mullan's work crew could carry on.[100]

That spring found his crew working both east and west of the camp where David Williamson had supervised boat construction. They encountered some of the toughest challenges of the entire project. At two places, where the mountains ran to the river, the crew blasted its way through rocky high ground, "an undertaking that I almost feared to attempt," Mullan later recounted. Dangerous work; Robert Booth "was severely stunned"; Frederick Sheridan blinded. Mullan took an unusual interest in Sheridan. He ordered an assistant, G. C. Tuliaferro, to accompany Sheridan to Washington, D.C., with a letter for Humphreys: "He is...blind and helpless....He is an Englishman and without friends in this country." Mullan asked that Humphreys place him in the Soldiers Home in Washington, paying for his care out of the road appropriation. Mullan's brother James also recommended that double-amputee Edward Murray, along with four other men from the escort who had become so disabled as to be "unfit to perform the duties of service," be discharged. Road construction had exacted a costly toll on many.[101]

In early June the raging waters of a spring freshet crashed into the ferry Williamson's crew had constructed, smashing it downstream, "leaving us in the unfortunate position of a portion of our wagons still on the left bank." Mullan dispatched a crew to build another ferry. "It may delay us a week," he apologetically informed Humphreys.[102]

Mullan was running out of time—and out of excuses for Humphreys. He learned from expressmen that Major Blake, with his three hundred troops, was steaming toward Fort Benton. The success of Mullan's road, his reputation, dictated that Mullan be there to greet him. He would have to cut corners.

Mullan made multiple crossings of multiple rivers. He could have avoided most with a little side hill excavation, but he could not spare the time. At the Big Blackfoot his crew hastily constructed a ferry. After a few crossings the flimsy craft tipped, dumping overboard a wagon and several men. Next, the boat got caught up on an island, and crew members, including Mullan, attempted to guide it across the river. But it quickly started filling with water, racing downstream out of control. Mullan, up to his waist in river water "stuck fast to the boat." It somehow found its way to a shallow, and the crew formed a human chain to rescue the lieutenant—the second time he had nearly drowned in a Montana river.[103]

Mullan had considered his discovery of the "celebrated pass through the Rocky Mountains...known as Mullan Pass" one of his great accomplishments. He was never happier to see it than on July 18, 1860. Here, six years earlier, he had ascended the treeless summit with a wagon. Now, descending its "gradual slope," Mullan realized his road-building slog had ended. "East of the Rockies we came to what was a new country compared with the wilderness and desolation...in which we had spent nearly a year," he later reminisced.[104]

The crew moved rapidly once over the pass. Only Medicine Rock slowed them, "by far the most difficult of any point along the entire line from Hells Gate to Fort Benton." Here they dug and graded for four days. When they reached Sun River on July 28, "our work proper ceased, for the remaining distance of fifty-five miles to Fort Benton was over an easy and almost level prairie road." He arrived at Benton, as he said he would, on August 1, 1860. "I have the honor to report the arrival of my expedition," Mullan jubilantly wrote Humphreys, "the road of 633 miles from Fort Walla-Walla to Fort Benton being opened." It should have been a triumphal entrance to the town. But it commenced acrimoniously.[105]

John Mullan had hoped to find his astronomer John Wiessner at the summit of Mullan Pass, preparing for the expedition's most anticipated astral event—a solar eclipse on July 17. Wiessner had already performed yeoman duty, trudging fragile instruments hundreds of miles, meticulously accumulating data. But on the day of the magnificent solar event, Wiessner sat not on a Rocky Mountain top, but on the comfortable deck of the steamer *Key West*, boating down the Missouri. "The eclipse of the sun occurred," wrote a disgusted Mullan, "but as our astronomical party had now descended the Missouri for St. Louis we were deprived of the opportunity of observing it."[106]

Mullan fumed not at Wiessner, always reliable, but rather at Major George Blake, who had arrived at Fort Benton in early July, awaiting Mullan. Wiessner had established an astronomical station at the fort, and he planned to backtrack to Mullan Pass for the eclipse. But when Major Blake left the East, he carried orders from the War Department to disband Mullan's crew. The countermanding orders carried by Walter Johnson—who traveled via Panama while Blake steamed up the Missouri—had not yet reached him. So Blake had unceremoniously sent Wiessner packing to St. Louis. Wiessner, though not at fault, nonetheless apologized to Mullan: "I was ordered by you…to go back to the divide of the Rocky Mountains, but before I went, got discharged by an order of the Secretary of War….I followed the demon….I went down the river….I was mislead."[107]

Mullan was livid. "It is with extreme regret and mortification that I have learned of the summary disbanding of my astronomical party," he wrote in a letter blasting Blake. "And at a time too when the data about to be collected were of the most marked value….For the last six months we have anxiously looked forward to the observation of the eclipse…. Willingly would I have paid out of my own pocket the amount necessary for securing the observations."[108]

Mullan and Blake were getting off to a poor start. Mullan simmered even more when he learned that Blake had also dismissed another of his scientists.

As Mullan's crew cut its way east in late 1859, John Pearsall traveled up the Missouri on the steamer *Spread Eagle*. Typical of nineteenth century military expeditions, the Smithsonian Institution had sent Pearsall to join Mullan and gather specimens for the burgeoning national museum. While awaiting the road crew's arrival, Pearsall collected material between Fort Benton and Fort Owen, where he spent the winter. There he met up with Mullan during Mullan's winter visit. Mullan assigned him to Wiessner's astronomical party. But by July 1860 Pearsall unexpectedly found himself embittered and unpaid, heading downriver with Wiessner, having also been brusquely dispatched by Blake.[109]

Until then, he had worked dutifully, gathering and drying plants, chiseling fossils from boulders, skinning snakes, toads, lizards, rodents, and birds. He labeled each specimen, noting the place and time he had collected it, its name, and anything else of interest, keying each entry to his field notebooks. While he continued collecting, he sent some of his specimens to Fort Benton and on to the Smithsonian.[110]

Fielding Meek and Ferdinand Hayden, the two young scientists Mullan had met seven years earlier in St. Louis, analyzed Pearsall's fossils, enthusiastically noting specimens "for the first time made known… very unlike anything hitherto known in our Nebraska series." [111]

But when Major Blake suspended him, Pearsall refused to ship the most valuable portion of his collections to the national museum. "No one [h]as any right to [the collections] but myself," Pearsall angrily responded to Spencer Fullerton Baird, the Smithsonian's curator. "Let those who find fault pay me my wages….Until then I shall treet their conduct with the contempt which it deserves." [112]

Like the great railroad surveys of the 1850s, Mullan had hoped his expedition would expand scientific knowledge. Mullan himself had gathered specimens for the Smithsonian when he had the opportunity. His expedition did add to scientific knowledge, though not to the extent he desired.[113]

❦

John Mullan would probably have been disposed to dislike George Blake under the best of circumstances. Blake, always irascible, soured even more on the steamboat to Fort Benton when several of his men deserted. In no trifling mood by the time he reached Benton, he grew more irritated while awaiting Mullan. Though Mullan could justifiably claim he arrived on schedule, he did not look forward to meeting Blake. He had by then received Walter Johnson's letters informing him that the War Department had denied his request that Blake's troops be "turned over to my command," eliminating his opportunity of leading them triumphantly into Walla Walla. Instead, Mullan was to transfer his men, wagons, and teams to Blake's command, a decision that rankled him.[114]

As Mullan approached Fort Benton, he sent the impatient Blake a "long communication...prolific of suggestions." Blake brooded, already "very much irritated at Mullan's reproaches for having discharged his astronomers." Mullan's former West Point classmate Augustus Kautz, then serving under Blake, wrote, "We are becoming very impatient for Lt. Mullan's arrival." When Mullan finally appeared on August 1, he failed to make the customary audience before a superior officer, "much to the Major's disgust." But he did meet Kautz. After a long talk with his old friend, during which time Mullan complained about "his troubles," Kautz penned the most succinctly accurate description of Mullan's personality ever written: "He is decidedly more monomaniacal in his demonstrations than I ever knew him. He imagines everybody who is not in favor of his road to be against it." Mullan lumped George Blake into that category.[115]

Fort Benton witnessed some notable events in the summer of 1860. On July 2, two steamboats owned by Pierre Chouteau Jr.—the *Chippewa* and *Key West*—moored at the town's levee, having achieved "one of the most celebrated feats of steam navigation." They had reached a point farther from the sea than any other motorized boat. A summer before the *Chippewa* had come within fifteen miles of the post. Prior to that Fort Union had served as head of steam navigation on the Missouri. But in 1859 and 1860 the War Department contracted with Chouteau to provision Mullan's party, enticing Chouteau to advance the frontier of American steam navigation.[116]

In addition to Mullan's provisions, the two boats disgorged Blake and his 300 troops, instantly quadrupling Fort Benton's population. Two weeks later another notable expedition arrived. Mullan had hoped, once he reached Benton, to send a party southeast to explore the feasibility of connecting his road with Fort Laramie, creating a new east-west overland route to rival the Oregon Trail. The Topographical Bureau's Captain Andrew Humphreys beat him to it. In the spring of 1859 he dispatched Captain William Raynolds on the last of the major western explorations undertaken by that department. Pierre Chouteau's *Chippewa* took them as far as Fort Union. Guided by legendary trapper Jim Bridger, the Raynolds party, including scientist Ferdinand Hayden, then made the first significant explorations of the Yellowstone basin, and arrived at Fort Benton two weeks after Blake. Raynolds reported what Mullan had long suspected—that a viable connection could be made to Mullan's road from the east. Mullan hoped to make that link, and would unsuccessfully seek authorization to do so in 1861. But a civilian entrepreneur, John Bozeman, would be the one to lay out his namesake trail connecting Fort Laramie with the Montana mines.[117]

John Mullan finally arrived at this destination two weeks after Raynolds. Fort Benton consisted of "a bakery, blacksmiths', carpenters' and coopers' shops; trade offices...and also shops for retail." Here Mullan would rest only five days before returning to Walla Walla.[118]

Mullan would make that westward journey in advance of Blake with a stripped-down crew. Most of his party drifted down the Missouri to St. Louis in Mackinaw boats. His initial road building had concluded, and the parting at Fort Benton proved bittersweet, as crew member John Strachan recalled:

> Our party here broke up....There are few who can realize the emotion felt...when friends gather round to bid farewell. We had faced privation and danger side by side—had become united as one brotherhood and always ready to stand by each other in the hour of danger. Speeches were made and guns boomed from the Fort; we shook hands, exchanged wishes, and one party left for the Pacific and the other for the Atlantic.[119]

We do not know whether Mullan shared that sentimentality. He could at times be given to emotion, but his reports from Fort Benton are businesslike. He turned over his wagons and most of his stock to Major

Blake. He also provided Blake two of his ablest assistants—Gustavus Sohon, guide and interpreter, and John Creighton, wagon master. "To their joint good services Major Blake was largely indebted for the success of his march," Mullan wrote. Indeed, Mullan relinquished so much to Blake that he believed even that cantankerous officer "had nothing of which to complain."[120]

On August 5, without ceremony—despite having at long last fulfilled Thomas Jefferson's vision of connecting the Columbia and Missouri Rivers—John Mullan and his remaining crew departed Fort Benton, two days ahead of Blake. They would make minor repairs to the road as they traveled. Returning to Walla Walla, Mullan preceded the only military expedition that would ever journey the entire length of what he had ostensibly constructed as a military road.

Mullan left Fort Benton with sixty-five pack animals, four light wagons, and a small civilian crew with military escort. In a few days, dysentery struck the normally robust lieutenant. He turned over control of his party to Walter Johnson. The infirmity lingered. August 13: "Dysentery much worse today and compelled to retire with much pain." August 14: "Compelled to be carried in a wagon." And then suddenly the illness passed and Mullan rejoined the work efforts.[121]

The road west of Fort Benton was a good stretch on which to be sick. Little work was needed and the party moved briskly to stay ahead of Blake. Mullan knew, up ahead, more toil awaited. Until then, they blazed some mile markers, did a little grading. Ten days out they built a twenty-foot bridge. Mullan noted other places he should span—when he had more time. Now he simply forded streams, eighteen crossings in one particularly wet day. It took two days to construct a thirty-foot bridge over the Little Blackfoot west of the continental divide. On August 30, a group driving cattle from Walla Walla to John Owen's fort met the crew. Mullan, surprisingly nonchalant in noting the event, was surely delighted that his road had already become a transportation corridor. But it was one thing to build a cattle trail, another a wagon road. Mullan's did not yet qualify for the latter designation. "Several wagons...broken," he noted on August 29. "Went back with carpenters to repair. Teams have much difficulty in passing steep places....Had much trouble in descending Mt.—rough—locked wheels and had men on with ropes."[122]

On September 3 his crew began its mountain crossing. Sixteen men wielded axes and saws to trim stumps to ground level. On their initial pass they had only been able to cut trees to the snow line. Another fourteen men removed rocks. The remainder corduroyed swamps. The work through the mountains continued for three weeks until they reached the Coeur d'Alene Mission. At one point Mullan remarked, "Men at work 12 hours and without anything to eat. Much fatigued." Hard traveling, but Mullan knew even more work awaited on his next road-building passage. His journal notes dozens of river crossings where "bridging... will be very severe"; other places would require grading. But for now, he had again made it through the mountains. Still, Mullan had to admit that when he returned to road building he would need to cut a new route, for he now realized he had made a mistake in 1859 when he followed the southern flank of Lake Coeur d'Alene.[123]

After arriving at Fort Benton in August, Mullan had informed Humphreys of his miscalculation. "The flats of the Coeur d'Alene and St. Joseph's rivers...are impassable for a wagon before late in July or early in August," he wrote. "A radical change of location" would be required to avoid this marsh. When the crew arrived at the mission in September, Mullan sent Walter Johnson on a reconnaissance to find a better route. Johnson hired a guide, Antoine Plante, a "man over fifty years of age." Few knew the interior better than Plante. Lieutenant Rufus Saxton had engaged him in 1853 to lead his party from The Dalles to Fort Owen with supplies for Isaac Stevens. Plante had lived along the Spokane River for sixteen years, operating a ferry at a placid crossing a few miles east of present-day downtown Spokane. Plante guided Johnson over an Indian trail along the northern edge of Lake Coeur d'Alene that, conveniently, converged at his ferry. Johnson recommended this as the route of Mullan's future road. Plante would profit handsomely by ferrying future Mullan Road travelers over the Spokane River.[124]

The remainder of Mullan's trek to Walla Walla went uneventfully. Some grading, a little bridging, but always rapid progress. Mullan reached Walla Walla on October 8. He found Major George Blake waiting. Blake, having passed Mullan on the last part of the road, arrived four days earlier, making it from Fort Benton in fifty-nine days.[125]

Blake had moved easily out of Fort Benton on a good trail. He knew the hard part lay ahead, and he found it at Prickly Pear Creek, his men struggling over hills, winding back and forth across streams, the road "almost doubling on itself."[126]

Blake's troops made dozens of river crossings, double-teamed oxen to drag wagons up hills, wrapped ropes around trees and tied them to the carts to slow descents, pulled vehicles out of mud. Despite all this, Augustus Kautz did not "find the road so difficult as I anticipated." Mullan came to camp one night and "entertained us all in his flowing style...about his Road, what he has done." When someone reminded Mullan that the Secretary of War, not as enamored of the road as its builder, had nearly withdrawn funding, Mullan "threatened and cursed like a Liliputian Hector."

Tragedy struck when one of Blake's privates died a few days before reaching Walla Walla, but altogether the trip had been successful, and Mullan received accolades when he followed Blake into town. The "Liliputian Hector" became the toast of the Northwest press. "A great undertaking has been accomplished," trumpeted the *Weekly Oregonian*. "Let all credit be freely and cordially rendered to the indomitable officer who has carried through amid so much to obstruct and discourage." In another story, the paper claimed "it is seldom that an officer is found more zealous in the discharge of his duties than Lieutenant Mullan."[127]

Mullan was pleased with the town's progress since he had left Walla Walla in 1859. He had no doubt that his road would further enhance the community: "A settlement of seven houses when we started has grown to seventy on our return to Walla Walla. Farms have been opened along the line, and, with the improvements that we propose putting on the road, I am sanguine to say ere many years a continuous line of settlements from the Columbia to the Missouri." Years later, Mullan reminisced that getting Blake's men safely to Walla Walla was, "next to the building of the Mullan Road...the most successful of my achievements....I was assured my work had not been in vain." Mullan had successfully concluded the first phase of road building.[128]

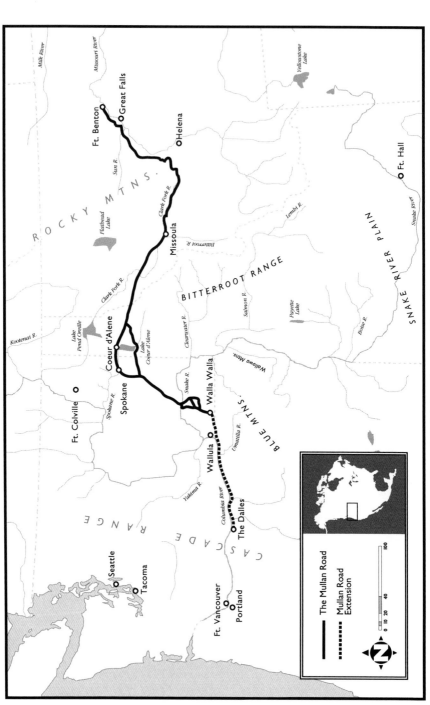

The 1859-60 and 1861-62 courses of Mullan's road varied slightly in a few places. The major change came when Mullan chose to re-route his road west and north of Lake Coeur d'Alene in 1861-62. *Courtesy David C. Hoyt; with thanks to Paul D. McDermott, Ronald E. Grim, and Philip Mobley.*

CHAPTER 9

Mullan's Road, 1861–1862

C HARLES SCHAFFT WAS A LITERATE MAN, but understated. "Alto-gether, it was not a very pleasant situation," he wrote. Unpleasant indeed. Schafft exited the month of January 1862 with two fewer legs than when he began. John Mullan had once again pushed his road crew hard and far, and yet another winter found them in a ramshackle wilderness camp, shivering in the elements. But this was the winter of 1861–62, the killer winter, one of the harshest on record. Charles Schafft, a member of the crew, became a casualty. Mullan had obviously not contemplated this situation on a warm May 13, 1861, when he led 120 men out of Walla Walla with assurances that he would make final improvements on his road "in good season."[1]

After leading Major Blake's command across his road in 1860, John Mullan received orders to remain at Fort Walla Walla, compile maps, and make plans for his final road-building season. But following orders was not always Mullan's strongest suit, and it seems unlikely he ever intended to work out of Walla Walla that winter. He had sent Theodore Kolecki to Washington, D.C., with all of his field notes. It would have been difficult for Mullan to complete maps with his best cartographer and all of his notes thousands of miles away. Mullan now used Kolecki's absence as an excuse for another cross-country excursion.

Mullan wanted to pitch an idea for dramatically expanding his road. So in January 1861 he once again journeyed to the nation's capital without authorization, a $1,338 trip. Captain A.A. Humphreys had grown impatient with Mullan's continued independent actions. The Topographical Bureau would eventually reimburse Mullan—but left him holding that bill for two years.[2]

Mullan made his way down the Columbia, boarded the steamer *Pacific*, disembarked in San Francisco, and spent most of his unauthorized travel expenditure on a twenty-two day, 2,800-mile stagecoach passage to St. Louis. Through Arizona, New Mexico, Texas, and Indian Territory he rode, twenty-four hours a day. To grasp the misery of such a trip requires suspension of Hollywood-induced notions of romantic stage travel. Instead, conjure three weeks in a cramped box, riding above unforgiving wooden wheels, over unsmoothed roads. Think dust. Noise. Unbathed seatmates. Think of sleeping upright for twenty-one consecutive nights. Think cold if you traveled, like Mullan, in winter. Mark Twain went overland a year later. "Every time we flew down one bank and scrambled up the other, our party inside got mixed somewhat," he wrote. "First we would all lie down in a pile at the forward end of the stage…and in a second we would shoot to the other end and stand on our heads." Even for Mullan, anxious to reach the capital the fastest way possible, the trip had to be excruciating. "I know what Hell is like," wrote another overland passenger of the era. "I've just had 24 days of it."[3]

Mullan arrived in Washington in mid-February, intent on making a case for changing the route of his road, running it from Fort Laramie in what would become Wyoming to connect with his existing road east of the Bitterroots. Mullan's road could then capture traffic traveling on Missouri River steamers to Fort Benton or going overland along the Oregon Trail. But he found Washington "in a somewhat chaotic state." It was a place where "a First Lieutenant's bars unlocked few doors." Besides, while Mullan made his way east, Humphreys had approved Mullan's original proposal of simply improving the route from Walla Walla to Fort Benton. Given the times and Humphreys's irritation at Mullan, he was ill-disposed to a change.[4]

"Somewhat chaotic" hardly describes Washington, D.C., in February 1861. On one end of the city's mall stood the capitol, its partially completed dome topped by a construction crane and surrounded by scaffolding. Here on February 13—about the day Mullan would have arrived—armed soldiers and plain-clothed policemen stood guard as senators tallied electoral votes before officially declaring Abraham Lincoln the new president. The Senate by then had been considerably reduced in number, as seven southern states had already seceded. Jefferson Davis, advocate for Mullan's road while secretary of war, but in

1861 a senator from Mississippi, had walked out of the chambers a few weeks earlier. On February 18, he would deliver his inaugural address as president of the Confederate States of America.[5]

At the other end of the mall, past the red towers of the Smithsonian Institution, past the stinking, sewage-filled city canal, stood the Willard, Washington's eminent hotel. Recently, the Willard had, boa-like, engulfed a Presbyterian church. Workers transformed its nave into a secular conference center, called Willard's Hall. To this hall, in that same February, the State of Virginia called a last-gasp peace conference to save the Union. Headed by former president and slave owner John Tyler, the conferees proffered no solution other than tired bromides that perpetuated slavery. The northern-dominated Senate easily rejected their proposal.

Washington that spring had the look of an armed camp, the city split between southern and northern sympathizers. With the failure of the peace conference, Mullan's native Virginia would soon secede. If the state where he grew up—Maryland—followed, a Confederate sea would surround the Union capital. Mullan no doubt visited his family in Annapolis and Rebecca Williamson in Baltimore, encountering hot-houses of secessionism. Only one resident of Annapolis had voted for Lincoln, and in February city leaders gathered to debate disunion. Once he took office, Lincoln sent federal troops to occupy the city.[6]

Still, Annapolis proved relatively quiet compared to Baltimore. In February Lincoln made his way to Washington by train to assume office. He had planned to stop in Baltimore, but at the last minute decided instead to slip into the capital under disguise. Allen Pinkerton, hired to protect the president, feared a Baltimore assassination attempt and convinced the president to avoid the city where he had received only 3 percent of the vote.[7]

Mullan left no record of his thoughts about Maryland's secessionist debates. But he seems never to have considered leaving the army for the Confederacy. He no doubt remained in Washington for Lincoln's March 4 inauguration, a windy day with little of the optimistic pageantry normally surrounding the change of presidents. Sidewalks held subdued crowds, some of whom proposed three cheers—for the Confederacy. It was a hiatus when, as historian Adam Goodheart noted, "Americans were in a trance, a fugue state, as they awaited whatever was to come."[8]

Mullan soon realized that, in this atmosphere, the War Department had little inclination to consider his plans for a different route. "Seeing so many difficulties interpose," he wrote, "I was forced to relinquish my Laramie scheme and proceed back to Walla Walla." But first he met with Isaac Stevens. It would be the last time he would see the man who had so instrumentally shaped his career.[9]

While making his way to the capital, Mullan had written to James G. Swan, an Indian agent in Washington Territory, clandestinely seeking advice about running for Stevens's position as territorial delegate to Congress. Mullan claimed that residents of Walla Walla and Vancouver had encouraged him. "I have ever been identified with Stevens in all matters," Mullan wrote. But Stevens had enemies scheming against his reelection. "I am assuming that a great effort will be made to defeat him," Mullan accurately predicted, "and in that case my name" could be entered into nomination, though "as long as Stevens stands a chance...I shall not be in his way." Mullan sought Swan's "advice and counsel." We do not know Swan's reply, but Mullan quickly gave up the idea after Stevens informed him he intended to seek reelection. Mullan had, however, gauged the political climate accurately; Stevens did not win renomination. But Mullan would not challenge his mentor.[10]

Mullan failed to win approval for a route change in his road; he had been rebuffed in his first contemplated foray into politics. Yet, amid the chaos of Washington, Mullan was fortunate to have held onto his authorization to improve the road. Had he remained in the District of Columbia after the war started in April, it is unlikely the War Department would have dispatched a West Point officer to build a road in the strategically insignificant Northwest. Except for his project, federal wagon road construction in the West virtually halted during the Civil War.[11]

✳

Mullan returned to Walla Walla on April 22. His trip east had set him behind schedule. He now hustled to hire crew and order provisions, finding it difficult to engage workers due to "the excitement" of the Clearwater River gold rush in what would become Idaho. But finally on May 13, about six weeks behind his target date, he marched out of Fort Walla Walla with a party that once again included his long-trusted aides Gustavus Sohon, Theodore Kolecki, Walter Johnson, and David Williamson.[12]

Mullan found the country between Walla Walla and the Snake River considerably changed. Farms filled the rich valley, just as Mullan had predicted. His road in this section received so much traffic that Washington's territorial legislature had granted a charter for a ferry at the mouth of the Palouse River, where Mullan now crossed, altering his route from 1859, when the road had traversed the Snake further upstream.[13]

Making camp on the north side of the Snake, Mullan enjoyed a rare luxury—taking a day off. With Sohon, he rode to Palouse Falls, a geologic wonder already attracting tourists. As the catastrophic Missoula Floods tore through the country some twelve thousand years earlier, the deluge's enormous force ripped open a river canyon, as well as Palouse Falls, a dramatic, two-hundred-foot-high plunge pool. A "beautiful and interesting falls" Mullan termed it. "The whole river…here leaps in a single sheet over a rocky ledge…a picturesque scene well worthy a visit." Sohon made a sketch.[14]

"Work light to-day" characterized the party's efforts in May. Crew members moved some rocks, cut trees, did a bit of grading. Sometimes the day's work simply involved keeping everyone moving. Mullan had determined to abandon his previous swampy course to the south and east of Lake Coeur d'Alene. He now adhered to the easier route on the west. This diversion entailed three days of bridge construction, but generally the crew moved rapidly, arriving at Antoine Plante's toll ferry on the Spokane River on June 1. This is just what Plante hoped Mullan would do when he had, with Walter Johnson, scouted a route north of the lake in 1860. Disappointed when Mullan first chose to take his road south of Lake Coeur d'Alene, Plante now anticipated a bonanza as Mullan's road crossed his farm.[15]

Voyageur, trapper, mountaineer, guide, businessman, farmer—the tall, burly Plante made the acquaintance of most everyone who roamed the Inland Northwest. Mullan considered the part-French, part-Indian Plante "a very worthy man." Along with his Flathead wife Mary, Plante owned a handsome house and productive farm along the Spokane River "from which he obtains corn, wheat, and vegetables." Mullan described Plante's ferry as "a good one, consisting of a strong cable stretched across the river, and a boat forty feet long." Mullan located his road to take advantage of this crossing, and for five years, until Spokane Bridge spanned the river upstream, Plante's ferry prospered.[16]

Mullan spent a day ferrying his party over the river, making camp on the opposite side. He sent Sohon to re-scout the route east of the ferry that Johnson and Plante had hastily explored in 1860. The remaining eighty members of the military escort joined Mullan here, arriving from Fort Colville.[17]

Mullan did not anticipate problems with Indians. But he acknowledged they were "all excited in reference to the large gold discoveries" made near the Clearwater River in 1860. Mullan appreciated the additional troops. Still, their primary responsibility turned out to be road construction, for Indians gave Mullan no problems.[18]

Mullan rode from the Plante ferry camp on June 4 to meet Sohon, who had disappointing news: he had found no better route north of the lake than had Johnson and Plante. The crew would have a hard slog.

"We are now in very dense timber," Mullan reported as he moved east. "The...making of a road [is] a difficult and irksome task, and, what with the myriads of mosquitos that annoy us, are well calculated to try one's patience." For two months Mullan's crew slashed through a woodland morass. "The whole country is now one immense bed of densely-timbered mountains, and the bottoms are covered with...dense underbrush," Mullan wrote. The crew felled trees on steep slopes, grubbing stumps from the rocky hills, a "slow, heavy, and tedious" task "hard on tools," not to mention backs. Mullan's men graded the best they could, and on occasion bridged creeks and swamps, including a 540-foot-long span at Wolf Creek that took thirty men four days. They split fifteen hundred cedar logs for the corduroy top, built derricks to support the blocks and tackle required to lift and place the timbers, and worked in water "icy cold." Despite constructing this and other bridges seven feet above the water's surface, upcoming spring freshets would splinter most of them.[19]

Independence Day found Mullan's crew on a mountain corridor that has since carried the name Fourth of July Pass, in today's Idaho. Here Mullan granted his men a well-deserved day off. The crew was by this time aware of events at Fort Sumter, the beginning of civil war. Raising the flag, firing guns, and enjoying their meal of ham, pickles, and whiskey provided an opportunity for both patriotism and repose.

Here, men from both North and South spent the day "pleasantly and harmoniously." They took time to commemorate the occasion by branding the date on a large white pine, the tree that stood until 1988. The last marker along the Mullan Road, it was a sentinel that welcomed more than a century's worth of tourists.[20]

A month later the crew arrived at the Coeur d'Alene Mission. From this point they would be repairing what they had built before, not constructing a new route. They had hacked and grubbed their way fifty miles in two months, less than a mile a day. This new route north of the lake took Mullan a month longer than he had anticipated, raising the specter of another harsh winter in the Bitterroots. Still, Mullan was proud of his accomplishment, accurately terming it "a creditable piece of mountain work" that "will compare favorably with any turnpike of the same length and through a similar difficult country." He had opened what would become a major avenue to the Northwest, eventually to be retraced by an interstate highway, along whose corridor the cities of Spokane, Post Falls, and Coeur d'Alene would rise.[21]

At the mission, Mullan received dispiriting news. The War Department had contracted with Pierre Chouteau to carry 10,000 rations for Mullan's crew to Fort Benton aboard the steamer *Chippewa*. While making its way up the Missouri, a deckhand discovered that the boat's cargo included whiskey. Thirst got the better of wisdom one night when he ventured into the hold, guiding his way with a candle—which promptly ignited a fire. The captain made it to shore in time to unload passengers, then set the boat adrift, where it blew up, destroying all its cargo. Mullan now had to purchase supplies from Walla Walla at "exorbitant prices," a cause of concern for an expedition rapidly burning through its congressional appropriation.[22]

Mullan hoped to work during the winter. But winter came early. He recorded snowfall on November 1, and river ice flows a couple weeks later. Determined to escape another winter in the mountains, he hurried his crew to Hellgate valley and split it into five groups. Some would construct a large bridge over the Blackfoot River; others would cut road bed in sidehills. Desperately behind schedule, he thought his remaining crew could work in advance to "put the road…to Fort Benton in…repair." But he had not planned on one of the harshest winters in Northwest history.[23]

☙

"Severe cold set in about December 1," recorded Granville Stuart from his home on the eastern section of Mullan's road. "The thermometer registered above zero only four times in three months." Things were no better to the west. Dan Drumheller reported from Walla Walla that "there were weeks at a time during that winter when the thermometer registered 40 degrees below zero." When spring finally arrived it brought gruesome sights. "You cannot walk out one thousand yards from the main street of Walla Walla but you encounter the festering and decaying remains of animals," noted one observer. "Cattle in unprecedented numbers succumbed," wrote historian J. Orin Oliphant, who called that winter "probably the worst in the history of the Pacific Northwest."[24]

In the mountains it got even worse. Mullan recorded the death of "many of our animals." His men once again trudged supplies to winter camp on hand sleds. "The Indians had never before experienced so severe a winter," he wrote. Despite his best intentions, another brutal winter found Mullan's men surviving in hastily constructed log huts.[25]

Mullan sent part of his military escort ahead to build the main camp at the confluence of the Hellgate (Clark Fork) and Big Blackfoot Rivers, a few miles east of today's Missoula. That Mullan still had a military escort was in itself remarkable.

The army was furiously consolidating troops in the East for Civil War duty. Construction of a wilderness road in the far Northwest plummeted on the military's list of priorities, and army officials recalled Mullan's escort. But Mullan alternately suffered and benefitted from poor communications. Having received instructions in October to recall the troops, Fort Vancouver officials sent a messenger to Fort Walla Walla. The post commander gave the orders to John Owen, who was at the fort purchasing supplies. Owen caught up with Mullan on November 4. By then snows had set in. "Taking either wagons or a pack train over the Bitter Root Mountains" would be "absolutely impossible," the escort's commander, Lieutenant Salem Marsh, wrote his superiors. No troops would march out of the mountains during that winter's onslaught. Mullan had secured the services of his escort for another season.[26]

Marsh supervised construction of "30 substantial log houses." Mullan named it Cantonment Wright, in honor of that "warm friend of our enterprise," George Wright. The location was dispiritingly cold. "The camp was...exposed to the bleak winds that at times came down the valley of the Blackfoot," Mullan wrote. "It was...an abode of not over much comfort."[27]

Mullan surely welcomed the invitation to spend Christmas at Fort Owen, an opportunity to escape the winds of Cantonment Wright, as well as one that afforded Mullan a chance to speak in public. He seldom declined such opportunities. So, on December 23 Mullan, Marsh, and Kolecki rode through the snow to John Owen's comfortable outpost. There on Christmas Day 1861, following a "very nice dinner... and a large eggnog," John Mullan gave the first public lecture in what became Montana. Owen invited him as part of an effort to raise money for orphans, and Mullan addressed "the largest audience of white persons...ever assembled at Fort Owen." He spoke on Lewis and Clark. A reporter later lauded his choice of topics, for "probably no other man in America was so practically competent to the subject chosen." Before Mullan's party returned to its winter quarters on December 27, Owen asked Mullan for a copy of the speech for his personal library, thus preserving one of Montana's significant historical documents.[28]

Charles Schafft also ventured out of Cantonment Wright that winter. His excursion proved less pleasant.

Born in Germany in 1838, Charles Schafft emigrated to the United States in 1849 to join his father, owner of a New York import shop. "Not liking the business," Schafft apprenticed himself to a jeweler, but like so many young nineteenth century immigrants seeking a foothold in America, soon enlisted in the army—as a fifteen-year-old musician. The 5'3" Schafft served in the Southwest until receiving his honorable discharge in 1858.[29]

The Fraser River gold rush of that year lured Schafft north. He found himself on the *Columbia* steaming to Portland, along with Lieutenant John Mullan. Schafft had read newspaper accounts of Mullan's road expedition, and must have been drawn to the adventure, because he agreed to join Mullan's road crew.

Colonel Edward Steptoe's defeat in the spring 1858 "put a stop" to road building, so Schafft taught school in the Willamette Valley. When construction commenced again in 1859, Schafft joined as a cattle herder. He watched helplessly as most animals died during the miserable mountain crossing that winter. "Having driven the few cattle that had not perished to the Bitter Root River," Schafft and three companions quit the road crew, leaving Cantonment Jordan in the midst of winter and making their way through "seven feet of snow" to the Coeur d'Alene Mission. He eventually got back to the Willamette Valley. He rejoined Mullan's expedition in 1861, this time as a clerk.

Schafft disdained winter mountain camps. On January 8, 1862, with temperatures south of minus forty degrees, Schafft quit Mullan again and headed for Deer Lodge, carrying a few letters that Mullan—never missing an opportunity to send mail—asked him to deliver. Schafft was an experienced outdoorsman, but his timing was bad. That winter brooked few accidents, and Schafft exercised his margin of error when he broke through ice into a slough, soaking his clothes. He turned back but, arriving at the bank of the Hellgate River, ironically found its ice too weak to hold him. "I had to walk up and down before a small fire to keep from freezing...until the ice should be strong enough to bear me," he wrote.

When the river solidified, he hobbled on, "feeling warm, yet not knowing that my feet were freezing all the time. At daylight I discovered that both my feet were frozen up to the ankle joint." Miraculously—a testament to his survival skills—Schafft crawled to one of the camps outlying Cantonment Wright. A messenger took word to Mullan, who sent a crew to sled Schafft to the main encampment. It took three days. They arrived to learn that the expedition's surgeon, Dr. George Hammond, was snowed in at Fort Owen. In the doctor's absence, crew members thawed Schafft's feet in a tub of water. "The flesh fell off," recorded Mullan. A week passed before Hammond appeared. By then, "my case was hopeless," Schafft recalled. Hammond amputated both Schafft's legs. "I was henceforth a cripple."

Mullan's crew took a collection and transported Schafft to St. Ignatius Mission, where Jesuit priests nursed him to health. He lived another thirty years and always spoke highly of John Mullan, who "stood by my bedside" and did "everything possible for me."[30]

Mullan, having reached Cantonment Wright behind schedule, ordered his men to work through that harsh winter. Even his ally, George Wright, questioned "whether it would not be advisable to suspend the operations...until a more favorable opportunity." Mullan could not fathom that; his reputation depended upon completing the road on time. A few days after he had delivered the first public lecture in what became Montana, Mullan approved the first arrests within its borders, conscripted the horse-stealing scofflaws, and promptly put them to work on his road. He would resort to most any means to finish his task.[31]

Mullan set some crew members to digging five sidecuts—seven miles of excavation—thereby avoiding ten crossings of the Hellgate River. But he could not escape bridging the Blackfoot, and here Mullan concentrated most of his workers. The Blackfoot bridge would have been a notable engineering accomplishment under any circumstances, but more so during that winter. Mullan's men felled trees from which they hewed timbers and whipsawed planks. They then ingeniously constructed a 235-foot boom across the river, creating an ice dam that allowed them to walk over the water and sink rock cribs into the river. Gus Sohon's sketch shows a bridge of four spans, each supporting thick timbers over which the men laid surface planks seventeen feet long and three inches thick.[32]

With the bridge completed and his road-building drawing to a close, Mullan ordered Lieutenant Marsh and David Williamson back to Walla Walla. They were to improve bridges hastily erected the previous fall. Mullan proceeded to Fort Benton with crew members who wished to depart the Northwest for St. Louis. He arrived on June 8 and purchased a Mackinaw—a flat bottomed, open boat—on which he sent crew members downstream, their work on the wagon road complete.[33]

Mullan turned back west, discouraged to find that spring runoff from that winter's massive snows had already "thrown out of shape" the Blackfoot bridge. Three months later Randall Hewitt, traveling with a wagon train over Mullan's road, described the scene: "The bridge was once a substantial structure...but at this time it was showing evidence of dilapidation." Mullan hired local rancher Sam Hugo to repair the structure. Despite the road crew's Herculean efforts and Mullan's engineering creativity, none of his bridges survived more than a season or two of western spring torrents.[34]

While dilapidation of the Blackfoot bridge dismayed him, the actions of Lieutenant Marsh angered him. Mullan had hoped that Marsh's escort, along with Williamson's civilians, could complete bridge reconstruction in the Bitterroots. "Learning...that...Marsh was pushing on...without having done what had been contemplated by myself," Mullan intercepted him at the Spokane River. Marsh was confused by a mishmash of orders. He assumed the instructions he received from Fort Vancouver took precedence over Mullan's and moved rapidly toward Walla Walla to make his troops available for Civil War duty. A discouraged Mullan wrote, "to me it was a source of regret, and militated strongly against the best interests of the road, and the amount of work which might have been judiciously performed in replacing certain bridges." But in that bloody spring and summer of 1862, the army had more pressing need for troops than constructing bridges in the West. Mullan realized that with Marsh's exodus, road building had essentially ceased. He led the remnant of his civilian work party to Walla Walla.[35]

For a perfectionist like Mullan, the final months of construction had been discouraging. Although he wrote that he had "succeeded... in accomplishing the full object of our mission," he knew that was a tenuous claim. His summary of that spring's work is not so much one of detailing road-building success as it is of tasks yet to be done. Still, his road "was the federal government's greatest contribution to transportation development in the Pacific Northwest" in the mid-nineteenth century, and it essentially marked the end of the nation's construction of military wagon roads.[36]

❧

John Mullan arrived in Walla Walla on a hot Wednesday, August 13, 1862. The remaining fifty members of the road crew accompanied him. So did a party of emigrants, among the first to cross his road, who had caught up with Mullan at Latah Creek. Hardly anyone in town took notice. The newspaper editor devoted two sentences to Mullan's arrival—on page three. Perhaps the town's inhabitants were too busy "selling whiskey and gambling and worse" to recognize Mullan's accomplishment.[37]

That same observer who noted Walla Wallan's propensity for whiskey also found that the town's "principal business appears to be selling horses." That served Mullan well, for he disposed of his stock and property at auction and disbanded all of his crew, except Gustavus Sohon. As he released men who had served him well and with whom he had become friends—David Williamson, Walter Johnson, Theodore Kolecki—he reflected on their creditable accomplishment:

> Thus ended my work in the field, costing seven years of close and arduous attention, exploring and opening up a road of six hundred and twenty-four miles from the Columbia to the Missouri river, at a cost of $230,000....It is impossible here to give those details of construction where special difficulties arose day by day for solution, the many trying positions in which I found myself placed during so long a period, the many discomforts put up with by my men, who yet retained all their cheerfulness.[38]

Despite some disappointment that the road failed to meet his exacting standards, Mullan had reason to be pleased. He had performed admirably and had enhanced his reputation, which, in many ways, was his ultimate goal. Although Raymond Dees, publisher of the Walla Walla *Washington Statesman,* lapsed slightly by devoting little space to Mullan's arrival in August, he proved overall to be a reliable booster of the road, which he figured would bring emigrants and their business his town's way. "The Mullan Road...will...become one of the most extensively traveled thoroughfares on the western slope," he exuberantly wrote in one edition. In another: "All honor to the men under whose auspices and direction this great work has been carried forward....Isaac I. Stevens and John Mullan merit the grateful homage of the people."[39]

The Washington territorial legislature passed a resolution thanking Mullan "for his industry, energy, and ability in constructing the Military Road." Even more significantly, Mullan received promotion to captain, and also learned that his former commanding officer, George Wright, now a brigadier general, recommended a further promotion to major as a reflection of "his perseverance, zeal, and ability." Just as Mullan had hoped, opportunities seemed to be opening.[40]

On September 7 Mullan and Sohon caught a stage out of Walla Walla, the first leg of a long journey taking them through Portland and San Francisco to Washington, D.C., where they would compile the official report of their road building. At Wallula on the Columbia River, thirty miles from Walla Walla, Mullan made note of the "long line of wagons and pack trains, heavily freighted for the interior," making their way to Walla Walla. He envisioned a better, profitable link with his road. "The prospective wants of the country are...in favor of a railroad connection," he wrote. "I feel warranted in believing that another twelve months will not roll around before the matter is taken up with a view to its practical execution."[41]

As it turned out, Mullan himself would lead that railroad effort.

CHAPTER 10

"Capt. Mullan Wishes to be Made Governor of Idahoe"

IN OCTOBER 1862, AS GUS SOHON and John Mullan bumped their way east in the crowded coach of the overland stage out of San Francisco, they noticed telegraph wires along the route—wires that had recently delivered them sad news. A Confederate bullet had caught General Isaac Stevens in the temple at the Battle of Chantilly on September 1. The nine years since Mullan's first trip west had seen a revolution in communication. In 1853 it took two months and an Isthmus crossing to deliver news from the East coast to the West. With completion of transcontinental telegraph service in October 1861, the information of Stevens's death traveled nearly instantaneously.

Patriotism had won over Stevens a year earlier and, despite previous disillusion with the army, he had rejoined the military after the outbreak of the Civil War, quickly rising to brigadier general. A division commander by September 1862, Stevens had been ordered at Chantilly to halt the advance of Confederate General Thomas "Stonewall" Jackson and protect the Union's retreat following a calamitous engagement at the Second Battle of Manassas. Stevens's brave action—picking up a tattered flag and leading his men in a charge against enemy lines—turned the Battle of Chantilly to the Union's favor. But a bullet from a retreating Confederate caught Stevens, who "fell dead clutching the colors in his hands." No one had more influenced Mullan's life. And Mullan could have used his mentor's sage advice that winter in Washington, D.C., where he did political battle with an old Stevens nemesis and got the worse of the encounter.[1]

Mullan and Sohon took the excruciatingly uncomfortable overland stage because it would most quickly transport them to the capital, where Mullan had been ordered to complete a report on the road project. Upon arrival, he moved into a residence at 215 F Street and began writing, under the scrutiny of the Corps of Topographical Engineers.

Mullan had grown up in the home of an army sergeant and, for the most part, had accepted strict discipline while a West Point cadet. But his service in the West had nurtured an independence influenced by Stevens, who believed "commanding officers on the frontiers should have entire discretion in matters of clothing, subsistence, and transportation....Directions from Washington...should be of the most general character." Mullan shared those sentiments. He wore buckskin, hardly standard army attire, during his hand-to-hand combat in the 1858 George Wright campaign. While building his road, Mullan often operated independently because of haphazard communications with the East. His independence vanished as he began work in Washington under Topographical Bureau supervision.[2]

Mullan found the bureau stifling. It declared some of his expenses "exorbitant," and others "entirely unauthorized by law or regulations." It refused his request to work from home, insisting upon "supervision of work as it progresses here [rather] than in a remote part of the city." It informed Mullan that his "report is desired without delay," and in the same letter chastised him for hiring personnel to rush the job: "You will please report your authority for...employing additional assistants." Mullan believed his maps could be significant contributions to western cartography. Yet when he suggested incorporating the compilations of other explorers to provide for a more thorough picture of the West, the bureau bluntly rebuked him. "I am led to believe that you mistake the scope of your duties," wrote Colonel Stephen H. Long. "The surveys of Fremont, Raynalds and Mendell have no connection with the wagon road expedition with which you were charged."[3]

When Mullan proposed undertaking another expedition to incorporate a better crossing of the mountains for his road—around Lake Pend Oreille—Colonel Long exasperatingly replied: "There is no authority or law nor are there funds available for the purpose....The instructions already given to you will claim your entire attention, so as to bring [your report]...before Congress at the earliest day possible."[4]

Mullan's reputation depended upon compiling the report, so he labored diligently despite the bureau's intractability. Although the bureau sought a document without flourish, the indefatigable Mullan successfully balked at this demand. As one scholar has noted, Mullan wrote "with the verdict of history in mind." Where his field notes are usually brisk and to the point, his road report meanders and posits. More than a mere military document, it is also an emigrant guide, beautifully illustrated with Sohon's paintings. Mullan provided a day-by-day itinerary, forty-seven days in all, for those traveling his road from Fort Benton to Walla Walla, indicating where wood, water, and grass could be found and supplies purchased. He advised travelers on the equipment they should carry and the Indians they would meet. He outlined the region's agricultural potential, its grazing possibilities, its mineral wealth. He discussed Catholic missions and regional climate. He devoted thirty-six pages to his official construction report, and forty-seven to counseling travelers. The report was typical Mullan, intended as a platform from which to launch a business or political career. And in that winter of 1862–63 he would be drawn into politics, engaging William Wallace, an old rival of his mentor; a man for whom Isaac Stevens had professed "a most profound contempt" when defeating him for Washington territorial congressional delegate in 1859. Wallace had replaced Stevens as delegate in 1861 and would now antagonize Mullan in the District of Columbia, where they both resided that winter.[5]

When Elias D. Pierce and twelve companions trespassed on land that the Stevens treaty of 1855 had reserved for Nez Perce Indians, they set off a rush that transformed the Northwest. As word spread of the promising diggings, prospectors and provisioners sped to the Clearwater region. A booming city of tents and hastily constructed frame buildings at the confluence of the Clearwater and Snake rivers took the name Lewiston—soon to be one of the largest communities in the Northwest. Almost overnight the region boasted thousands of settlers who clamored for a new territory.[6]

The Pierce discoveries propelled a dramatic population shift to what was then eastern Washington Territory. Washington's three candidates for territorial delegate to Congress in 1861 had many differences. But as they campaigned in the new gold region, they all agreed with the miners living far removed from the territorial capital on Puget Sound at Olympia: whoever won would do whatever he could to secure separate territorial status for the mining country.[7]

As Washington's eastern population grew, Olympia's hold on the capital became ever more tenuous. "Of what use to us is a capital located at Olympia?" pondered Lewiston's newspaper editor. "During four months of the last year no communication could be had with the place at all." Lewiston residents hoped for their town to become the capital. Citizens in Walla Walla, booming as the terminus of the Mullan Road, also made a play for capital city. Residents of Olympia realized their best chance of retaining the capital rested with lopping off the mining districts into a new territory, for if Washington retained its existing borders, Walla Walla and Lewiston had more logical claims as capital based on more centralized locations. Residents of Olympia, Walla Walla, and Lewiston could all agree on the logic for a new territory, but had different ideas as to its shape, each city advocating boundaries that bettered its case.[8]

Walla Walla sought a boundary for Washington that extended the current Washington/Oregon border east so that Washington would include what is now the Idaho panhandle and western Montana—exactly the shape of Washington Territory as originally created in 1853. (It had been awkwardly enlarged in 1859, when Oregon became a state, to include all of current Idaho.) Walla Walla's vision included the new Clearwater mines in Washington. Their community conveniently sat near the center of this territorial vision, and they could stake a valid claim as capital.

Before Sohon and Mullan headed out of Walla Walla to Washington, D.C., Mullan met with community leaders who advocated these boundaries and sought his assistance in advancing them once he got to D.C. It did not take much to persuade Mullan. By this time, he had purchased property in Walla Walla and planned to return as a businessman. He had a vested interest in the economic advantages if Walla Walla became the capital.[9]

Olympia and Lewiston sought a border that separated the eastern mines into a new territory apart from Washington. They wanted a boundary drawn directly north to Canada from Oregon's eastern border—the current edge of Washington State. Olympia would remain as capital of Washington, allowing Lewiston to make a case for being capital of the new territory, leaving Walla Walla capital-less.

It is unlikely that Congressman James Ashley of Ohio knew about any of this border intrigue transpiring in America's far northwest corner. Ashley chaired the House Committee on Territories. Since few knew the Northwest as well as John Mullan, it made sense for Ashley to seek Mullan's help drawing boundaries for a new territory—one that would gain the name Idaho that winter. Ashley apparently had only one prerequisite: any new territories should be rectangular, longer east and west than north and south—more like Kansas than Illinois. Ashley's geometric concept meshed perfectly with Mullan's aspirations for Walla Walla. Irritated at the stifling supervision of the Topographical Bureau, Mullan spent increasing time creating a map encapsulating his vision of a future Idaho.[10]

By mid-December, Mullan had completed a plat of territorial boundaries. His map of Washington shows an east-west rectangle, as Ashley and Walla Walla residents desired. A straight line runs from the Oregon border due east to the Rocky Mountains. All of what became the Idaho panhandle, including Lewiston, and a portion of western Montana, is included. Olympia lies ridiculously isolated on the western fringe of this version of Washington; Walla Walla sits conveniently central. Areas to the south and east form a new territory; Mullan originally labeled it Montana.[11]

Just before Christmas, Ashley introduced legislation creating the new territory and setting boundaries as Mullan had drawn. On February 12, 1863, the House of Representatives easily passed the measure. Mullan had triumphed, or so he thought.[12]

William Wallace, a resident of Puget Sound, naturally favored the Olympia plan for Washington's eastern border, and thus had a different idea about the territory's shape. By the time the House-passed Ashley/Mullan measure reached the Senate, Wallace had carefully plotted its defeat.

While Mullan worked on his map, Wallace quietly sketched one of his own. It showed Washington Territory shaped exactly as the current Washington State. A huge new territory he labeled Idaho encompassed all of the current states of Idaho and Montana, and virtually all of Wyoming—a region larger than Texas. But Wallace did not at first reveal his proposed boundaries. Instead he blocked the Ashley bill by encouraging Senate passage of a measure that differed from Ashley's only in technicalities, mostly whether the new territory should be named Idaho or Montana. Ashley paid the Senate bill little notice. He believed the minor differences between the Senate and House bills could be easily resolved in a conference committee, unaware that Wallace was actually working with the Senate on a totally different vision for the new territory's shape.

Congress, overwhelmed with Civil War concerns, did not take time to reconcile differences between the two bills until the final evening of the final session of the thirty-seventh Congress. And by then Wallace had laid a skillful trap.

Late in the evening of March 3, 1863, the Senate passed a new territorial bill with Wallace's proposed boundaries. The measure did much more than change the name of the new territory: it rewrote the Ashley/Mullan boundaries. And it took Ashley by surprise. Anxious to end the session, the House agreed to take up consideration of the Senate version, rather than vice-versa. An angry Ashley vigorously sought a conference committee to hash out differences. But by then it was near midnight, congressmen were exhausted, and Ashley found little support for prolonging the session over something as trivial as borders for a territory thousands of miles away. At about 2:00 a.m. on March 4, the House agreed to the Senate bill. At dawn, President Abraham Lincoln signed the act creating the new territory of Idaho.[13]

Wallace had completely outmaneuvered Ashley, but in the process created an Idaho of unmanageable geographical divisiveness. When Congress established Montana one year later, carving hard into Idaho's east, it left behind an awkward-looking Idaho with a narrow, isolated northern panhandle—just the type of non-geometric shape Ashley abhorred. While Mullan had lost the political battle with Wallace, he had been cartographically more prescient, for there was more at stake than mere aesthetics. Mullan believed the Idaho boundaries absurd. For several years he advocated a new territory—one including parts of what are now eastern Washington, northern Idaho, and western Montana, a region of much greater geographical logic as a political unit—a proposition supported by the majority of northern Idaho residents. The Idaho Wallace created, with mountains and rivers segregating north and south, led to political and cultural fractiousness that defined the state into the twenty-first century.[14]

William Wallace not only got his way with the borders, he also won the president's appointment as Idaho's first territorial governor—a position Mullan aggressively sought. "It would appear that the redoubtable Captain Mullan has beat the bush and somebody else has caught the bird," mocked the Sacramento *Daily Union*. Wallace rebuffed Mullan again.[15]

Mullan's courting the governorship has a quixotic feel about it. It is unlikely Abraham Lincoln ever gave his appointment serious consideration. But Mullan honestly believed he held the vantage ground. Until March 3 he remained oblivious to William Wallace's counter-boundary proposal. He believed his map the only one under consideration by Congress. Wallace had campaigned for territorial delegate in what became the Idaho panhandle, and therefore knew that section slightly. But that caused Mullan little concern, for he believed that area would remain part of Washington. Wallace had never stepped foot in the country Mullan proposed for Idaho; indeed, few people knew that land as well as John Mullan. He would stake his claim for the governorship based upon that superior awareness of the field. But the acceptance of Wallace's map cut that advantage from under him, for now Idaho included the panhandle, a region holding much of the new territory's population, and an area with which Wallace was familiar.

Ostensibly residing in the nation's capital to complete his road report, Mullan spent inordinate time that winter not only working with Ashley but also lining up politicians to support his appointment as governor of the new territory. Mullan's "knowledge of the country…is superior to that of any living man," wrote Oregon Senator James Nesmith to President Lincoln. Senator Henry Rice of Minnesota recommended that Lincoln appoint Mullan because of "his intimate knowledge of the great North West, and his universal popularity." William Dole, Commissioner of Indian Affairs, noted Mullan's knowledge of tribes. Congressman Thaddeus Stevens of Pennsylvania, learning that "Capt. Mullan wishes to be made governor of Idahoe," called him a man of "great achievements….I have derived more benefit from [him] with regard to a knowledge of our Western territories than from all other sources." Senators James McDougall of California and Thomas Hicks of Maryland, Territorial Delegate John Todd of Dakota, and Supreme Court Justice Robert Grier also endorsed Mullan. Mullan had hoped to lay his case before the president in his typically deliberate and systematic fashion. But on March 4 he learned that William Wallace had not only outdone him on the territorial boundaries, but had also inveigled his own supporters to write Lincoln, recommending that he be appointed governor. Mullan's quest became urgent.[16]

On the morning Lincoln signed the territorial act, Mullan hastily scrawled a handwritten appeal to the president, tucked it into the packet of support letters he had assembled, and delivered it to the White House. "For the last ten years I have resided within the region now organized into a Territory," Mullan wrote, "and...by my labors and Explorations have added to the development and progress of that region by opening a communication from the head Waters of the Missouri to the Head Waters of the Columbia River....I have spent three winters amid the Rocky Mountains in my labors to add to the development of that region to which I am attached and which I desire to make my permanent home." He informed Lincoln how a previous president had assisted him, obviously hoping Lincoln would do likewise: "I would state...that I am a self-made man—that I was taken by the hand by President Polk and by him educated at West Point." But he concluded resignedly, aware Wallace held the upper hand: "I would ask at least...of the President a special investigation in regard to my case before any appointment is made." The next morning, at Mullan's request, Senators Hicks, Nesmith, and McDougall met Lincoln at the White House, repeating Mullan's request for an investigation and seeking to "solicit at [Lincoln's] hands the appointment of Capt. John Mullan."[17]

The senators found Lincoln somewhat preoccupied. Having relieved the dilatory George McClellan from his command of the Army of the Potomac in November, Lincoln was now suffering through the ineffectual tenure of its third general in five months. Army morale lagged. Just the day before, Congress had passed the nation's first wartime draft to feed the military's insatiable demand for troops. The president had no intention of initiating an investigation to determine who best to head a distant territory. Besides, Lincoln knew Wallace and did not know Mullan. Most significantly, Wallace was a Republican. On March 10, Congress approved Lincoln's appointment of Wallace as Idaho's first governor.[18]

Wallace's victories represented the first serious setbacks in Mullan's professional career. They would not be the last.

❧

Exactly one month after Lincoln signed the act creating Idaho Territory, Captain John Mullan resigned from the army. He had contemplated the move for years, informing Rebecca Williamson of his plans as early as 1859. We do not know Rebecca's reaction to John's 1863 resignation, but in 1859 she worried. She could not be "certain of" Mullan's entrepreneurial success. But "in the Army you can always maintain your position as a gentleman." Of course, much had changed in America since 1859, and Rebecca now might well have supported John's decision, which would protect him from bloody war.[19]

One author attributed Mullan's resignation to umbrage, refusing to serve "a country which…denied him the governorship of the new territory." But in December 1862, long before Lincoln appointed Wallace, Mullan wrote the editor of the Walla Walla *Statesman* about his desire to enjoy "the pleasures of a quiet home in the beautiful valley of Walla Walla, where I trust soon to be." Lincoln's decision embittered Mullan, but he had already made up his mind to return west as a civilian—a governor, if that had worked—but in any event, not as an army officer.[20]

Some have speculated that Mullan resigned because of conflicted sentiments as a Virginian raised in the border state of Maryland. "The decision to leave the army was undoubtedly in part due to his Southern heritage which would not allow him to fight for the Federal cause," suggested one historian.[21]

Mullan lamented that the war appeared to be "waged for the negro." But there is no evidence that he considered resigning the army to serve the Confederacy. In his only exposition on the war, he called the southern "revolution" a "fraud…which will sink its perpetrators and its abettors into eternal infamy. Valuable lives may be sacrificed, the material development of our country paralyzed, and devastation and ruin make desolate many a now happy home, before the storm shall have abated;

but I verily believe that from thence forward shall date the commencement of a better and more stable government to be handed down to those who are to bear our names."²²

Mullan resigned so he could make money. Had he been assigned to go west again to take his road over the Pend Oreille route, he would have remained in the army for awhile, as that task would have further burnished his reputation. But he always viewed army service as a means to prosperity, not a patriotic duty. From the time he admiringly gazed upon Annapolis mansions as a child, Mullan coveted material success. Having made a reputation as a western explorer and road builder, he intended to reap economic rewards from those accomplishments by returning west as a businessman. He had plotted that course before the war began, and he saw no reason in the spring of 1863 to deviate from his plan. And it seemed at first that Mullan had planned well. That spring, the incorporators of the new Walla Walla Pacific Railroad company named him a commissioner. They wanted Mullan to lead them in constructing a short line from the Columbia River to Walla Walla. Mullan would be heading west with an impressive title and, he thought, legitimate prospects for success.

John and Rebecca married on April 28. It seems likely that before they left D.C., John attended the wedding of his old friend Gus Sohon, who married Julia Groh in Washington that same April. Like Mullan, Sohon had purchased property in Walla Walla before traveling to the capital to assist Mullan on the road report. He lost his property in a land swindle and never made it back to Walla Walla. But he did move west—to San Francisco—where he briefly operated a daguerreotype studio; on one occasion he photographed Father Pierre-Jean DeSmet, one of his few photographic likenesses. He had returned to Washington, D.C., where one of the outstanding artists of the American West spent the rest of his life as a shoe salesman. Mullan and Sohon remained friends. Mullan wrote letters of support on a couple of occasions when Sohon unsuccessfully sought positions as an Indian agent. The letters are heartfelt, products of an obvious bond between the men. At the end of one typically long, detailed recommendation, Mullan added a postscript: "What I have said is not the one hundredth part of what I could & possibly should say, but I fear to extend my endorsement to too great a length." Sohon died in September 1903. Newspaper obituaries made no mention of his extraordinary contributions to western exploration and art. It would remain for future generations to posthumously pay this man, Mullan's most trusted assistant, his deserved recognition.[23]

John Mullan said goodbye that spring to another man, one who had, along with Isaac Stevens, been the most influential in his life: his father. Mullan could not have known as Rebecca and he traveled west that he would not see his father again. John Mullan Sr. died in December 1863, shortly after winning election as an Annapolis city alderman, his first and only elected office.[24]

Following their wedding John and Rebecca journeyed to New York where John gave an invited address to the American Geographical and Statistical Society and met with the Walla Walla railroad investors. The newlyweds then boarded a coal-fired steamship, beginning their journey west to a new life. If recollections of passengers on similar boats at the time are any indication, the Mullans rode a filthy, overcrowded, understaffed steamer, dining on rancid meat served atop dirty tablecloths, enduring a wretched ten-day voyage to the Isthmus of Panama. People slept on benches, in lifeboats, and on decks, doing their best to dodge fellow passengers retching from seasickness. It might not have been the honeymoon Rebecca had fancied.[25]

The Mullans disembarked in Aspinwall, a squalid village with streets of mud. Luckily, they arrived after 1855, when completion of the Panama Railroad reduced to a few hours a crossing that had previously taken days on foot or mule. Once on the Pacific side of the Isthmus, the Mullans boarded another steamer for San Francisco.[26]

From there they caught a boat north to the Columbia River, then traveled to Walla Walla, the town John had promised Rebecca would soon blossom with pleasant homes and burgeoning businesses. Rebecca's two new brothers-in-law greeted them, John's siblings who had tended Mullan's property while John had gone east to prepare his road report. A new home, new family, and seemingly assured prosperity ostensibly awaited the Mullans at this community with a redundant name, a place that knew and appreciated John Mullan. The future appeared bright. Neither John nor Rebecca had an inkling they would soon be making the same laborious trip in reverse—down the Pacific, across the Isthmus, up the Atlantic—retreating to Baltimore, broke and in the midst of an ugly family feud that pitted brother against brother. Walla Walla proved far less propitious than either John or Rebecca had envisioned.

Northern Pacific Railroad Survey expedition
leader Isaac Stevens. Stevens gained confidence in the young Lieutenant John Mullan
during their trek west and would become
the most significant mentor in Mullan's life.
*Washington State University Libraries, Manuscripts,
Archives, and Special Collections.*

Gustavus Sohon was a young private on the
Stevens railroad survey when he met Mullan.
The two became lifelong friends. Sohon, an
exceptional self-taught artist, served as Mullan's
ablest assistant during the two road building
expeditions. *Courtesy of Paul D. McDermott and the
Sohon family.*

From this small base camp that he named Cantonment Stevens after his mentor, Mullan undertook some of the most significant explorations of the American West in 1853-54. Sohon's image of the camp, located about twelve miles from today's Stevensville, Montana, shows an enclosed facility with numerous teepees in close proximity. *Washington State University Libraries, Manuscripts, Archives, and Special Collections.*

This, the most dramatic image of the many that Sohon drew for the Northern Pacific Railroad Survey and Mullan's road building expeditions, shows Mullan nearly drowning in the Hellgate River (today's Clark Fork). Mullan and a group of men were returning from an exploration to Flathead Lake in the spring of 1854 and had constructed a small raft to cross the engorged river. The raft crashed into a tree and nearly swept Mullan to his death. *Washington State University Libraries, Manuscripts, Archives, and Special Collections.*

Another dramatic Sohon image shows Mullan's team crossing an iced-over Hellgate (Clark Fork) River on their return from a winter exploration to Fort Hall. Mullan described this as one of the most miserable of his many western adventures, and it is easy to see why, contemplating the bone-chilling cold of crossing such icy rivers. *Washington State University Libraries, Manuscripts, Archives, and Special Collections.*

Sohon captured Mullan's party as it prepared to head over Lolo Pass in September 1854, the last of Mullan's expeditions seeking a railroad route. Mullan, following the course of Lewis and Clark a half century earlier, found this passage through the Bitterroots as disagreeable as had those earlier explorers. *Washington State University Libraries, Manuscripts, Archives, and Special Collections.*

Sohon's quick sketch shows part of Mullan's road building crew approaching the mouth of the Tucannon River in 1859. The bluffs named in honor of Captain Oliver Taylor and Lieutenant William Gaston, killed during the Steptoe disaster of 1858, flank the road. *Washington State University Libraries, Manuscripts, Archives, and Special Collections.*

Constructed a few years before Mullan began his road building, and now Idaho's oldest building, the Coeur d'Alene Mission proved a welcome respite for the road building crew. Mullan, a devout Catholic, took mass here whenever in the area, and sought information on routes across the mountains from the priests and resident Indians. *Washington State University Libraries, Manuscripts, Archives, and Special Collections.*

John Creighton served as wagon master for both of Mullan's road building expeditions. This image shows Creighton's wagon train, probably preparing to supply Mullan—an

intricate undertaking as the road building crew constantly worked its way farther away from supply depots. *Overholser Historical Research Center, Fort Benton, Montana.*

This remarkably detailed Sohon image shows Mullan's engineering crew at work at Cantonment Jordan, the crew's first winter encampment, located near today's De Borgia, Montana. It is rare to find an image of nineteenth century mapmakers at work. The illustration details what Mullan called "the office," and shows a drafting table, book shelves, and pegs supporting maps and manuscripts along the walls. Mullan took his cartography so seriously that he had his crew construct a skylight to better assist the work. *Courtesy of Paul D. McDermott and the Sohon family.*

Mullan established his second winter camp at Cantonment Wright on the Blackfoot River, near its confluence with the Hellgate (Clark Fork), and close to today's Bonner, Montana. This lithograph, from a Sohon image, also features the Blackfoot bridge, one of Mullan's major construction undertakings. *Washington State University Libraries, Manuscripts, Archives, and Special Collections.*

As Mullan exited the Northwest having completed his road in 1862, he made his way to California and left a glowing description of John Bidwell's Rancho Chico. A few years later, Bidwell and Mullan would partner in an unsuccessful attempt to provision Boise Basin miners from Chico. *California State University, Chico Meriam Library, Special Collections, donated by City of Chico Parks Department.*

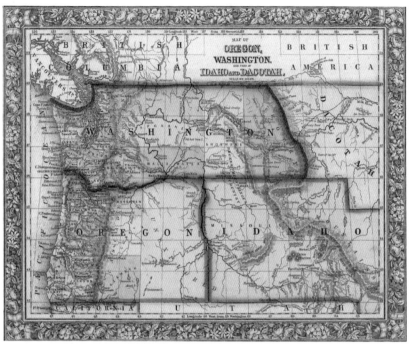

In 1863, Congress created Idaho Territory, and debated two maps that outlined different boundaries. John Mullan's concept included what became the Idaho panhandle and western Montana with Washington. William Wallace's map had the panhandle as part of Idaho. Mullan's map made more geographical sense, but Congress's last-minute decision to approve the Wallace version set the climate for the next 150 years of oftentimes contentious Idaho politics. *Idaho State Historical Society.*

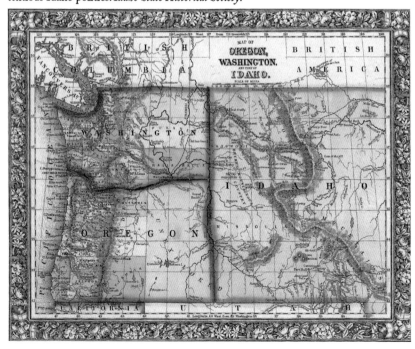

Following completion of the road, Gustavus Sohon briefly
operated a photographic and ambrotype gallery in San
Francisco. In 1863, having just journeyed on the Mullan Road,
Father Pierre-Jean DeSmet stopped by Sohon's studio, where
Sohon captured this image of the Catholic missionary whose
extraordinary wanderings in the American West profoundly
influenced Mullan. *Montana Historical Society Research Center
Photograph Archives, Helena, Montana.*

The Mullan Road brought an economic boom to Fort Benton. Steamboats unloaded tons of materials at the Fort Benton wharf, to be shipped out to miners and settlers, much of it along Mullan's road. *Overholser Historical Research Center, Fort Benton, Montana.*

Mullan posed for this photograph while living in San Francisco in the 1870s. *John Mullan Papers, Georgetown University Library, Special Collections Research Center, Washington, D.C.*

Mullan began courting Rebecca Williamson of Baltimore in the 1850s. They married in 1863. She posed for this photograph while they lived in San Francisco in the 1870s. *John Mullan Papers, Georgetown University Library, Special Collections Research Center, Washington, D.C.*

The Mullans' oldest daughter, Emma. As Mullan's health failed late
in his life, he asked Emma to move west to pursue legal and political
avenues to attain payment for legal fees he believed western states owed
him. *John Mullan Papers, Georgetown University Library, Special Collections Research Center, Washington, D.C.*

The Mullans' daughter May supported John in his last years and worked throughout her life to preserve the record of his western accomplishments. For half a century she retained boxes of his personal papers, which she donated to Georgetown University upon her death in 1962. *John Mullan Papers, Georgetown University Library, Special Collections Research Center, Washington, D.C.*

The Mullan's son Frank. He became estranged from his father following Frank's scandalous marriage to a divorcée in 1903. *John Mullan Papers, Georgetown University Library, Special Collections Research Center, Washington, D.C.*

A Mullan family photograph, probably from the 1890s. John's few demerits while attending West Point mostly came from his penchant for growing long hair and mustaches. After leaving the army, he had a full beard most of his life, which turned white as he aged. His daughter May wrote, "With his white beard, merry blue eyes, and rosy cheeks he looked the ideal Santa Claus." *John Mullan Papers, Georgetown University Library, Special Collections Research Center, Washington, D.C.*

Rebecca Mullan posed for this photo inside the Mullan home in Washington, D.C. For a time, the Mullans experienced the economic success that John had always sought. They filled their home with antiques and artwork brought back from extensive travels in Europe. *John Mullan Papers, Georgetown University Library, Special Collections Research Center, Washington, D.C.*

Day Allen Willey interviewed the famous road builder shortly before Mullan's death. Willey's article appeared in *Sunset Magazine* in 1910. It featured this image by Willey—probably the last photograph taken of John Mullan. *John Mullan Papers, Georgetown University Library, Special Collections Research Center, Washington, D.C.*

More than two dozen monuments—and even more interpretive signs—in three states commemorate events associated with John Mullan. Aside from Civil War battlefields, few American people or events are more thoroughly monumentalized. This statue commemorating Mullan's road is located in Mullan, Idaho. Twelve other identical massive monuments are located along the road in Idaho and Montana. Washington's monuments are even greater in number, though each has a unique design. *Keith C. Petersen photograph.*

Prelude

NO JOUNCING CROSS-COUNTRY STAGECOACH RIDE for John Mullan this time. No crammed steamship and sultry Isthmus crossing. On this trip Mullan traveled comfortably by rail from the East Coast to California. He might have reflected on his first journey west thirty-six years earlier, then a trailblazer laying the foundation for America's transcontinental railroads, like the one on which he now rode.

So much had changed—how he traveled, but also who he had become. As he rode west to meet the governor of California, Mullan perhaps reminisced about other recent travel, across the Atlantic to join his family on a grand tour of Europe. The Mullans made society news in those days: "Mrs. John Mullan, 1310 Connecticut Avenue, who left New York June 3 on the French steamer Normandie with all her children, arrived in Havre June 10 and will be absent over two years. Capt. Mullan...will join his family in Europe next year after the adjournment of Congress." Shortly before leaving for Europe the Mullans had attended President Grover Cleveland's inaugural ball, where "Mrs. John Mullan... wore a blue and white striped silk with front of yellow satin covered with lace." John provided well for his family as counsel for three western states and the Territory of Washington, testifying before Congress, arguing cases before the Supreme Court. He had become one of the prominent lawyers of Washington, D.C. Perhaps, riding on the train, he proudly recalled the newspaper story a year earlier about his eldest daughter, Emma, "a debutante this season...she has made the tour of the world... [and] during her residence abroad...continued her vocal lessons."[1]

John had gone broke twice early in his marriage, but the Mullans now lived comfortably. So what a jolt it must have been when Mullan received a February 1888 letter from California's Governor Robert Waterman, threatening to revoke his lucrative position as state counsel: "I wish you to distinctly understand that I do not recognize your authority to act in behalf of California...you never having been appointed by any competent authority for that purpose." At first John thought there had been a misunderstanding, that his supporters in Sacramento would clear things with the governor. But now nearly a year had passed; the governor had not relented. John would settle things himself. He would travel to Sacramento and face Waterman personally. He had met with so many prominent people before—presidents, senators, governors, generals, Indian chiefs. He had confidence in his ability to persuade. His family's livelihood depended on his success.[2]

Mullan's Central Pacific coach arrived at the Sacramento depot on Second and G streets on a January day in 1889. He rode the city's street railway to the Golden Eagle Hotel, a four-story Italianate building with a popular oyster saloon next door. Mullan took a room, and prepared for his upcoming meeting with the governor, once more reviewing the meticulously detailed letter over which he had labored so long, itemizing facts the governor might not know. How the federal government had reneged on obligations to reimburse California for expenses incurred during "the suppression of Indian hostilities." How the interest on that debt had grown over the years. How three previous governors had appointed Mullan to secure this and other federal payments. How the legislature had confirmed those appointments, setting his pay at 20 percent of whatever sums he recovered. How he had labored for years at his own expense, and succeeded in forcing the federal government to honor its obligations. And how it was only appropriate that the state now pay him for his services. He had penned a precise, methodical appeal that would surely convince Waterman.[3]

On the afternoon of January 18, 1889, Mullan walked to the capitol for his appointment. He met the governor in his private office. Mullan read his letter, then presented it to Waterman. The governor refused the document, curtly informing Mullan, "My secretary will read you my reasons for not accepting your drafts." The secretary then notified Mullan that the governor had nullified his appointment as state agent.

Mullan "in a laughing mood" according to a reporter, addressed Waterman: "All right, Governor, we don't care to have any words about it; and I believe this ends our business."

That meeting did essentially end Mullan's business with the State of California, though he would not have laughed had he thought so at the time. Mullan believed his Democratic allies in the legislature would overrule this Republican governor, whose behavior was driven more by politics than legal authority. In characteristically partisan fashion, California's newspapers entered the controversy. "Just what [Mullan] was to do under his ostensible authority is…a little misty, except that he was to intercept a large sum of money due from the United States to the State of California, and to levy toll upon it in transit," mocked the Republican San Francisco *Call*.[4]

Countered the Democratic San Francisco *Chronicle*, "Governor Waterman has no power to set aside an act of the Legislature…. He makes himself the laughing stock of the State and the country at large….Mullan has a legal right to receive [his money], and no act of the Governor can prevent him from doing so."[5]

But the governor certainly had the ability to complicate Mullan's life, and he did. Other states recognized they also could save money by reneging on agreements to pay Mullan. Mullan's financial affairs spiraled out of control. He would live another twenty years, nearly all his energy focused on legal efforts to obtain payments he believed justly due.

As he rode the transcontinental train back across America, John Mullan did not yet recognize that his confrontational meeting with Governor Waterman signaled the apex of his financial success. He would die virtually penniless. His debutante daughters would open a laundry in an effort to pay family bills. His reputation, so carefully whetted, would suffer the incrimination of a rabidly partisan press.

CHAPTER 11

❧

Family Feud

WELCOME TO WALLA WALLA, August 1863, the city that greeted John and Rebecca Mullan.

A dusty, half-mile long main street bisects the town, lined with rambling one-story businesses. Carpenters scramble to transform mounds of lumber into buildings. They constructed fifty last summer and look to beat that record this year. A few stores have wooden sidewalks, but for the most part pedestrians negotiate "miring mud or flying dust according to the weather," all the while sidestepping fetid manure. Walla Walla's streets, "nasty and dirty," are crowded with freight wagons and pack animals. Each week hundreds of miners make their way from Portland to this place, booming as a supply center for recently discovered gold diggings in the Boise Basin and in a place some folks are already calling Montana, though at this time it remains part of Idaho. Walla Walla is the biggest city in Washington Territory, a couple thousand residents serving miners' needs. It's not a place for the prim. One observer has called it, politely, "socially…below par." Another tagged it more accurately. Walla Walla, he said, is "quite low down the scale of civilization… overrun with thieves, gamblers and women of the demi-mode…reaping their…harvest from the reckless prospectors….Shooting and death attract…very little attention." Gambling houses operate day and night, "all the games known to the guild…running in full blast unceasingly."[1]

At least Rebecca had not arrived earlier, when things were really rowdy. By 1863 a vigilance committee had facilitated "the purification of the moral atmosphere" after stretching some necks. A few families had moved into town, formerly a bastion of single men. Walla Walla boasted businesses that dispensed not only shovels, gum boots, bacon, and beans, but also "fancy coffee and teas, stylish men's and women's clothing, including French cashmere pants and vests and silk velvet clothes [and]…bolts of…expensive cloth."[2]

Walla Walla in the summer of 1863, still rough, also promised opportunity. "Stages arrive and leave almost every day," wrote one eyewitness. "Long trains of mules and horses may be seen constantly coming in and quietly emerging with well assorted cargoes, to the different mining camps....Freight wagons, with long strings of oxen and mules attached...literally obstruct the highways."³

Walla Walla's aspirations to become territorial capital had ended, but Mullan still believed in the town's future. Why not? What a transformation he had seen. The Walla Walla of 1859 consisted of a handful of houses and businesses. No nearby gold had yet been discovered, and businesses existed to supply the neighboring fort, itself not much more than an extensive parade ground surrounded by wooden barracks.⁴

Now Walla Walla teemed, primarily because of Mullan's road, completed just in time to coincide with the gold rushes. It became the super highway of a vast region and, terminating in Walla Walla, that city flourished as a result. Mullan took great pride in Walla Walla's boom, courtesy of his road, and foresaw continued growth. "So long as men shall desire pleasant homes,—where the eye is as desirous of drinking in draughts of...beauty as the pocket is of accumulating wealth,—where mills, farms, gardens, and pleasant enclosures can be had,—where the products of the fields are garnered with a short transportation to a ready market—just so long will Walla Walla...be the chief emporium and point of business for the interior," he wrote. Here, Mullan could "accumulate wealth." At least, that was the plan. And it would begin with construction of a shortline railroad.⁵

❦

Mullan had noted long lines of wagons and pack trains at Wallula on the Columbia River when he and Sohon had passed through the previous year. By 1863 the Oregon Steam Navigation Company operated a fleet of steamers between Portland and Wallula. There they disgorged prospective miners and camp followers. Most then made their way thirty miles to Walla Walla. Mullan estimated forty thousand people a year took that trek. Anyone observing the men and supplies arduously wending their way would be, as was Mullan, "convinced that...some more rapid and economical means is positively demanded in order to connect the heart of the [Walla Walla] valley with the Columbia River."

Mullan's solution: a railroad. Walla Walla would then "become the commercial centre which will supply the large and rich mining region."[6]

At a Walla Walla meeting in January 1863, a group of businessmen incorporated the Walla Walla Railroad Company and appointed Mullan, then still in Washington, D.C., as commissioner, believing his reputation would encourage investors. "Capitalists will do well to look into this project, which appears to possess elements of profit and public usefulness in no ordinary degree," editorialized *Railway Times*. "Capt. Mullan…is every way well informed upon the subject."[7]

Mullan believed this the opportunity he had long awaited, a way of profiting from his road-building notoriety. While he and Rebecca honeymooned in New York, he pitched his case to prospective investors. With a goal of raising $600,000, he boldly guaranteed the railroad would "pay its stockholders the rate of two per cent per month on all capital…invested."[8]

Notwithstanding Mullan's enthusiasm, the railroad scheme quickly fizzled. Or, in the words of W.W. Baker, "nothing tangible resulted." Baker was in a position to know. His father, Dorsey Baker, had been one of the thirty Walla Walla residents who incorporated the railroad. Dorsey shared Mullan's zeal for Walla Walla's future. In 1875 he finally brought rail service to the town, his Walla Walla & Columbia River Railroad fulfilling Mullan's dream. But by then, John Mullan had long exited Walla Walla, his first effort to capitalize on his fame a complete flop.[9]

John and Rebecca made their home on a farm a couple of miles out of town, on some of "the finest [land] there is anywhere in this locality," with a beautiful spring of clear water. Mullan had purchased a part interest in the 480-acre farm, along with a sawmill, in 1858 when he partnered with local businessman A.H. Robie. Shortly after the purchase he sent his brothers Louis and Charles to Walla Walla to oversee the farm and mill. The newlyweds followed in August 1863 and "found abundant work to do…plowing, planting, fencing."[10]

In October 1863 they had a guest at their modest house. Sixty-two-year-old Father Pierre-Jean DeSmet had made his way to Walla Walla over the Mullan Road from Fort Benton on this, his last visit to the

Northwest. On the first Sunday in October "church services were held in the small parlor of the Mullans' farmhouse," DeSmet officiating.[11]

DeSmet described Walla Walla as "barely a town...yesterday, but already...over 2,000 inhabitants, with all the signs of civilization in full swing." One symbol of civilization it lacked: a Catholic church. Walla Walla's Catholics attended mass in a pole-roofed structure with a slab floor. Father Jean Baptiste Brouillet—who would appear prominently in John's life twenty years later—officiated. DeSmet's visit inspired the town's Catholics to raise money for a proper church, and Rebecca helped lead the effort. Walla Walla women sponsored a fundraising dinner and auction, with Rebecca "donating my pin cushions and various odds and ends given me at my wedding....Without laying out a penny, we realized $3,000." The attractive Rebecca enticed a considerable share of that money herself: "Miners from Idaho in their buckskin suits were much the most liberal in their contributions. Several times in one evening I was asked to take supper, which I made the pretense to eat for charity sake, and these men would weigh out of their leather pouches $5 and $10 of gold dust." With the earnings, parishioners constructed a small church.[12]

Given DeSmet's affection for Indians, he no doubt complimented the Mullans for taking care of a young Indian boy name John, who also lived at the farm. In 1858, pickets with Colonel Wright's troops, on guard at Fort Taylor, captured three Indian brothers as the expedition prepared to cross the Snake River. Wright sent the two older boys to Walla Walla. Mullan convinced Wright to let him take the younger on the expedition. "After myself and Uncle John...of Kentucky I have called him John," Mullan wrote, "and my present determination is to educate him and take him with me to the States....Poor little fellow. His fate has been a hard one, an orphan and then a captive and slave."[13]

There is no indication that Mullan took John "to the States." Instead the young boy went to live with Mullan's brothers on the farm. When Rebecca and John moved there in 1863, they found the younger John, "where he remained till the fall of 1864 when the ranch was abandoned." What happened to the Indian John is unclear. But the ranch abandonment was not something the elder John undertook willingly. That occurred only after a bitter family feud.[14]

❧

John Mullan might have longed for his old desk under the stifling watch of the Topographical Bureau after a few months with his brothers. Mullan's loyalty to family ran deep. As the oldest child of a large clan with limited means, he felt obliged to assist his younger siblings, and sent brother Louis and later Charles to Walla Walla. John described the twenty-year-old Louis as "houseless, homeless, penniless, (&) without occupation" until John entrusted him with his Walla Walla interests. John probably did not know Louis well; he had been ten years old when John left the family's Annapolis home. John at times had lapses in character judgment. He certainly misjudged Louis.[15]

In addition to the mill and farm that John owned in partnership with Robie, Mullan also purchased a livery stable. He sent the "homeless, penniless" Louis to manage these complex concerns. In December 1860 Robie sold John his shares in the property and business. John then owned everything outright.

John soon realized that Louis lacked the maturity to oversee his diverse interests, so he sent brother Charles—three years Louis's senior—to help. Things did not improve, neither brother having a knack for business, though Louis did have a talent for irritating people. "A fool, and a low-bred hanger-on," one contemporary labeled him. When John completed the road, he asked future brother-in-law David Williamson to manage the farm. Louis refused to cooperate with him.[16]

Under this sloppy arrangement John's investments began to unravel even before he moved to Walla Walla. His brothers, serving as his agents, regularly appeared before the U.S. District Court in Walla Walla to defend against lawsuits, cases they almost invariably lost. A man who worked in the mill won a suit for back wages. Creditors sued over unpaid debts. A man John contracted to deliver mail to Colville sued over lack of payment. The men who provided feed for the Mullans' livery sued; the sheriff confiscated $160 worth of equipment from the Mullans' stable in lieu. John's former road crew wagon master John Creighton sued for $363.25, an amount that increased to $426.68 with interest by the time John paid.[17]

In some cases plaintiffs filed suit against John; in others, against a firm called the Mullan Brothers. In the most complicated legal action, pitting Louis against brothers John and Charles, John claimed there was no such firm; that he alone owned the businesses and farm. But he would lose that case, and when he did, what money and assets he had managed to accumulate were also lost.

The crux of the complicated lawsuit was this. In the spring of 1864, Louis filed a claim against John and Charles, alleging that Louis was a partner in the firm known as the Mullan Brothers, and that the company owed him $25,000. John responded that he alone had purchased the farm and business; that "Mullan Brothers" was a "pretended firm"; and that Louis and Charles were merely his agents. He allowed them to operate under the name Mullan Brothers because he did not wish "to disgrace or mortify" them. A host of witnesses—including brothers James and Ferdinand, drawn into the increasingly ugly family spat—testified.[18]

It seems unlikely that Louis brought any money into the association. And, given that John had to bring in Charles and David Williamson to create order out of Louis's messes, his sweat equity seems to have had dubious value. But Louis was shrewd. He staked out 160 acres of the farm and claimed it as his share of the Mullan Brothers partnership. Louis then sued his two brothers for "forcible entry" when they came onto the property. Louis had maneuvered himself into ownership of a farm at no personal expense. John had also given Louis power of attorney, and allowed him to operate under the name Mullan Brothers. Both proved legal mistakes. When John and Rebecca moved next door to Louis, all semblance of family tranquility disintegrated. By December 1863 John had endured all he could. Two days after Christmas he attempted to remove Louis from the farm, precipitating the legal case. Louis asserted that John had no right to "oust and dispossess" him. Louis further charged that John and Charles were preparing to sell company assets without his approval "for the purpose of defrauding" Louis of his share as an equal partner. John, countering that no partnership existed, vouched that he did not owe Louis "any sum whatsoever."

Brothers Ferdinand and James had by this time also moved to Walla Walla and got drawn into the dispute. Ferdinand attested that he "heard John Mullan say they were all in [business] together, Louis, Charles and himself....John said he knew he was wrong...and was sorry....Said that he would sell out and pay off the debts first and give Louis one third." James testified that he, too, knew "of a partnership existing" between the three brothers.

The squabble pained the family-oriented John. By early 1864, just as the lawsuit commenced, the brothers would have learned of their father's December death. John Mullan Sr. had worked his entire life to provide for his family. As the eldest son, John Jr. had assumed much of that responsibility, providing opportunities for his brothers. There is no doubt that John made all the Walla Walla investments; Louis and Charles had no money. It is unlikely there ever was a partnership. But John trusted his siblings and Louis took advantage. By late 1864, the legal case had really become moot. John was bankrupt. He sold what assets he had and paid what debts he could. Louis remained on the 160 acres, living there a few more years. He then practiced law in California—having learned something about the profession in Walla Walla—before moving to Arizona where he edited a newspaper. There is no record that John and Louis ever spoke again.[19]

Louis's actions hurt John, but not nearly as much as those of James, the second-oldest brother, who was much closer to John. John had worked hard to advance James's career. While stationed at Fort McHenry, John had taken a leave so he could accompany James to medical school. He had hired him as a young physician on the road crew. To have James side with Louis had to aggrieve John.

John's issue with James ran much deeper than merely his brother's testimony. As soon as James arrived in Walla Walla in September 1863, ostensibly to take up "the practice of his profession," he began conspiring with Louis to swindle John. "That Capt. John Mullan was prevented from 'proving up' on his land through the connivance of his brother Louis and perhaps with the help of brother James, there is no doubt," recalled the granddaughter of the man who purchased the Mullans' farm. James's name, along with that of Louis, appears on the deed of sale for that property. How James gained an interest is unclear. But by November 1864 his collusion with Louis was clear. In that month, with one family lawsuit winding down, John filed another suit against James and Louis to prevent them from selling his personal property. James testified that John did "not speak" to him. "I would be friendly if John would." But it is difficult to befriend a person attempting to cheat you, even if he is your brother. There is no evidence John and James were ever friendly again. Brothers John, Charles, Horace, Dennis, and Ferdinand Mullan are all buried in St. Mary's Cemetery in Annapolis, evidence of a close-knit family. James and Louis are conspicuous by their absence.[20]

🌿

John Mullan's first effort to capitalize on his road-building renown ended in absolute failure. He found no investors for the Wallula railroad, perhaps because he could devote less time than necessary to that task as he struggled to save his Walla Walla business ventures.

Imagine Rebecca's distress as she retreated to her family in Baltimore. The future had seemed so bright when she and John had honeymooned in New York, less than a year earlier, where John gave a speech before so many prominent men. Their plans had unraveled so fast. John finished his legal affairs and joined Rebecca in Baltimore, his Walla Walla investments worthless.

But John and Rebecca had resilience, and John still believed in the latent value of his carefully honed reputation and the promise of the West. They would return.

CHAPTER 12

The Chico to Boise Line

THE 1841 WAGON TRAIN OUT OF Westport, Missouri, that included Father DeSmet, split into three parts at Soda Springs in today's Idaho. Twenty-one-year-old John Bidwell helped lead the group that went south to California, pioneering the California Trail.

Bidwell's caravan straggled to the Pacific, battered by harsh elements, tough travel, and marauding Indians. There he left the group and went north to New Helvetia, established by John Sutter, soon to be called Sacramento. If you survived the emigration ordeal and were a young white man with energy, it was a fine time to land in California, and Bidwell took full advantage. Sutter hired him to manage some of his growing business concerns. Bidwell carried the golden stones discovered at Sutter's mill to San Francisco in 1848 to have them tested. Before the subsequent gold rush arrived, Bidwell discovered his own rich lode and then acquired a prime piece of property north of New Helvetia in the Sacramento Valley he named Rancho Arroyo Chico.[1]

At the twenty-four-thousand-acre Rancho Chico, Bidwell became one of California's leading agriculturalists. He experimented with grains; he established a dairy; he grew grapes; he operated California's largest fruit tree nursery. He surrounded his spacious mansion with rare roses, imported shrubs, and Asian trees.[2]

As the farm grew, Bidwell needed workers. So in 1860 he platted a town and offered free lots to anyone willing to build a house. He called the place Chico.[3]

Rancho Chico impressed many travelers, including John Mullan, who ventured past after completing his road in 1862. Mullan did not meet Bidwell on that trip, but what an impression Bidwell's ranch made:

> We passed through the extensive and rich fields of Major Bidwell, where eleven thousand acres of grain were being threshed—where his

own mill stood ready to convert into flour the produce of his own fields; where his own mammoth store furnished hundreds of his employees with all the wants of life; where his own energy was opening...a wagon road from the Sacramento River to the Humboldt mines; and where his own purse has already paid out $35,000, and backed by a willingness to pay as much more, in order to open up a new market for the exuberant products of so rich a soil....The center of his large estate is the beautiful village of "Chico," where...live an educated and contented peasantry, all more or less supported by the means of this bachelor millionaire—whose residence...is one of those architectural gems hid away amidst shrubs, trees, orchards, and groves....May Major Bidwell long live...to dispense his bounties to a people who respect him for the liberal and generous manner in which he shares his wealth with those not similarly blest.[4]

Rancho Chico exemplified the ostentatiousness that Mullan extolled, and Bidwell epitomized a man who had capitalized on western opportunity. In a few years the lives of Mullan and Bidwell would closely intertwine. About the time Mullan needed a fresh start after his Walla Walla debacle, John Bidwell went looking for someone to help him establish a transportation route into Idaho to better market his farm produce. But he did not seek out the famed road builder. Instead, he sought help from one of Mullan's Northwest contemporaries.

On August 2, 1862—just a couple of weeks before John Mullan rode into Walla Walla having completed his road—George Grimes, Moses Splawn, and a small party of prospectors stumbled upon one of the renowned gold discoveries of the American West at a place called the Boise Basin. "Every town and village in Oregon and Washington Territory is sending into our midst its entire male population," noted one who witnessed the flood. By 1864, nearly forty thousand miners had fanned over a three-hundred-square-mile area as one extravagant lode topped another in what seemed an unending flow of mining opportunity.[5]

But what a torturous place to reach. Miners traveled east up the Columbia River by steamer to Umatilla, Oregon, then backtracked on the Oregon Trail more than 250 miles overland across sagebrush desert before heading into the mountains. Provisions often lagged, particularly in winter if the Columbia froze. Here lay opportunity if a person could cut a dependable supply route into the isolated, mountain-rimmed Boise Basin. The prospect of a market for his ranch produce enticed John Bidwell. He engaged a man who knew Idaho even better than Mullan to plot a course from Chico to the Boise diggings.

Thousands of argonauts had rushed into California in 1849. Elias D. Pierce was one, leaving Missouri in May. By the time his train of fifty-two wagons reached Soda Springs where it turned south to California, Pierce had been elected captain, a title he proudly carried the rest of his life. The party reached Sacramento in September. Pierce, whose name for a time flashed as brightly as any in the nineteenth century mining West, discovered no golden riches in California. But, like many others, he found profit by supplying miners.[6]

Then Pierce's partner absconded with their money, and Pierce moved north. In 1852 he opened a trading post at Lapwai in what would become Idaho, near the farm of William and Isabel Craig, selling goods to Nez Perce Indians. The Nez Perce country intrigued him. He believed it contained gold. Pierce began exploring the mountains east of Lapwai in search of mineral, trespassing onto country that Isaac Stevens had reserved for the Nez Perce in his 1855 treaty. In February 1860 he panned some color, convincing himself he had found "a rich and extensive gold field." "I had the…destiny of that country…at my own option," he wrote. His discovery would unleash a rush that led to the creation of Idaho.[7]

But at first, Pierce kept his discovery quiet. In the summer of 1860 he set out for the mountains again with eleven men, laboring through a rugged landscape. "I am quite confident there never had been a human being in the country before," he wrote.[8]

That isolation soon ended. In October they found gold. "I never saw a party of men so much excited." This time Pierce made no effort to secret the news, and another western gold rush ensued. All those miners quickly claimed any area that seemed promising. So prospectors pushed on, seeking unoccupied ground, sweeping south to the Boise Basin.[9]

Pierce, who believed the way to prosperity lay in building roads to connect miners with suppliers, determined to move south with the mining excitement. "The question of opening up a new over land route to [Boise] was the topic of the day," Pierce later recalled. He traveled to

California in 1864 and made his way to Chico, where he "found general Bidwell willing to do any thing in the bounds of reason" to support construction of a wagon road to the Boise mines—as long as Chico became "the starting point."[10]

Bidwell was not quite as eager "to do any thing" as Pierce had assumed. He had invested heavily in 1862 to connect Chico with Frederick Lander's Fort Kearney, South Pass and Honey Lake Wagon Road. That secured him access to Humboldt River mines, but the connection did him little good, as the mines fizzled and Bidwell lost money. He would gamble again only cautiously.[11]

Still, it could not hurt to have a man of Pierce's reputation scout a potential supply route to Boise. So in January 1865 Bidwell hired Pierce to chart a wagon path into Idaho. It was a tough time of year to travel, so Bidwell engaged a couple of veteran mountaineers to teach Pierce to ski. "It was my first experience [skiing] and I traveled a little heavy," he recalled.[12]

Tottering along, he reached Susanville and enlisted sixteen men to help him survey the road, which they did with the loss of one man, killed by Indians. By spring he convinced Bidwell of the route's feasibility and "we…decided to start a saddle train once a week from Chico to Idaho." In April, Pierce led a pack train into Boise, pronouncing his a much faster course than the traditional Columbia River route. By summer, stages had begun negotiating the new line. From the East Coast, John Mullan followed the developments.[13]

After their Walla Walla disappointment, John and Rebecca retreated to Baltimore. By then the genre of literature that John Bidwell inaugurated a quarter century earlier when describing his overland trek to California had proliferated. If nineteenth century overland travelers owned one book, it would be an emigrant guide; if two, they might also possess a Bible. New guidebooks appeared annually. The manuals informed readers of the comparative merits of oxen versus mules, provided primers on firearms, recommended routes, and advised where to find grass and water. John Mullan now had both the time and knowledge to enter this burgeoning field. In 1865, he published his *Miners and Travelers' Guide*.[14]

Preparing the *Guide* proved light duty. Captain Andrew Humphreys of the Topographical Bureau had provided all the incentive Mullan needed to compile abundant emigrant information as he constructed his road: "You will forward...a report...[to] include a description of the country along each part of the road, with reference to the supplies of grass, wood, and water that would be available, at different seasons, to emigrant parties." Mullan did just that, and when the government published his construction report, he insisted it include a day-by-day itinerary for travelers, data Mullan duplicated in his *Travelers' Guide*.[15]

Mullan divided his volume into three parts. The first lent practical advice: "Never maltreat [pack animals], but govern them as you would a woman, with kindness, affection, and caresses, and you will be repaid by their docility and easy management." This section reiterated the itinerary included in his road report.[16]

Section two carried Mullan's 1863 lecture to the American Geographical and Statistical Society on the region's topography and resources. The third part was a curious addendum. Mullan transcribed newspaper articles and provided a hodgepodge of other information about recent mining activity. While hastily thrown together, it confirmed his proclivity to keep appraised of the latest news from the West—including efforts to supply Boise Basin miners.

Compiling the *Guide* kept the restless Mullan somewhat occupied. But he remained focused on western opportunity. By early 1865, he learned that E.D. Pierce, a man whose "boldness and...judgment [are] worthy every commendation," had teamed with the wealthy John Bidwell on a road project. Mullan wanted part of that potentially lucrative action.[17]

By the summer of 1865 Mullan had again moved west. There he joined Pierce and his partner J.B. Francis of Boise, operating a freight and stage line into Idaho. Bidwell had no money in the firm, but did provide a few stagecoaches; he no longer needed them after his abortive Humboldt endeavor. In July, Mullan led a party out of Boise to improve the road to Chico.[18]

A few months later Mullan guided a stage from Chico to Ruby City, an Idaho mining boom town. Ever the promoter, he brought with him not only "a full load of...passengers," but also peaches, apples, and grapes from Bidwell's ranch, which he presented to the publisher of the *Owyhee Avalanche*. The *Avalanche* praised Mullan's efforts: "The Idaho and California wagon and stage routes are beginning to assume an importance which we have for a long time predicted they would." A few weeks later the Idaho and California Stage Line began advertising in the *Avalanche*, promoting tri-weekly service to Chico, "Fare 60 Dollars." The Boise *Idaho Statesman* also took notice. It believed the partnership of Pierce and Mullan—two of the region's best-known men—guaranteed success: "There is now no more doubt that the Idaho and California stages will continue to run with regularity."[19]

But the *Avalanche* soon soured on Mullan. Despite his grand entrance to Ruby City in a "coach and four" on September 1, 1865, and the advertisements proclaiming three stages weekly, "no coaches have as yet arrived" the paper noted in October. The publisher perceptively pinpointed the problem. Mullan "is doubtless engineer enough, but his present income would not permit him to furnish the necessary rolling stock for a bowling alley, to say nothing of establishing a tri-weekly line of stages....We confess to being beautifully bilked."[20]

All stage travel was adventuresome, but the Chico to Idaho route particularly so, featuring a rugged road and serious Indian threats. The Portland *Oregonian* called it "a very pleasant route for a gentleman to take his wife, who wishes to get rid of her." Mullan's first months at his new venture proved disappointing. But the Chico *Courant* urged patience: "Let the *Avalanche* and the people of...Idaho hold their temper. Next spring will give them a stage line...from Chico direct and continuous."[21]

Mullan left California for the East in October, determined to salvage his second entrepreneurial effort. He pursued two avenues to infuse his company with capital, lobbying for a mail contract and enticing investors, particularly John Bidwell.

John and Rebecca stayed with the Williamsons in Baltimore again that winter. But John spent most of his time in Washington, seeking a mail contract. He immediately sought out Idaho's territorial delegate, Edward Holbrook, and California's newly elected representative, John Bidwell. Those were hectic days in Washington; the thirty-ninth

Congress witnessed the assassination of Lincoln and the surrender of the South, while approving more legislation than any other to that time. Bidwell and Holbrook had much requiring their attention, and relied on Mullan to undertake the brunt of negotiations for the mail contract.[22]

It proved fortunate that Mullan had both time and energy, for the Chico advocates faced serious opposition. The Oregon Steam Navigation Company fought the contract because it threatened that company's near monopoly of provisioning Idaho via the Columbia River. Nevada's congressman sought an alternate mail route into Idaho through his state. And the Central Pacific Railroad, laying track east for its eventual meeting with the Union Pacific to form America's first transcontinental, hoped to land the contract to help establish a feeder stage route into Idaho. Despite those powerful adversaries, Mullan, Bidwell, and Holbrook prevailed. Because Mullan was in the East, he suggested the contract be assigned to a surrogate in the West, Rebecca's brother, L.T. Williamson of San Francisco. "I got the mail contract for his brother in law, against terrific opposition," Bidwell proudly wrote, assuming more credit than he had earned.[23]

They had hoped for a $100,000 contract, but settled for $75,000. Bidwell claimed they could have had more except for all "the adverse interests...here to match me." Bidwell needed Mullan to oversee the complicated negotiations, but Mullan's bulldogged tenacity grated on him. "I had to make a fight for a mail contract for some one," he wrote, "and Mullan edged himself in continually so that I could not strike anywhere without hitting him." Late in his life Bidwell proved unwilling to give Mullan any credit. "I won my [mail route] alone, with nobody to help me," he erroneously and petulantly wrote in 1891.[24]

Mullan did not yet recognize it, but he had simultaneously triumphed and failed. Despite Bidwell's later revisionism, there would have been no mail contract without Mullan. But Mullan so irritated Bidwell that he smothered any chance of a Bidwell partnership. Bidwell wished Mullan success—a line to Idaho would be a fiscal bonanza for Chico. But he refused to provide capital. "Mullan must succeed," Bidwell wrote. "Everything must be done to aid him, without incurring pecuniary liability." Of course, there were other reasons for Bidwell's reticence. By this time, Chico's founder had overextended himself, whirling into a debt from which he would never recover.[25]

Mullan worked tirelessly, a "small steam engine." He sought financial backing in Baltimore and New York. He drew up incorporation papers. He tried to land a telegraph line adjacent to the stage route, "two projects...natural hand-maids of each other." He gave the endeavors "all the energy that I possess." He wrote Bidwell once that "Mrs. Mullan will have an operation of the womb performed on Monday next." Yet even that would not deter him from business: "If my presence is needed [in Washington]...I shall obey any telegram you may send me."[26]

Bidwell would have preferred someone else to head the stage line. "Capt. Mullan...may be in the new concern, perhaps, but I prefer, if possible, to get the whole thing out of his hands." Bidwell thought Mullan built "castles in the air," and found him "too visionary." Most significantly, he believed the captain provoked as many financiers as he induced. "There were plenty of Idaho people here," Bidwell wrote. "They all said that Mullan was not the right kind of man....There were... men of means seeking investment...who would have put on the line, but [for] Mullan." But Bidwell never had a chance against the Mullan onslaught. "Mullan kept waging his cause and was so omnipresent that I was obliged to let him in," he wrote. "Mullan with his pamphlets was everywhere."[27]

"If Mullan had never" lobbied for the stage line, "I believe the result would have been different and better," Bidwell lamented. "But now if Mullan fails the route fails—which it must not do." Mullan gave success his best effort. He failed to raise as much money as he hoped, but he did secure enough "to begin the line." He hurried back to California, arriving in May, and announced the incorporation of the California and Idaho Stage and Fast Freight Company, with himself as president.[28]

Mullan hired "one or two hundred Chinamen," and sent them under the direction of J.B. Francis to repair the road and construct stations. He built a blacksmith shop and purchased coaches and stock. He hired drivers who wheeled up and down Chico's streets—which "look like a perpetual stage line"—breaking in animals and equipment. Despite all the bustle, the *Owyhee Avalanche* remained skeptical: "Should Mullan succeed he'll astonish himself, friends and enemies."[29]

At midnight on July 1, 1866, the day the mail contract took effect, the first stage left Chico. It arrived in Ruby City, Idaho, three days and five hours later, John Mullan aboard. The *Avalanche* finally had something positive to report: "We say 'bully for Mullan.' He has persevered." The publisher looked forward to "the permanent success of the line."[30]

And for a time, things looked rosy. Idaho businesses placed large newspaper advertisements touting a vast array of goods "Just Received from San Francisco! Via CHICO"—stoves, tinware, boots, shoes, liquor. Mullan's freight company "has perfected its line," the *Avalanche* now boasted. "More stock will be put on and the time reduced." The capital city's paper, too, praised Mullan, who "intends to extend his line to Boise."[31]

Bidwell, however, remained dubious. He desperately hoped for success, but refused to provide financial support. "When I found it was a Mullan…or nothing—I resolved to make it the best Mullan in the country," Bidwell wrote his ranch manager D.D. Harris. But the extent of Bidwell's effort consisted of providing suggestions. "Give him advice," Bidwell wrote. " But I must not be made responsible for Mullan's debts." Bidwell was torn. "It is life or death with us….All of our hopes are with Mullan." He needed a successful stage line to help lift him out of his financial abyss. [32]

When first viewing Rancho Chico in 1862, before he met Bidwell, Mullan had praised the Californian's "generous manner." Mullan could have used some of that generosity now. But it was not to come. Mullan's second entrepreneurial endeavor would soon collapse.[33]

"Chico stage makes its last trip to-morrow," ran a notice in the November 17, 1866, issue of the *Owyhee Avalanche*. "Staging will be resumed in early spring." But come spring, the Chico *Courant* reported more accurately: Mullan was out of business, selling stock and equipment. "Thus for a second time he was left without resources," remembered Rebecca, "completely broken financially." The *Owyhee Avalanche* showed little sympathy, having roller-coastered along with Mullan's ambitions too long: "Thus concludes the farce commenced nearly two years ago—a continually distracting subject."[34]

Mullan had encountered a number of difficulties. His lack of capital became particularly apparent when Indians, enraged by years of intrusion into their lands following the California gold discovery, made a stand against this stage line. "At the commencement of opening up the route the Indians gave us but little trouble," recalled Pierce. But by the end of the 1865 season they had "destroyed over fifteen thousand dollars worth of our Stock besides burned a number of valuable Stations."[35]

Mullan took advantage of his influence with the military to plead for protection. The army established a number of posts along the line—including one named Fort Bidwell. "Whatever advantage Idaho and California may derive from dispelling the Indian difficulties…is due…to the energy and perseverance of Capt. Mullan," reported the Boise newspaper.[36]

But the protection proved insufficient. Mullan suffered not only from the loss of property, but also deteriorating revenues when people refused to ride the stage out of fear of Indian attack. Even had the military patrols succeeded in defending the line, Mullan faced increasing competition for the lucrative Idaho market.

The *Avalanche* had hoped Mullan would succeed, as an antidote to the Oregon Steam Navigation Company's exorbitant charges. The *Avalanche* editorially bantered with Oregon newspapers. "Columbia advocates, you may as well toot your horn for another market," it mocked. "You might as well insist upon cutting your own throats—financially—as upon continuing the Owyhee trade." Mullan held all the advantages, the *Avalanche* believed, at least initially.[37]

But the Steam Navigation Company would not give up easily. Indeed, the OSN proved so desperate to retain its monopoly that it destroyed a prized boat in the process. The *Colonel Wright*, the steamer that had so ably assisted Mullan's road building, suffered such extensive damage during its attempt to ascend the Snake River to reach the Idaho mines that only its engine could be salvaged. Eventually, Columbia River freight did move regularly to Boise, with improvement to the road out of Umatilla. Ironically, Mullan then faced competition from another former ally from his road-building days when George Creighton, Mullan's wagon master, began hauling freight from Umatilla.[38]

Mullan also had challenges from rivals who, like himself, sought to supply Idaho from the south. Hill Beachey had recognized the commercial potential of Mullan's Fort Benton road. During the first session of Idaho's territorial legislature he received approval to operate a toll road connecting Lewiston with the Mullan highway. Beachey did not act on that authorization because the mining rush moved south from the Clearwater country to Boise. He would chase profits there, instead. [39]

Beachey had been a successful hotel keeper in Lewiston, but sold his business to seek his fortune in the Boise Basin. On a steamboat bound for San Francisco Elias D. Pierce and Hill Beachey met and exchanged ideas about a freight route to Boise. They made their way to Rancho Chico to meet with John Bidwell, who so inspired Pierce that he set off on that winter ski trip. But Beachey remained unconvinced that Chico provided the best avenue to Idaho. Instead, he would establish an alternate route to rival that of Pierce, Bidwell, and Mullan.[40]

Beachey thought the best way to Idaho lay through Nevada. "If such a line can be made a permanent institution, Mr. Beachey is the man to do it," glowed one newspaper. After less than a month of operation, in June 1865, when Indians drove off his stock and burned two stage coaches, Beachey temporarily gave up. But Beachey, "a man of intense energy, indomitable when aroused," would try again.[41]

The next year, with support from the Central Pacific Railroad, Beachey was back. His competition proved Mullan's demise. With the assistance of the Nevada congressional delegation and backing from the powerful railroad, Beachey wrested from Mullan the contract to deliver mail to Idaho, dooming Mullan's company. Mullan's effort had proven "to be a miserable abortion," lamented the Boise *Idaho Statesman.* "It soon dwindled down to a pony line."[42]

John Mullan earned a reputation as an explorer of railroad routes. Ironically, "his failure to foresee the impact of the railroad" undermined his Chico enterprise. Eventually, railroads also ruined Hill Beachey's venture. Ironically, when he died in San Francisco in 1875, a train carried his body to his former home in Marysville for burial.[43]

Elias Pierce married in 1869 and moved to Oakland. In 1871 he had a son. He named him Hill Beachey Pierce, after the man he met on that steamboat to California as they both sought their fortunes. Pierce died penniless in 1897.

John Bidwell, who died in 1900, ran unsuccessfully for governor of California four times, and once for president as head of the Prohibition Party. Bidwell's experimentation at Rancho Chico played a crucial role in the development of California agriculture. After laying out the city of Chico, he founded a state normal school that is today the campus of

California State University, Chico. There, in the archives of the Meriam Library, are John Bidwell's papers. They detail the hopes and frustrations of his partnership with John Mullan in the attempt to forge a stage line to Idaho.

In May 1866, during the second—and last—season of Mullan's stage company, a group of men on horseback approached the swollen crossing of the Owyhee River. They were riding along the portion of Mullan's freight route that cut through southeastern Oregon, on their way to prospect in Montana. One of the men slipped off his horse into the icy water. A well-seasoned traveler, he probably did not think much about the dunking. Maybe his friends laughed at the seemingly insignificant incident as they accompanied him in his wet clothes to a nearby stage station used by Mullan's coaches. There the man developed "mountain fever"—probably pneumonia. He died on May 16, and his companions buried him in the desert. His grave attracted little attention. Then, more than a century after his death, the Oregon Historical Society erected a sign that read:

> This site marks the final resting place of the youngest member of the Lewis and Clark Expedition. Born to Sacajawea and Toussant Charbonneau at Fort Mandan on February 11, 1805, Baptiste and his mother symbolized the peaceful nature of the "Corps of Discovery."[44]

As John Mullan had set out to explore the West in 1853, one of his few aids had been the journals and maps of Lewis and Clark. Now, as the youngest member of that expedition died along his stage route, Mullan was about to be bankrupted by a railroad. In half a century, the West had rocketed from a time of intrepid exploration to the comforts of train travel. Despite his financial troubles, Mullan recognized the opportunity this ease of transportation presented. As always, he believed the West held promise. As the region filled, lawyers would be required. Mullan determined that his next entrepreneurial effort would be as an attorney.

CHAPTER 13

"The Notorious Captain John Mullan"

IN 1892, LOOKING BACK ON NEARLY thirty years of marriage, Rebecca Mullan set out to reclaim her husband's tarnished reputation. John had come under criticism as an attorney of questionable ethics. In a reminiscence intended for her children, Rebecca assumed the role of hagiographer. Her piece is filled with praise—often exaggerated—for a heroic husband. But there are times when Rebecca provides insight. After briefly describing the failure of the Chico stage venture, Rebecca outlined an indomitable will. John had just gone bankrupt for the second time, but his "strong constitution and stronger energy and will power sustained him." Indeed, John Mullan recovered from the Chico fiasco remarkably quickly. The Mullans moved to San Francisco. The local paper reminded readers that Mullan was "well known in this city as a man of great administrative capacity, energy and worth." He focused his undeniable vigor on a new goal. He would become a California lawyer.[1]

Both Mullans took jobs in a San Francisco bank. John also worked for the U.S. Surveyor's Office. He fleetingly considered another road-building project when it appeared Congress might authorize a wagon route along Lake Pend Oreille. Oregon Senator Henry Corbett "will try to have me assigned to the charge of the work," he wrote. But Congress provided no appropriation, and John spent most of his time reading law. He had contemplated a legal career before. "I have been a student of Law for the last five years," he wrote President Lincoln in 1863 when seeking the Idaho territorial governorship. It took him only a few additional months to pass the California bar exam.[2]

Mullan brought to his new vocation considerable skill. His legal briefs flowed logically, their reasoning clear. Where some attorneys might take five pages to make a case, Mullan would use ten, peppering his arguments with historical references. Mullan had a fine legal mind, though not a particularly original one. His forte was to outwork everyone. He also brought a solid educational background and literary flare often lacking in lawyers practicing in the nineteenth century West.

Mullan's engineering background helped him land his first significant assignment. The city hired him to provide both legal and engineering expertise in a water rights case. "For this he received the sum of $8000," Rebecca proudly noted. Mullan soon retired his Chico debts.[3]

Another job provided Mullan an avenue into California's minimally regulated but potentially lucrative public lands arena. By 1868 he was managing agent of the California Immigration Association. In that year the association published a booklet, probably written by Mullan, instructing immigrants how to acquire public lands. Part of the association's intended audience was farm families, entitled to free homesteads. But there was another clientele. California contained vast tracks of public lands for sale, and "parties buying are not compelled to reside upon them." In short, California was ripe for land speculators. Mullan quickly learned the nuances of that trade. He would spend the next decade negotiating land deals that skirted both ethical and legal boundaries—a practice that brought him the prosperity he had long cherished, but at the cost of his carefully honed reputation. He advertised himself as both an attorney practicing land law and a real estate agent. He had "the largest practice of the kind in the state," Rebecca recalled, "enabling him in a short time...to buy a very handsome house...on Post Street."[4]

Mullan soon allied with a shrewd, if ethically challenged partner, Frederick A. Hyde. The Mullan and Hyde firm promoted itself as "Attorneys for Land Claimants, Dealer in Land Warrants and College Scrip, will perfect Titles and Procure Patents from the State and United States for all Kinds of Lands." The letterhead also noted their office's convenient location "next door to the U.S. Land Office." That favored position proved a great boon.[5]

Upon statehood, the federal government relinquished to California thousands of acres, intending land sales would support education and the construction of public buildings. The government planned that these lands be sold to small farmers. The system worked well in some states, but in California it devolved into money-grubbing chaos. The legislature did not establish an agency to oversee sales of public property until ten years after statehood, and hamstringed the chronically understaffed bureau with little authority even then. California surveyors in the post-Civil War era often colluded with land jobbers.[6]

Mullan and Hyde soon mastered this underregulated system, becoming "one of the largest land speculators in California." They cozied up so close to the state land agency that they gained access to records theoretically open only to state employees, a practice "of inestimable value in land jobbing operations." Sometimes the land office simply copied official documents free of charge for the law firm, despite legal mandates requiring payment of fees. "The business of Mullen & Hyde with the state land office became so voluminous," wrote historian Gerald Nash, "that the state…printed…envelopes with the firm's letterhead at the state's expense." At least that saved California money by eliminating the need to hand-address all the envelopes required to keep up with the firm's flood of demands.[7]

Mullan and Hyde perfected an even more efficient means of circumventing the system. They hired people to file for land on which they falsely swore they would reside. These dummy owners then transferred their holdings to "the notorious firm" of Mullan and Hyde. The legal partners purchased public land through surrogates at the state price of $1.25 an acre and sold it for considerably more. "The law never contemplated that the purchaser should be at the expense of one cent beyond [the state's]…price," recalled one former state land employee familiar with Mullan and Hyde. "Yet the land cost him nearly $5 an acre, of which the state school fund got but $1.25." Mullan and Hyde pocketed the remainder.[8]

Sometimes Mullan and Hyde literally stole land. Occasionally, applicants seeking title to land that had been set aside to benefit public schools found their preferred parcels already occupied. This happened frequently—and sometimes legitimately—in the chaotic California system. Some property supposedly "set aside" for public sale actually had lawful owners dating back to Mexican claims. In such cases, both federal and state laws allowed applicants to choose "in lieu" from other land in the public domain. Mullan and Hyde gained access to those applications at both the U.S. and state land offices. They copied in lieu selections and entered them onto their own dummy applications. When the legitimate in lieu occupant sought to obtain title to the property, they found it already taken. Fighting this rigged system nearly always proved fruitless for poor settlers who could ill-afford attorneys. Speculators often came away with free title to land they could then profitably sell. There was really no downside for the unscrupulous, for even if they lost a few cases, they had no investment in the process and plenty more dummy filings from which to profit. Mullan and Hyde became "the leading specialist in this dubious operation," blocking up thousands of acres of school in lieu lands.[9]

Mullan, operating independently of Hyde, also took advantage of the flawed system designed to support higher education. Under the Morrill Act of 1862, the federal government gave states vast tracks of property to support land-grant colleges. The University of California received 150,000 acres, which individuals could purchase using government-issued scrip. In an ideal system, colleges would hold onto this land for long-term investment. But legislators appropriated insufficient funds for the University, forcing fire sales of scrip lands. John Mullan was perfectly positioned to benefit. He had access to land records. He also understood the scrip system because he had clients who made scrip acquisitions. Mullan pounced, acquiring thousands of acres of scrip land, holding it until he could sell at a profit.[10]

Mullan had fabricated an interlocking system, prospering at every nexus. The California Immigration Association paid him to lure immigrants to the state, supposedly to acquire small parcels of public land and establish farms. That process in itself was complicated, and virtually necessitated the legal services of land agents like Mullan. Thus Mullan received fees from both the Immigration Association as well as from people it drew to the state. Yet few of the immigrants could actually purchase public land. Instead they found it had been gobbled up by speculators like Mullan and Hyde—eager to sell to them, but at a much higher price than the government. As a sidelight of their practice, Mullan and Hyde also represented large landowners against squatters, many of whom built on private property after being shut out of public lands. Albert Dibblee of San Francisco "on consulting Mullan & Hyde...[learned] with surprise and disgust" the "miserable outrage" that he needed to engage lawyers to establish property boundaries, or risk losing some of his land to squatters. So he hired Mullan and Hyde, who worked every nefarious angle of California land deals.[11]

Mullan became one of San Francisco's prominent lawyers and a Democratic Party activist. He supported William Irwin in his successful run for governor. He attended state Democratic conventions.[12]

California's Democrats and Republicans in 1875 strove to determine which could most vehemently oppose Chinese immigration. A Republican Party plank lamented the incoming "hordes of servile Chinese [who are] inimical to our advancement as a nation," and chastised Democrats for being soft on the issue. The Democrats responded, refusing to be outflanked in their hostility toward Asian aliens: "No Chinese immigration. It is so thoroughly obnoxious to our people and institutions, that its prohibition is imperatively demanded."[13]

Mullan marched in lockstep with his party. In September 1876 he wrote San Francisco Police Chief Henry Ellis requesting protection at a Democratic mass meeting where party members, including Mullan, unanimously demanded that Congress prohibit "the residence of Chinamen in the United States for other than those connected with commercial interests." A month later he represented his party in a debate with Republican attorney A.P. Van Duzer before an audience "numbering several hundred," including Governor Irwin, the lieutenant governor, and San Francisco's mayor. In his hour-and-fifteen-minute address, Mullan blasted Republicans for leniency toward Chinese. Republicans, he thundered, approved of the "right of the Mongolian to sever his allegiance from the Emperor of China, and become a citizen of the United States." America was "a white man's government," he argued. Its laws were to be administered "by white men, for the benefit of white men." If California did not oppose Chinese suffrage, it would be forced upon the state, just as "negro suffrage was forced upon the people of the south." While Van Duzer was "more logical in...tone and character than...Captain Mullan," he was no less rabid. Both fed a growing nativist movement that led to the San Francisco anti-Chinese riots nine months later, resulting in four deaths.[14]

There is no way to whitewash Mullan's racism. Even for his time and that place, his opinions were vile. They served a political purpose. Mullan proved himself a dutiful Democratic foot soldier and Governor Irwin would soon reward him.

The federal government assisted new states in efforts to fund public schools through the transfer of public lands. The income generated on the property benefited education. Beyond this the government had traditionally delivered 5 percent of proceeds from sales of federal lands within a state's borders to school aid. California rushed to statehood so quickly after the gold discovery that Congress neglected to enact this provision. In 1858 the California legislature "respectfully" sought payment of 5 percent of all federal land sales dating back to the time of statehood, but this feeble effort gained no traction in Congress.[15]

In 1878 Mullan brought the dearth of compensation to the attention of Governor Irwin, recommending the governor appoint "a competent party conversant with the subject matter" to secure "a…grant to California." The legislature passed a joint resolution authorizing the action. Not surprisingly, on November 1, Irwin selected Mullan as his "competent party."[16]

Mullan would work at his own expense, retaining 20 percent of any proceeds he might gain for the state. "Armed with this authority," Mullan wrote, "I proceeded from California to Washington City in the month of November, 1878."[17]

John and Rebecca held onto their San Francisco home for a few years, perhaps thinking they would return. But the Mullans, now numbering five with the San Francisco births of Emma, May, and Frank, would make Washington, D.C., their permanent home, though Mullan's future remained tied to the West, the location of his client base.

The exit from California closed the "notorious" chapter of Mullan's legal career. He labored diligently, honestly, and successfully as a D.C. attorney. For the next ten years he enjoyed the lifestyle he had long sought. But prosperity would be fleeting.

Mullan left California and his affiliation with Frederick Hyde at the right time. Eventually their shenanigans caught up with his former partner.

In December 1908—one year before Mullan's death—the *New York Times* announced the result of a scandalous trial: "Frederick A. Hyde of

San Francisco, recently convicted of conspiracy to defraud the United States of large tracks of land…was sentenced…to-day to pay a fine of $10,000 and to serve two years in the penitentiary at Moundsville, West Va., the maximum penalty under law."[18]

The trial, "one of the longest in the history of the District of Columbia," had cost the government dearly. Yet it was so consequential to halt western land grabs that Congress appropriated $60,000 to prosecute Hyde, the most odious of the malefactors.[19]

The government, after a five-year investigation, charged Hyde with engaging dummy applicants to acquire lieu land certificates that he redeemed to block up enormous aggregations of public school land. While prosecutors accused Hyde of this offense in several states, including California, the court found him guilty in only two—Oregon and Washington. The system that Mullan and Hyde refined had worked well in California, with its lax regulations. Hyde ran afoul of the law when he extended that model elsewhere.[20]

Hyde, "said to be a very wealthy man," appealed. Four years later, the United States Supreme Court upheld his conviction and Hyde went to federal prison.[21]

By the time of Hyde's 1908 conviction, John Mullan was old and sick. He left no record of his reaction to Hyde's predicament. But the renewed publicity about his former deeds with a criminal partner did Mullan no good. He was in the midst of his own legal struggle to recoup fees he believed California owed him. But he had enemies in the West determined to bring a comeuppance. His reputation as a shyster lawyer endured. Mullan was one of "the land sharks who have been the curse of this state," claimed a former clerk in the California Surveyor General's office, labeling him "the notorious Captain John Mullan." Hyde's case provided additional fodder for Mullan's critics.[22]

Mullan quit his land manipulation ways in time to escape the fate of his former partner. But he never outran his California notoriety. John Mullan—the dashing young army officer who had engineered a highway through an unforgiving wilderness, an explorer and road builder of renown—had finally found an occupation that did not lead to bankruptcy. But it did tarnish a carefully whetted reputation—one that never fully regained its former luster.

CHAPTER 14

※

Rise and Fall

WASHINGTON TERRITORIAL GOVERNOR Watson Squire wrote to
John Mullan in 1886: "The last legislative Assembly passed a
bill authorizing the Governor to appoint an agent for the collection of
certain claims alleged to be due from the U.S. government. I have had
several applicants for this position…but have concluded to tender it
to you." The choice made sense. No lawyer had more experience winning western claims against the federal government. Like the states of
California, Oregon, and Nevada, the Territory of Washington engaged
Mullan to make its case.[1]

Mullan recouped expenses incurred by states and territories during
Indian wars. He won federal reimbursement for the expenses of recruit-
ing, organizing, and paying volunteers who served in the Union Army
during the Civil War, and recovered tax overpayments levied on states
during that war. He sought indemnity for underpayments from sales of
public lands. He wrote bills for Congress; met with cabinet members;
drafted dozens of petitions and legal documents.[2]

The case with the greatest potential for compensation was a claim
by California seeking redress for 5 percent of the proceeds from sales
of federal lands within its borders. According to Mullan's contract, he
would receive 20 percent of all revenue he brought to California for this
and other claims, an arrangement similar to that he had with Nevada,
Oregon, and Washington. Most of the claims on which he worked garnered returns in the thousands of dollars. The 5 percent suit would eventually generate more than $1 million for California. Mullan's fee would
be more than $200,000 according to his contract. By the 1880s, Mullan
led the lifestyle he had always desired. But he overextended himself, for
he lived largely in anticipation of big payments, most of which never
materialized.[3]

❦

When Mullan moved to Washington, D.C., he leased a handsome house and office at 1310 Connecticut Avenue. His flowery letterhead, crowded with information Mullan thought pertinent, barely reserved room for messages. Below his new address it announced:

Washington City Offices
State Agent for California, Oregon, Nevada
Law, Land and Claim Offices
of
Captain John Mullan
Attorney and Counselor at Law
Land titles perfected, Patents procured, Cases argued before U.S. Supreme Court, and Claims of all Classes prosecuted before the Court of Claims, Congress, National and International Commissions, and the Executive Departments of the United States at Washington, D.C.[4]

The Mullans furnished their house with European finery—much acquired by Rebecca during the two years she and the children spent abroad in the 1880s. It featured Venetian lamps, oil paintings, lace curtains, bronze statues, Italian vases, Bellagio blankets, Swiss curtains. John and Rebecca hosted parties and receptions, employed two domestic servants, and hobnobbed with the upper echelons of Washington society.[5]

So it was not surprising when John received an invitation in 1883 to join western governors, industrial tycoons, foreign dignitaries, cabinet officers, and former president Ulysses Grant on an excursion to the West. Among all those notables, none had greater credentials than John Mullan to participate in ceremonies commemorating completion of the Northern Pacific Railroad. He had helped to chart its course. On September 8 the dignitaries gathered in a grassy meadow in western Montana, participants in an event "so pretentious, so glittering in spangled brilliance that the whole world would have to pay attention."[6]

Of the 2,500 observers that day, most had come by horse and carriage from Helena. But 332—including Mullan—arrived as Northern Pacific President Henry Villard's special guests. They had ridden cross country in private cars on four trains, traveling at the company's expense. They made celebratory stops in communities along the way. Villard hoped, erringly as it turned out, that the townspeople's boisterous enthusiasm would entice his invited entrepreneurs to invest in his struggling company. Few put money into the railroad, but Villard's guests witnessed elaborate exhibits of mine specimens, met Chief Sitting Bull and watched a Crow war dance, and toured demonstration farms. The rail cars finally convened at the ceremonial last spike grounds on that grassy field, where workmen had constructed a platform. The Fifth U.S. Infantry band performed amidst flags and banners.

None of the speakers that day mentioned John Mullan. Villard welcomed the guests, followed by cabinet members, governors, ambassadors, and a senator. Only when "loud cries for Gen. Grant" brought the former president forward did anyone allude to that time, long before, when Stevens and Mullan had laid the path for this transcontinental route. Grant jokingly told the crowd that he deserved credit for the day, for he had been serving at Fort Vancouver during Stevens's expedition and helped provision that party. He did not note Mullan's much more critical role in those events.

After all the speeches, "300 men with brawny arms" took thirteen minutes to ceremoniously lay the last 1,200 yards of track. At 10:00 p.m. the trains departed. At long last, the old Oregon Country had been connected to the East by rail.[7]

The last spike ritual put Mullan in a reflective mood. Frank Worden, one of the founders of Missoula and a former Mullan Road crew member, wrote to him in advance of the event. Mullan replied with a letter made public nearly thirty years later, full of his typical braggadocio, but also the vision that had sustained him during those formidable road building days:

> You say: "Just to think that 20 odd years ago, you and I were struggling through Hell Gate canyon, never dreaming of making the trip in Pullman sleepers." Now, sir, permit me to say that if there was ever any conviction firmly lodged in my mind, it was the conviction that the day was coming when a line of Pullman sleepers would cross down through Hell Gate canyon....It was for that purpose that our surveys were made and our wagon-road construction was conceived and, under my direction, were executed and, while there were plenty of persons who, 25 or 30 years ago, conceived that I had a mania on wagon roads and railroads, yet I thought I could see in the distance, coursing across

the plains from Minnesota to Oregon...through the Mullan pass... this same line of Pullman sleepers...so that now...you can well imagine that my heart wells up with gladness at seeing realized one of the germs of my life and fulfillment of so many years of hard and patient toil in the mountains, where I was so largely a pioneer, 30 years ago.[8]

Mullan had hit upon a theme to which he would frequently return. In 1884 he wrote to an Idaho newspaper editor:

I am...not surprised to see today as I saw last September, when going out to assist in driving the last spike on the N.P. railway, countless herds of stock grazing...the entire road dotted with towns and villages...nor to know that the great waters of the Coeur d'Alene river and lake are being ploughed by steamers...because all these were foreseen and officially reported by me thirty years ago.[9]

By 1889 he had refined the sentiment. In an interview with a Tacoma newspaper that year he provided what would become his most-repeated quotation:

Night after night, I have laid out in the unbeaten forests, or on the pathless prairies with no bed but a few pine leaves, with no pillow but my saddle, and in my imagination heard the whistle of the engine, the whirr of the machinery, the paddle of the steamboat wheels....In my enthusiasm I saw the country thickly populated, thousands pouring over the borders to make homes in this far western land.[10]

Both Mullan's pride and his foresight are encased in this poetic quote, often cited as an example of the rapid change that Mullan helped foment. But there is also melancholy here, a proud man holding fast to evanescent glory. For by the time of the Tacoma interview, his career was reeling downhill. States were reneging on payments for his services, and Mullan had been booted from his most prestigious honorary position.

When serving at Fort Vancouver, Ulysses Grant wrote a letter to his wife. She worried about her husband residing among Indians. Grant replied in March 1853 in a manner most tolerant for that time: "You charge me to be cautious about riding out alone lest the Indians should get me. Those about here are the most harmless people you ever saw. It really is my opinion that the whole race would be harmless and peaceable if they were not put upon by the whites."[11]

On another March day, sixteen years later, newly elected President Grant devoted a remarkably progressive portion of his inaugural address to Indians, calling for their "civilization and ultimate citizenship." A man who made his reputation as a warrior now sought peace. During his administration, the army did fight more than two hundred battles in America's long Indian wars. Yet what became known as Grant's Peace Policy was instrumental in gradually changing the conscience of a nation. Even after George Custer's inglorious defeat near the end of Grant's presidency, an event leading to renewed calls to let "the army... finish the job on the Indians," the adherents of Grant's policy helped stifle calls for annihilation. As John Mullan rode west with the former president in Henry Villard's lavishly appointed trains in 1883, the two army veterans might well have discussed the Peace Policy, for Mullan knew by then that he would soon be appointed to a post in which he hoped to help accomplish one of Grant's primary intents.[12]

A component of Grant's policy promoted Indian education. Grant disdained corrupt Indian agents. "I determined to give all the agencies to such religious denomination as had heretofore established missionaries among the Indians," Grant informed Congress in 1870. Religious groups would deliver the services—particularly education—that civil authorities had botched.[13]

Grant's policy precipitated a scramble among religious denominations to provide services on reservations—in return for lucrative federal subsidies. Catholics were overwhelmed by anti-Catholic prejudice and Protestants' sophisticated lobbying. Given their historical record of missionary activity, Catholic dioceses had anticipated winning federal awards to provide schools at thirty-eight of the nation's seventy-three reservations. But when the new policy took shape, only seven came under their purview.[14]

Catholics objected, but found no relief. So in 1872 the bishops of Oregon and the Territory of Washington sent Father Jean Baptiste Brouillet to Washington to encourage more equitable representation. Brouillet had arrived in the Northwest in 1847 at a mission in Walla Walla. Over the years he served at a variety of posts. No one knew Northwest Indians better, and Brouillet had experience lobbying on behalf of Catholic missions in the capital. He was a natural choice to argue the Catholic case. Even so, Brouillet soon recognized the need for an experienced lay person with time and skill to help promote the Catholic cause. He convinced the church hierarchy in 1873 to appoint Charles Ewing, a Washington, D.C. attorney, as Commissioner of Catholic Indian Missions.[15]

General Ewing, a Catholic, brought many assets to his new task. A Civil War hero, he had an outstanding reputation as a lawyer. His father, Thomas, had been a United States Senator and member of two presidential cabinets; the family commanded respect. Thomas Ewing had also raised a young orphan by the name of William Tecumseh Sherman, who would one day marry Thomas's daughter, Ellen. Thus Charles Ewing was both the foster brother and brother-in-law of the man closest to President Grant, guaranteeing him access to the highest echelons of government. No person was more passionate about Catholic Indian schools than Ellen Ewing Sherman. By retaining Charles, the bishops had actually engaged a powerful brother-sister team.[16]

But the job overwhelmed even the dedicated Charles Ewing. In 1874 Brouillet urged the church to provide him help. It established a central agency in Washington, later known as the Bureau of Catholic Indian Missions, supervised by the archbishop of Baltimore. Brouillet became its first director. The bureau would establish Indian schools and raise funds for Catholic missions. Brouillet and Ewing forged an effective team. By 1882 Catholics operated seventeen Indian boarding schools.[17]

President Chester Arthur terminated the Peace Policy in 1882. But the government continued to fund efforts of religious orders to "Americanize" Indians, and the Bureau of Catholic Indian Missions continued promoting the education of Native Americans. John Mullan would soon be at the center of that effort.[18]

Forty-eight-year-old Charles Ewing died suddenly in June 1883, leaving his sister Ellen Sherman "desolate at heart." For ten years he had borne the bulk of the Catholic Bureau's work. The bureau would miss the man whose "conscientious and faithful labor in behalf of the religious rights and educational interest of the Indians" had so advanced the cause of both the bureau and Indian education.[19]

Father Brouillet immediately championed John Mullan as Ewing's successor. "It will be a great pleasure…to have you…with me as one of my associates in this work," Brouillet wrote in July 1883. "We are old acquaintances."[20]

The bureau sought an attorney, preferably Catholic, who knew his way around the federal bureaucracy. No Washington lawyer better suited its needs. Mullan had already done legal work for the bureau and had a long association with Jesuits. "I have ever enjoyed their kind cooperation and zealous support," he had written in the 1860s. Jesuits returned the praise. Catholic missionaries "keep your name in benediction," Father Pierre-Jean DeSmet once wrote Mullan. Seconded Father Adrian Hoecken of St. Ignatius Mission, "I can only pray, poor missionary that I am, that the Lord may repay [Mullan's] generosity and kindness a hundredfold in blessings of time and eternity."[21]

Mullan had long advocated education as the only way "to save any portion of the Indian tribes." And he had known Brouillet for more than twenty years. In September 1883, Brouillet requested that the archbishop of Baltimore appoint Mullan to the bureau, which he did the following month.[22]

By then, Brouillet was seriously ill, suffering the effects of a trip to an Indian school in Dakota the previous winter. Caught in a blizzard with temperatures below zero, he never fully recovered and died early in 1884. Possibly the old friends Mullan and Brouillet could have advanced the progress initiated by Brouillet and Ewing. But in May, James Gibbons, archbishop of Baltimore, appointed Father Joseph Stephan to replace Brouillet. It proved an ill-fated choice for Mullan, who never formed an effective bond with the new director.[23]

Mullan worked diligently for the bureau. When he became a commissioner, it operated eighteen boarding schools, teaching fewer than five hundred students. Three years later, it administered twenty-seven, teaching nearly fourteen hundred. Still, the bureau was underfunded, and Mullan spent much of his time lobbying on its behalf with members of Congress and the Interior Department "for an increased per capita compensation for our schools."[24]

During Mullan's tenure, largely due to his efforts, the government's annual student allotment rose from $39,000 to $149,000. The federal government mandated that its funds be used exclusively for education. The bureau itself operated on a shoestring. Its total annual administrative budget amounted to a little more than $3,000, mostly used to pay the director and secretary; the other three commissioners, including Mullan, served gratuitously. "The Bureau is without the means necessary to further carry out its proper operations," Mullan wrote in one fundraising appeal to wealthy Catholics. To encourage donations, Mullan spearheaded publication of a book noting the bureau's accomplishments and coordinated an article in the *Catholic World* praising its work. He arranged for free mailing of bureau letters and gave speeches soliciting donations.[25]

Mullan became president of the bureau shortly after his appointment. He attended nearly every weekly meeting, hosting many in his Connecticut Avenue home. At his own expense, he spent months on the road visiting mission schools. He performed his volunteer tasks admirably.[26]

Yet from the beginning of their tenure together, Mullan and Joseph Stephan clashed. Charles Lusk, who served with both men, noted that Stephan's "zeal for the Indians was unbounded and his courage great," but that his "zeal might have been tempered with greater discretion." Stephan and Mullan, equally obstinate, proved a toxic mix.[27]

A few months after his appointment as director, Stephan convinced the bishops to rescind the authority of lay commissioners like Mullan from transacting business with the Department of Interior, giving all such jurisdiction to Stephan, a man much less experienced than Mullan. Mullan objected and the bishops reinstated his authorization.[28]

Stephan detested that interference. The fragile relationship between the two completely ruptured in September 1886. That month, at a meeting Stephan did not attend, Mullan introduced a resolution that his other commissioners approved. Prior to his appointment to the bureau, Stephan had served under Bishop Martin Marty in Dakota Territory. Marty's advocacy proved instrumental in Stephan's selection to the bureau. Mullan's resolution sought an investigation into "whether the total sums donated" to Marty's Rosebud Agency school "have been expended, and if not, where the unexpended balance is deposited and in whose name." Mullan must have caught a scent of impropriety, for he sent a copy of the resolution to his wife, then in Paris, asking her to forward it to the French benefactor who had donated the money. Mullan's ardor got the better of common sense. The Rosebud school received no federal funds and did not come under the bureau's purview. Stephan exploded, claiming the resolution had been "introduced for the purpose of injuring me personally." The commissioners rescinded the recommendation in December, but Mullan had effectively sealed his fate.[29]

Bishop Marty fired a letter to Archbishop Gibbons demanding Mullan's removal from the bureau. He spewed a profusion of accusations. Mullan had attempted "to destroy the work of Father Brouillet," cheated Indians out of land, tried to abscond with $10,000 of the bureau's money. Unfocused rant, those charges held no truth. But Mullan had challenged Marty's ethics and tarnished his relationship with a major donor, allegations Mullan could not defend—though he tried. In typical fashion, Mullan dashed off a thirty-one page rebuttal. He expertly turned aside the nonsense—particularly accusations that he had tried to destroy Brouillet and embezzle money. But when attempting to deflect the crux of Marty's blast, he could only whimper. He reminded Archbishop Gibbons that other bureau commissioners had approved the resolution, and questioned why Marty's diatribe was "aimed solely at me." Could it have been because Mullan composed and introduced the document? To the most damning charge of requesting Rebecca to furtively deliver the resolution to the French donor, he meekly responded, "I had good and pure and sufficient reasons which if needed…I can…disclose and which I only refrain from doing here…lest I might touch upon a terrain it were better…to leave untouched."[30]

The bishops had no intention of hearing Mullan's full disclosure; he had initiated a fight he could not win. They stood with Marty and Stephan; they could easily replace a lay attorney. But Mullan refused to resign. At a meeting in March 1887, Stephan informed the commissioners that "one of the members of the Bureau had proved unfaithful to his duties, whereupon his resignation was requested, which request this member declined to comply with." Mullan protested, but Stephan simply adjourned the meeting. When the bureau next met in July, it operated under new bylaws, with Mullan no longer a commissioner. Longtime bureau treasurer Charles Jones resigned in protest. But the Bureau of Catholic Indian Missions had effectively ousted John Mullan.[31]

For the devoutly Catholic Mullan, the dismissal was excruciating. Still, he continued to hold his lucrative legal practice. Money can salve a battered ego. But, though he did not yet know it, John Mullan's finances were about to freefall. He would soon become the subject of a vitriolic campaign that would shatter both his reputation and his livelihood.

🌱

Mullan's first glint of an assignment gone sour came in the spring of 1886. Former California Governor George Perkins sent a letter attempting to distance himself from Mullan in a controversy mounting in the California press. Perkins, a Republican, had succeeded William Irwin, the governor who first named Mullan as state counsel, and had reappointed Mullan to that position. Now he had doubts. "I am charged with having frittered away the school money of California in having commissioned you to represent the state," the governor wrote. "I fear that I have made a mistake in allowing you so large a commission....[I now must] shield myself." He should not have granted Mullan "a commission of 20% out of all amounts collected!" The letter shocked Mullan. But soon the governor's backpeddling seemed mild. The California press was about to excoriate him "for what the boys call 'a fat racket.'"[32]

Three successive governors—Democrat Irwin, Republican Perkins, and Democrat George Stoneman—had appointed Mullan state counsel, Stoneman's praise in doing so being typical: "The intelligence and fidelity displayed by Captain Mullan fully reflect the confidence reposed in him by his selection for this special work and I therefore recommend that the Legislature confirm the executive appointment." Inevitably, the legislature ratified the decisions, resolving to pay Mullan "20 per cent of each of the sums...that may be by him collected from the United States."[33]

In Washington Mullan toiled earnestly and successfully, gaining for California—and his other state clients—small sums of money, from which he parceled his fee. But the California 5 percent case had the potential for serious remuneration for both California and Mullan. Mullan's work had largely gone unnoticed in the press, but the probability of substantial commissions led to publicity and to his harassment, spearheaded by former California Surveyor General Robert Gardner who, in 1886, initiated a twenty-year campaign to smear Mullan. He alleged the state was "the subject of insidious attack" by the greedy captain. For two years, California newspapers carried Gardner's accusations. When Republican Lieutenant Governor Robert Waterman became governor in 1887 upon the death of Democrat Washington Bartlett, he promptly revoked Mullan's appointment. "I do not recognize your authority to act in behalf of California," he wrote Mullan in early 1888, prompting

Mullan's transcontinental train trip to meet with the governor, and commencing a legal battle destined to persist the rest of Mullan's life.[34]

The reasons for Gardner's vitriolic campaign remain a mystery. He served as state surveyor general from 1871 to 1875, the land grab era that had so benefitted Mullan and Hyde. Gardner was hardly above controversy. The state sued him for absconding with $40,000 in public funds. After "perhaps the most controversial [term] of all the Surveyors General of California," the disgraced Gardner left office. But in 1886 he ran again for surveyor general, the same year he began crusading against Mullan. It could have initially been a political tactic, a way of gaining publicity. Gardner lost that election, but not his ardor for denigrating Mullan. He found a confederate in Waterman.[35]

Gardner claimed Mullan would have never received the appointments had he honestly stated the nature of the legal work involved and the size of his potential claims. Mullan convinced governors and legislators that the cases involved issues so intricate they required constant vigilance, a claim Gardner challenged. When it became clear that Mullan's commissions might total hundreds of thousands of dollars, Gardner struck. "In what terms can we fitly characterize a scheme which makes it possible for one man by questionable methods to secure $251,021.27 as a fee for pretended services," Gardner railed. He asserted that the legislative resolutions under which Mullan operated had no legal power: "His audacity is equaled only by his success in securing appointments made without authority of law."[36]

Mullan responded typically. He wrote a 580-page book, meticulously detailing the legal authority for his work and exhaustively refuting charges against him. He reminded readers that he had moved to the nation's capital and undertaken the various cases "at my own expense." He noted the tedious nature of the work, alleging it could have been successfully executed only by someone willing to devote years of toil. And, also typical for Mullan, he considered his future reputation. He wrote, he said, "especially for the purpose of having an authentic record of the history" of his efforts.[37]

"I have waded through" the book, responded Gardner. "It was a clear waste of time, money and the raw material to print." Gardner and his allies centered their opposition to Mullan on two arguments. He had no legal authority to act on behalf of California, and the results could have been accomplished just as effectively by the state's congressional delegation—at no expense.[38]

Mullan's authority came from joint legislative resolutions. But Gardner and the Republicans argued those had no legal validity. Resolutions "are without any force or effect whatever," Gardner wrote, "as the Constitution declares...that 'no law shall be passed except by bill.'" Beyond this, Republicans claimed that Mullan really accomplished nothing. Congress would have acted on California's behalf anyway. As Senator Leland Stanford stated, "The services of Captain John Mullan are in no wise necessary for the passage of any of these bills."[39]

The Republican press piled on, suddenly outraged over "the large sums of money that will be diverted from the State Treasury...for supposed services." Those concerns had not surfaced during the years Mullan labored on cases returning small sums. The size of potential payouts changed all that. The federal money Mullan attained for California was earmarked for education. Republicans now depicted Mullan as a money grubber depriving poor school children of books, desks, and teachers. The "Public School Fund...is the subject of insidious attack" from Mullan's "unlawful and unconstitutional" actions, they railed.[40]

Mullan had supporters. Democratic Senator George Hearst countered the arguments of Stanford in a letter to Mullan:

> It gives me great pleasure to bear witness to your persistent diligence, fidelity, and usefulness in presenting and urging the settlement between the U.S. and the State of California of all unpaid claims due California....
>
> You have performed a task which could not be expected from a Representative in Congress, and which would be impossible for him to perform.[41]

Mullan alleged that the governor had no authority to dismiss him. He derived his employment from the legislature, which had approved various governors' appointments. Mullan wanted the legislative branch to determine his fate. There he had advocates and a salient argument—the state could lose a large amount of money if it fired Mullan. "The Governor has been led into defeating the State out of 80 cents to defeat Mullan out of 20 cents," stated assemblyman M.D. Hyde, brother of Mullan's former law partner. "It looks to me like cutting off the nose to spite the face.[42]

"In view of the importance and amount of the unpaid claims," the legislature in 1889 appointed a seven-man committee to investigate the Mullan affair. It proved a victory for Mullan. "John Mullan has actively, diligently and faithfully performed all the duties devolving upon him," the committee found. "Justice, as well as the honor and good faith of this State, demands that John Mullan…should be fully paid all the commissions which he has already earned." The assembly unanimously accepted the committee's recommendations, and only seven senators dissented when the upper house voted.[43]

But Mullan's victory was fleeting, his difficulties with California just beginning. The legislature agreed to pay Mullan "all the commissions which he has already earned." Deciphering that language engulfed Mullan in a legal battle still unresolved at his death.

The United States mandated that states bill the federal government by 1874 for reimbursement of expenses incurred organizing Civil War volunteers. California missed that deadline, and would have received no restitution except for Mullan, who pressed the claim anyhow. Remarkably Mullan won, and the federal government paid California $228,000. Mullan's work occurred before the legislative action of 1889. But the federal check arrived after that decision. When Mullan presented his claim for $45,600, California balked.[44]

Mullan sued. The case made it to the state supreme court in 1896, where Mullan lost. The court ruled that legislative resolutions, like the ones under which Mullan operated, held no force of law. The state owed Mullan no money, regardless of whether his work occurred before or after the 1889 legislative action.[45]

Unsuccessful legally, Mullan sought a political solution. He received more testimonials, including one from California Republican Congressman Grove Johnson: "Our state ou[gh]t to be very grateful to Captain Mullan. At present he is reaping the reward meted out usually to persons who labor for the state, viz: suspicion and envy." In 1897 and 1899 the California legislature passed bills authorizing payment to Mullan; governors vetoed them.[46]

By the time of Republican Governor Henry Gage's 1899 veto, Mullan suffered from a lingering illness from which he would never recover.

"I am weak as a kitten and thin as a rail," he wrote to his children. "I have fallen off to a shadow of my former self." Unable to press his own case, Mullan's appeals went nowhere. In 1905 he asked his oldest daughter Emma to move to California to lobby on his behalf.[47]

Emma proved as energetic as her father. Still, she faced a daunting task. "I have known Captain John Mullan for the past forty years, and have always believed he had a just claim," former California Surveyor General Theodore Reichert wrote her. "I regret to say that most of the men that stood by your father...[have] passed away." But Emma persevered. "Your daughter...is the boss lobbyist of the world," Grove Johnson wrote a proud Mullan in 1906.[48]

A key ally enhanced Emma's effectiveness. When appearing before the legislature in 1905, she met State Senator George Russell Lukens, who "not only helped her...but did a little lobbying on his own account by which he succeeded in winning a bride." Together, Senator and Mrs. Lukens pursued the Mullan case.[49]

The 1905 legislature again passed a bill to pay Mullan $45,000. Republican Governor George Pardee faced a difficult choice. The bill had vocal adherents and opponents. Any decision regarding the legislation would be controversial. In a time-honored tradition, Pardee compromised. He signed the bill, but agreed to pay Mullan only $25,000, a concession with little appeal to anyone. Mullan's old nemesis, former Surveyor General Robert Gardner, railed against Pardee: "The passage of this iniquitous measure, with your hasty and ill-advised approval, after so many years of pernicious activity...by Mullan...proves that the forces of corruption never sleep." The San Francisco *Chronicle* claimed the action cost Pardee his party's nomination in 1906.[50]

At first Emma accepted Pardee's offer, having been advised by California's deputy controller "to agree to the compromise rather than lose it." The payment would come in two installments. Emma redeemed the first check for $23,000. But when the second arrived, she refused it and once again pursued legal action seeking full compensation.[51]

The courts sided with Emma, finding the governor had no authority to simultaneously sign a bill and tinker with its contents. The legislature had authorized full payment; Governor Pardee signed the act; the Mullans were due $45,000. Finally in 1910—after John had died—the State of California paid Mullan's children the final installment on the $45,000 commission, after two decades of legal and political contention.[52]

John Mullan had expected much more. His work to recoup 5 percent of sales of federal lands in California always held the greatest opportunity for compensation. By 1908, the U.S. Treasury Department had paid California more than $1 million on those claims. According to terms of Mullan's appointment, he believed he was due more than $200,000. He encouraged Emma and Senator Lukens to continue the legal struggle: "It worries me a good deal to think that I shall be robbed of what I have worked for so earnestly and so long, because it would go to you children in the case of my death," he wrote Emma.[53]

But California would prevail this time. The state retreated to its old argument: Mullan had not been legally appointed; therefore the state owed him nothing. California drew a distinction between the Civil War claims and the 5 percent issue, an ethically questionable stance. But Emma and Lukens were exhausted; indeed, both would die while continuing the struggle. With their deaths, the long legal strife between the Mullans and California finally ceased.

Officials in other states watched the California proceedings with interest, sensing an opportunity to renege on old agreements. With the exception of the 5 percent case, Mullan labored on essentially the same causes for Oregon and Nevada as he did California, mostly claims for reimbursement of expenses incurred during the Indian conflicts and Civil War. Like California, the arrangement worked well while Mullan recouped small amounts. But as he attained success and commissions loomed large, Oregon and Nevada followed California's lead. "It seems the greed of 'Capt.' Mullan can never be satisfied," protested a former Oregon state senator in 1889, inviting residents to encourage Oregon's leaders to halt "this leech of the public crib," just as had California. In 1894 as the federal government was set to reimburse Nevada $400,000 and Oregon $350,000, the states' congressional delegations maneuvered to withhold payment from Mullan. They drafted legislation requiring the Treasury Department to send funds directly to the states. Allowing Nevada and Oregon to deal with Mullan as they saw fit would mean no compensation for him.[54]

The cases dawdled on. Finally, in 1905, Mullan decided "it would be wise for Emma to go to Oregon." She partially succeeded in winning recompense. Oregon agreed to pay Mullan $9,465. Though only a fraction of what he believed he deserved, Mullan basked in praise for Emma. "Congratulations," telegraphed a Portland friend, "for possessing such a magnificent daughter." [55]

❦

There were those, particularly in California, who relished Mullan's reversals—just desserts, they believed, for his nefarious land dealings years earlier. But despite obvious personal foibles, Mullan was a diligent and methodical worker on the states' behalf. Notwithstanding melodramatic rants about robbing poor school children, or wishful assessments that states' elected officials could have won federal payments without Mullan's persistence, the evidence argues otherwise. Numerous representatives in Congress, both Republican and Democrat, testified to the critical nature of Mullan's work. They also noted that their schedules did not permit the vigilance required—over many years—to win settlements. As Mullan accurately noted, no congressman had "the time and few even the disposition" to carry out such painstaking work. Their relatively short terms prevented successful attention to legal cases that spanned decades. "To-day there is not a single member in our California delegation...who was in Congress at the time I took hold of these several claims," Mullan wrote—just eight years after his initial appointment. Only Mullan's bulldogged determination enabled states to win the federal claims. Despite attempts to justify their rebuff of Mullan, essentially state officials entered into contracts they did not honor. [56]

"Every laborer is worthy of his hire, of which he should not be defrauded," wrote former Oregon Republican Governor Z.F. Moody in 1907, chastising the legislature for refusing Mullan his fee. "Captain Mullan in good faith entered into a contract with the State, under which he unquestionably performed valuable service and recovered to Oregon...large sums of money, at his own expense,...the State having enjoyed the benefit thereof these many years." John Mullan deserved better by the states he ably served. [57]

CHAPTER 15

Dear Papa

T HE NEWS SPREAD ACROSS THE COUNTRY, a human interest story
ripe for society pages in 1905. In the shadow of the British embassy,
along "the sacred precincts of Dupont circle" in Washington, D.C., two
young society women, "belles of many dances given in the most elegant
ballrooms in the city," had opened a laundry. How charming. They were
"not compelled to go into business. Their father...accumulated a comfortable fortune in California." They simply wanted to try something
new, a whimsical "labor of love." The women had "acquired the art of
laundering fine laces, tapestries and exquisite fabrics which it is unsafe
to entrust to the colored lady who comes to your back door." These
"plucky girls" showed abundant "feminine independence," then so much
in vogue.[1]

But beneath this sugary story that briefly titillated America's newspaper readers lay a contrary reality. Emma and May Mullan started the
DeSales Hand Laundry not on a capricious lark, but because their family was broke. Being a laundress held no glamorous allure for Emma. As
she wrote to her aunt, both she and May despised the need "to take in
washing." Family finances dictated their course.[2]

John Mullan appreciated the efforts of his "plucky" daughters. Still,
a 1905 newspaper headline about their business hurt a proud man who
had spent his life scaling social ladders. "Washington's Smart Set Sniffs
at Mullans Venture," blared the stinging banner. But any money Mullan's daughters brought to the family coffers would help. John Mullan
was destitute, reduced to begging. In 1905 he wrote to "My Dear William" King, a long-time legal associate:

> I have waited with great patience for a satisfactory reply to my letter
> requesting an advance of $250.00 to be repaid from the first appropri-
> ation [we receive] in reference to any of our joint cases....I know that

> you are not in the business of advancing money, but I assumed that under all the circumstances of my case & as my request was modest... that you would do it unhesitatingly as a personal favor to me. I would not have written had I not needed the amount asked for, & I beg to say that the circumstances are now just the same as at the date when I wrote you.

Four years later, John Mullan died, possessing "no real or personal property." The dreams of John and Rebecca so many years earlier, when they had ventured across a nation to stake claims to prosperity in the West, had completely shattered.[3]

John Mullan's finances did not collapse overnight. While battling states for his commissions, Mullan retained other legal business. He took on cases for individuals, "the friend and defender of the miner and farmer before the interior department." He did considerable work for Northwest Jesuit missions. Such employment had always been a sidelight, but it paid some bills. Into the 1890s, living beyond their means in anticipation of winning suits against various states, the Mullans kept a standing among Washington's socialites. Rebecca, with Mrs. Henry Cabot Lodge, Mrs. George Westinghouse, and other grande dames, served as a patron of Washington's Glee, Banjo, and Mandolin Club. In 1897 a Washington newspaper reported that "Capt. and Mrs. John Mullan and the Misses Mullan" attended the annual Thanksgiving Tea of the Alibi Club, "a brilliant gathering" that also included families of the British and Swiss embassies. John served a term as secretary of the Goodwill Pleasure Club. Two servants, Paul and Anne, lived with the family. John's old home town of Annapolis, where his sisters retained the family house, selected him to chair its delegation to the National River and Harbor Congress.[4]

Beneath this veneer lay economic reality. Rebecca proudly wrote in 1892 that "John says he will never accept a [military] pension." But the previous year, increasingly desperate for any revenue, John had unsuccessfully applied for money he claimed the War Department had underpaid him while in the army.[5]

While Rebecca surely understood the family's financial predicament, John's sisters Annie and Virginia seemed oblivious. John had treated his sisters generously when he could. When their mother died, he surrendered to them his portion of her estate. He later transferred to them his interest in their brother Ferdinand's estate; at one point he provided them more than $10,000 and throughout his life he furnished free legal services. The sisters had become accustomed to such gratuity. When circumstances prevented further beneficence, they sulked.[6]

Having read that John was to receive part of his long-anticipated commission from Oregon, Annie wrote in 1907: "Now John I think it is justice to us to know something in regard to...the Oregon money you promised us....It is now the 10th of July and still no money has been sent us." John snapped back that he had already spent the Oregon money "to cancel many back debts of long standing," and continued, "I am in no position financially to make free gifts....You seem to have completely overlooked all my acts of generosity to you and Virginia, to whom I gave freely and lavishly whenever I had it to give."[7]

Annie suspected Mullan's daughters had written the letter. John would have never penned such an "impertinent" response she angrily wrote Emma and May. "Such a letter never should have been written to me." Emma's reply was so livid the handwriting is barely decipherable: "You must know that Papa has but one duty in the world and that is to those children he brought into the world and he would slip up indeed if he [did]...not help us when he had the means—in place of giving his two sisters several thousands of dollars....Did you ever put your hand in your pocket...to spend anything for him?"[8]

In the midst of this family fracas, John wrote a new will. He reminded his sisters that he had surrendered to them his interest in their mother's estate. He now had second thoughts. Given "the great love, admiration and gratitude" which his sisters bore for him, he stated his "earnest desire" that they bequeath his former share of the estate, including "the family heirlooms," to his three children.[9]

There is no indication that Annie and Virginia left anything to Mullan's children, but relations between John and his sisters improved in John's last years. He visited them as frequently as his health allowed, and both are buried in the family plot in an Annapolis cemetery near John. Absent from that same plot is Rebecca.

John Mullan spent a long life writing reports, legal documents, and professional letters. Portions of his personality emerge from those records. He was proud, meticulous, determined. Still, one wishes for more personal correspondence. Particularly absent is any communication between John and Rebecca. She, even more so than John, remains a skeleton in search of flesh. In all the time the couple spent apart—while John traveled west for the Catholic Bureau, when Rebecca vacationed in Europe—they must have corresponded. But what they wrote is frustratingly lacking in the preserved annals of their lives.

Virtually all we know of Rebecca comes from two documents. One is the diary of a love-struck teenager devoted to the army lieutenant she has just seen off to the far West. The other, an adulatory reminiscence penned as a fifty-four-year-old, was written from the perspective of a mother determined to rescue for her children the reputation of their father.

We know Rebecca was shy. We know she bore five children, two of whom died very young. We know she at one time deeply loved John, and there is no reason to assume their shared love did not continue throughout their long marriage. We know she lived modestly most of her life, though, with John, she had a few years of mostly perceived prosperity. Did she, like her husband, long for greater wealth and social prominence? We cannot tell from this vantage.

We also know that, before she died on September 4, 1898, she chose to be interred in the Williamson family crypt at Bonnie Brae Cemetery in Baltimore. Surely she knew of John's intention to be buried near his parents in Annapolis. Just why these two people, by all accounts faithful through thirty-five years of marriage, chose separation at death is a matter for conjecture. About all we can conclude is that for each, devotion to their birth families bested allegiance to one another when it came time for this end-of-life decision.[10]

❧

By the time of Rebecca's death, John found himself "quite an invalid." He had lost use of his left arm, perhaps because of a stroke. His penmanship, always atrocious, descended into nearly indecipherable loops and scrawls. He went days without sleep and endured long periods unable to eat solid foods. He spent much of 1898 and 1899 under the care of a nurse who rubbed various liniments on his useless arm. Letters to his children, signed "Affectionately Papa" in response to their inevitable "Dear Papa," were filled with details of various ailments and anguish over finances.[11]

Mullan spent most of his last ten years with his daughters in Washington. "I have depended solely on Emma and May for my comforts," he wrote in 1907, "and must look to them for the same in the future." But he traveled to his beloved Annapolis as frequently as his health permitted, where his sisters cared for him. At times the trips worried his daughters. But John remained obstinate, even in his decline. "I did not say anything about your Father going to Annapolis as I knew you did not want him to go," a cousin wrote Emma in 1907 while she was in California. "You ask why May and I let him go? Could we stop the wind from blowing or the rain from falling? We had just about the same amount of influence to prevent your dear Papa from his visit."[12]

He exerted himself to the extent his ailments allowed. Once he journeyed to Annapolis to witness a visiting armada of twenty ships. "It was a grand picture, such as I never saw before or never expect to see again," he informed his daughters in 1905—his letters now typed by a neighbor. A few months later, Emma sent him a suit to wear to a concert in the governor's home. When in Washington he worked in his Connecticut Avenue office, and loved to read. "The Captain is very well but you can hardly see him for newspapers and letters," a friend wrote to Emma.[13]

Though his finances and health had soured, Mullan retained a fierce pride—and a strong recollection of times when his family had hobnobbed with Washington's elites. His son Frank's 1903 decision to marry beneath that social status rocked their relationship. Despite Frank's assurances that his new wife, Mary Knapp, was their "social equal in every respect," John never believed it. Knapp was a divorcée, anathema to Mullan's strongly held Catholic beliefs.[14]

John apparently expressed his disapproval in an August 9, 1903, letter. Though it has not survived, Frank's livid response has. "I well see that you have taken some determined stand against me," he penned, chastising his father for a letter "written neither in courtesy or affection....I object strongly to receive any such communication from you or anyone else which reflects on your daughter-in-law—whether you have a mind to recognize her as such or not." To a father ever mindful of finances, he assured John that "I can & am supporting both myself & wife. I am not incurring bills in your name, nor looking to you or anyone else for any maintenance." He concluded obdurately, "I tell you frankly, that unless your future communications...can be couched in a greatly altered tone, I desire to receive none of them."[15]

John and Frank eventually reached a rocky accord, though John never again treated Frank commensurately with his daughters. John included Frank in his will, to "share and share alike" with Emma and May all his real and personal property. But that was a shallow gift of equanimity, for John had no property of monetary value. He did bequeath Frank "the gold watch which...formerly belonged to his great-grandfather, David Williamson, Senior." But John recognized that the only real value of his estate lay in potential commissions from the states he had served as counsel—and rights to those funds he assigned exclusively to Emma and May.[16]

One week after John dictated that last will and testament, he attended Emma's wedding to California State Senator George Russell Lukens. It was a happier affair.

The two exchanged vows in June 1907 in an "extremely quiet and informal" wedding at the Mullan house in Washington. Frank escorted his sister into the drawing room, where a Catholic priest presided. May stood as maid of honor, and "the bride was given away by her invalid father," who attended in a wheelchair.[17]

May soon moved out of that Connecticut Avenue home into a place on 18th Street, where John spent his last two years. A writer for *Sunset* magazine visited him there in 1909, John's last interview. Photos taken for the story show John with "flowing hair and beard...whitened until he resembled the patriarchs of old." He sits in a parlor epitomizing the Victorian clutter popular at the time, possessions he and Rebecca had gathered over many years. "His body had become enfeebled," wrote the interviewer. "But his mind, still alert, went readily back the fifty odd years to the route through the wild that was his lifework."[18]

Mullan's health took a sudden downward turn in December 1909. May telegraphed Emma to rush to Washington. Before she could depart, May sent another telegram: their dear Papa died on the morning of December 28. He was seventy-nine years old. The *Sunset* article, appearing after his death, was his finest obituary, capturing the personality of this proud man far more accurately than the brief notices that ran in a handful of papers. San Francisco, Richmond, and Washington newspapers printed obituaries; perhaps some others, though remarkably few, if any, in Washington, Idaho, or Montana, the states intersected by his road. The obituaries summarized Mullan's life in two or three brief paragraphs and garbled his achievements. Mullan "distinguished himself as an explorer in the Indian campaign back in the early sixties with the discovery of Mullan Pass," reported the Richmond *Times Dispatch*. "Captain Mullan had a prominent place in military affairs" in Washington, D.C., the San Francisco *Call* erroneously stated. A West Point publication ran a longer obituary, but it, too, ran wide of the mark: Mullan "engaged against the Seminole Indians"; he served "on frontier duty in Oregon"; he was an agent for California who prosecuted claims for which "millions of dollars were recovered."[19]

Far more captivating than the brief accounts of Mullan's death are the stories appearing near them. An advertisement for the Royal Laundry, including a telephone number, ran above Mullan's obituary in the Richmond paper. The page with the Mullan announcement in the San Francisco paper carried the banner headline, "Aeroplane's Flight Marred by Lack of Suitable Starting Field." A man remembered for engineering a wagon road through Indian country had lived into the age of telephones and the embryonic beginnings of human flight.

On December 30, a priest from Washington officiated at Mullan's funeral at St. Mary's Church in Annapolis. His body was transported to St. Mary's Cemetery, where he was buried next to his father and mother. Years later, May fondly remembered her father in a comment that revealed both daughters' love for their dear Papa:

> My father…had a masterful air, a keen sense of humor, loved a joke and a good story, his blue eyes twinkling with merriment. He had a wonderful skin, cheeks like winter apples, and with his white beard, merry blue eyes, and rosy cheeks he looked the ideal Santa Claus—and children on the street would so call him.
>
> He was paralyzed for five years before his death, the last two years being confined to bed and a wheelchair. He bore his affliction with amazing patience, grateful to everyone for the smallest service rendered.[20]

CHAPTER 16

America's Great National Highway

"**W**HEN WE REACHED BENTON," John Mullan later reminisced, "we had completed a route over which a loaded wagon could journey a distance of 624 miles, crossing three mountain ranges and connecting with navigable waterways, reaching from ocean to ocean."[1]

The first emigrant wagon train to make that passage traveled over the road even before Mullan's work crew completed construction. And in 1860 Christopher Higgins and Frank Worden recognized the road's commercial merit. They packed $7,000 worth of merchandise across the Mullan Road, virtually on the heels of the road builders. They constructed a log store on the north bank of the Hellgate River, convinced the convenience of their position on the new road would lure customers. It did, and they prospered. The first picks and shovels used by miners in Montana's fabulous gold rush traveled over the Mullan Road from Walla Walla to the Higgins and Worden store. In 1865 the two relocated a few miles away, helping to establish the city of Missoula, a place that owed its start to a favorable location on the road.[2]

By 1862 the Walla Walla newspaper noted the arrival of several emigrant parties over the road. Twenty-two wagons reached the town in August; the paper claimed their journey was "a trip [of] health, pleasure, and bold Rocky Mountain scenery." Six more wagons appeared a few weeks later, and in September the paper reported eighteen wagons approaching town. One 1862 emigrant proclaimed the route to be America's "great national highway." That was an exaggeration, but the term stuck, and it was this vision of the road's potential that inspired Captain James Fisk. He believed the northern route across the country pioneered by Isaac Stevens, with its critical mountain crossing via the Mullan Road, could compete with the foremost emigrant road of its day, the Oregon Trail.[3]

✿

Even as civil war ravaged the East, western politicians conjured economic growth for their region. They convinced a cash-strapped Congress to appropriate money for military escorts to protect western emigrants from Indians. Congress originally intended the money for the Oregon Trail. But hard times in Minnesota convinced many in that state to seek new lives in the West. The Oregon Trail lay far to the south. Minnesotans exerted political pressure to corral $5,000 for an escort along a northern track to Fort Benton. Captain James L. Fisk would lead them. Fisk hired a former member of the Stevens expedition as guide, and in July 1862 directed 130 people west on what he called the Northern Overland Route.[4]

The Fisk party entered Fort Benton on September 5. Here his official obligations ended, but the emigrants requested he escort them to Walla Walla on Mullan's new road. Fisk's group arrived there on November 1. He had seemingly established the viability of a northern competitor to the Oregon Trail.[5]

But the anticipated surge of emigrants to Walla Walla over Mullan's route never materialized. Henry Lueg made the trek in 1867 with 115 other people. His experiences reveal why his was the last large emigrant train to attempt Mullan's mountain passage. Mullan had estimated that his route from the Clark's Fork River to Wolf Lodge, west of the Coeur d'Alene Mission, would take nine days. Lueg's party spent seventeen, a time of absolute misery. Downed trees and landslides blocked the road. Bridges had washed out. Wagons overturned or broke down while negotiating stumps in the road and boulders in the streams. One girl died, and by the time the party finally straggled into Walla Walla, many were "prostrate with mountain fever disease."[6]

The eastern and western portions of Mullan's road, connecting communities like Walla Walla with Spokane, and Missoula with Fort Benton, would witness heavy wagon traffic as corridors providing north-south access. But it proved a bust as an east-west, cross-mountain wagon highway. Still, the mountain passage would see expansive traffic of a different sort once gold discoveries enticed hordes of fortune seekers to the region.

✿

"A flood of picks and pans" spread rapidly over the Inland Northwest in the 1860s. Mining strikes lured thousands of prospectors. So many people swarmed to Grasshopper Creek that Congress created Montana Territory in 1864, splitting it from the recently established Idaho. By 1865, Montana boasted a non-Indian population of about thirty thousand.[7]

It takes a transportation network to sustain mining activity. "A mining town without market connections is like a seed without water," wrote historian Kent Curtis. Had Mullan's road not existed, someone would have had to construct it, for it served as the vital artery enabling development of a vast region, while becoming one of the West's most heavily traveled highways.[8]

Traffic on the Mullan Road moved in multiple directions to various gold camps. Word of Elias Pierce's 1860 discovery in what became Idaho brought a rush of fortune seekers from the East, some by steamers to Fort Benton. There they took Mullan's new road toward the Clearwater and Salmon diggings. Others going to the Idaho fields traveled the Oregon Trail to Fort Hall and then north to Deer Lodge, there to connect with Mullan's highway. The road outside Granville Stuart's home buzzed in 1862. "En route for Salmon river gold mines…five emigrants arrived last night and twelve or fifteen today," he noted in July. Later that month he recorded "many emigrants arriving every day."[9]

In the fall of 1863 a prospector who found about $500 worth of "beautiful gold" along a creek in southeastern British Columbia touched off another rush, isolated from Canadian supply sources. But Walla Walla lay only four hundred miles south, "one day's journey closer to the Kootenai than any other route." Mullan's road north out of Walla Walla now became the connector between that community and the Canadian mines. So tempting were these prospects that they lured Mullan himself from his Walla Walla home.[10]

John and Rebecca had lived in Walla Walla only briefly before John realized he needed more money to keep his fledgling businesses afloat. So, along with brother-in-law David Williamson, guided by old friend Antoine Plante, he led a party of about twenty people north to investigate the Kootenai prospects. But the group returned disappointed, finding the profitable claims already staked.[11]

Mullan's road, though, continued to serve as the essential transportation link for a growing Northwest mining region. The gold discoveries in what became western Montana fully established the road as the area's principal supply line. Packers and freighters had to carry every scrap of food, piece of cloth, and hunk of metal to isolated camps. A new trade route north from Salt Lake eventually rivaled Mullan's mountain course, but initially the bulk of goods reached the Montana mining towns via the Mullan Road. Indeed, the road's stiffest competition came from itself. Fort Benton received steamer goods from St. Louis that then traveled the eastern part of the road to the camps, while Walla Walla tried to monopolize trade from the west.

"During...the summer and fall of 1865, the road was literally lined with men and animals on their way to the new El Dorado," recorded a contemporary. "So great was this trade, that hundreds and even thousands of pack mules were employed." Sometimes as many as five pack trains a day, of about twenty-five to thirty animals each, left Walla Walla. In some places along the narrow road they created traffic jams. In 1865, an estimated 750 tons of freight moved from Walla Walla to Montana. The Walla Walla newspaper claimed in September that year that five hundred pack animals were "en route or to start in a few days" for the mines.[12]

Mules transported the bulk of goods. More sure of foot than horses, mules could also carry heavier burdens, up to four hundred pounds or more. Snaking their way over Mullan's road, averaging about fifteen miles a day, mules carried the usual—bacon, flour, beans. But also the latest fashions, California wines, caskets, and, at least once, a piano.[13]

Mules proved dependable, but the drive for profits often leads to innovation. The most bizarre sight ever seen along Mullan's road came when packers tried their hands with camels. It seemed logical. Camels could cover forty miles a day, ferrying much more weight than mules. "They could carry all you could pile on them and...go up and over the mountains in the roughest and steepest of places," recalled one Montanan. The War Department introduced camels to Texas in the 1850s to transport military supplies. Shortly afterward, entrepreneurs imported them for the western trade, and they eventually made their way to the gold camps of Canada and Montana. Small strings of camels traveled the Mullan Road, supplying camps from Helena, and at least one camel train crossed from Walla Walla. The animals spooked mules, sometimes causing stampedes, and traditional packers loathed them. When Jim McNear shot a camel he mistook for a moose, the brief, colorful era of Mullan Road camel freighting came to an end.[14]

Walla Walla—with the completion of Mullan's road—mushroomed into Washington Territory's largest city, a position it held for two decades, dominating Pacific Northwest trade. The valley's productive farms, as Mullan had predicted, became the region's breadbasket. The community featured stores selling the latest European fashions and gourmet foods; boasted a regional library, churches, and schools. The reach of the city's influence could be seen on the distant main street of Helena, Montana, where the Walla Walla Store, the Walla Walla Hotel, and the Walla Walla Restaurant all conducted business. And yet, it would be an exaggeration to say no city benefitted more from its Mullan Road connection. For, 624 miles across the mountains in Montana, at the nether end of John Mullan's highway, Fort Benton's growth proved nearly as spectacular.[15]

Small communities sprang up every few miles along the Mullan Road in Montana. Twenty-eight Mile Springs, Dearborn, New Chicago, and Sun River were born due to travel along the road. Helena became a metropolis, at least by Montana standards, as well as the capital. Though it owed its origin to gold, Helena's growth came courtesy of easy access to the Mullan Road. Supplies for Montana's burgeoning population landed there via the road from both Walla Walla and Fort Benton. Warehouses bulged. Yet among all the Montana towns bolstered by Mullan's road, none boomed more flamboyantly than Fort Benton.[16]

The adobe-walled trading post that had greeted Isaac Stevens and John Mullan in 1853 began a gradual transformation when Mullan, seven years later, punched his road through to this Missouri River community. Still, by 1865 the town consisted of only a dozen log buildings facing Broadway. "We shall have six streets here as soon as we get 5 more," noted one wag. Walter DeLacy, late of Mullan's road crew, laid out those additional streets, creating the town's first plat. And suddenly, Fort Benton blossomed. "It was a wonderful metamorphosis, scarcely paralleled in any other city of the country," noted historian Hiram Chittenden.[17]

Each spring, when high water permitted navigation, St. Louis newspapers advertised sailing dates for Montana-bound steamers; seventy-five left in 1866. Those going as far as Fort Benton landed several weeks later at the town's levee. What a sight: "It was fascinating to watch the unloading of a boat and wonder what would come off next," recalled one observer. "There were stoves, barrels of flour, barrels of whiskey, buggies, chickens."[18]

In 1867 the steamers also disgorged eight thousand tons of freight. Goods stretching for nearly a mile piled high on the levee. Warehouses filled, and when those reached capacity, shippers commandeered every available building, storing goods until the glut could find its way out of town on Mullan's road. Unlike Walla Walla with its pack trains, here streets were jammed with wagons. Fort Benton thronged with ox teams, sometimes as many as twenty pulling three or four wagons strung together.[19]

As a city, Fort Benton compared poorly to Walla Walla. When the last parcel of freight disappeared down the Mullan Road, the place hibernated. "Waiting…for spring seems to be the sole occupation of our townsman," recorded one resident. But Fort Benton posed a serious threat to Walla Walla's economic hegemony. The freight wagons that clogged Fort Benton's streets carried larger loads at less expense than could Walla Walla's mule trains. But Walla Walla would not easily yield to that seeming superiority.[20]

❦

John Mullan had anticipated Walla Walla's challenge as early as 1862: "Supplying these mines from the Pacific slope is a matter to which the merchants and capitalists of Walla Walla would do well to give some attention, in order that St. Louis may not alone be the supply depot." What Mullan had not foreseen was that Walla Walla merchants would also have to battle Salt Lake and Portland interests.[21]

Say you were a miner finding yourself in the mountains of western Montana. Once the thrill of potential instant fortune abated, reality set in. And the reality was this: you had taken up mining a long way from any source of supplies. You might purchase goods transported from Walla Walla. You could get merchandise via Salt Lake, a city more than 350 miles away. Or you could buy stock carried by steamboat to Fort

Benton. No matter from which direction your provisions came, they had one commonality: all traveled at least part of the way on Mullan's road. But this shared link did not still fierce competition among the various cities.

It would seem that Fort Benton held the advantage. The broad-bottomed, shallow-drafted stern- and side-wheelers plying the Missouri River could carry huge amounts of goods. Once the boats unloaded, bushwhackers guided wagons out of town, carrying quantities that dwarfed the capabilities of the sturdiest pack mule.

But the steamers had limitations. None made it to Benton in 1863; two in 1864. "Of about 20 Boats which have left St. Louis this year for this place," wrote Hiram Upham from Fort Benton in 1865, "only four have reached here. 3 have sunk and the balance have been compelled, on account of low water, to discharge their freight hundreds of miles below from whence it has to be hauled to this point by teams."[22]

The river's testy nature created an opportunity for other towns. Salt Lake freighters reached Montana over Monida Pass, the course Mullan had explored in December 1853 on his trek to Fort Hall. Tons of cargo traveled this route, proffering a more dependable supply line than Mullan's road over the Bitterroots, posing a menace to Walla Walla.[23]

Walla Walla also suffered a rival from the west. Until 1866, Portland shippers had sent goods to Walla Walla for transport to Montana. But the powerful Oregon Steam Navigation Company recognized a potential for greater profits via the Lake Pend Oreille route that Mullan had rejected for his road. It pushed its steamers up the Columbia to White Bluffs. From there, goods and people traveled overland to Lake Pend Oreille, and—via three steamboats and intervening portages—reached the Montana camps after connecting with Mullan's road on the eastern side of the mountains. On its initial trip in April 1866, the company's lake steamer, the *Mary Moody*, carried eighty-five pack animals, ten thousand pounds of freight, and fifty passengers.[24]

The Pend Oreille route bypassed the mountainous portion of the Mullan Road. "In the saloon of the vessel eating a sumptuous dinner we crossed the dreaded Bitterroot mountains," wrote one *Mary Moody* passenger in 1866. But exorbitant fares and the inconvenience of portages partially offset this advantage. Steamboat transportation to White Bluffs also proved about as fickle as steamer travel to Fort Benton.[25]

Still, Walla Walla merchants recognized that winning the trade war would require improving the mountain passage, a route that, as early as 1865 when only three years old, had already gained the sobriquet "The Old Mullan Road."[26]

🌿

Phillip Ritz arrived in Walla Walla in 1861 and began purchasing rich valley farm land. He eventually had an estimated million trees in his orchards and sold fruit seedlings "into the farthest country where trees would grow." No one proved more earnest in his advocacy of Mullan's road:

> What the country most needs is a direct route opened up; one which heavy wagons, after loading at Walla Walla...can go directly through to the mines without unloading...and over which the settlers...can roll right along without detention....If the road had been open so that teams could have passed over it loaded this season [1866] it would have been of immense value to this valley....Instead of [farmers] selling their wheat for 60 cents per bushel, it would have readily commanded one dollar....This route only needs to be known to become the most popular one on the continent.[27]

But for the road to "become the most popular on the continent" would require work. It had sunk into disrepair almost as soon as Mullan had it completed. Heavy winds downed trees across its course and by 1865 every bridge Mullan had so laboriously constructed had either been destroyed or so weakened that travelers refused to trust them. What Mullan had designed as a mountain wagon road became a trail navigable only by sure-footed pack animals. A traveler in 1863 advised that "any other method of crossing from the Pacific to the Atlantic is preferable to the Mullen route."[28]

Conditions degenerated from there. An 1866 traveler found "the road over which we passed yesterday...was 'horrible,' but to-day I am satisfied that no word in the English language can convey an idea of its condition." Three years later another described Mullan's mountain passage:

> It...is decidedly the longest, hilliest, stoniest, muddiest, crookedest road ever attempted to be built by human hands....For days we floundered thro cedar swamps in bottomless mud, only to ascend and wind

around the summits of heaven-kissing mountains, where a single mis-step would have hurled [us] down their almost perpendicular sides into the rushing waters.[29]

In 1865 Walla Walla residents began a campaign to "open the road." The city's future depended upon this vital link to lucrative Montana trade. Walla Walla demanded more than a pack trail. Its citizens sought funding to complete what they claimed the government had originally intended: a viable wagon route.

But Walla Wallans had a skewed view of what Mullan had been sent to accomplish. Certainly, when Congress authorized military roads, it recognized that emigrants and settlers would also use them. But military road builders were to undertake the bare minimum to open routes. They could fell trees, bridge streams, move boulders, and excavate side hills where necessary. The army would, in other words, create a passage, "but it was up to the local inhabitants to see to their improvement if they so desired."[30]

Walla Wallans would try. Inspired by Phillip Ritz, their "open road" campaign at first encouraged local efforts. "Let Walla Walla take the lead," recommended the *Washington Statesman*. The newspaper sought local pledges for "the small sum required" to "make the Mullan road one of the best mountain roads on the continent."[31]

For a while the campaign seemed to gain traction. San Francisco businessmen pledged $5,000 if Walla Walla would match it. Oregon newspapers encouraged the effort—at least until the Oregon Steam Navigation Company opened its competing route across Lake Pend Oreille. And the *Statesman* encouraged Montanans: "Why the people of Montana do not undertake the clearing of this great highway, and thus open up a route by which they may receive supplies at rates 1/2 to 2/3 cheaper than at present, is a mystery."[32]

But, unwilling to contribute themselves, Walla Wallans' campaign for private subscriptions elsewhere quickly collapsed. "It is a decided indication of local weakness in our Western neighbors to ask the peo-ple of [Montana] to render assistance in removing obstructions from the 'Mullen Road,'" the publisher of the *Montana Post* observed. "It is like the merchant asking the patron to make the pavement leading to his store."[33]

John Mullan and Phillip Ritz came up with another solution: ask Congress for the money. "Capt. John Mullan is now in Washington trying to stir up the War Department to take some action," The Dalles newspaper reported in 1866. The following year, Ritz spent six months in the capital "endeavoring to secure an appropriation from Congress." Ritz proved unsuccessful, to the chagrin of the *Statesman*: "It is greatly to be regretted that Congress could not drop the 'negro' for a few moments, and attend to a question in which people of the Pacific slope are so greatly interested." Nonetheless, the publisher remained optimistic: "Congress may yet come to our relief." Ritz journeyed to Washington again the next year, "endeavoring to get an appropriation."[34]

The territorial legislatures of Washington and Montana petitioned Congress for road improvements. Washington sought $100,000 to mend the "great national highway." When constructed, Mullan's road traversed "an uninhabited region, infested throughout by bands of hostile Indians. Now the scene has changed....What was then a wilderness now contains a large and rapidly increasing population." Attempting to cement their case, the legislators tried hyperbole: "Not less than 20,000 persons have passed over the 'Mullan road' to and from Montana during the past season."[35]

By 1866 Mullan's trusted assistant, Walter Johnson, was serving in Montana's territorial legislature. He introduced House Joint Memorial Number 3, requesting money from Congress. Johnson sought a more modest $75,000, but did not shun the hyperbole. The congressional investment would yield "the most extensively traveled road" across the Rockies, "practically uniting over this great national highway the waters of the Atlantic with those of the Pacific." When Johnson's petition failed to stir Congress, the Montana legislature tried again in 1868 and 1879.[36]

"The concurrent action of the Legislatures of the two Territories, and the united influence of the Washington and Montana Delegates in Congress, cannot fail to secure the opening of this great national highway," enthused the *Statesman*. "It will certainly be a very easy task to secure a trifling appropriation." But the *Statesman* did not understand Congress. From a Northwest perspective, logic dictated that a government that had invested $230,000 to construct an impassable wagon road should complete "a work already commenced." But Congress faced huge expenses in the Civil War's aftermath. And many members clung to beliefs that federal funding of roads not required by the military exceeded Congress's constitutional authority. Besides, Montana and Washington were hardly the only places clamoring for roads. "Urging federal appropriations for internal improvements had become shop-worn," summarized historian W. Turrentine Jackson. It would take the influence of a great national hero, William Tecumseh Sherman, to convince Congress to improve the road. Sherman justified his request on military necessity.[37]

Only one commander, Major George Blake, would lead troops over the Mullan Road from Fort Benton to Walla Walla. Some historians have emphasized this paucity to criticize the road. "By the time of its completion in 1862 the military urgency of the road greatly diminished… because Northwest Indians had been quieted," noted one. This led to the oft-repeated declaration that "the military used the road only once"—when Blake passed through. Finally came the assertion that as a military road it was a "fiasco." The "truly astonishing thing about Mullan," wrote one, is that "he is celebrated for a failure."[38]

Those pronouncing the road a military failure are similar to ones who condemn it as a civilian flop. Critics focus on that part of the road across the mountains, and there it can hardly be termed a success. But it was a long road. The military, like civilians, made extensive use of its western and eastern portions as north and south passages. The frequent condemnation that the army used it "only once" is fallacious.

In the west Mullan's road linked Forts Walla Walla and Colville, with a branch to Fort Lapwai. By the late 1870s the road also connected with the new Camp Coeur d'Alene, later known as Fort Sherman. Accounts from Lyon's Ferry, along Mullan's road north of Fort Walla Walla, record that in 1873 the army paid passage for mule teams, ambulances, a horse coach, and a pack train. "After 1873…large numbers of soldiers and government horses and mules used the ferry every year," recorded historian Alex McGregor.[39]

In the east the road also joined a number of army posts. Shortly after completing his road, Mullan recommended the army "establish a military depot…at the mouth of the Sun River," and there Fort Shaw opened in 1867, primarily to protect Mullan Road travelers. Fort Benton became a military post two years later. And by 1877, Mullan's road tied both of these with the army's new Fort Missoula.[40]

General of the Army William Sherman knew something about moving armies, and he believed the Inland Northwest needed a way to convey troops rapidly. He recognized that Mullan's road worked effectively for north and south traffic. But an inability to efficiently negotiate the mountains concerned him.

Sherman, accompanied by Mullan's West Point classmate General Phil Sheridan, traveled west in 1877. Their journey came just a year after Custer's defeat, and during the same summer that the army chased the Nez Perce before Chief Joseph's surrender near Canada. Sherman believed the military still had an important function in this country. Taking Mullan's "well traveled" road out of Fort Benton, Sherman and his party arrived in Helena in August and prepared to continue west. "There was once a wagon-road hence to Walla Walla—the Mullan Road—on which a good deal of money was spent," Sherman wrote as he contemplated the upcoming trip.[41]

It would be an adventure, as Sherman noted: "We found many persons who had crossed this route all of whom thought we could not possibly come with wagons over to Walla Walla." But Sherman relished challenges. "I thought the attempt necessary," he wrote. "The time seems to have come when there should be intercourse between Montana and Oregon."[42]

Sherman sent for an army escort. Sixty-one men of the First Cavalry arrived from the west via Lewis and Clark's Lolo trail. Their stories of that perilous trip convinced Sherman that the best course over the mountains remained Mullan's road. Sherman left Missoula on September 4 with his escort, five wagons, and eighteen days of provisions. His trip account reads much like Mullan's when he initially cut the route:

> The road is obstructed by fallen trees....The road ascends the valley of the Regis Borgia, crossing it some forty times; all the bridges long since gone....The troopers...were kept ahead with axes....Our men persevered in a tangled wood....By perseverance we reached the mission.[43]

Traveling the "villainous" road west of the Coeur d'Alene Mission, "progress was slow and the labor severe." Things improved when Sherman's party continued south on Mullan's route—"a creditable piece of road making"—arriving in Walla Walla at 2:30 p.m. on September 18.[44]

The trip had been an ordeal for the fifty-seven-year-old Sherman, but he and his party found much to commend about the route. Sherman's aide-de-camp, Colonel Orlando Poe, had served as Sherman's chief engineer during his march to the sea; after the Civil War he designed lighthouses and ship locks on the Great Lakes. He knew good engineering, and respected Mullan's work. "Often...we remarked upon the pluck, the energy, the endurance, and the executive ability of Captain Mullan," Poe wrote. "Its inception was creditable, and its execution worthy of any man's ambition."[45]

"This road should be reopened for travel," Sherman avowed. Had it been passable that summer, Sherman believed General O.O. Howard "could have reached Missoula before the Nez Perces," intercepting Joseph and bringing a more expeditious halt to what became a long, running war. Sherman recommended constructing a military post on Lake Coeur d'Alene and employing troops from there and Missoula to improve the mountain crossing: "I am sure they can nowhere else be better employed."[46]

In August 1879 two detachments of infantry "commenced work on the old Mullan road," gleefully announced one newspaper. Some soldiers worked east from Coeur d'Alene while others labored west from Missoula. They cleared timber, constructed bridges, and smoothed grades. In September the army announced the opening of the road to wagon travel. The public took immediate advantage. "During the time I was engaged on this work," reported Captain William Mills, "several...wagons, with families and their baggage, made the trip....I was surprised to meet so many travelers." Army troops undertook additional work each of the next two summers, and the road, for the first time, became the wagon highway that Mullan had originally intended.[47]

In 1883 Sherman returned to the Northwest, arriving at Fort Missoula on July 26. But this time the general's party continued west in comfort on the new Northern Pacific Railroad. The company had just completed its line around northern Lake Pend Oreille, the route Mullan had recommended for rail travel after his arduous road building across the mountains.[48]

Sherman did not see either Walla Walla or Fort Benton on that trip. The railroad bypassed them, going instead through Spokane. That city soon supplanted Walla Walla, beginning its long reign as the transportation and economic hub of the Inland Northwest. Walla Walla did not bust so much as it treaded water, settling in as a pleasant, livable community, but never again with the commercial influence it held when Mullan's road served as the region's primary transportation link.

Fort Benton plummeted much more dramatically. Dozens of steamboats reached that community during a string of high water years in the late 1860s, and the city prospered. A newspaper editor in 1869 prophesied a wonderful future. Steamer traffic had "achieved last year a success that is a sure guarantee of future importance in the commercial history of Montana." Then on May 10, 1869, celebrants in Utah pounded a golden spike at Promontory Point, signaling completion of America's first transcontinental railroad. Suddenly, it became cheaper to ship goods by rail to Utah, and then by wagon to Montana. Fort Benton competed for awhile. Eight boats arrived in 1870; twelve in 1872. A few straggled through until 1890. But by then, railroads had Fort Benton in a stranglehold. The Northern Pacific in 1883 slashed the economic vitality of steamers. That same year, the Canadian Pacific reached Calgary, virtually eliminating traffic into Canada via Fort Benton. And finally in the late 1880s, as the Great Northern laid track nearby—the northernmost of America's transcontinentals—all reason to ship products by river to Fort Benton vanished. "Even the most loyal river men then had to acknowledge their defeat," wrote one Montanan. Fort Benton metamorphosed into a quiet village, not too dissimilar from its days before the arrival of Mullan's road.[49]

Few people risked Mullan's road across the mountains after completion of the Northern Pacific. It again deteriorated. In 1884, Lieutenant Augustus Egbert reported it "impassable from the…absence of bridges." William R. Wallace—nephew of Mullan's old nemesis, Idaho's first territorial governor, William W. Wallace—wrote Mullan that "the old road…is soon to be a thing of the past." Wallace, who had a namesake town along the road in Idaho, just west of one named for Mullan, proved too pessimistic, though for a while his prediction seemed prescient.[50]

✣

In 1880 A.J. Prichard, traveling via Mullan's road into the valley of the Coeur d'Alene River, discovered gold, setting off another mining stampede. Gold seekers from both east and west took Mullan's road to the diggings. Railroad builders looked again at the mountain route they had at first spurned. Soon they would lay track, in places directly over Mullan's wagon path.[51]

The wagon road rapidly decayed. Stories of those few who hazarded its passage rivaled earlier attestations of its formidable challenges. Young Ermal Steiner traveled with her family on the Mullan Road in 1900. "Our means of transportation was a common covered wagon, pulled by two horses," she recalled. "The Mullan Road was nothing fancy….In places the railroad was built on this road. We would straddle the railroad tracks with the wagon and send my brothers both behind and ahead of us to stop any train that might be coming." The railroad "took a great deal of the old road bed, which for many years put the old road practically out of commission," noted another observer in 1912.[52]

While a few families like the Steiners, unable to pay rail passage, continued to negotiate the Mullan Road, for a quarter century this route through the mountains essentially reverted to a rail line. But Mullan's road would enjoy new life. In 1910 the *Missoulian* newspaper praised county commissioners for agreeing to survey an automobile route that would become "the connecting link…of an…interstate highway" joining Montana and Idaho along "the old Mullan road." And had John Mullan lived just two more years, he would have heard the extraordinary news that the first automobiles had crossed Fourth of July Pass, where his men had spent that rollicking Independence Day in 1861. Indeed, two cars that summer of 1911 raced over Mullan's road from Spokane to Wallace, the winner covering the distance in five hours and fifteen minutes. Imagine Mullan's astonishment had he received that news.[53]

In the early twentieth century, automobile associations blossomed. Much like advocates for rail routes in the mid-nineteenth century, the groups touted various interstate road options. There was the Jefferson Davis Highway, Dixie Highway, Midland Trail, the Lincoln, the Lee. Most existed only in the promoters' imaginations, "outlets for sloganeering and self-promotion." But up north, contemplating an automobile highway paralleling Isaac Stevens's cross country trek and the Fisk Northern Overland Route, advocates advanced a highway with a euphonic name. The Yellowstone Trail Association held its first meeting in South Dakota in 1912 with the lofty goal of connecting Plymouth

Rock to Puget Sound, 3,700 miles of continuous road. To accomplish that would require the collaboration of road boosters across the continent, and in towns along the Mullan Road the association found automobile enthusiasts eager to cooperate. Mullan's road would again become a thoroughfare.[54]

In August 1913 C.F. Wupper, an automobile dealer from Milwaukee, became the first person to drive a car into Idaho from the east. With two passengers, he motored from Wisconsin to Spokane. Had John Mullan been alive, he would have appreciated their ordeal in Idaho. "For 15 miles east of Mullan," reported the Spokane newspaper, "they were compelled to cut their way through windfalls, build bridges…and many times drive their machine up creek beds. It took a week to traverse the distance." The following June, two men from Spokane initiated automobile traffic into Montana from the west "over the Mullan…highway."[55]

Two weeks after that trip, picnickers celebrated near the old Coeur d'Alene Mission. They had just received notice that the Yellowstone Trail Association had added Mullan's mountain link to its interstate route. In a promotional booklet published that year, the association encouraged travelers to take the Yellowstone Trail, "the best long road in the world….The climate is most bracing….The scenery is most delightful." In 1915, another brochure specifically touted the Mullan Road section. "At no point will the traveler be far from a phone. A ring calls central in Wallace….A car or team will be rushed out to bring in the tourists and the car, or to take a supply of gasoline, as necessities may require. For this service there is absolutely no charge."[56]

By 1917 road builders, seeking a mountain passage with less snow, veered south of Mullan's original course over Sohon Pass, taking Lookout Pass instead. But, aside from this, the Yellowstone Trail essentially followed Mullan's route.

In the 1920s automobile traffic over Mullan's road became common. Much of the route by then had been paved, and the former Yellowstone Trail had become part of one of America's original long-haul highways, U.S. Route 10, running from Detroit to Seattle. In 1930, five hundred cars a day negotiated Fourth of July summit, still a precarious pass in winter. In 1931 the Federal Bureau of Public Roads authorized construction of a 394-foot tunnel under the pass. Opened in 1932, it became an integral part of an ongoing effort to transform the old Mullan Road into an advanced highway. By the 1940s, when engineers created a "four-lane, modern superhighway," they paid the ultimate respect to Mullan by following his course. A 1941 Spokane *Spokesman-Review* article lavishly praised Mullan's engineering acumen. He had chosen the best route; it remained only for twentieth century engineers and advanced technology to create and maintain the highway he envisioned:

> When, traveling eastward from Spokane, you realize how closely the new wide ribbons of cement follow the path blazed nine decades ago, you are almost forced to reflect admiringly on the engineering genius of Captain John Mullan....
>
> For "U.S. No. 10" from Spokane far beyond the continental divide, follows and will continue to follow so closely on Captain Mullan's wagon trail that hardly anywhere are the new route and the old route more than a few hundred yards apart.
>
> Where Mullan went over a mountain, the modern highway builder goes through it. Where he kept to the water's edge around a bay, the modern road engineer puts up a "fill" or builds a bridge. Where Mullan blazed a curve to avoid crossing a stream, his 20th century successor moves the stream. Where Mullan devised a laborious switchback up a narrow canyon or down a steep-sloped ridge, the 1941 road builders take out the kinks.[57]

That progress would have stunned Mullan. Even more so if he realized that, just seventeen years later, this "superhighway" would become outmoded, to be replaced with yet another road—again laid over Mullan's route through the Bitterroots.

President Eisenhower signed the Federal Highway Act in 1956, creating the Dwight D. Eisenhower System of Interstate and Defense Highways. At nearly 47,000 miles, this is perhaps the greatest public works program in world history. The longest of all the highways—the one known as I-90, running 3,099 miles from Boston to Seattle—took Mullan's route over the Bitterroots. At a time when engineers had the equipment, the time, and the money to choose a different course, they instead followed Mullan. As a 1964 engineering study noted, "U.S. Highway 10, long...an important east-west arterial...follows closely the route of the historic Mullan Road....The natural topographic features which controlled the alignment of these earlier facilities also were of major significance in planning the location for Interstate Highway 90." It was the ultimate verification of Mullan's route.[58]

Begun in 1958, construction crews finally completed Interstate 90 in 1991 when cars bypassed the city of Wallace, Idaho, on a viaduct constructed above the town, preserving the historic community. It was an engineering solution Mullan would have appreciated.

During a bitterly cold and snowy December in the 1980s, my wife and I spent an unexpected night in Wallace, deep in Idaho's Silver Valley along the old Mullan route, while on the way to a cousin's funeral in Helena, Montana. We stopped because a snowstorm had closed the interstate. Despite modern snow-clearing equipment, there are times when nature still prevails over the road through the Bitterroots.

We made our way across the pass the next day, and it would not have occurred to us to call the interstate a failure—any more than it would have occurred to Walla Walla businessmen in the 1860s to label Mullan's road a fiasco. Commentators of later generations invented that designation. It is as inaccurate as it is unfortunate. One of Montana's earliest historians better understood the real nature of Mullan's course. "It never attained…the importance as a through military and emigrant road anticipated…by its originators and promoters," wrote James Bradley. "But that it [has]…been of great value to the territories of Montana, Idaho and Washington is undeniable….It will be only a just tribute to its energetic and painstaking builder if [his] name is not permitted to become lost."[59]

With the completion of Interstate 90, the Idaho Transportation Department installed large highway signs visible to those entering Idaho from the west and east. They officially proclaim this seventy-five mile stretch of the interstate through the Idaho panhandle, simultaneously the most scenic and the most difficult passage of that long transcontinental freeway, as the "Captain John Mullan Highway." His name has not been "permitted to become lost."

Epilogue

❦

All these emigrants...were journeying safely and pleasantly towards the setting sun. The safe passage...proves the value of this line for emigrant purposes, and will yet cause it to stand in competition with other lines across the continent.

> Captain John Mullan
> *Report on the Construction of a Military Road*
> *from Fort Walla Walla to Fort Benton*, 1863

THE CAR MADE ITS WAY UP the pass from Montana, then wound down the precipitous descent into Idaho; New Years Day 2001 in the frigid Northwest. Cold, but not comparable to that day in 1860 when John Mullan, near here, recorded temperatures of minus forty degrees. The emaciated carcasses of starved horses littered his path to Cantonment Jordan, casualties of a road-building winter. Not equal to another raw day in 1862 when Charles Schafft ventured out of Cantonment Wright, slipped into an icy pond, and hobbled back to camp on two frostbit feet, flesh peeling from his bones.

Still, as the car topped Lookout Pass heading west on Interstate 90, the outside temperature stung; snow flurried. The two occupants had just entered what Idaho officially recognizes as the Captain John Mullan Highway, a seventy-five-mile segment of America's longest interstate traversing Idaho's panhandle—John Mullan's perilous mountain crossing.

They had been traveling in a land of Mullan. To their backs in Montana his name adorned Missoula's expanding Captain John Mullan and Mullan Road neighborhoods, Mullan Trail Realty, Mullan Trail Little League, and a string of Mullan Trail Banks.

Ahead, in communities to the west, lay Mullan Road Elementary School, Mullan Trail Elementary School, Mullan KinderCare, and a Mullan Street in virtually every municipality along Interstate 90 west to Spokane.

And there was also the town of Mullan, Idaho, just six miles west. Here the two exited, a place neither had visited before. Late afternoon on a numbing day, they found the town closed, the streets empty. They paused at the Captain John Mullan Museum and slipped a note under its locked door. They drove to the Mullan statue at the far western end of town, one of more than two dozen monuments in three states paying tribute to the road builder. Here John Mullan perpetually gazes upon the main street of his namesake community. They got out, shivered while reading the plaque, and rushed back to the comfort of their heated car.

And then they left, headed toward the interstate.

Abruptly, the car stopped. Turned around. Circled back to the statue. "It seemed that we had done all we came to do," recalled the passenger. "But Wes parked by the statue and wanted us to get out. I was freezing. He was being really odd." But she courteously complied.

And there, on that piercing cold New Years Day, under the watchful attention of the marble image of her great-great-great uncle, Caitlin Mullan accepted the surprise marriage proposal of Wes Crain. "I guess he had some jitters on our first stop," she remembered, "or maybe wanted to see if there was anywhere in town more appropriate."

But surely there could be no place more suitable for a Mullan engagement than this, a monument marking the event, nearly a century and a half earlier, when John Mullan struggled through these same mountains, engineering the predecessor of the interstate on which they traveled.

Now the two returned again to the warm car and, on their way out of town, stopped for snacks "at the only thing open," a small convenience store. "I wanted to tell everyone there that I was a Mullan—and I just got engaged."[1]

But she refrained.

They quietly left town, continuing west on the Captain John Mullan Highway.

The road would take them—like so many who had come before, so many yet to come—toward the setting sun.

Appendix

※

MULLAN'S CHILDREN

FOLLOWING HIS WESTERN EXPLORATION in 1853–54, John Mullan recorded "heartfelt regret" upon leaving the Bitterroot Valley, "a place and a people we shall not soon forget." Did he have Flathead Indian Rose Laurant particularly in mind?

On March 20, 1939, eighty-four-year-old Peter Mullan died on the Coeur d'Alene Reservation in Idaho. His father, according to the obituary, "directed the building of the road from Fort Benton...to Fort Walla Walla." Peter Mullan's family history posits that Flathead Indian Rose Laurant gave birth to Peter, precisely nine months after John Mullan left the Bitterroot Valley. John never officially recognized Peter as his son, and the documentary evidence of the relationship is thin. Still, historians draw conclusions based upon the best available evidence. It does not take a leap of imaginative fancy to conclude that John Mullan's first child was born in Washington Territory in 1855.[1]

We do know this. On a November day in 1853, Father Louis Vercruysse administered marriage vows to Peter Roi and Mary Ann Finley, a granddaughter of famed Northwest fur trader Jocko Finlay. On June 9, 1855, the Catholic records at St. Paul's Mission near Fort Colville record the birth of Peter, son of Peter and Mary Ann Roi. Then things get complicated, for this is also the exact information that an adult Peter Mullan would provide as his birth date and place. But Catholic priests recorded only one Peter as being born at St. Paul's that day, and Peter Mullan claimed John Mullan as his birth father, not Peter Roi. Reconciling how John could have fathered this child, whose recorded father is Peter Roi, has confounded researchers.[2]

In the 1990s Glen Adams, who lived near the Coeur d'Alene Reservation and knew members of Peter Mullan's family, attempted to prove or disprove the story of John Mullan's child, but grew frustrated. Adams knew John Mullan had ventured to Fort Colville in 1854, but that trip took place more than a year before Peter's birth. So Adams, assuming that Peter's conception occurred at the same location as his birth, concluded "it does not seem possible that John Mullan could have fathered the child." Further, "both Mary Ann Finley and Peter Roi were persons of good reputation," and Adams discounted the potential of an adulterous affair.[3]

Writing thirty years earlier, Louis Coleman and Leo Rieman had access to a key source not available to Adams—Christine Mullan Witt, the only child of Peter Mullan and his wife, Susan Inkster Mullan. Still, they too grappled with the inconsistencies that perplexed Adams. Despite their yeoman efforts, they also came to a wavering conclusion, "baffled over the apparent discrepancy in the date of Peter's birth with the times the records show that Mullan could have been visiting Mary Ann."[4]

Yet, establishing a connection between John and Peter is not as great a stretch as those earlier writers imagined, if one substitutes Rose Laurant as the birth mother in place of Mary Ann Finley. It seems that Adams, Coleman, and Rieman did not know of the existence of Rose. And she is admittedly a mystery. But one of the Coleman and Rieman Indian informants did tantalizingly—but mistakenly—state that Mary Ann was a member of the Laurant family—a statement that threw the authors off course, for they knew she was a Finley.

More recent family genealogies provide a possible explanation. These family histories claim Rose—a Flathead Indian—as the birth mother, not Mary Ann. If Rose lived with the Bitterroot Flatheads, which she certainly could have, that could explain the discrepancy between the time of Mullan's trip to Colville and Peter's birth date. Peter could have been conceived in the Bitterroot Valley. There were Laurants living in the Colville area in the 1850s, and Rose could have chosen to move near them when she gave birth. Family tradition states that Rose died in childbirth, and that Peter and Mary Ann Roi adopted her child—thus, according to this, Mary Ann was indeed Peter's mother, but his adoptive mother. Family members had also told Adams that Peter's mother had died in childbirth, but not knowing the possible existence of Rose, Adams had been unable to reconcile this—because he knew that Mary Ann Roi, who he assumed to be the birth mother, had lived a long life after 1855.[5]

What can be verified by documentary records is this: Peter Mullan did exist. He married Susan Inkster in 1880. He died in 1939 and she in 1954. They had a daughter, Christine, born in 1882. We know, too, that by 1894, Peter Mullan was farming on the Coeur d'Alene Reservation. In 1909 and 1916 Peter and Susan filed land claims as part of the reservation's allotment, blocking up 480 acres of good farm land about three miles from DeSmet, Idaho, on which they lived for the rest of their lives. And we know that in 1917 Peter Mullan donated a pistol to the Eastern Washington State Historical Society in Spokane—a gun he stated his father John had given to him.[6]

A lawyer would call the thread connecting Peter to John circumstantial evidence. And that it is. But who determines the burden of proof? Mid-nineteenth century vital records in the Inland Northwest are scanty, particularly when it comes to Indians and illegitimate births. There are enough inconsistencies in the line of evidence for any person to doubt Peter Mullan's lineage. But there seems little doubt that Peter, who proudly changed his last name to Mullan as an adult, authentically believed John Mullan to be his father. There is no overpowering reason to disbelieve that family oral tradition. And it could well be that the reason John so lamented departing the Bitterroot Valley in 1854 was because he was leaving Rose behind.

Emma Mullan met state senator George Russell Lukens in California while working on her father's behalf on contested legal cases. Ironically for the staunchly Democratic Mullans, Lukens was a Republican.

Marriage came late for the thirty-nine-year-olds. Lukens "has [long] been the despair of mothers of marriageable daughters," reported one paper. The same story called Emma "a perfect blond, slender, as all golden-haired women should be, while Mr. Lukens is dark and heavy of figure."[7]

Emma returned to California following her father's funeral in 1909, where she and George lived comfortably in San Francisco. She continued pursuing John's claims against the states, but with limited success. Emma inherited a modest estate upon her husband's death in 1912. She signed her last will days before she died in March 1915. She left $150 each to two Williamson cousins; $100 to the Mullans' "colored servant,"

Paul Jones of Washington. She directed that a sum of money "sufficient to produce a net income of $100 per annum," be reserved for perpetual upkeep of the Williamson family vault at Bonnie Brae Cemetery in Baltimore.[8]

To Frank, who had never completely made his way back into her graces following his scandalous marriage, she bequeathed $500. To May she gave the remainder of her estate. Emma was buried in the Williamson family crypt—like her mother, separated from her husband. She was forty-six years old.

Frank, the youngest Mullan child, was born in 1873. He graduated from Cornell University in civil engineering, which must have pleased his father. He worked briefly as a railroad engineer, but spent most of his life as "a writer on topics of interest to society." He worked twenty-five years at *The Club Fellow*, a Washington, D.C., society magazine, then moved to New York to write for the *Tatler* and *Town Topics*.[9]

Frank and Mary had one daughter, Elizabeth Williamson Mullan. At the time Frank died in February 1936, he was separated from his wife and daughter, who resided in Washington. Frank lived in a small apartment "in a dismal neighborhood in New York City." After funeral services in a New York Catholic church, he was buried in the Williamson crypt in Baltimore.[10]

Mary Rebecca—who always preferred May—journeyed to that "dismal neighborhood" when her brother died to gather family effects. Frank's home contrasted fundamentally with her own. John Mullan never attained—for any length of time—the material success he so desired. But it came to the succeeding generation in the person of May.

On January 19, 1916, in a simple ceremony at her residence in Washington, May Mullan married Henry Hepburn Flather. He was forty-eight; she forty-four. May, still in mourning for Emma, invited only family to the ceremony officiated by a Catholic priest. Frank was among the few attendees.[11]

Henry Flather grew up in Washington. His career ascended steadily. He served as a cashier at Riggs National Bank, then became a director of the American Security and Trust Company, treasurer of the Georgetown Gas Company, and a stockholder of the Washington Gas Light Company. In 1909, he was an invited guest at President William Taft's inaugural ball. By 1918 he had the means to purchase a coveted $59,000 membership on the New York Stock Exchange and opened his own brokerage firm.[12]

At the time May married Henry, his daughter Lucy, from a previous marriage, was about to enter the "debutante lists." In 1919 May and Henry hosted a "large wedding" as Lucy married William Flammer of New York, a Princeton graduate. Prior to the wedding, Lucy had summered with Henry and May at "their estate in West River, Md." That estate was Tulip Hill.[13]

At the end of a long, narrow driveway just south of Annapolis, the mansion at Tulip Hill occupied the highest point of a fifty-two acre estate. Samuel Galloway, a Quaker shipping magnate, constructed the Georgian-style manor in the 1750s, naming it for a grove of tulip trees on his property. He entertained often, and as an architectural historian once said, Tulip Hill "is one of the few places where you can say 'Washington actually did sleep here,'" the first president recording his frequent visits in his journals.[14]

Tulip Hill remained in the Galloway family until Henry and May Flather purchased the 6,500-square-foot, two-story home in 1918. The Flathers restored the house, which retained virtually all of its original features. From the upstairs bedrooms, Henry and May enjoyed sweeping vistas of the West River and "perhaps the most impressive terraced gardens in the United States." The Flathers retained their home near Washington, but spent summers at Tulip Hill. Mariquita Mullan, who married John's grand-nephew Hugh, recalled that "Hugh and I went down to visit May at Tulip Hill in 1941, a few weeks before our wedding. She seemed to approve of me, invited us to stay for dinner. When we arrived she was working in the garden in a famous grove of English boxwood."[15]

Mariquita Mullan described May as "not very fashionable, rather plain in the manner of Mrs. Herbert Hoover, her friend—correctly dressed, with gloves and hat, but not showy. She was of medium height, and had a forthright manner, no-nonsense." After marrying Henry, May moved in the upper echelons of Washington society. "Mrs. [Franklin D.] Roosevelt will be glad to receive Mr. and Mrs. Flather on Wednesday afternoon," reads one invitation that May preserved. Another: "The President and Mrs. Roosevelt request the pleasure of the company of Mr. and Mrs. Flather on Tuesday evening."[16]

Henry Flather, "widely known in the financial district" of Washington, died in 1946. A Methodist minister officiated at his funeral. May, who always remained Catholic, would live another sixteen years. "I had lunch with her once at the Sulgrave Club in Washington," Mariquita Mullan recalled, "after which she walked me briskly to St. Matthew's Cathedral to show me some famous chandeliers that she had given the Cathedral." It would not be the last of May's Catholic philanthropy.[17]

May Mullan Flather died on December 23, 1962, at age ninety-one. In 1953 she had given to Georgetown University, a Jesuit institution, a gift of family heirlooms "in memory of my father John Mullan and his great friendship for Father DeSmet." She followed this with a $100,000 gift to the university four years later and then donated $300,000 to the Georgetown Hospital for the May Flather Endowment Fund. She left an estate worth nearly $1.5 million. She bequeathed $400,000 to Catholic University, $200,000 each to Providence Hospital, Little Sisters of the Poor, and Georgetown Hospital, and an additional $100,000 to Georgetown University. She gave $100,000 to her niece, Frank's daughter, Elizabeth. The remainder she donated to various Catholic charities, friends, and former employees. She, like her mother and siblings, was buried in the Williamson crypt, separated from her husband.[18]

At the time she died, she was living in Georgetown. Mariquita Mullan remembered a visit to her home there:

> The last time I saw her was in her Georgetown house. She was frail and had an attendant. The house was a handsome Colonial-style mansion. She was sitting in an alcove overlooking the back garden—and the house behind hers. She pointed to some cameras in the garden of that house and complained that they were there day and night taking pictures of some important young man who lived there. It was John Kennedy's house.[19]

No one did more to preserve John Mullan's legacy than his daughter May. About the only inheritance he had to leave her was a large collection of personal and legal papers. It must have been tempting for May, then living in a small home, to toss the material. Instead, she preserved the records for more than half a century. It is rather remarkable that she recognized their significance, for apparently only one historian in all the years the papers remained in her care sought access.

Helen Addison Howard grew up in Missoula. She earned a bachelor's degree from Montana State University and, after becoming interested in Mullan in the 1920s, contacted May. "It will give me great pleasure to give you as ample data concerning my Father...as you may desire," May responded to Howard in 1926. The two continued their correspondence while Howard wrote the first biography of Mullan.[20]

In 1934 Howard published her biographical account of John Mullan in the *Washington Historical Quarterly*, a piece she expanded in her 1963 book, *Northwest Trail Blazers*. Hers, the first serious account of Mullan's life, delighted May:

> Needless to say the reading of it gave me great pleasure, and we are all indebted to you for the research and the piecing together of the data collected into an interesting and graphic account. I feel this will be of permanent interest, as the years take us farther away from that early pioneer period, and time would have blurred the detail. It is just a thread in the web of that early history, but it is the weaving of these threads that make the picture stand out, like a vivid tapestry.[21]

Howard, though, made very sparing use of the large collection of John Mullan papers that May carefully retained, and no other historian used the papers during May's lifetime. Upon her death, May bequeathed to Georgetown University her Georgetown home, along with all of its contents. Among those contents were dozens of boxes of her father's papers. University officials moved the boxes to the university library archives, where they remained for decades, carefully preserved but unprocessed, there being no demand for access. But in the twenty-first century, nearly one hundred years after John's death, university archivists cataloged the collection. It is the largest and most significant compilation of Mullan papers anywhere, open at last to those desiring to research the life of the western road builder. May had found the best possible way to preserve the memory of her dear Papa.

Acknowledgements

M Y WIFE MARY REED, an outstanding historian, found time during
her retirement to serve as my over-qualified research assistant.
What a pleasure it was as we together explored historical repositories
from coast to coast in the search of John Mullan. The Idaho Humanities Council, a state-based affiliate of the National Endowment for
the Humanities, enabled travel to those collections by awarding me a
research fellowship.

In 2007 Janet Gallimore, executive director of the Idaho State
Historical Society, and the society's Board of Trustees honored me by
naming me the Idaho State Historian, opening opportunities for me
to explore the state's history. It has been a richly rewarding experience,
though they might have regretted their decision after suffering through
years of anecdotes about John Mullan.

My cousin, Ted Craig, faced a choice in college: deciding upon a
major between his two loves, chemistry and history. He chose chemistry,
and that proved wise, given his many professional achievements. But I
am pleased that in retirement he has found time for history. This book
is better because of that. Ted accompanied me on several research trips
and lent his editorial hand to every chapter.

Others who assisted by reviewing parts or all of the manuscript:
Robert Dunsmore, Kellogg, Idaho; Catherine (Kay) Strombo, the
guiding light of the Mineral County Historical Society in Superior,
Montana, and its outstanding Mullan research collection; Jane Wilson
McWilliams and Jean Russo of Annapolis; Major Ryan L. Shaw of
West Point; Kimberly Rice Brown, Post Falls, Idaho; and Eileen Starr,
professor emeritus of science at Valley City State University, North
Dakota.

Paul (Dan) McDermott, an outstanding scholar of both Gustavus
Sohon and Mullan, proved ever patient in answering my inquiries.
Others who provided expertise on various topics included: Peggy Ann
Brown, historical consultant, Alexandria, Virginia; Glenn Campbell,

Historic Annapolis Foundation; William Dobak, U.S. Army Center of Military History; Walter Gary, Walla Walla; Bruce Kirby, Library of Congress; Sandy Kirkpatrick, Redemptorist Cemeteries, Annapolis; Rose Krause, Northwest Museum of Arts & Culture, Spokane; Shaun Miller, Davenport, Washington; John Missal, Seminole Wars Foundation; and Dan Torres, Baltimore City Historical Society.

I am very appreciative of the kind assistance and friendship of Fitzhugh and Anthony Mullan and Caitlin Mullan Crain. Mariquita Mullan died at the age of 99 while this manuscript was in process; she provided valuable insights into Mullan family history.

Tom Weitz allowed the use of his home while doing research in Helena. Richard Waldbauer, friend and colleague of many years, did the same in Washington, D.C., and, as always, provided thoughtful observation on Western history that helped put Mullan's story into perspective.

I first heard of Mullan and his road in an undergraduate class on Northwest history at Washington State University taught by David Stratton, who has been a friend and mentor for decades. I appreciate his support, insight, and his always gentle nudges to eliminate the extraneous.

To my friends at Washington State University Press, thanks again for taking on another book. For this project I particularly want to thank Beth DeWeese, manuscript editor; Nancy Grunewald, designer; Kerry Darnall, copyeditor; Caryn Lawton, marketing manager; and Robert Clark, editor-in-chief, who brings to that task not only skill and enormous patience, but also a great wealth of knowledge about Northwest history.

There are too many archivists, librarians, and curators to thank individually. Over the course of this project I researched in dozens of records repositories, from small county historical societies to some of the nation's largest research facilities. Regardless of size, and whether they were staffed by professionals or volunteers, I invariably found knowledgeable, dedicated, and helpful people willing to spend time uncovering obscure documents. Each place unlocked parts of a mystery, and I have fond memories of my research time at all. We are fortunate in this country to have so many diverse institutions safeguarding our historical records.

Endnotes

ENDNOTE ABBREVIATIONS

Bancroft: The Bancroft Library, University of California, Berkeley, California.

BCIM: Bureau of Catholic Indian Missions Records, Department of Special Collections and University Archives, Raynor Memorial Library, Marquette University, Milwaukee, Wisconsin. The bureau's records are available on microfilm.

CDA: Coeur d'Alene Tribe Historical Data Base, Cultural Resources Program, Tribal Headquarters, Plummer, Idaho. Mullan's "Field Notes" referred to from this collection are notes Mullan wrote while with Colonel George Wright in 1858 and during the first six months of road building; transcribed from National Archives.

Chico: Special Collections and University Archives, Meriam Library, California State University, Chico, California.

EWSHS: Research Library and Archives Collections, Northwest Museum of Arts and Culture, Spokane, Washington. This institution was known as the Eastern Washington State Historical Society at the time the materials referred to were collected.

Gonzaga: Special Collections Department, Foley Center Library, Gonzaga University, Spokane, Washington.

ISHS: Idaho State Archives, Idaho State Historical Society, Boise, Idaho.

MHS: Research Center, Montana Historical Society, Helena, Montana.

MINCO: Mineral County Historical Society, Superior, Montana.

MNI: Museum of North Idaho, Coeur d'Alene, Idaho.

Mullan, *Military Road 1861*: This is Mullan's road report for 1861, originally published as a congressional document. I have used the more accessible *Military Road from Fort Benton to Fort Walla Walla* from the Michigan Historical Reprint Series (Ann Arbor: University of Michigan University Library, n.d.).

Mullan, *Military Road 1863*: This is Mullan's final road report, 1863, originally published as a congressional document. I have used the more accessible *Report on the Construction of a Military Road from Walla-Walla to Fort Benton,* which includes useful introductory materials (Fairfield, WA: Ye Galleon Press, 1998).

Mullan Papers, Georgetown: John Mullan papers at Special Collections Division, Georgetown University Library, Washington, D.C.

NA: National Archives, Washington, D.C.

NARA: National Archives and Records Administration, College Park, Maryland.

Railroad Survey*: Reports of Explorations and Surveys to Ascertain the Most Practicable and Economical Route for a Railroad from the Mississippi River to the Pacific Ocean, 1853-54*, 36th Cong., 1st Sess., House Ex. Doc. No. 56, Serial Set No. 1054. In twelve volumes.

Smithsonian: Smithsonian Institution Archives, Washington, D.C.

UISC: Special Collections, University of Idaho Library, Moscow, Idaho.

University of Montana: Archives and Special Collections, Maureen and Mike Mansfield Library, University of Montana, Missoula, Montana.

West Point: Special Collections and Archives Division, U.S. Military Academy Library, West Point, New York.

Whitman: Northwest and Whitman Collection Archives, Penrose Memorial Library, Whitman College, Walla Walla, Washington.

WSA-Cheney: Records of the U.S. District Court of Walla Walla County, Eastern Region Branch, Washington State Archives, Cheney. There are seventeen cases involving John Mullan for the period 1861-66. The designation WAL is used to distinguish the Walla Walla Court, and the case numbers follow that abbreviation.

WSU: Manuscripts, Archives, and Special Collections, Washington State University Libraries, Pullman, Washington.

Yale: Beinecke Rare Book and Manuscript Library, Yale Collection of Western American, Yale University, New Haven, Connecticut.

PROLOGUE

1. Rebecca Mullan, in her unpublished reminiscences, 1892, mentions Mullan's talk in New York, and being escorted by Cyrus Field. Box 8, Fldr. 9, Mullan Papers, Georgetown. For the quote about Field, *New York Times*, 23 Aug. 1858.

2. *New York Times*, 10 May 1863. Mullan's lecture was published as "Remarks of John Mullan, 7 May 1863, on the Geography, Topography and Resources of the Northwestern Territories" in *Proceedings of the American Geographical & Statistical Society of New York*, 1864, Yale.

3. *New York Times*, 10 May 1863.

PRELUDE, SECTION I

1. For a description of the campus at the time, Tench Francis Tilghman, *The Early History of St. John's College in Annapolis* (Annapolis: St. John's College Press, 1984), esp. 70, 81-82.

2. For Bidwell, Michael J. Gillis, and Michael F. Magliari, *John Bidwell and California: The Life and Writings of a Pioneer, 1841-1900* (Spokane: Arthur H. Clark Co., 2004); Marcus Benjamin, *John Bidwell, Pioneer: A Sketch of His Career* (Washington: 1907); Doyce Nunis, *The Bidwell-Bartleson Party: 1841 California Emigrant Adventure* (Santa Cruz, CA: Western Tanager Press, 1991). For his own account of the 1841 journey, John Bidwell, *A Journey to California, 1841: The First Emigrant Party to California by Wagon Train* (Berkeley: Friends of the Bancroft Library, 1964).

3. Robert C. Carriker, *Father Peter John DeSmet: Jesuit in the West* (Norman: University of Oklahoma Press, 1995), 44.

4. Kit Oldham, "Robert Newell and Joseph Meek Reach Fort Walla Walla with the First Wagons Driven Overland to the Columbia River in September 1840," www.historylink.org, retrieved 24 Mar. 2013. Also, LeRoy R. Hafen, *Broken Hand: The Life of Thomas Fitzpatrick, Mountain Man, Guide and Indian Agent* (Denver: Old West Publishing Co., 1931).

5. For DeSmet's as the first wagons over Monida Pass see Betty M. Madsen and Brigham D. Madsen, *North to Montana! Jehus, Bullwhackers, and Mule Skinners on the Montana Trail* (Salt Lake City: University of Utah Press, 1980), 8.

6. For the Stevens courtship and marriage, Kent D. Richards, *Isaac I. Stevens: Young Man in a Hurry* (Pullman: Washington State University Press, 1993), 26-33; and Hazard Stevens, *The Life of Isaac Ingalls Stevens* (Boston: Houghton, Mifflin and Co., 1900), 1:76-78.

7. For the DeSmet quote, Lucylle H. Evans, *St. Mary's in the Rocky Mountains: A History of the Cradle of Montana's Culture* (Stevensville, MT: Montana Creative Consultants, 1976), 43.

CHAPTER 1

1. Jane Wilson McWilliams, *Annapolis: City on the Severn, a History* (Baltimore: The Johns Hopkins University Press, 2011); David Ridgely, ed., *Annals of Annapolis, comprising sundry notices of that old city from the period of the first settlements...in the year*

1649, until the War of 1812… (Baltimore: Cushing & Brother, 1841); Elihu S. Riley, *"The Ancient City": A History of Annapolis in Maryland* (Annapolis, 1887).

2. The quotes are from Annapolis municipal records, 1857-59, provided to the author by Jean Russo, historian for Historic Annapolis Foundation. See McWilliams, *Annapolis,* 160 for street garbage.

3. For background on Annapolis historic sites and Annapolis in the time of Mullan, I am indebted to Russo, who led me on a city tour in Mar. 2010 and subsequently provided additional information, as did McWilliams.

4. Tilghman, *Early History of St. John's.*

5. St. John's Matriculation Book, 1789-1860, MSA SC 5698-2-1, Maryland State Archives, Annapolis. Mullan would later receive an AM degree from St. John's in the 1850s, but the requirements consisted of little more than asking for the degree; his formal education at the school essentially ended in 1847.

6. The quote is in Tilghman, *Early History of St. John's,* 73. For Mullan family attendance, see St. John's Matriculation Book.

7. Riley, *"The Ancient City,"* 274-76.

8. Robert L. Worden, *Saint Mary's Church in Annapolis, Maryland: A Sesquicentennial History, 1853-2003* (Annapolis: Saint Mary's Parish, 2003), esp. 21-22, 33.

9. Riley, *"The Ancient City,"* 280. Russo, personal interview with the author, Mar. 2010. For a brief summary of the makeup of parishioners at St. Mary's, Worden, *Saint Mary's Church,* 44.

10. Riley, *"The Ancient City,"* 323. For the quotes, "A Brief History of the United States Naval Academy," www.usna.edu/VirtualTour/150years, retrieved 16 Apr. 2011.

11. George P. Upshur, Superintendent, U.S. Naval School, to General R. Jones, U.S. Army, Washington, D.C., 27 Apr. 1850, Records of the Office of the Superintendent, Letters Sent, 1849-1853, RG 405, Special Collections and Archives, U.S. Naval Academy, Annapolis. According to materials in John Mullan Jr.'s West Point Application Papers, 1847/158, West Point, Mullan Sr. entered the Army in 1823.

12. The first quote is in L.M. Goldsborough, Superintendent, Naval Academy, to Charles Morris, Chief of the Bureau of Ordnance & Hydrology, Washington, D.C., 3 June 1855, Records of the Office of the Superintendent, Letters Sent, 1855-1857, RG 405, Special Collections and Archives, U.S. Naval Academy, Annapolis. The second in Samuel Cooper, Acting Secretary of War, to J.C. Dobbin, Secretary of the Navy, 28 May 1855. Mullan's appointment to Seaman is confirmed in Dobbin to Goldsborough, 9 June 1855. The latter two documents provided in a letter to the author, 8 Mar. 2010, by Jennifer Bryan, Head of Special Collections and Archives, U.S. Naval Academy, Annapolis.

13. For Mullan Sr. as alderman, Russo, "Annapolis History Chronology, 1790-1975," unpublished, provided to the author.

14. The letters and petition are in Mullan's West Point Application Papers, 1847/158, West Point.

15. Rebecca Mullan, Reminiscences, Box 8, Fldr. 9, Mullan Papers, Georgetown.

16. For Mullan on Polk, see Mullan to Lincoln, 4 Mar. 1863, General Records of the Department of State, 1763-2002, RG 59, Series: Applications and Recommendations for Public Office, NARA. For Polk's personal interest in West Point, James L. Morrison Jr., *The Best School: West Point, 1833–1866* (Kent, OH: Kent State University Press, 1998), 26-28, 62-63. For the difficulty in determining the names of Polk's visitors, I am indebted to Bruce Kirby, Manuscript Reference Librarian at the Library of Congress, which houses the Polk papers; email to the author, 8 Jan. 2010.

17. Mullan to Emma and May Mullan, 10 Sept. 1905, Box 2, Fldr. 4, Mullan Papers, Georgetown.

CHAPTER 2

1. Descriptive List of New Cadets for the Year 1848, West Point. For descriptions of West Point in Mullan's time, Morrison Jr., *"The Best School"*; George Crockett Strong, writing under the pseudonym Benson J. Lossing, *Cadet Life at West Point by an Officer of the United States Army* (Boston: T.O.H.P. Burnham, 1862); Theodore J. Crackel, *West Point: A Bicentennial History* (Lawrence: University of Kansas Press, 2002); and Stephen E. Ambrose, *Duty, Honor, Country: A History of West Point* (Baltimore: The Johns Hopkins Press, 1966). Mullan's "Cadet Engagement for Service and Oath of Allegiance" is in a folder of that title, Adjutant, Class of 1852, West Point.

2. Mullan's daughter May Mullan Flather donated these artifacts to the Montana Historical Society in 1945; catalog #X1945.06. For details on cadets' first day on campus, Morrison, *Best School*, 64-65 and Lossing, *Cadet Life,* 57-58 (quote).

3. The quote is in Lossing, *Cadet Life*, 14, 206-07.

4. Morrison, *Best School*, 64-68, quote 65; Lossing, *Cadet Life*, 65-69. I am also indebted to Major Ryan L. Shaw for making available his unpublished paper, "The Making of an Explorer: John Mullan at West Point," 2011.

5. The quote is from an 1830 Board of Visitors report in William H. Goetzman, *Army Exploration in the American West, 1803–1863* (Austin: Texas State Historical Association, 1991), 13.

6. For the quote, Morrison, *Best School*, 101; also see 24, 94-98.

7. Morrison, *Best School*, 87-96; Lossing, *Cadet Life*, 185-86; Ambrose, *Duty, Honor, Country*, 128-29. The quote is in a letter to the academy from John Mullan Sr., 9 Dec. 1850, Mullan Application Papers 1847/158, West Point.

8. Morrison, *Best School*, 73; Lossing, *Cadet Life*, 112-21, 181-84; Crackel, *West Point*, 118-28.

9. Morrison, *Best School*, 69-71; Lossing, *Cadet Life*, 183-84; Ambrose, *Duty, Honor, Country*, 134-36.

10. Philip Henry Overmeyer, "George B. McClellan and the Pacific Northwest," *Pacific Northwest Quarterly*, 32:1 (June 1941), 3-60, quote 8; Morrison, *Best School*, 43, 58.

Sheridan entered with the Class of 1852, but did not graduate until 1853, having been suspended a year for fighting with a classmate.

11. Mullan's quote about French came as he encountered a camp of non-English speaking Flatheads in 1853. See *Railroad Survey* 12(1):308. For details on professors and classes at West Point at the time, Morrison, *Best School*, 47-51, 97; Lossing, *Cadet Life*, 105; Shaw, "The Making of an Explorer." Cadets' progress through various levels of classes can be tracked through Post Order Ledgers for the appropriate years, West Point. For Mullan's standing in various classes, *Official Register of the Officers and Cadets of the U.S. Military Academy, 1852*, 23, West Point. Mullan did best in infantry tactics, poorest in philosophy. For Mullan's ranking in his class, George W. Cullum, *Biographical Register of the Officers and Graduates of the U.S. Military Academy at West Point, New York, Since Its Establishment in 1802* (Cambridge: Riverside Press, 1901), 85.

12. For background on the library at this time, its holdings, and use by cadets, Morrison, *Best School*, 76-77, 89-91. Records of usage and the specific volumes checked out by various cadets can be found in the entries in U.S. Military Academy Library Circulation Records, West Point.

13. Library Circulation Records, West Point, for Mullan's reading habits.

14. Post Orders, Special Order 12, 23 Jan. 1850, provides background to Mullan's arrest; USMA *Regulations 1839*, Rule 114, was in effect at the time of the 1850 incident. Both West Point.

15. Post Orders, Special Order 12, 23 Jan. 1850; *Official Register of the Officers and Cadets of the U.S. Military Academy, June 1849*. Both West Point.

16. Carl P. Schlicke, *General George Wright: Guardian of the Pacific Coast* (Norman: University of Oklahoma Press, 1988), 88-89.

17. The demerits of each cadet are noted in *Official Register of the Officers and Cadets of the U.S. Military Academy*, West Point. Shaw, "The Making of an Explorer," tabulated demerit statistics for the class of 1852.

18. Mullan Demerit File, 1848-1852, West Point. For the demerit system generally, Morrison, *Best School*, 73-74.

19. The quote is from Morrison, *Best School*, 74.

20. For the bathing quote, Post Order No. 134, 22 Nov. 1849, West Point. For lack of privacy quote, Morrison, *Best School*, 72. Also see 77-78, 85, and Ambrose, *Duty, Honor, Country*, 151-55.

21. Post Orders, Special Order No. 65, 17 June 1850, West Point.

22. For the first quote, Lossing, *Cadet Life*, 285; for the second, Morrison, *Best School*, 70.

23. For the quote, Crackel, *West Point*, 115. Also see Morrison, *Best School*, 61. Shaw, "The Making of an Explorer," gathered the data for Mullan's class. For the poor graduation rates of this era and the significance of prep school, Morrison, *Best School*, 63, 89; and Ambrose, *Duty, Honor, Country*, 128-33.

24. Post Orders, Special Order No. 83, 15 June 1852, West Point, for Mullan's notice to proceed home. See Cullum, *Biographical Register* II, 482-83 for his promotion and initial placement.

CHAPTER 3

1. Stevens, *Life of Stevens*, 1:299.

2. For Stevens's access to the best people for his expedition, Richards, *Stevens*, 100.

3. For Stevens's physical characteristics, Richards, *Stevens*, 6. For the quote by expedition member George Suckley, Goetzmann, *Army Exploration*, 278-79.

4. For this period in Stevens's life, Richards, *Stevens*, 92-93; Stevens, *Life of Stevens*, 1:254-56, 272-74. Also see Richard Kluger, *The Bitter Waters of Medicine Creek: A Tragic Clash Between White and Native America* (New York: Alfred A. Knopf, 2011), 14-15.

5. For details on the Monticello Convention, *Cowlitz Historical Quarterly* 44(4), Dec. 2002, and 45(1), Mar. 2003.

6. Richards, *Stevens*, 96-98.

7. Stevens, *Life of Stevens*, 1:287-88.

8. For summaries of the vision and influence of Whitney, Philip Henry Overmeyer, "George B. McClellan and the Pacific Northwest," *Pacific Northwest Quarterly*, 32:1 (Jan. 1941), esp. 3-6; Alton Byron Oviatt, "The Movement for a Northern Trail: The Mullan Road, 1859-1869," Ph.D. diss., University of California, 1947, 2-3; Stephen Ambrose, *Nothing Like It in the World: The Men Who Built the Transcontinental Railroad, 1863-1869* (New York: Simon and Schuster, 2000), 27; and Goetzmann, *Army Exploration*, 262-78.

9. Goetzmann, *Army Exploration*, 305. Also, W. Turrentine Jackson, *Wagon Roads West: A Study of Federal Road Surveys and Construction in the Trans-Mississippi West, 1846-1869* (Berkeley: University of California Press, 1952), 321.

10. Goetzmann, *Army Exploration*, 274-75, 318, 331, 336 (quote); Jackson, *Wagon Roads West*, 242-43. Also, Ambrose, *Nothing Like It*, 59-60; and Paul D. McDermott, Ronald E. Grim, and Philip Mobley, *Eye of the Explorer: Views of the Northern Pacific Railroad Survey, 1853-54* (Missoula, MT: Mountain Press, 2010).

11. Ambrose, *Nothing Like It*, 60.

12. Stevens, *Life of Stevens*, 1:290; Richards, *Stevens*, 99, 128.

13. Richards, *Stevens*, 101-02, 109-10.

14. The quote is from an 1852 description of St. Louis by Adolphus M. Hart, in Lee Ann Sandweiss, *Seeking St. Louis: Voices From a River City, 1670-2000* (St. Louis: Missouri Historical Society Press, 2000), 176.

15. The Stevens quote is in *Railroad Survey*, 12(1):34.

16. Unless otherwise noted, details and quotes of the journey of the *Robert Campbell* come from the following sources. Fritiof M. Fryxell, *Ferdinand Hayden: A Young Scientist in the Great West, 1853-1855* (Rock Island, IL: Augustana Historical Society, 2010), 27-64; John Sunder, *The Fur Trade on the Upper Missouri, 1840-1865* (Norman:

University of Oklahoma Press, 1965), 149-57; Mike Foster, *Strange Genius: The Life of Ferdinand Vandeveer Hayden* (Niwot, CO: Roberts Rinehart Publisher, 1994), 35-53; Lesley Wischmann, *Frontier Diplomats: The Life and Times of Alexander Culbertson and Natoyis-Siskina'* (Spokane: The Arthur H. Clark Co., 2000), 217-45. Stevens summarized Donelson's official version of the trip in his *Railroad Survey* 12(1):79-82.

17. Foster, *Strange Genius*; James G. Cassidy, *Ferdinand V. Hayden: Entrepreneur of Science* (Lincoln: University of Nebraska Press, 2000).

18. Richard X. Evans, "Dr. John Evans, U.S. Geologist, 1851-1861," *Washington Historical Quarterly*, 26:2 (Apr. 1935), 83-89; Erwin F. Lange, "Dr. John Evans, U.S. Geologist to the Oregon and Washington Territories," *Proceedings of the American Philosophical Society*, 103:3 (June 1959), 476-77; "Benjamin Franklin Shumard," *The American Geologist*, 4:1 (July 1889), 1-6.

19. Foster, *Strange Genius*, 44-45; Fryxell, *Ferdinand Hayden*, 11-12, 45-49; Sunder, *Fur Trade on Upper Missouri*, 153-54.

20. Mullan could have had contact with survivors of tribes in the East, but his contact with Indians prior to 1853 it would have been limited.

21. Richards, *Stevens*, 13-14; Erwin N. Thompson, *Fort Union Trading Post: Fur Trade Empire on the Upper Missouri* (Medora, ND: Theodore Roosevelt Nature & History Association, 1986), 71-72.

22. Stevens's description of the fort is in *Railroad Survey* 12(1):85-86. Also see McDermott, et al., *Eye of the Explorer*, 58-61.

23. Stevens, *Railroad Survey*, 12(1):86; Sunder, *Fur Trade on Upper Missouri*, 155-56.

24. Details of the expedition from Fort Union to Fort Benton from Richards, *Stevens*, 114-18, and Stevens, *Railroad Survey*, 12(1):87-102.

25. For the quotes, Stevens, *Life of Stevens*, 1:313; Stevens, *Railroad Survey*, 12(1):95, 97; McDermott, et al., *Eye of the Explorer*, 70.

26. For Stevens's description of Fort Benton see *Railroad Survey*, 12(1):101-02. For a description from 1860, Martin D. Hardin, "Up the Missouri and Over the Mullan Road," *The Westerners, New York Posse Brand Book*, 5:2 (1958), 29.

27. For Stevens's time at Fort Benton and dividing his party, Richards, *Stevens*, 118-27.

CHAPTER 4

1. I will use the term Flathead rather than the preferred Salish, for it was the term used at the time. For a summary of the efforts of Flatheads to seek Black Robe missionaries, John C. Mellis, "Ignace Partui: Iroquois Evangelist to the Salish, ca. 1780-1837," *International Bulletin of Missionary Research*, 33:4 (Oct. 2009), 212-15. For the story of the various Flathead delegations to St. Louis, John Upton Terrell, *Black Robe: The Life of Pierre-Jean DeSmet, Missionary, Explorer, Pioneer* (New York: Doubleday & Co., 1964), 80-82; and Carriker, *DeSmet*, 18-30.

2. For descriptions of the mission, Evans, *St. Mary's in the Rocky Mountains*, esp. 89-97; Stevensville Historical Society, *Montana Genesis: A History of the Stevensville Area of the Bitterroot Valley* (Missoula: Mountain Press Publishing Co., 1971), 45; and Car-

riker, *DeSmet*, 48-54. The Jesuits would later return to the valley to construct another mission near the original location.

3. Evans, *St. Mary's*, 99-118; Merrill G. Burlingame, *The Montana Frontier* (Helena: State Publishing Co., 1942), 296-97.

4. The best source for the Owen trading post is George F. Weisel, ed., *Men and Trade on the Northwest Frontier as Shown by the Fort Owen Ledger* (Missoula: Montana State University, 1955), particularly Weisel's introduction and exhaustive footnotes. Also see *Montana Genesis*, 60-75. Nancy died in 1868, and Owen in his last years suffered an insanity of unknown cause. Because of large debts, he had to sell his Montana property, and in 1877 moved to Philadelphia. He died there in 1889. For Mullan's quote, John Mullan, *Miners and Travelers' Guide to Oregon, Washington, Idaho, Montana, Wyoming and Colorado* (Fairfield, WA: Ye Galleon Press, 1991), 48.

5. *Railroad Survey*, 12(1):122-23; Weisel, *Men and Trade*, xxii, xxv; Richards, *Stevens*, 100-03; *Montana Genesis*, 63.

6. Mullan's report of his trip is in *Railroad Survey* 1, 301-19, quote 319. Unless otherwise noted, details and quotes that follow about Mullan's expedition from Fort Benton to Fort Owen are from this source. For Stevens's summary of Mullan's exploration, *Railroad Survey*, 12(1):123-25. Mullan's instructions for the trip are in Stevens to Mullan, 8 Sept. 1853, in *Report of the Commissioner of Indian Affairs*, 33rd Cong., 1st Sess., Senate Ex. Doc. No. 1, Part 1, Serial Set No. 690, 462-63.

7. The best description of Cantonment Stevens comes in *Railroad Survey*, 12(1):181. Members of the Mullan party traveled regularly to Fort Owen to purchase coffee, tobacco, and other supplements to the rations Saxton had provided.

8. Mullan's report of the reconnaissance is in *Railroad Survey*, 1:319-22. Unless otherwise noted, details and quotes that follow about Mullan's expedition to Fort Hall are from this source. Weisel, *Men and Trade*, 67, suspects the "Mr. Owen" who guided Mullan was John's brother, Frank. Mullan does not say. But since John was the better known of the two, I have assumed if the guide was the other "Mr. Owen," Mullan might have noted that.

9. Mullan's report of this trip is in *Railroad Survey*, 1:322-49.

10. Weisel, *Men and Trade*, 5-7, 88-89; Evans, *St. Mary's*, 27, 38, 42, 72, 132, 139.

11. The classic study of western road building remains Jackson's *Wagon Roads West*. Also see Goetzman, *Army Exploration*; and Lawrence J. Malone, *Opening the West: Federal Internal Improvements Before 1860* (Westport, CT: Greenwood Press, 1998). In 1855 Congress established the Pacific Wagon Road Office under the Department of the Interior, partially in recognition of the value of roads to civilians, and for a time supervision of western road building was split between that office and the army.

12. For Cantonment Loring, Howard Stansbury, "The Bannock Montana Road," *Idaho Yesterdays*, 8:1 (Spring 1964), 10-15; John D. Nash, "The Salmon River Mission of 1855," *Idaho Yesterdays*, 11:1 (Spring 1967), 22-31; and Jennie Broughton Brown, *Fort Hall on the Oregon Trail: A Historical Study* (Caldwell, ID: The Caxton Printers, 1932), 309-10.

13. Mullan's quote is in *Railroad Survey*, 1:335. For Grant, Brown, *Fort Hall*, 316-23; Clyde A. Milner II and Carol A. O'Connor, *As Big as the West: The Pioneer Life of Granville Stuart* (New York: Oxford University Press, 2009), 47-48; and Weisel, *Men and Trade*, 80. Grant's son, Johnny, settled in Montana, where John Mullan's road eventually passed nearby. His memoir provides background about life along the Mullan Road in the 1860s. See Lyndel Meikle, *Very Close to Trouble: The Johnny Grant Memoir* (Pullman: Washington State University Press, 1996).

14. None of Sohon's biographers are able to pinpoint just when Mullan and Sohon met. By early 1854 Sohon was serving under Mullan at Cantonment Stevens. Most biographers assume he was there in the fall of 1853. Years later, Mullan recollected that "I became acquainted with him in October 1853," and that memory could well be accurate. Mullan to H.M. Teller, Secretary of the Interior, 24 June 188?, in the possession of Paul D. McDermott, who made it available to the author. In any event, Mullan and Sohon no doubt met at Cantonment Stevens. For Sohon, John Ewers, *Artists of the Old West* (Garden City, NY: Doubleday & Co., 1965), 164-73; Ewers, *Gustavus Sohon's Portraits of Flathead and Pend d'Oreille Indians, 1854* (Washington: Smithsonian Institution, 1948), Smithsonian Miscellaneous Collections 110(7); David Nicandri, *Northwest Chiefs: Gustav Sohon's Views of the 1855 Stevens Treaty Councils* (Tacoma: Washington State Historical Society, 1986); and McDermott, et.al., *Eye of the Explorer*. Also extremely helpful is Paul D. McDermott and Ronald E. Grim, *Gustavus Sohon's Cartographic and Artistic Works: An Annotated Bibliography* (Washington: Library of Congress, 2002), Philip Lee Phillips Society Occasional Paper Series No. 4.

15. Day Allen Willey, "Building the M.R." *Sunset*, 24:6 (June 1910), 638.

16. *Railroad Survey*, 1:350.

17. Salem *Oregon Statesman*, 16 May 1854; *Railroad Survey*, 1:349-52; and McDermott, et. al, *Eye of the Explorer*, 142-45.

18. For Mullan's account of this trip, *Railroad Survey* 1:516-27.

19. For Ogden, Weisel, *Men and Trade*, 103, and Albert J. Partoll, "Fort Connah: A Frontier Trading Post, 1847-1871," *Pacific Northwest Quarterly*, 30:3 (Oct. 1939), 399-415.

20. Sohon's painting of the raft incident is the most dramatic image to appear in all of Stevens's railroad reports. The image appears in *Railroad Survey*, 12(1) following 179.

21. Mullan, *Military Road 1863*, 6.

22. Details of Mullan's May-June trek, and all quotes, are in *Railroad Survey*, 1:527-29, and Mullan, *Military Road 1863*, 4-6.

23. For St. Ignatius Mission at this time—Mullan refers to it as the Pend d'Oreille Mission—Weisel, *Men and Trade*, 99-101. The mission would be moved to a different site, south of Flathead Lake, a few months after Mullan's visit.

24. Weisel, *Men and Trade*, xxxiv, for a description of Fort Colville at this time. The original mission site selected by DeSmet in 1842 was about thirty-five miles south, but was subject to flooding. In 1846 the Jesuits moved the mission to the site Mullan

visited. Stevens wrote a description of the mission from his 1853 visit. See *Railroad Survey* 12(1):133-34. For other contemporary accounts of the mission and construction details, Lawrence Kip, *Army Life on the Pacific: A Journal of the Expedition Against the Northern Indians* (New York: Redfield, 1859), 78-79; Ella E. Clark, "The Old Mission," *Idaho Yesterdays*, 15:3 (Fall 1971), 19-27; and Donald R. Tuohy, "Horseshoes and Handstones: The Meeting of History and Prehistory at the Old Mission of the Sacred Heart," *Idaho Yesterdays*, 2:2 (Summer 1958), 21-27. The church is now a National Historic Landmark and Idaho's oldest standing building.

25. Goetzman, *Army Exploration*, 283.

26. Stevens's analysis is summarized in Richards, *Stevens*, 140. Stevens noted that, "the Coeur d'Alene route is entirely practicable." Stevens to George Gibbs, 30 Aug. 1855, Box 1, Fldr. 7, WA MSS 443, Yale.

27. William Clark, 16 Sept. 1805, in Gary E. Moulton, ed., *The Journals of the Lewis and Clark Expedition* (Lincoln: University of Nebraska Press, 1988), 5:209.

28. Mullan's quote is in James McClellan Hamilton, *From Wilderness to Statehood: A History of Montana, 1805-1900* (Portland: Binfords & Mort, 1957), 127.

29. Mullan's description of the trip over Lolo is in *Railroad Survey*, 1:529-37. For a summary of the difficulty of this passage, Lynn N. Baird and Dennis W. Baird, *In Nez Perce Country: Accounts of the Bitterroots and the Clearwater after Lewis and Clark* (Moscow: University of Idaho Library, 2003).

30. Lin Tull Cannell, *The Intermediary: William Craig among the Nez Perces* (Carlton, OR: Ridenbaugh Press, 2010). Also, Benjamin Baughman, "Such Deeds of Darkness: Story of William Craig," *Idaho Yesterdays*, 46:2 (Spring/Summer 2005), 7-21.

31. Mullan's quotes are in *Railroad Survey*, 1:534-35. For contemporary accounts of the Craig home and farm, Cannell, *The Intermediary*, 52, 71, 78-82.

32. Hamilton, *Wilderness to Statehood*, 128. For the Stevens quote, *Railroad Survey*, 1:538.

33. *Railroad Survey*, 1:635. Also see Richards, *Stevens*, 116-18.

34. Gary L. Ecelbarger, *Frederick W. Lander: The Great Natural American Soldier* (Baton Rouge: Louisiana State University Press, 2000), 17, 28.

35. Ibid., 14; Richards, *Stevens*, 100, 155-56.

36. The quote is in *Railroad Survey*, 12(1):107. Also see Ecelbarger, *Frederick Lander*, 20-22; Richards, *Stevens*, 125.

37. For Lander's expedition for an alternative route, Ecelbarger, *Frederick Lander*, 22-31.

38. Ambrose, *Nothing Like It*, 23-39.

39. Ecelbarger, *Frederick Lander*, 34-65, quote 65; Mullan, *Military Road 1861*, 48.

40. Ecelbarger, *Frederick Lander*, 27.

41. For McClellan's efforts—or lack thereof—Overmeyer, "George B. McClellan"; Goetzman, *Army Exploration*, 280-301; Jackson, *Wagon Roads West*, 90-93; and Richards, *Stevens*, 136-42.

42. Richards, *Stevens*, 137.

43. Goetzman, *Army Exploration*, 299-304.

44. *Railroad Survey*, 12(1):181.

45. Richards, *Stevens*, 160-78.

46. For a description of the survey offices, Stevens, *Life of Stevens*, 1:421-22.

47. *Report of the Secretary of War, 1856*, 34ᵗʰ Cong., 3ʳᵈ Sess., Senate Ex. Doc. No. 5, Serial Set No. 876, 18.

CHAPTER 5

1. Henry M. McKiven Jr., "The Political Construction of a Natural Disaster: The Yellow Fever Epidemic of 1853," *Journal of American History*, 94:3 (Dec. 2007), 734-42; JoAnn Carrigan, *The Saffron Scourge: A History of Yellow Fever in Louisiana, 1796-1905* (Lafayette: University of Southwestern Louisiana, 1994); and for the numbers killed, "Yellow Fever Deaths in New Orleans, 1817-1905," Louisiana Division New Orleans Public Library, nutrias.org/facts/feverdeaths.htm, retrieved 12 Apr. 2012.

2. For a history of the Second Regiment, Theophilus F. Rodenbough and William L. Haskin, eds., *The Army of the United States: Historical Sketches of Staff and Line with Portraits of Generals-in-Chief* (New York: Maynard, Merrill & Co., 1896), 312, ff. Mullan's orders can be traced in "Returns from Regular Army Artillery Regiments," Microfilm M727, NA. Roll 12 covers the Second Regiment. Brief remarks on the postings—such as Mullan's AWOL status—help to explain troop activities, but contain little detail.

3. For Mullan's transfer request, Mullan to Col. S. Cooper, Adjutant General, 27 July 1855, M567, "Letters Received by the Office of the Adjutant General," Roll 522, year 1855, M file, 481-856. The epidemic quote is in the 1855 Annual Return of the Second Artillery, Company H, M727, Roll 12. Both NA. The report states the epidemic was cholera, which it could have been. But since some symptoms of yellow fever and cholera are similar, the cause could just as likely been the rampant yellow fever.

4. For the Topographic Engineers, Goetzman, *Army Exploration*; and Henry P. Beers, "A History of the U.S. Topographical Engineers, 1818-1863," www.topogs.org/history.htm, retrieved 16 Oct. 2011.

5. Ray B. Seley Jr., "Lieutenant Hartsuff and the Banana Plants," *Tequesta* 23 (1963), 3-14.

6. The best account of the Seminole Wars is John Missal and Mary Lou Missal, *The Seminole Wars: America's Longest Indian Conflict* (Gainesville: University Press of Florida, 2004). For the Third Seminole War, James V. Covington, *The Billy Bowlegs War, 1855-1858: The Final Stand of the Seminoles Against the Whites* (Chuluota, FL: The Mickler House Publishers, 1982).

7. Covington, *Billy Bowlegs*, 81-82.

8. Cullum, *Biographical Register* 2:483; Rebecca Mullan, Reminiscences, Box 8, Fldr. 9, Mullan Papers, Georgetown.

9. Dan L. Thrapp, "Captain John Mullan," *Encyclopedia of Frontier Biography* II (Glendale: The Arthur H. Clark Co., 1988).

10. Mullan's postings from 1855 on can be followed in Returns from the Regular Army Artillery Regiments, June 1821-January 1901, M727, Roll 12, Second Regiment: Jan. 1851-Dec. 1860, NA. George Cullum assembled much of his information from West Point graduates themselves or their families. So, at times the material in his *Register* is no more accurate than what he was told. Although Rebecca Mullan wrote her reminiscences a year after Cullum's *Register*, it seems likely she could have provided Cullum with the information about John's service in Florida. Is this something John told her—perhaps in a boastful moment? On the other hand, if John began courting Rebecca in 1856—as he could have since he was stationed most of that year at Baltimore's Fort McHenry—she might have had first-hand knowledge of his service in Florida. We will probably never know exactly. However, it is true that Rebecca's reminiscences contain several exaggerations that John could have corrected, but did not. A search of National Archives records turned up no evidence that Mullan applied for a military pension; such a record might have clarified whether or not he ever appeared in Florida.

11. Mullan's acceptance of the first lieutenant commission is in Mullan to Capt. P.T. Euaish (?), 18 July 1856, Letters Received by the Office of the Adjutant General Main Series, M567, Roll 542, 1856, M 121-620, NA. Mullan left West Point as a brevet second lieutenant in the First Artillery. In the fall of 1852 while at Fort Columbus he wrote that he would accept promotion to second lieutenant in the Second Artillery, but that promotion failed to materialize. However, a vacancy as a second lieutenant in the Second Artillery came open while Mullan served in the West with Isaac Stevens. A War Department circular stated that for brevet second lieutenants to "accept the promotion to which…they may become entitled," they had to approve the promotion. But communication with Mullan as he scouted railroad routes in 1853-54 was exceedingly slow. A letter caught up with Mullan regarding a promotion in Nov. 1853 while he was at Cantonment Stevens; Mullan was unable to reply until he reached Fort Hall the following month. In his letter of 15 Dec. 1853, Mullan seemed confused by a couple of vacancies for which he might be eligible. He agreed to accept one promotion but not another. As it turned out, the position Mullan seemingly declined came open, and the War Department—believing it was acting in Mullan's best interests and unable to correspond with Mullan in a timely fashion—promoted him anyhow. A report from the Adjutant General's office explained why Mullan had received a promotion he had not specifically accepted, summarizing, "There being then several vacancies in the 2nd Artillery the filling of which had been delayed by the failure to hear from Lieut. Mullan the Secretary of War decided that as he had once [while at Fort Columbus] signified his willingness to accept promotion to the 2nd Artillery, and this promotion could be advantageous to him…he should be promoted." Thus, Mullan went from the First Artillery to the Second, and became a second lieutenant. The promotion occurred in 1854, but became retroactively effective to fill a vacancy that had occurred in May 1853. The Adjutant General's "Report on the Case of 2nd Lt. J. Mullan, Jr. 2nd Arty," 26 July 1854, along with accompanying correspondence, is in Registers of Letters Received

by the Office of the Adjutant General, Main Series, 1812-1889, M711, Roll 26, Year 1854, Referencing Vol. 30, M211. Mullan's 15 Dec. 1853 letter from Fort Hall and a 12 Jan. 1854 letter from Cantonment Stevens, in both of which he laments the difficulty of sending and receiving mail, can be found in Letters Received by the Office of the Adjutant General, Main Series, M567, Roll No. 501: 1854, M2-595, M211. All sources in this note in NA.

12. Richard D. Scheuerman and Michael O. Finley, *Finding Chief Kamiakin: The Life and Legacy of a Northwest Patriot* (Pullman: Washington State University Press, 2008), 22, 44; Richards, *Stevens*, 132.

13. Scheuerman and Finley, *Kamiakin*, 35. For the Puget Sound treaties, Kluger, *Bitter Waters*.

14. For the best description of the council, Richards, *Stevens*, 215-26, and Scheuerman and Finley, *Kamiakin*, 37-42. For Craig being featured in the painting, Cannell, *The Intermediary*, 84.

15. The complete treaty text can be found at History Link, www.historylink.org.

16. Scheuerman and Finley, *Kamiakin*, 40-42.

17. For Stevens hearing of the gold discovery while in Walla Walla, Richards, *Stevens*, 219-20. For "Eldorado," Robert Ignatius Burns, *The Jesuits and the Indian Wars of the Northwest* (Moscow: University of Idaho Press, 1966), 125.

18. Stevens to George Gibbs, 30 Aug. 1855, Box 1, Fldr. 7, WA. MSS. 443, Yale; Richards, *Stevens*, 212-13; William J. Trimble, *The Mining Advance Into the Inland Empire* (Fairfield, WA: Ye Galleon Press, 1986), 15-23, newspaper quote 16; Scheuerman and Finley, *Kamiakin*, 45.

19. William Norbert Bischoff, "The Yakima Indian War, 1855-1856," Ph.D. diss., Loyola University, 1950, 65; Richards, *Stevens*, 236-37; Scheuerman and Finley, *Kamiakin*, 45.

20. Scheuerman and Finley, *Kamiakin*, 45; Richards, *Stevens*, 237.

21. Richards, *Stevens*, 239-41; Burns, *Jesuits and Indian Wars*, 128.

22. Richards, *Stevens*, 241; for the Rains message, Bischoff, "Yakima Indian War," 126-27. Also see Scheuerman and Finley, *Kamiakin*, 49-51.

23. Richards, *Stevens*, 245-48; Scheuerman and Finley, *Kamiakin*, 51, 59.

24. Schlicke, *George Wright*, 106-19.

25. Richards, *Stevens*, 289-312.

26. Ibid., 313-26.

27. Mullan, *Military Road 1863*, 7; "Remarks of John Mullan, 7 May 1863," 8.

28. John J. Killoren, *"Come Blackrobe": DeSmet and the Indian Tragedy* (Norman: University of Oklahoma Press, 1994), 217, 219.

29. Richards, *Stevens*, 318, 323-26.

30. Stevens, *Life of Stevens*, 2:276.

31. Mullan, *Military Road 1863*, 8.

PRELUDE, SECTION II

1. For first person accounts of events at Latah Creek, John Mullan, "Field Notes," CDA; for Wright's account, *Report of the Secretary of War, 1859*, 35th Cong., 2nd Sess., House Ex. Doc. No. 2, 35th Cong., 2nd Sess., Serial Set No. 998; Erasmus D. Keyes, *Fighting Indians in Washington Territory* (Fairfield, WA: Ye Galleon Press, 1988), 21-41; and Kip, *Army Life on the Pacific*. For secondary accounts, Scheuerman and Finley, *Kamiakin*, 69-90; Burns, *Jesuits and Indian Wars*, 298-317; Benjamin Franklin Manring, *Conquest of the Coeur d'Alenes, Spokanes & Palouses* (Fairfield, WA: Ye Galleon Press, 1975); and Schlicke, *George Wright*, 141-96.

2. *Railroad Survey* 1:518.

CHAPTER 6

1. War Department to Mullan, 12 Mar. 1858, RG 77, Entry 359, Box 3, NA.

2. Mullan to Capt. A.A. Humphreys, Topographical Engineers, 12 Mar. 1858, ibid.

3. For the quote on the importance of the road and Mullan, San Francisco *Globe*, 1 May 1858; that paper also reprinted a glowing report on the road that had appeared in the 5 Apr. 1858 New York *Journal of Commerce*. The Vancouver description is from Father DeSmet's 1854 observation, quoted in Burns, *Jesuits and Indian Wars*, 331. For Mullan's departure from New York, Mullan, *Military Road 1863*, 8. For a description of the *Sonora*, John Haskell Kemble, *The Panama Route, 1848-1869* (Berkeley: University of California Press, 1943), 247.

4. The first quote is from Charles W. Frush, who hired on with Owen out of The Dalles, "A Trip From The Dalles of the Columbia, Oregon, to Fort Owen, Bitter Root Valley, Montana, in the Spring of 1858," *Contributions to the Historical Society of Montana* 2 (Helena: State Publishing Co., 1896), 337. Also see Kip, *Army Life*, 21.

5. Mullan, two letters to Humphreys, 12 Mar. 1858; the second includes the crossed-out name of his brother as a suggested assistant. The quote is in Mullan to Humphreys, 3 Apr. 1858. All in RG 77, Entry 359, Box 3, NA.

6. McDermott and Grim, *Gustavus Sohon*, 37.

7. Mullan to Commanding Officer, Fort Walla Walla, 27 May 1858, RG 77, Entry 359, Box 3, NA. For the initial exaggerated report of Steptoe's losses, Burns, *Jesuits and Indian Wars*, 236.

8. The quote is from an 1859 description of the country in Strachan, *Blazing the Mullan Trail*, 25. Mullan's confirmation that he has received Steptoe's express is in Mullan to Steptoe, 1 June 1858, RG 77, Entry 359, Box 3, NA. For work on the road before receiving Steptoe's message, Mullan, *Military Road 1863*, 8-9, and Pal Clark, ed., "Journal from Fort Dalles O.T. to Fort Wallah Wallah W.T. July 1858, Lieut John Mullan U.S. Army," in *Sources of Northwest History*, No. 18 (Missoula: State University of Montana, c. 1932), 3-4.

9. Steptoe to Major W.W. Mackall, San Francisco, 23 May 1858, RG 77, Entry 359, Box 3, NA.

10. Mullan to Steptoe, 1 June 1858, ibid.

11. Mullan to Humphreys, 14 June 1858, ibid.; Mullan, *Military Road 1863*, 9. The quote is in Burns, *Jesuits and Indian Wars*, 237.

12. John A. Hemphill and Robert C. Cumbow, *West Pointers and Early Washington* (Seattle: The West Point Society of Puget Sound, 1992), 167-80; Jackson, *Wagon Roads West*, 140-44; Manring, *Conquest*, 266-73; Richards, *Stevens*, 303.

13. Steptoe later supervised the move of Fort Walla Walla to higher ground. Both of these forts were located about thirty miles from an earlier Hudson's Bay Company post of the same name on the Columbia River, which Mullan usually referred to as Old Fort Walla Walla. See Larry Hussey, *Fort Walla Walla: Then and Now* (Walla Walla: Privately Published, 1994).

14. Hemphill and Cumbow, *West Pointers*, 178.

15. Trimble, *Mining Advance*, 32; *Message of the President of the United States, 1858*, 35th Cong., 2nd Sess., House Ex. Doc. No. 2, Serial Set No. 998, 344-45.

16. The quote is from Father DeSmet's springtime description of the country, in Burns, *Jesuits and Indian Wars*, 196. Various authors have estimated the size of Steptoe's force. In all probability, it was 160, including Steptoe and a surgeon. For the best effort to verify the force's strength see Hussey, *Fort Walla Walla*, 164-65.

17. Rodney Frey, *Landscape Traveled by Coyote and Crane: The World of the Schitsu'umsh* (Seattle: University of Washington Press, 2001), 80.

18. For the quote, Burns, *Jesuits and Indian Wars*, 196. For suspicions over Steptoe's circuitous route, Laura Woodworth-Ney, "Tribal Sovereignty Betrayed: The Conquest of the Coeur d'Alene Indian Reservation, 1840-1905," Ph.D. diss, Washington State University, 1996, 114; Frey, *Coyote and Crane*, 80. Part of Steptoe's purpose was to investigate the deaths of the two miners. He also wanted to impress the Indians with a show of strength. Neither purpose could be accomplished by marching directly to Colville.

19. Steptoe to Mackall, 23 May 1858; Wright to Mackall, 26 May 1858, both in *Message of the President, 1858*, 350-51.

20. The first quote is in Schlicke, *George Wright*, 146. The second is in *Message of the President, 1858*, 346. For Steptoe's arms and ammunition, also see Hussey, *Fort Walla Walla*, 166-67; Burns, *Jesuits and Indian Wars*, 202; and Manring, *Conquest*, 71-73. The best recent analysis of the Steptoe campaign is Mahlon E. Kriebel, "Battle of To-hots-nim-me: The U.S. Army vs. the Coeur d'Alene Indians," *Bunchgrass Historian*, 34:2/3 (2008), entire issue.

21. For Steptoe's quote, *Message of the President, 1858*, 347.

22. Steptoe to Major W.W. Mackall, 23 May 1858, ibid., 349.

23. Scott's statement is in ibid., 348. The second quote is from a history of the U.S. Cavalry published at the end of the Civil War, cited in Burns, *Jesuits and Indian Wars*, 230.

24. For the quote, Stevens, *Life of Stevens*, 2:283. Also, Richards, *Stevens*, 331-32.

25. Schlicke, *George Wright*, 154; Wright to Mackall, 26 May 1858, *Message of the President, 1858*, 351.

26. Burns, *Jesuits and Indian Wars*, 152. Also, Frush, "A Trip from The Dalles to Fort Owen."

CHAPTER 7

1. Kip, *Army Life*, 12. For the movement of troops from Kentucky and Utah, Burns, *Jesuits and Indian Wars*, 269-70. Many of the troops traveling great distances arrived after hostilities ceased.

2. For Clarke's instructions to Wright, W.W. Mackall, Assistant Adjutant General to Wright, 4 July 1858. Clarke also demanded that Inland tribes return the booty collected after Steptoe's battle and relinquish to the army the warriors instrumental in the attack on Steptoe. *Message of the President of the United States, 1858*, 35th Cong., 2nd Sess., House Ex. Doc. No. 2, Serial Set No. 998, 361-64.

3. Keyes, *Fighting Indians*, 5, 21-22. For Mullan as a Keyes student, Rebecca Mullan, Reminiscences, Box 8, Fldr. 9, Mullan Papers, Georgetown.

4. Mullan to Captain A.A. Humphreys, 21 June 1858, RG 77, Entry 359, Box 3, NA.

5. For Mullan's offer to volunteer, Mullan to Mackall, 26 June 1858; for Wright's acceptance and his quote, Wright to Mullan, 14 July 1858, ibid. For Mullan's quote, *Military Road 1863*, 9.

6. Kip, *Army Life*, 24-27. Clark, ed., "Journal from Fort Dalles." Mullan's official account of his time with Wright, including the march from The Dalles to Walla Walla, is in his *Topographical Memoir of Col. Wright's Campaign*, 1859, 35th Cong., 2nd Sess., Senate Exec. Doc. No. 32, Serial Set No. 984. UISC holds a unique copy of this volume. The government document had been sent to Mullan, probably in the 1870s or 1880s, apparently with the request that he correct his memoir—which he had written hurriedly in the winter of 1858-59 while in Washington, D.C.—and add other notations, which Mullan did. The volume was then re-bound with Mullan's handwritten notations set side-by-side with the original pages of the document, and eventually donated to UISC.

7. Clark, "Journal from Fort Dalles," 5, 7. For "brutally butchered," Mullan, *Topographical Memoir*, 10.

8. Clark, "Journal from Fort Dalles," 10.

9. For Craig in Walla Walla, Cannell, *The Intermediary*, 145; "Nez Perce Agency," Idaho State Historical Society Reference Series No. 761, 1983. For Wright's treaty with the Nez Perce, *Message of the President, 1858*, 370-71.

10. Kip, *Army Life*, 35. The schism among the Nez Perce is cogently summarized in Burns, *Jesuits and Indian Wars*, 174-78. For background on the peace treaty, Wright to Mackall, 23 May 1858, 349 and Mackall to Wright, 4 July 1858, 363-64. Both *Message of the President, 1858*. Mullan described the treaty scene in *Topographical Memoir*, 11.

11. The "eagle-eyed" quote is in Wright to Mackall, 31 Aug. 1858, *Message of the President, 1858*, 385. Mullan's quote is in his Field Notes, 31 Aug. 1858, CDA. For how the Nez Perce selected the thirty warriors, William Compton Brown, *The Indian Side of the Story* (Spokane: C.W. Hill Printing Co., 1961), 230.

12. For Mullan on the Nez Perce, *Message of the President, 1858*, 632-34. For "am I among savages," *Railroad Survey* 1:308.

13. Kip, *Army Life*, 39-40; Lieutenant P.A. Owen, Orders No. 3, 3 Aug. 1858, 381; General N.S. Clarke to Lt. Col. L. Thomas, 12 Aug. 1858, 369. Both *Message of the President, 1858*.

14. Kip, *Army Life*, 40-42.

15. The first quote is in Kip, *Army Life*, 41-42; the second in Henry Harrison Walker to James McPherson, 25 Aug. 1858, "Affairs at Fort Vancouver in Washington Territory During the Indian Wars of 1858," WA MSS S-930, Yale. Mullan did not leave an account of the fight, but did note laconically, "a number of incidents, on the part of both friendly and hostile Indians, occurred while we lay at Fort Taylor, that served to break the monotony of camp life." *Topographical Memoir*, 13.

16. As the main body of troops moved on, a company of artillery remained at Fort Taylor to protect the crossing in the event of a hasty retreat. Kip, *Army Life*, 42; Mullan, *Topographical Memoir*, 13; and Schlicke, *George Wright*, 360-61.

17. Wright to Mackall, 19 Aug. 1858, *Message of the President, 1858*, 384.

18. Wright to Mackall, 31 Aug. 1858, ibid., 385.

19. Manring, *Conquest of the Coeur d'Alenes*, 184.

20. Wright to Mackall, 31 Aug. 1858, *Message of the President, 1858*, 385; Kip, *Army Life*, 44-45; Burns, *Jesuits and Indian Wars*, 282; Schlicke, *General George Wright*, 161-62. The size of the force has been variously estimated. Wright stated his force consisted of 570 army regulars and 100 civilians; Kip gave the figures as 680 and 200. The "animals of all kinds" included horses, pack animals, and cattle.

21. Burns, *Jesuits and Indian Wars*, 273-74.

22. The quote is in Mullan's Field Notes for the period 24-28 Aug. 1858, CDA. For daily life on the march, Kip, *Army Life*, 25; Schlicke, *George Wright*, 163.

23. Mullan, Field Notes, 24-28 Aug. 1858, CDA; Wright to Mackall, 31 Aug. 1858, *Message of the President, 1858*, 385.

24. For Mullan's association with an odometer, *Owyhee Avalanche*, 30 June 1866. For the abandonment and destruction of Mullan's cart, Kip, *Army Life*, 77, 86; and Mullan, Field Notes, 12 Sept. 1858, CDA. Mullan never described his odometer carts, but those in common usage in the West at this time were two-wheeled, pulled by one horse.

25. Mullan, Field Notes, 30 Aug. 1858, CDA; Wright to Mackall, 31 Aug. 1858, *Message of the President*, 1858, 385-86.

26. Mullan, Field Notes, 31 Aug. 1858, CDA.

27. Kip, *Army Life*, 52-60; quotes, 53, 55. Also see Wright to Mackall, 2 Sept. 1858, *Message of the President, 1858*, 386-90.

28. For the arrangement of the Indian forces, Scheuerman and Finley, *Kamiakin*, 83-84; for the Indian tactics, Kip, *Army Life*, 85. Wright estimated the size of his enemy at 400-500. In 1935, the Spokane County Pioneer Association and other groups erected a monument in Four Lakes that reads, "On this historic ground, Sept. 1, 1858, 700 soldiers under Col. Geo. Wright U.S.A. routed 5,000 allied Indians." In more recent years, in an act of historically accurate vandalism, someone has eliminated one of the zeros in the figure estimating the number of warriors.

29. Kip, *Army Life*, 57-58.

30. The quote is in Burns, *Jesuits and Indian Wars*, 292. Also see Kip, *Army Life*, 85. Wright's forces suffered no casualties.

31. Wright to Mackall, 2 Sept. 1858, *Message of the President, 1858*, 386-90; Burns, *Jesuits and Indian Wars*, 292-93.

32. Wright to Mackall, 2 Sept. 1858, *Message of the President, 1858*, 386-90; Mullan to Capt. A.A. Humphreys, 2 Sept. 1858, RG 77, Entry 359, Box 3, NA.

33. Kip, *Army Life*, 63.

34. Mullan, Field Notes, 5 Sept. 1858, CDA; Kip, *Army Life*, 63-64. Kamiakin was not the only Indian leader, but he, more than any other, was responsible for assembling the alliance.

35. Sohon's sketch is in Scheuerman and Finley, *Kamiakin*, 85. Mullan, Field Notes, 5 Sept. 1858, CDA for the quote.

36. Mullan, Field Notes, 5 Sept. 1858, CDA.

37. Burns, *Jesuits and Indian Wars*, 297.

38. Mullan, Field Notes, 8-10 Sept. 1858, CDA. Also, Schlicke, *George Wright*, 176-77.

39. Keyes, *Fighting Indians*, 28-29; Mullan, Field Notes, 8-10 Sept. 1858, CDA. Manring, *Conquest of the Coeur d'Alenes*, 215, notes that the bones were clearly visible in 1911. Kip, *Army Life*, 75, states that most of the 100 horses that the troops retained either escaped or were shot, "entirely too wild to be of any use."

40. Mullan, Field Notes, 8-10 Sept. 1858, CDA; Wright to Mackall, 30 Sept. 1858, *Message of the President, 1858*, 402-03; Kip, *Army Life*, 70, 76; Thomas Beal, "Pioneer Reminiscences," *Washington Historical Quarterly* 8:2 (Apr. 1917), 85. Joset is quoted in Burns, *Jesuits and Indian Wars*, 300.

41. Kip, *Army Life*, 83-85, and Mullan, Field Notes, 16-19 Sept. 1858, CDA, described the treaty council. This treaty and the one Wright later signed with the Spokanes—essentially identical—can be found in *Letters from the Secretary of War*, 36th Cong., 1st Sess., House Ex. Doc. No. 65, Serial Set 1051, 89-90.

42. Mullan, Field Notes, 24 Sept. 1858, CDA.

43. For the Hercules quote, Keyes, *Fighting Indians*, 34. For the other quotes, Kip, *Army Life*, 103.

44. Beall, "Pioneer Reminiscences," 83-90. Also see Cannell, *The Intermediary*, 147, 156. Manring, *Conquest*, originally published in 1912, states (255) that Mullan's odometer wagon was used as a "handy platform for the gruesome" hangings that Wright ordered, although he does state that soldiers pulled Qualchan into the air, and so therefore does not claim the wagon's use for that particular hanging. But Manring's story of Mullan's wagon serving as a moveable platform has been often repeated. Altogether, Wright probably hanged sixteen Indians in 1858, the first on Sept. 8, and Qualchan, being the second, on Sept. 24. If Mullan's wagon was used at all, it could only have been for the Sept. 8 hanging. As Mullan recorded, on Sept. 12 the fallen timber on Wright's route along Lake Coeur d'Alene became so dense that "it soon became evident that we must abandon our odometer wagon which thus far had accompanied us on our journeys." Mullan, Field Notes, CDA. Kip, *Army Life*, 77 confirms the loss of the wagon. Mullan and Kip both provide great detail of the events of Sept. 8, but neither mention the use of Mullan's wagon in the hanging.

45. The number of Indians executed by Wright that fall has been variously estimated at between twelve and sixteen. The higher number seems the most plausible.

46. Kip, *Army Life*, 105.

47. Ibid., 116-17.

48. Keyes, *Fighting Indians*, 36-37; Manring, *Conquest of the Coeur d'Alenes*, 245.

49. Mullan to Humphreys, 2 Sept. 1858; Wright, Special Order No. 9, 30 Sept. 1858; Mullan to Humphreys, 10 Oct. 1858, all RG 77, Entry 259, Box 3, NA. Salem *Oregon Statesman*, 23 Nov. 1858, 30 Nov. 1858.

50. Michael Kenny, writing from Fort Walla Walla, to "Brother," 10 Oct. 1858, "Fort Walla Walla—Military," Box 2, N153.7, Whitman, described carrying the bones in a "bag," which was probably a parflesche. For the ceremonial burial see Kip, *Army Life*, 123-24. A few years later the remains of Captain Oliver Taylor and Lieutenant William Gaston were disinterred and reburied side by side at West Point cemetery.

51. "Slaughter and destruction" is in Wright to Mackall, 15 Sept. 1858, *Message of the President, 1858*, 396. For the high assessment of the campaign, Durwood Ball, *Army Regulars on the Western Frontier, 1848-1861* (Norman: University of Oklahoma Press, 2001), 51 (quote), 141. Kip, *Army Life*, 128.

52. Schlicke, *George Wright*, 213-356.

53. Scheuerman and Finley, *Kamiakin*, 92-95, 115-21.

54. Wright, Special Order No. 9, 30 Sept. 1858, RG 77, Entry 359, Box 3, NA; Keyes, *Fighting Indians*, 40.

CHAPTER 8

1. Mullan to Humphreys, 2 Sept. 1858, RG 77, Entry 359, Box 3, NA.

2. Mullan, *Military Road 1863*, 9.

3. Mullan to Humphreys, 30 Nov. 1858, RG 77, Entry 359, Box 3, NA.

4. Mullan to Humphreys, 4 Sept. 1858, ibid. As Mullan worked in D.C., word reached the capital of a memorial from Washington Territory enthusiastically seeking congressional funding for the road. Olympia *Pioneer and Democrat*, 17 Dec. 1858.

5. Mullan to Humphreys, 7 Jan. 1859, RG 77, Entry 359, Box 3, NA for the inadequacy of the appropriation. Oviatt, "The Movement for a Northern Trail," 18-25. Also see Jackson, *Wagon Roads West*, 104-06.

6. Mullan to Humphreys, 7 Jan. 1859, RG 77, Entry 359, Box 3, NA. For Mullan's report of the Wright campaign, Mullan, *Topographical Memoir*.

7. Mullan, *Military Road 1863*, 10; Ecelbarger, *Lander*, 47-48.

8. Humphreys to Mullan, 15 Mar. 1859; Mullan to Humphreys, 15 Mar. 1859 (multiple letters); 16 Mar. 1859; 17 Mar. 1859. All RG 77, Entry 359, Box 3, NA.

9. U.S. Passport Applications, 1795-1925, "Rebecca W. Mullan," search.ancestry.com, retrieved 23 Oct. 2011. Details for this section from Rebecca Mullan, Reminiscences, 1892, Box 8, Fldr. 9; and Rebecca's 1859 Diary, Box 8, Fldr. 14, both Mullan Papers, Georgetown. All quotes in the pages that follow are from her diary.

10. Charles B. Tiernan, *The Tiernan and Other Families* (Baltimore: William J. Gallery & Co., 1901), 15-18; "Murrill v. Neill," United States Supreme Court, 49 U.S. 414, Syllabus by Justice Peter Vivian Daniel, en.wikisource.org/wiki/Murrill_v._ Neill, retrieved 25 Jan. 2012; "Luke Tiernan Comments," trees.ancestry.com/ tree/13250491/person/320293937, retrieved 26 Mar. 2011.

11. *Oregon Union*, 7 May 1859, as quoted in Oscar Osburn Winther, *The Old Oregon Country: A History of Frontier Trade, Transportation, and Travel* (Stanford: Stanford University Press, 1950), 203; Olympia *Pioneer and Democrat*, 28 Jan. 1859, 29 Apr. 1859.

12. Clark, ed., "Journal from Fort Dalles"," 4; Mullan, *Military Road 1863*, 153-54; Mullan to Humphreys, 7 Jan. 1859, RG 77, Entry 359, Box 3, NA.

13. Rebecca's Diary, Box 8, Fldr. 14, Mullan Papers, Georgetown.

14. Mullan, *Military Road 1861*, 5; Salem *Oregon Statesman*, 12 July 1859. RG 77, Entry 359, Box 3, NA, for the period 1859-60, contains numerous letters from Mullan justifying expenses. For example, see Mullan to Humphreys, 4 Sept. 1859 where Mullan writes, "the difficulties and length of the route & the manner of overcoming them have been so often and in such detail set before the Dept. in my previous reports, that it would hardly seem necessary to call attention to them again."

15. Humphreys to Mullan, 15 Mar. 1859, RG 77, Entry 359, Box 3, NA. Mullan, *Military Road 1861*, 5; Mullan, *Military Road 1863*, 10.

16. Ken Robison, "Mullan's Hardworking Wagonmaster John A. Creighton," *150th Anniversary Mullan Road Conference* (Fort Benton, MT: May 20-22, 2010), 4-5; "Family History of Mullan's Wagonmaster," Mineral County Historical Society *Mullan Chronicles*, 11:1 (Autumn 2006), 3. Strachan, *Blazing the Mullan Trail*, 31.

17. For Howard's illness, Mullan, *Military Road 1861*, 4. For DeLacy's 1859 explorations, Mullan, *Military Road 1863*, 89-94, 118-26.

18. It is likely Stevens remembered DeLacy from West Point, for the two attended the academy at the same time.

19. Walter W. DeLacy Papers, Mss. Coll. 52, and "Walter W. DeLacy" Vertical File, both MHS; William F. Wheeler, "Walter Washington DeLacy," *Contributions to the Historical Society of Montana* 2 (Helena: State Publishing Co., 1896), 241-51.

20. Kolecki described one of the more spectacular 360 degree viewsheds in America—a place that would become a National Natural Landmark. His report is in Mullan, *Military Road 1863*, 103-05. Today the word "steptoe" is a geological term used to describe an isolated protrusion of bedrock in a lava flow. Though named for Colonel Edward Steptoe, his encounter with Indians did not occur here, as is often mistakenly assumed. The battle took place at the current town of Rosalia, several miles to the north.

21. Sohon's account is in Mullan, *Military Road 1863*, 95-100. For Jesuits requesting a route away from the mission, Lieut. J. L. White to Capt. A. Pleasonton, 17 July 1859, in Donna M. Hanson, ed., *Frontier Duty: The Army in Northern Idaho, 1853-1876* (Moscow: University of Idaho Library, 2005), 52.

22. Mullan, *Military Road 1861*, 4. Jesuits rightfully feared the impact of Mullan's road. Lieutenant James White, of the military escort, reported to Captain Alfred Pleasonton that he believed "the Fathers to be more opposed to the route than are the Indians." Hanson, *Frontier Duty*, 63. Mullan recognized the problems his road created: "I fear that the location of our road, and the swarms of miners and emigrants that must pass here…will so militate against the best interests of the mission that its present site will have to be…abandoned." *Miners and Travelers' Guide*, 47. The prediction proved accurate. In 1877 the Jesuits relocated to a new mission site at DeSmet, many miles southwest.

23. Rebecca's Diary, Box 8, Fldr. 14, Mullan Papers, Georgetown.

24. A lawsuit involving Mullan, WAL 757, WSA-Cheney, documents Mullan's purchase of Walla Walla property in 1858. It is unclear just when Mullan left Walla Walla. In a July 3 correspondence with Humphreys he states "we moved from Walla Walla on the 25th of June," but he is probably referring to his advance party; Mullan, *Military Road 1861*, 2. In *Military Road 1863*, 12, he notes "we started again [from Walla Walla] on the 1st of July," which is probably the date he left.

25. Mullan, *Military Road 1863*, 12-13; Mullan, *Military Road 1861*, 2.

26. Strachan, *Blazing the Mullan Trail*, 32.

27. For the quote, ibid. I am taking some liberties here, as there is no description of a camp on the south side of the Snake. But it is likely that before facing a hazardous crossing, where some of the advance crew had spent five days making it to the northern side of the river, tents went up. In any event, the Sibley and A tents would be mainstays of the crew's existence in the following months. See Mullan to Humphreys, 22 Nov. 1860, RG 77, Entry 359, Box 3, NA.

28. Strachan, *Blazing the Mullan Trail*, 32; Robison, "Mullan's Hardworking Wagonmaster," 4; Willey, "Building the M.R.," 638; Mullan, *Military Road 1861*, 2-3; Mullan, *Military Road 1863*, 12-13.

29. The quotes are from White to Pleasonton, 2 July 1859, in Hanson, *Frontier Duty*, 30. Hanson transcribed White's handwriting for the drowned private's last name as Lancaster, an easy mistake given his handwriting. For the correct spelling see Mineral County Historical Society, *Mineral County Pioneer* 6 (Summer 1989), 8.

30. For Brown, see White to Pleasonton, 2 July 1859, in Hanson, *Frontier Duty*, 30. For the fight, Strachan, *Blazing the Mullan Trail*, 32. The Mineral County Historical Society in Superior, Montana, has collected biographical information on members of Mullan's road crew. These are arranged alphabetically in the society's research files. Much of the information that appears in this book regarding crew members came from these files.

31. For early navigation and the *Colonel Wright*, Randall V. Mills, *Stern-wheelers Up Columbia: A Century of Steamboating in the Oregon Country* (Palo Alto: Pacific Books, 1974), esp. 40-43; Carlos A. Schwantes, *Long Day's Journey: The Steamboat and Stagecoach Era in the Northern West* (Salt Lake City: Gibbs-Smith, 1999); Fritz Timmons, *Blow for the Landing: A Hundred Years of Steam Navigation on the Waters of the West* (Caldwell, ID: Caxton Printers, 1973), esp. 2-21, 141-43; and Lulu Donnell Crandel, "The Colonel Wright," *Washington Historical Quarterly*, 7:2 (Apr. 1916), 126-32.

32. The Dalles *Journal*, 4 June 1859.

33. Mullan to Humphreys, 4 Sept. 1859, RG 77, Entry 359, Box 3, NA.

34. Mullan established a series of supply depots convenient to his road work where provisions were off-loaded.

35. Strachan, *Blazing the Mullan Trail*, 32-3; and Mullan to Pleasonton, 17 July 1859, Hanson, *Frontier Duty*, 53.

36. Mullan, quoted in Willey, "Building the M.R.," 638. Also see Oscar Osburn Winther, "Early Commercial Importance of the Mullan Road," *Oregon Historical Quarterly*, 46:1 (Mar. 1945), 24.

37. Mullan to Pleasonton, 26 July 1859, RG 77, Entry 359, Box 3, NA; Mullan Field Notes, 8 June-31 Dec. 1859, CDA; Thomas Hughes to Indian Agent A.I. Cain, 18 Aug. 1859, Hanson, *Frontier Duty*, 67.

38. Mullan, *Military Road 1861*, 18; Willey, "Building the M.R.," 638; Mullan, *Military Road 1863*, 175. For the sophistication of the maps, Paul D. McDermott and Ronald D. Grim, "The Mapmaker as Artist: Early Visuals of the American West," *Mercator's World*, 1:1 (1996), 28-33. The meteorological observations of Wiessner, the expedition's astronomer, are in Mullan, *Military Road 1863*. Eileen Starr, professor emeritus of science, Valley City State University, North Dakota, provided me with copies of two unpublished analyses she wrote concerning Mullan's measurements, "How High Am I: Or Determining the Elevation of the Mullan Road," 2012; and "How the Mullan Expedition Knew Their Location When Building the Military Road Between Fort Walla Walla and Fort Benton," n.d.

39. Mullan, *Military Road 1863*, 3.

40. Solar chronometer No. 7691 was broken in Feb. 1860.

41. Mullan, *Military Road 1861*, 12.

42. Starr maintains that Wiessner's initial elevation for Walla Walla was high, and he carried this error through all later measurements. Still, Starr found the calculations to be "remarkably close to the actual values."

43. Mullan, *Military Road 1863*, 13-15. For the precaution near Steptoe's battlefield, Strachan, *Blazing the Mullan Trail*, 35.

44. War Department to Mullan, 12 Mar. 1858, 15 Mar. 1859, RG 77, Entry 359, Box 3, NA. Olympia *Pioneer and Democrat*, 12 Aug. 1859.

45. Mullan, *Military Road 1863*, 16; Mullan, *Military Road 1861*, 8.

46. Willey, "Building the M.R.," 638; Mullan, *Military Road 1861*, 8.

47. For Mullan's quotes, Willey, "Building the M.R.," 638. DeSmet gave the description about the sun unable to penetrate, quoted in Burns, *Jesuits and Indian Wars*, 305.

48. Schafft was writing about the area east of the Coeur d'Alene Mission, but the challenges were the same in the densely forested areas the road crew encountered southwest of the mission. "Blazing the Mullan Road: Reminiscences," fortbenton. blogspot.com/2008/08/blazing-mullan-road-reminiscences.html, retrieved 24 Feb. 2009.

49. Mullan, *Military Road 1863*, 15; Mullan, *Military Road 1861*, 7; Mullan to Humphreys, 11 Mar. 1860, RG 77, Entry 359, Box 3, NA, contains reports and details of the construction effort, as does Mullan's Field Notes, 8 June-31 Dec. 1859, CDA.

50. The quotes are from Mullan, Field Notes, 1859, CDA.

51. For details on the boats see Mullan, *Military Road 1861*, 7, 11; Mullan, *Military Road 1863*, 16; and Mullan to Humphreys, 11 Mar. 1860, RG 77, Entry 359, Box 3, NA. General William T. Sherman, traveling the Mullan Road in 1877, noted that the flatboats were still in use. *Travel Accounts of General William T. Sherman to Spokan Falls, Washington Territory, in the Summers of 1877 and 1883* (Fairfield, WA: Ye Galleon Press, 1985), 126-27.

52. For Mullan as a worker, Schafft, "Blazing the Mullan Road: Reminiscences." For work on Sundays, Mullan, *Military Road 1861*, 22. For the reprimand, Humphreys to Mullan, 10 Sept. 1859, RG 77, Entry 359, Box 3, NA.

53. Mullan records taking mass at the mission in his Field Notes, 1859, CDA.

54. Willey, "Building the M.R.," 638; Mullan, *Military Road 1863*, 18; *Military Road 1861*, 17-18.

55. For the first quote, Mullan, *Military Road 1863*, 18; for the second, Mullan, Field Notes, 1859, CDA. For additional details on Sohon's sortie, Mullan, *Military Road 1861*, 18, 24. Despite Mullan's complete confidence in Sohon, he understood the complexity of this mountain range and the hurried nature of Sohon's reconnaissance. He accurately predicted "a more thorough examination of this special locality...shall...discover a better pass." *Military Road 1861*, 34. When Interstate 90 came through the area, it went over nearby Lookout Pass—200 feet lower in elevation than the one Mullan named for Sohon. Sohon Pass was later renamed St. Regis Pass.

56. For the quotes, Mullan to Humphreys, 12 Mar. 1858, RG 77, Entry 359, Box 3, NA; Mullan, *Military Road 1861*, 13.

57. The quotes are in Strachan, *Blazing the Mullan Road*, 38; Mullan, *Military Road 1863*, 18; Mullan, *Military Road 1861*, 20, 24; and White to Pleasonton, 3 Sept. 1859 and 5 Oct. 1859 in Hanson, *Frontier Duty*, 68, 70.

58. The first quote is in Mullan, *Military Road 1861*, 16; the second in a report from Johnson attached to Mullan's letter to Humphreys, 11 Mar. 1860, RG 77, Entry 359, Box 3, NA.

59. Mullan, *Military Road 1861*, 16. Constructing sidecuts above the flood plain was out of the realm of possibility, given Mullan's resources. Even the builders of Interstate 90 in the twentieth century yielded to geography here. Present-day freeway travelers cross bridges over the crooked river at frequent intervals.

60. Mullan provided a detailed description of only one bridge—across the Blackfoot River. It was the most substantial of all, but the construction methods would have been basically the same for all bridge work. See Mullan, *Military Road 1863*, 32. He noted a few construction details on smaller bridges in *Military Road 1861*, 2, 7. For a description of bridges in the region shortly after Mullan's time, Jon Axline, *Montana's Historic Highway Bridges, 1860-1956* (Helena: Montana Historical Society Press, 2005), 11-22.

61. For the quotes, Mullan, *Military Road 1861*, 26; White to Pleasonton, 14 Nov. 1859, RG 77, Entry 359, Box 3, NA. The final quote, from a letter written 17 Oct. 1859, published in the *New York Times*, 23 Feb. 1860.

62. Mullan, *Military Road 1861*, 27; White to Pleasonton, 14 Nov. 1859, RG 77, Entry 359, Box 3, NA.

63. White to Pleasonton, 14 Nov. 1859, RG 77, Entry 359, Box 3, NA; Mullan, *Military Road 1861*, 23, 27.

64. Strachan, *Blazing the Mullan Trail*, 38.

65. Mullan to Pleasonton, 26 July 1859; Mullan to Humphreys, 4 Sept. 1859. RG 77, Entry 359, Box 3, NA.

66. Strachan, *Blazing the Mullan Trail*, 38; Olympia *Pioneer and Democrat*, 12 Aug. 1859 (quote), 26 Aug. 1859; The Dalles *Journal*, 6 Aug. 1859.

67. Mullan, *Military Road 1861*, 4 for the first quote; 19 for trading procedures. For the second quote, Mullan to Major Pinkney Lugenbeel, 19 July 1859, in Hanson, *Frontier Duty*, 59. Mullan's Field Notes, 1859, CDA, record the nearly daily contact with tribal members.

68. Mullan, *Military Road 1861*, 10, 19; Mullan, Field Notes, 1859, CDA.

69. Hughes to A.J. Cain, 18 Aug. 1859 in Hanson, *Frontier Duty*, 67.

70. Strachan, *Blazing the Mullan Trail*, 39.

71. For "eternal spring," Helen Addison Howard, *Northwest Trail Blazers* (Caldwell, ID: The Caxton Printers, 1963), 146. For the temperature, Mullan, *Military Road 1861*, 29. For Sibley tents, Mullan to Humphreys, 15 Mar. 1859, RG 77, Entry 359,

Box 3, NA. Mullan does not state for whom he named the winter camp, and some sources claim it was named for Charles D. Jordan, a West Point graduate, 1842. But it does not appear his path and Mullan's crossed. Since Mullan, *Military Road 1863*, 8, praised Thomas Jordan, it seems most likely he named the camp for him. Mullan called the river St. Regis de Borgia; Lieutenant White referred to it as St. Francis de Borgia. It is now more simply known as the St. Regis.

72. Mullan described Cantonment Jordan in *Military Road 1861*, 29, and Willey, "Building the M.R.," 639. For Kautz, Martin F. Schmidt, "From Missouri to Oregon in 1860: The Diary of August V. Kautz," *Pacific Northwest Quarterly*, 37:3 (July 1946), 227. "Journal of the March of a Detachment of U.S. Recruits for Oregon Commanded by Major George A.H. Blake," WA MSS S-1721, Yale, is the official record of the expedition that included Kautz. The entry for 10 Sept. 1860 briefly described the "good log building" that had served as the storehouse. For the earthen embankments still being visible in 1915, Weisel, ed., *Men and Trade*, 89.

73. Mullan, *Military Road 1863*, 18; also Mullan, *Military Road 1861*, 27-29.

74. For the quote, Mullan, *Military Road 1863*, 18; also Mullan, *Military Road 1861*, 28-29.

75. Mullan, *Military Road 1861*, 31 for the quotes. Also see White to Pleasonton, 8 Jan. 1860, in Hanson, *Frontier Duty*, 76.

76. Strachan, *Blazing the Mullan Trail*, 40. For news of Murray, St. Louis *Missouri Republican*, 1 Apr. 1860.

77. Mullan, *Military Road 1861*, 25, 36.

78. Three of Toohill's trip reports are published. See Mullan, ibid., 98, 152-55, and Hanson, *Frontier Duty*, 77-78. See Mullan to Humphreys, 16 Jan. 1860, RG 77, Entry 359, Box 3, NA for the time required for cross-country mail delivery.

79. Mullan, *Military Road 1863*, 21-22. One assumes that Williamson returned with mules, but Mullan is unclear. For additional background on Williamson, Weisel, *Men and Trade*, 202-03.

80. *Weekly Oregonian*, 31 Dec. 1859; The Dalles *Journal*, 7 Jan. 1860.

81. Mullan's first quote is in a letter to Pleasonton, 1 June 1860, Hanson, *Frontier Duty*, 85; his second in *Military Road 1861*, 30. Johnson's letter to the editor is reprinted in Schafft, "Blazing the Mullan Road: Reminiscences."

82. Mullan, *Military Road 1863*, 19.

83. "Journal of the Survey of the 49th Parallel, 1857-1861," 9 May 1860 entry, George Clinton Gardner Papers, Bancroft.

84. Mullan, *Military Road 1863*, 19-20.

85. Mullan, *Military Road 1861*, 42-43; Willey, "Building the M.R.," 639; White to Pleasonton, 2 Apr. 1860, Hanson, *Frontier Duty*, 80. The fresh vegetables from the mission no doubt helped, particularly if the provisions included potatoes, carrots, and cabbage. More significant is the fact that the civilians ate frozen beef, including, no doubt, organs. Though not understood at the time, fresh meat and animal

organs such as liver contain enough vitamin C to prevent scurvy. Lynn Goebel, "Scurvy," *Medscape Reference,* emedicine.medscape.com/article/125350-overview, retrieved 16 Mar. 2012.

86. For Mullan's quote, *Military Road 1861,* 28; Strachan, *Blazing the Mullan Trail,* 8.

87. The quote is in Mullan, *Military Road 1863,* 20. For the efforts of settlers and Flatheads, Mullan, *Military Road 1861,* 40, and Willey, "Building the M.R.," 639.

88. Biographical details on Johnson are in "Walter W. Johnson," undated typescript, MINCO. Details on Johnson's mission in Mullan, *Military Road 1861,* 31-32, 36.

89. Mullan, *Military Road 1861,* 16-17.

90. Ives to Mullan, 18 Apr. 1860, RG 77, Entry 359, Box 3, NA.

91. Mullan to Humphreys, 16 Jan. 1860, ibid.

92. *Message of the President of the United States,* 36th Cong., 1st Sess., Sen. Ex. Doc. No.2, Serial Set No. 1024, 13. For gold discoveries, *Military Road 1861,* 18. For Mullan's efforts to keep the gold discovery quiet, Salt Lake *Herald,* 25 Dec. 1889. Mullan effectively hushed the news about gold even among his own crew. Lieutenant James White of the military escort wrote, after he received Floyd's report, "I was surprised to see…a statement…of the existence of valuable mineral deposits, in the mountains through which the road passes. If any such discovery has been made by any one attached to this expedition, he has kept his secret well." White to Pleasonton, 31 May 1860, Hanson, *Military Duty,* 83.

93. The quote is in Mullan, *Military Road 1863,* 21.

94. Mullan to Humphreys, 27 July 1858, RG 77, Entry 359, Box 3, NA.

95. Mullan, *Military Road 1862,* 17, 33.

96. Strachan, *Blazing the Mullan Trail,* 40-41; Mullan, *Military Road 1861,* 30, 37, 41; Mullan, *Military Road 1863,* 20.

97. Strachan, *Blazing the Mullan Trail,* 42; Mullan, *Military Road 1863,* 20; Mullan, *Military Road 1861,* 46.

98. For Fort Owen at this time, Stevensville Historical Society, *Montana Genesis,* 60-75, and Weisel, *Men and Trade,* xxiv-xxx. For Mullan's arrival, *Military Road 1861,* 38.

99. Weisel, *Men and Trade,* 77-79, detailed supplies Mullan purchased. For the rise and fall of Fort Owen with the military road, see xxx. Mullan, *Military Road 1861,* 38 for Engle and the stock.

100. Strachan, *Blazing the Mullan Trail,* 46; Mullan, *Military Road 1863,* 212; Mullan, *Military Road 1861,* 39-40.

101. For Booth, Mullan, *Military Road 1863,* 23. For Sheridan, Mullan to Humphreys, 4 Aug. 1860. For the five disabled, James Mullan to John Mullan, 28 July 1860. Humphreys tried to pay for Sheridan's care out of the road appropriation—even writing the Secretary of War to seek assistance—but it is unclear if he succeeded, writing once, "I have not much expectation of its success." See Humphreys to B. Blake, Commissioner of Public Buildings, 27 Sept. 1860, and to William Drinkard,

Acting Secretary of War, 28 Sept. 1860. All correspondence in RG 77, Entry 359, Box 3, NA.

102. Mullan to Humphreys, 8 June 1860, RG 77, Entry 359, Box 3, NA.

103. Strachan, *Blazing the Mullan Trail*, 46-47; Mullan, *Military Road 1861*, 50-51; Mullan, *Military Road 1863*, 23-24.

104. The first quote is in Olympia *Pioneer and Democrat*, 21 May 1858. For Mullan's later recollections, Willey, "Building the M.R.," 640.

105. Mullan described the route beyond Mullan Pass in *Military Road 1863*, 25-26. His letter to Humphreys is in *Military Road 1861*, 50.

106. Mullan, *Military Road 1863*, 24. Also see Mullan, *Military Road 1861*, 47 for the anticipation with which Mullan awaited the eclipse.

107. Mullan, *Military Road 1863*, 179.

108. Mullan to Lieutenant LaRhett L. Livingston, Adjutant, Third Artillery, 17 July 1860, RG 77, Entry 359, Box 3, NA.

109. Correspondence, lists of specimens sent, and other materials relating to Pearsall's collecting can be found in Accession Numbers 269 (1859), and 173, 186, 233, and 253 (1860), Smithsonian.

110. For a description of field methods used by Smithsonian-trained scientists of this era, Cassidy, *Hayden*, 48-51.

111. F.B. Meek and F.V. Hayden, "Descriptions of New Cretaceous Fossils from Nebraska Territory, Collected by the Expedition Sent Out by the Government Under the Command of Lieutenant John Mullan," *Proceedings of the Academy of Natural Sciences of Philadelphia*, 14 (1862), 21-28. John L. LeConte, "New Species of Coleoptera Inhabiting the Pacific District of the United States," *Proceedings of the Academy of Natural Sciences of Philadelphia*, 13 (1861), 335-90. LeConte harshly criticized Pearsall for withholding part of his collection from the Smithsonian.

112. Pearsall to Baird, 7 Apr. 1861, Accession No. 186 (1860), Smithsonian.

113. For Mullan gathering specimens, Mullan to Baird, 3 Oct. 1859, Accession No. 269 (1859), Smithsonian.

114. For the quote, Mullan, *Military Road 1861*, 33. For Blake's trip upriver, Schmitt, "Diary of August V. Kautz," 193-230, and John E. Parsons, ed., Martin D. Hardin, "Up the Missouri and Over the Mullan Road," a two-part story in *The Westerners, New York Posse Brand Book*, 5:1 (1-18), 5:2 (29-38), 1958. For Blake, "Brevet Generals," www.generalsandbrevets.com, retrieved 2 Apr. 2012.

115. All quotes from Schmitt, "Diary of August Kautz," 217-18.

116. For the 1859 trip, see Chouteau's personal account in "Early Navigation of the Upper Missouri River," *Contributions to the Historical Society of Montana* 7 (Helena: Montana Historical and Miscellaneous Library, 1910), 253-56. For the significance of the 1860 landing at Fort Benton, James McClellan Hamilton, *From Wilderness to Statehood: A History of Montana, 1805-1900* (Portland: Binfords & Mort, 1957), 145-46.

117. For Mullan's anticipation of what became the Bozeman Trail, *Military Road 1861*, 49. Summaries of the Raynolds expedition and its connections to Mullan's work can be found in Goetzman, *Army Exploration*, 417-26, and Jackson, *Wagon Roads West*, 266-69, 283-84.

118. The quote is from Strachan, *Blazing the Mullan Trail*, 53. Also Mullan, *Military Road 1863*, 27.

119. Strachan, *Blazing the Mullan Trail*, 55-56; Mullan, *Military Road 1863*, 27. Strachan, 12-13, reported that on the party's return to St. Louis, "as we were of the long lost expedition which was reported through the press at one time all frozen and starved to death, and other times massacred by the Indians, we found many enquirers and no little attention."

120. Mullan, *Military Road 1863*, 27.

121. Mullan stated in a letter to Humphreys that he would "retain one assistant and a force of about 25 men," *Military Road 1861*, 53. In his Field Notes, Whitman, he reveals that he actually had a larger crew, because of his custom of providing extra wages for members of the escort. On Aug. 13 he reported thirty-three men at work; on Aug. 17, forty-eight. On Aug. 8 he recorded the number of wagons and animals, and daily entries for Aug. 9-13 describe the dysentery. For the latter also see *Military Road 1861*, 56, and *Military Road 1863*, 28.

122. Mullan provided daily details of his trek in his Field Notes, Whitman, which contain the quote. The journey is summarized in *Military Road 1861*, 54-70.

123. The quotes are in Mullan's Field Notes, Whitman, for, respectively, 7 Sept. and 4 Sept.

124. Mullan, *Military Road 1861*, 54, 67, 70; and for Johnson's report, 161-68.

125. Ibid., 54.

126. There are three accounts of the Blake expedition. The official "Journal of the March," Yale, from which the quotes are taken, is the only account of the trip from the Coeur d'Alene Mission to Walla Walla. Blake's party split at the mission, with some continuing to Walla Walla and others ordered to Fort Colville. Schmitt, "Diary of August Kautz," and Parsons, "Up the Missouri and Over the Mullan Road," both record the travel as far as the mission and then—off the Mullan Road—to Colville.

127. Portland *Weekly Oregonian*, 20 Oct. 1860; 9 July 1860.

128. Mullan, *Military Road 1861*, 70. Mullan's recollections were recorded in the Sacramento *Daily Record-Union*, 19 Apr. 1889.

CHAPTER 9

1. For the Schaaft quote, Vivian A. Paladin, "Sketch of a Life," *Montana: The Magazine of Western History*, 26:1 (Jan. 1976), 30. The second quote is in Mullan, "United States Military Road Expedition from Fort Walla Walla to Fort Benton, W.T.", *Report of the Secretary of War, 1861*, 37th Cong., 2nd Sess., Sen. Ex. Doc. No. 1, Serial

Set No. 1118, Vol. II, 549. Mullan would later pick up an additional seventy-nine men as part of his military escort.

2. For Kolecki, Mullan, *Military Road 1863*, 28; also Mullan from the "Steamer Pacific, Bakers Bay, Wash. Ter." to Capt. James Hardie, 18 Jan. 1861, *The War of the Rebellion: A Compilation of the Official Records of the Union and Confederate Armies*, Series I, Vol. L, Pt. I (Washington: Government Printing Office, 1897), 434. For the denial and eventual acceptance of Mullan's travel reimbursement request, see Lt. Col. Hartman Bache, Topographical Engineers, to Mullan, 31 Aug. 1861, Reel 23; and Major J.C. Woodruff, Topographical Engineers, to Mullan, 26 Dec. 1862, Reel 24. Both in "Letters Sent by the Topographical Bureau of the War Department and by Successor Divisions in the Office of the Chief of Engineers," RG 66, NA.

3. Mullan, *Military Road 1863*, 29 notes that he traveled by stage on the southern overland route. For the Twain quote, "Riding the Overland Stage, 1861," www.eyewitnesstohistory.com/stage.htm, and for the quote by journalist Waterman Ormsby, "Butterfield Overland Mail," www.parks.ca.gov, both retrieved 4 May 2012.

4. Mullan's quote is in *Military Road 1863*, 29. The second quote is from Oviatt, "Northern Trail," 42. For Humphreys's approval of Mullan's original road improvement concept, Humphreys to Secretary of War, 24 Jan. 1861, RG 77, Entry 359, Box 3, NA.

5. Margaret Leech, *Reveille in Washington, 1860–1865* (Alexandria, VA: Time-Life Books Inc., 1980), esp. 1–55; and Adam Goodheart, *1861: The Civil War Awakening* (New York: Alfred A. Knopf, 2011).

6. McWilliams, *Annapolis*, 166–74.

7. Goodheart, *1861*, 124–25.

8. Ibid., 131.

9. Mullan, *Military Road 1863*, 29.

10. Mullan to Swan, 12 Jan. 1861. The letter is in the personal collection of Thomas Minckler of Thomas Minckler Fine Art. A copy was made available to the author by Major Ryan Shaw of West Point. Mullan dated his letter, written from Portland, 1860, an obvious mistake, for he was in Cantonment Jordan in January 1860. But in January 1861 he was in Portland on his way to D.C. For Stevens's unsuccessful bid for a third term as territorial delegate, Richards, *Stevens*, 354–58.

11. For the dearth of road building during the war, Jackson, *Wagon Roads West*, 281.

12. For Mullan arriving in Walla Walla on Apr. 22, Hartman Bache to Mullan, 14 Aug. 1861, RG 66, Microfilm Reel 23, NA. For delays due to difficulty in hiring crew, Mullan to Humphreys, 14 May 1861, *Report of the Secretary of War, 1861*, 549. For leaving on May 13, Portland *Daily Oregonian*, 20 May 1861.

13. Mullan, *Military Road 1863*, 29.

14. Ibid.

15. Mullan to Humphreys, 4 June 1861, *Report of Secretary of War, 1861*, 552–55; Mullan, *Military Road 1863*, 29–30.

16. The quotes are in Mullan, *Military Road 1863*, 30. For Plante, see Jack Nisbet and Claire Nisbet, "Antoine Plante," www.historylink.org, retrieved 8 May 2012; Jerome Peltier, *Antoine Plante: Mountain Man, Rancher, Miner, Guide, Hostler and Ferryman* (Fairfield, WA: Ye Galleon Press, 1983).

17. Mullan to Humphreys, 4 June 1861, *Report of Secretary of War, 1861*, 554.

18. The quote is in Mullan to Major Hartman Bache, 1 Aug. 1861, *Report of Secretary of War, 1861*, 564. For Sohon, 554, 557. Details on the number of troops, supplies, etc. are provided in Major W.W. Mackall, Special Order No. 50, 8 Apr. 1861, in *War of the Rebellion*, 461-62.

19. Details of this section of road construction and the quotes are in Mullan to Major Hartman Bache, Bureau of Topographical Engineers, 20 June 1861, 14 July 1861, 1 Aug. 1861, and 16 Aug. 1861, *Report of Secretary of War, 1861*, 555-66.

20. Mullan to Bache, 14 July 1861, ibid., 560.

21. Mullan to Bache, 1 Aug. 1861, ibid., 563.

22. The quote is in Mullan to Bache, 5 Sept. 1861, ibid., 569. For Mullan receiving word of the *Chippewa* disaster, Bache to Mullan, 20 Sept. 1861, RG 77, M66, "Letters Sent by the Topographical Bureau of the War Department and by Successor Divisions in the Office of the Chief of Engineers, 1829-1870," Reel No. 23, NA. For details of the *Chippewa* fire, Hiram Martin Chittenden, *History of Early Navigation on the Missouri River*, 2 volumes (New York: Francis P. Harper, 1903), 1:220-21.

23. Mullan, *Military Road 1863*, 31-32; Mullan to Bache, 5 Sept. 1861, *Report of Secretary of War, 1861*, 569.

24. Paul C. Phillips, ed., *Forty Years on the Frontier as Seen in the Journals of Granville Stuart* (Lincoln: University of Nebraska Press, 1977), 200; "Uncle Dan" Drumheller, *"Uncle Dan" Drumheller Tells Thrills of Western Trails in 1854* (Spokane: Inland-American Printing Co., 1925), 61-65; J. Orin Oliphant, "Winter Losses of Cattle in the Oregon Country, 1847-1890," *Washington Historical Quarterly*, 23 (Jan. 1932), 8-9.

25. Mullan, *Military Road 1863*, 32.

26. The quote is in Second Lieutenant Salem S. Marsh to First Lieutenant A.C. Wildrick, Fort Vancouver, 6 Nov. 1861, *War of the Rebellion*, 790. A variety of dispatches to and from various posts in the West attempting to get word to Mullan can be found in this volume, 676, 726, 730, 732, 738, 745, 750, 897, 957, 972-73, and 1119-20.

27. For the first quote Salem *Oregon Statesman*, 7 Apr. 1862; for the latter two, Mullan, *Military Road 1863*, 33.

28. The first quote and information on Mullan's party is in Thomas W. Harris, "Fort Owen Journal, 1860-62," Small Collection No. 231, Fldr. 4. Mullan's original handwritten lecture, preserved by Owen, is in Small Collection No. 547. Both MHS. Owen loaned a copy of Mullan's talk to the Deer Lodge *New Northwest*, which published it on 8 Apr. 1870. The editor's introduction contains the other quotes.

29. Schafft left two autobiographical accounts. His handwritten "Sketch of a Life," 1887, is in Small Collection No. 1234, MHS. Vivian A. Paladin edited this and published it in *Montana: The Magazine of Western History*, 26:1 (Jan. 1976), 26-37. Schafft also

wrote in the Fort Benton *Record Weekly*, 2 Jan. 1880, reprinted with a foreword and afterword by Ken Robison as "Blazing the Mullan Road: Reminiscences." Mullan, *Military Road 1863*, 32-33, does not mention Schafft by name, but does give a brief account of his "sad accident."

30. Schafft died in 1891. He served variously in Montana as a county clerk, justice of the peace, Indian agency clerk, bookkeeper, postmaster, and newspaper reporter.

31. George Wright to L. Thomas, Adjutant General, 1 Mar. 1862, *War of the Rebellion*, 897-98. Mullan did not mention the arrest. Details come from Schafft in Paladin, "Sketch of a Life," 30, and "Blazing the Mullan Road: Reminiscences." Schafft claimed it as the first arrest in Montana, which is probably accurate.

32. Mullan, *Military Road 1863*, 32. For Sohon's sketch, McDermott and Grim, "The Mapmaker as Artist," 30.

33. Mullan, *Military Road 1863*, 34. Mullan had discretionary authority to discharge his crew either at Walla Walla or Fort Benton. A.A. Humphreys to J. Jolt, Secretary of War, 24 Jan. 1861, *War of the Rebellion*, 439-40.

34. Mullan, *Military Road 1863*, 35. Randall H. Hewitt, *Across the Plains and Over the Divide: A Mule Trail Journey from East to West in 1862, and Incidents Connected Therewith* (New York: Broadway Publishing Co., 1906), 373. Hewitt found most bridges on the road "weakening with age" (370), "unsafe," (402), "sadly demoralized," "destroyed by fire," or "serious obstructions to travel" (397).

35. Mullan, *Military Road 1863*, 35. For the continuing confusion over, and conflicting nature of Marsh's orders, *War of the Rebellion*, 119-20, 790, 1136-37, 1143.

36. Mullan, *Military Road 1863*, 36. Jackson, *Wagon Roads West*, 325-26.

37. Walla Walla *Washington Statesman*, 16 Aug. 1862. The quote describing Walla Walla in Oct. 1862 is from Helen Addison Howard, ed., "Diary of Charles Rumley from St. Louis to Portland, 1862," *Frontier and Midland*, 19:3 (Spring 1939), 200. Mullan noted the meeting with the emigrants at Latah (Hangman) Creek in *Military Road 1863*, 36.

38. Howard, "Diary of Charles Rumley," 200; Mullan, *Military Road 1863*, 36.

39. Walla Walla *Washington Statesman*, 1 Feb. 1862, 12 July 1862.

40. For the territorial resolution, Rebecca Mullan, Reminiscences, Box 8, Fldr. 9, Mullan Papers, Georgetown. For Mullan's promotion to captain, Cullum, *Biographical Register*, 2:483. Wright's recommendation came in an 18 Oct. 1862 letter to Major General Henry W. Halleck. Mullan later provided this "unsolicited" letter to the Topographical Bureau. Letters Received by the Topographical Bureau of the War Department, 1824-1865, M 275, Microfilm M506, Roll 54, NA. Wright noted that Mullan had served "far removed…from the seat of war ever since the commencement of the rebellion" and had "not accrued that promotion which he was so justly entitled to."

41. Mullan stated, *Military Road 1863*, 36, that he left Walla Walla on Sept. 11. But the Walla Walla *Washington Statesman*, 6 Sept. 1862, stated that he and Sohon "will leave here tomorrow." Mullan wrote two long dispatches to the *Washington States-*

man about their trip. They were reprinted as "From Walla Walla to San Francisco," *Oregon Historical Quarterly*, 4:3 (Sept. 1903), 202-26; quotes, 202-03.

CHAPTER 10

1. Richards, *Stevens*, 359-87.

2. Stevens, *Life of Stevens*, 1:261.

3. Long to Mullan, 7 Nov., 10 Nov., 17 Nov. 1862, Letters Sent by the Topographical Bureau of the War Department and by Successor Divisions in the Office of the Chief of Engineers, 1829-1870, RG 77, M66, Reel 24, NA. The seventy-eight-year-old Long had once operated as independently as had Mullan, undertaking one of the most significant army explorations of the early nineteenth century West, but clearly was unwilling at this stage of his life to grant such latitude to Mullan.

4. Long to Mullan, 11 July 1862, Letters Sent by the Topographical Bureau, RG 77, M66, Reel 23, NA.

5. For the first quote, Jackson, *Wagon Roads West*, 276; for the second, Richards, *Stevens*, 344.

6. J. Gary Williams and Ronald W. Stark, eds., *The Pierce Chronicles: Personal Reminiscences of E.D. Pierce as Transcribed by Lou A. Larrick* (Moscow: Idaho Research Foundation, 1976).

7. [Merle W. Wells], "Idaho's Centennial: How Idaho was Created in 1863," *Idaho Yesterdays*, 7:1 (Spring 1963), 48-49. Also see Wells, "The Creation of the Territory of Idaho," *Pacific Northwest Quarterly*, 40:2 (Apr. 1949), 106-23. When Stevens withdrew his name from consideration for territorial delegate in 1861, the Democrats, unable to agree on a single candidate, instead ran two. With division in the Democratic ranks, Wallace won with 43 percent of the vote. See Richards, *Stevens*, 352-58. Anne Laurie Bird documented Wallace's life in a multi-part biography that appeared in *Idaho Yesterdays*, beginning with 1:1 (Spring 1957), through 3:1 (Spring 1959), under the title, "Portrait of a Frontier Politician." See 2:3 (Fall 1958), for detail on the territorial boundary issue.

8. The quote is in Wells, "Idaho's Centennial," 52.

9. Ibid., 53-56.

10. Ibid., 53.

11. The name Idaho for the proposed new territory had been discussed previously, but for some reason Mullan and Ashley referred to their new territory as Montana.

12. Wells, "Idaho's Centennial," 53-54; David H. Leroy, "Lincoln and Idaho: A Rocky Mountain Legacy," *Idaho Yesterdays*, 42:2 (Summer 1998), 12.

13. Wells, "Idaho's Centennial," 54; Leroy, "Lincoln and Idaho," 12-13.

14. Mullan advocated for a new territory in his *Miners and Traveler's Guide*, 68-69. Idaho's awkward boundaries and the difficulties of governing in a territory/state with such significant geographic and transportation challenges has been the subject of work by several historians. The best synopsis of the theme is Carlos A. Schwantes,

In Mountain Shadows: A History of Idaho (Lincoln: University of Nebraska Press, 1991). Well into the twentieth century, residents of northern Idaho lobbied for either annexation to Washington or the formation of a new territory/state as advocated by Mullan.

15. Sacramento *Daily Union*, 6 Apr. 1863.

16. The letters are in General Records of the Department of State, 1763-2002, RG 59, Series: Applications and Recommendations for Public Office, NARA.

17. Mullan to Lincoln, 4 Mar. 1863; record of senators meeting with Lincoln, 5 Mar. 1863, ibid.

18. Mullan might have also given some consideration to campaigning for Idaho's new position as territorial delegate to Congress. As early as Feb. 1863, the Sacramento *Daily Union*, noting Mullan's efforts to establish the new territory, stated, "it is expected that the grateful Salmon river miners will return Lieut. Mullan as their first Delegate to Congress in default of his being the recipient of the office of Governor, for which he is now the contingent applicant." Quoted in Walla Walla *Washington Statesman*, 14 Feb. 1863. The *Daily Union*, no friend of Mullan's, gleefully noted on 6 Apr. 1863, "Captain Mullan is understood to be a candidate for the delegateship from the new Territory, but he has failed to make much of a stir." If Mullan gave consideration to the office, it was probably fleeting. Newly married and with business concerns in Walla Walla, the prospect of campaigning in the huge new territory could not have been inviting. William Wallace would become Idaho's first congressional delegate and thus served as governor—the position Mullan truly did covet—for only a few months.

19. Mullan submitted his resignation to Colonel S.H. Long, 4 Apr. 1863, RG 77, Records of the Office of the Chief of Engineers, M 506, Roll 54, Letters Received by the Topographical Bureau of the War Department, 1824-1865, NA. Quote from Rebecca's Diary, Box 8, Fldr. 14, Mullan Papers, Georgetown.

20. Glen Adams believed the loss of the governorship "the most likely explanation" for Mullan's resignation. See his introduction in *Military Road 1863*, 9A. Mullan wrote his letter on 2 Dec. 1862; it appeared in the Walla Walla *Washington Statesman* on 14 Feb. 1863.

21. Weisel, ed., *Men and Trade*, 72.

22. The first quote is in Walla Walla *Washington Statesman*, 14 Feb. 1863; the second is from the transcription of a 14 May 1861 clipping, probably the Portland *Oregonian*, in the May 1861 file, MINCO.

23. The *Washington Times* carried Sohon's death notice on 8 Sept. 1903, and a brief notice on 25 Dec. 1903 that he left his estate to his wife Julia. For a brief biographical account of Sohon's life, McDermott and Grim, *Gustavus Sohon*, 54. McDermott made available to the author copies of three letters of recommendation for Sohon written by Mullan, which McDermott had received from members of the Sohon family. The quote is from Mullan to H.M. Teller, Secretary of the Interior, 24 June 188?, recommending the "eminently qualified" Sohon as an Indian agent in Washington Territory.

24. Historian Jane McWilliams of Annapolis provided information about Mullan's brief tenure as alderman.

25. Neither John nor Rebecca left an account of their voyage. John had previously traveled via the Isthmus and would have prepared Rebecca for the unpleasant trip. Still, the travel was easier than taking the overland stage. For descriptions of the journey see John Haskell Kemble, *The Panama Route, 1848–1869*, University of California Publications in History 29 (Berkeley: University of California Press, 1943).

26. The description of Aspinwall's streets, as they appeared in 1854, is in Stevens, *Stevens*, 1:433–44. Passengers complained far less about the West Coast steamers then they did their East Coast counterparts.

PRELUDE, SECTION III

1. For the European trip, Washington *Sunday Herald*, 14 June 1885; inaugural ball, Washington *National Republican*, 5 Mar. 1885; Emma as debutante, Sacramento *Daily Record-Union*, 3 Nov. 1887.

2. Waterman's letter appeared in Sacramento *Daily Record-Union*, 6 Feb. 1888.

3. Mullan's letter is recorded in ibid., 19 Jan. 1889, which also contains the details of the meeting between Mullan and the governor. For the hotel, Edith E. Pitt, "History of the Golden Eagle Hotel," www.sonoma.edu/asc/projects/golden_eagle/1_01_History_Golden_Eagle_Hotel.pdf, retrieved 25 Jan. 2011.

4. San Francisco *Call*, 8 Feb. 1888.

5. San Francisco *Chronicle*, 7 Feb. 1888.

CHAPTER 11

1. For "miring mud," and "quite low down," T.C. Elliott, "The Organization and First Pastorate of the First Congregational Church of Walla Walla Washington," *Washington Historical Quarterly*, 6:2 (Apr. 1915), 90-99, quotes 92. "Nasty and dirty" is in C.S. Kingston, "The Northern Overland Route in 1867: Journal of Henry Lueg," *Pacific Northwest Quarterly*, 41:3 (July 1950), 234-53, quote 251. For "below par," Hussey, *Fort Walla Walla*, 72. "All the games" in Hewitt, *Across the Plains*, 463. Also, James W. Watt, "Experiences of a Packer in Washington Territory Mining Camps During the Sixties," *Washington Historical Quarterly*, 19 (Oct. 1928), 285-93; G. Thomas Edwards, "Walla Walla, Gateway to the Pacific Northwest Interior," *Montana: The Magazine of Western History*, 40:3 (Summer 1990), 29-43; and Robert A. Bennett, *Walla Walla: Portrait of a Western Town, 1804-1899* (Walla Walla: Pioneer Press Books, 1980).

2. For the quotes, Hussey, *Fort Walla Walla*, 72-73; Edwards, "Walla Walla," 36.

3. Quoted in Edwards, "Walla Walla," 35.

4. For Walla Walla in 1859, Bennett, *Walla Walla*, 47-48. Also, "Founding of Walla Walla," published in *Up-to-the Times Magazine* in Jan. 1910, and reprinted by the Fort Walla Walla Museum Complex, n.d. A copy is in Box 3, Fldr. 49, Mary Avery

Papers, EWSHS. Fort Walla Walla had been moved in 1859 from the site first selected by Colonel Edward Steptoe. For the fort in 1859, Strachan, *Blazing the Mullan Trail,* 30.

5. Mullan, "From Walla Walla to San Francisco," 202, 204. For an analysis of the impact of the Mullan Road on Walla Walla, Alexander Campbell McGregor, "The Economic Impact of the Mullan Road on Walla Walla, 1860-1883," Honors thesis, Whitman College, 1971.

6. For the first quote, Mullan, "From Walla Walla to San Francisco," 203; for the second, *Railway Times,* 28 Mar. 1863.

7. *Railway Times,* 28 Mar. 1863.

8. Ibid.

9. W.W. Baker, "The Building of the Walla Walla & Columbia River Railroad," *Washington Historical Quarterly,* 14:1 (Jan. 1923), 3-13; quote 4.

10. The quote about the quality of the land and information on the spring is from an interview by Louis C. Coleman with Gail Dunkenbert, granddaughter of James Lasater, who acquired the Mullan property in 1866, Louis Coleman Papers, EWSHS. Rebecca's quote is in her Reminiscences, Box 8, Fldr. 9, Mullan Papers, Georgetown. John's purchase of the Robie property and the involvement of brothers Charles and Louis are detailed in various testimonies in the drawn-out legal case of Louis Mullan vs. John and Charles Mullan, WAL No. 757, WSA-Cheney.

11. Killoren, *Come Blackrobe,* 249. DeSmet's arrival from Fort Benton on the Mullan Road is noted in the Walla Walla *Washington Statesman,* 3 Oct. 1863.

12. Rebecca Mullan, Reminiscences. For DeSmet's quote, Killoren, *Come Blackrobe,* 249. For Brouillet as priest and a description of his primitive church, Elliott, "Organization and First Pastorate," 93. Rebecca mentions that Brouillet was a frequent guest at the Mullan house.

13. Mullan, Field Notes, 24 Aug. 1858, CDA. Kip, *Army Life,* 47-48, records the capture of the three brothers. Rebecca Mullan, in her Reminiscences, claims that John gained custody of the boy at the camp where Wright slaughtered hundreds of horses. She states Mullan "begged for [the boy's] life" when Wright was about to hang him. "This boy called himself John in gratitude to his protector." Rebecca's account has been repeated frequently. But both Kip and John Mullan are clear that the boys were captured on Aug. 24 along the Snake River, long before Wright engaged in any conflict. Wright hanged a number of warriors, but there is no indication he hanged boys, nor that this boy's life was threatened. Whether Rebecca ever showed her reminiscences to her husband is not clear. If he did see them, he did not take the opportunity to correct embellishments. But John was not above overstating his accomplishments.

14. Quote in Rebecca Mullan, Reminiscences.

15. Statement of John Mullan, Louis vs. John and Charles, WAL No. 757, WSA-Cheney. Unless otherwise noted, the details of the Mullan businesses in Walla Walla and the brother-vs.-brother lawsuit come from testimony in this case.

16. The quote, by William Beggs, appeared in the Salem *Oregon Statesman*, 14 Dec. 1858.

17. There are several cases against John Mullan or the Mullan Brothers for the period from 1861 to 1866 in the records of the U.S. District Court of Walla Walla County. The final decisions for some are unclear, but in most cases, judgments came down against the Mullans. See WAL case numbers 274, 281, 429, 588, 593, 594, 595 (Creighton), 747, 768, 851, 899, and 1141, WSA-Cheney.

18. All details and quotes in this account of the case, unless otherwise noted, are from WAL No. 757, WSA-Cheney.

19. A brief biography of Louis appears in his obituary, Yuma *Sentinel*, 9 Aug. 1884.

20. For the quote about James moving to Walla Walla, Walla Walla *Washington Statesman*, 19 Sept. 1863; for James's name on the deed and the quote about the brothers' connivance, Dunkelberg interview. John's suit against Louis and James is WAL No. 587, WSA-Cheney.

CHAPTER 12

1. Gillis and Magliari, *John Bidwell*; Benjamin, *John Bidwell*.

2. Bidwell Park in Chico, one of the nation's largest urban recreation areas, is a remnant of Rancho Chico. Bidwell's mansion is operated as a California State Parks property.

3. George C. Mansfield, *History of Butte County, California with Biographical Sketches* (Los Angeles: Historic Record Co., 1918), 240-42; *Reproduction of [Harry Laurenz] Wells' and [W.L.] Chambers' History of Butte County, California, 1882, and Biographical Sketches of its Prominent Men and Pioneers* (Berkeley: Howell-North Books, 1973), 222-24.

4. Mullan, "From Walla Walla to San Francisco,", 222-23.

5. Merle W. Wells, *Gold Camps and Silver Cities: Nineteenth Century Mining in Idaho* (Moscow: Idaho Bureau of Mines and Geology, 1983); "Placer Mining in Southern Idaho," Idaho State Historical Society Reference Series No. 166, 1980. For the quote, C. Aubrey Angelo, "Impressions of the Boise Basin in 1863," *Idaho Yesterdays*, 7:1 (Spring 1963), 11.

6. Williams and Stark, *The Pierce Chronicle*.

7. Ibid., 78-79.

8. Ibid., 81. Pierce had made a second trip into the Clearwater region in the spring, but quickly abandoned the effort. His party discovered gold on his third venture.

9. Ibid.

10. Ibid., 103.

11. Clarence F. McIntosh, "The Chico and Red Bluff Route," *Idaho Yesterdays*, 6:3 (Fall 1962), 12. Also, Alan Patera, "The Chico Route to Idaho," *Western Express*, 40 (Apr. 1990), 8-33.

12. Williams and Stark, *The Pierce Chronicle*, 102.

13. Ibid., 105–06; McIntosh, "Chico and Red Bluff Route," 14.

14. Rebecca Mullan, Reminiscences, Box 8, Fldr. 9, Mullan Papers, Georgetown, mentions their move to Baltimore. Mullan, *Miners and Travelers Guide*.

15. Humphreys to Mullan, 30 May 1860, RG 77, Entry 359, Box 3, NA.

16. Mullan, *Miners and Travelers' Guide*, 34.

17. Ibid., 49.

18. McIntosh, "Chico and Red Bluff Route," 14–15. The Boise *Idaho Statesman*, 11 July 1915, contained a "50 Years Ago" column that noted Mullan's July 1865 road improvement efforts.

19. *Owyhee Avalanche*, 2 Sept. 1865; the first ad appeared on 23 Sept. 1865. As a reward for standing with him during the ugly family dispute in Walla Walla, John hired brother Charles as an agent; he is listed in advertisements.

20. *Owyhee Avalanche*, 28 Oct. 1865.

21. The Chico *Courant* is quoted in the *Avalanche*, 23 Dec. 1865. The *Oregonian* quote is from W. Turrentine Jackson, "Wells Fargo & Co. in Idaho Territory: Old and New Routes 1865," *Idaho Yesterdays*, 26:1 (Spring 1982), 21. This is part one of Jackson's six-part series on Wells Fargo.

22. Patera, "Chico Route to Idaho," 11–14 for the mail contract. Also Jackson, "Wells Fargo & Co.: Into the Inland Empire and Idaho Territory," *Idaho Yesterdays*, 25:4 (Winter 1962), 136.

23. For the quote, Bidwell to D.D. Harris, 13 Apr. 1866, Box 3, Fldr. 4, Bidwell Papers, Chico; McIntosh, "The Chico and Red Bluff Route," 18.

24. First quote, Bidwell to Harris, 8 Mar. 1866, Box 3, Fldr. 3; second, Bidwell to Harris, 28 Apr. 1866, Box 3, Fldr. 4. Both Bidwell Papers, Chico. The third quote is from an 1891 typescript Bidwell provided to the University of California, quoted in Gillis and Magliari, *John Bidwell*, 212.

25. Bidwell to Harris, 28 Apr. 1866, Box 3, Fldr. 4, Bidwell Papers, Chico. Gillis and Magliari, *John Bidwell*, 150.

26. For "small steam engine," McIntosh, "Chico and Red Bluff Route," 19. For the telegraph line, Mullan to Western Union Telegraph Co., 4 Feb. 1866. See also Mullan to Bidwell, 5 Feb. 1866; John Berry to Mullan, 15 Feb. 1866; and J.H. Wade to Mullan, 19 Feb. 1866. For the other quotes, Mullan to Bidwell, 18 Feb. 1866, and Mullan to Bidwell, 5 Feb. 1866. These and other letters detail the work Mullan undertook to gain financial backing. All in Box 3, Fldr. 3, Bidwell Papers, Chico.

27. Bidwell to Harris, 13 Apr. 1866 and 4 July 1860, Box 3, Fldr. 4. Bidwell to Harris, 27 Nov. 1865, Box 3, Fldr. 1. All Bidwell Papers, Chico.

28. Bidwell to Harris, 10 June 1866, Box 3, Fldr. 4; Mullan to Bidwell, 22 Feb. 1866, Box 3, Fldr. 3. Both Bidwell Papers, Chico. The exact amount Mullan raised is variously listed. The Boise *Idaho Statesman*, 22 May 1866 noted the capitalization at $25,000; the Chico *Courant*, 12 May 1866, $200,000. Mullan, in his 22 Feb. 1866 letter to Bidwell, stated he had, as of then, raised $39,000.

29. *Owyhee Avalanche*, 23 June 1866, 2 June 1866; McIntosh, "Chico and Red Bluff Route," 19.

30. *Owyhee Avalanche*, 7 July 1866.

31. Ibid., 14 July 1866, 1 Sept. 1866; Boise *Idaho Statesman*, 25 Aug. 1866. Advertisements promoting goods from Chico can be found in issues of the *Avalanche* from July through the fall of 1866.

32. Bidwell to Harris, 13 Apr. 1866, 4 July 1855, Box 3, Fldr. 4, Bidwell Papers, Chico.

33. Mullan, "From Walla Walla to San Francisco," 223.

34. *Owyhee Avalanche*, 17 Nov. 1866, 27 Apr. 1867; Rebecca Mullan, Reminiscences. For the stage line, its impact on Chico, and the Chico *Courant's* reporting, Larry Francis Brurdeau, "The Historic Archaeology of Cabo's Tavern," Master's thesis, California State University, Chico, 1982, esp. 125-33.

35. Williams and Stark, *The Pierce Chronicle*, 108-09.

36. Boise *Idaho Statesman*, 5 Sept. 1865; "Camp Lyon," Idaho State Historical Society Reference Series No. 357, 1965; Williams and Stark, *The Pierce Chronicle*, 108; Gillis and Magliari, *John Bidwell*, 196.

37. *Owyhee Avalanche*, 7 Apr. 1866.

38. For the *Colonel Wright*, "Steamboat Down the Snake: The Early History of the 'Shoshone,'" *Idaho Yesterdays*, 5:4 (Winter 1961-62), 22-33; 27 for Creighton. Realizing it could not steam its way through Hells Canyon, the OSN constructed the *Shoshone* in Idaho to service a short stretch of river providing a link to Umatilla. Also for Creighton as a shipper of goods to Idaho mines see "Descendants of Samuel McCully" in *Condor Tales: The History and Genealogy Pages*, www.condortales.com, retrieved 29 Jan. 2012. For improvement of the Umatilla road, Jackson, "Wells Fargo & Co. in Idaho Territory: Old and New Routes, 1865," *Idaho Yesterdays*, 26:1 (Spring 1982), 18-19.

39. H.B. No. 63, 22 Jan. 1864, the act approving Beachey's toll road, is in Box 1, Territorial Records, ISHS. Beachey's name is spelled in both primary and secondary sources as either Beachy or Beachey.

40. Williams and Stark, *The Pierce Chronicle*, 103.

41. Victor Goodwin, "William C. (Hill) Beachey, Nevada-California-Idaho Stage-coach King," *Nevada Historical Quarterly*, 10:1 (Spring 1967), 4-46, "indomitable" quote 4. Walla Walla *Washington Statesman* quote about Beachey is in Jackson, "Wells Fargo & Co. in Idaho Territory: Old and New Routes, 1865," *Idaho Yesterdays*, 26:1 (Spring 1982), 8. Julia Conway Welch, "Hill Beachy," *Owyhee Outpost*, 20 (May 1989), 71-75.

42. For the quote, Boise *Idaho Tri-Weekly Statesman*, 13 Apr. 1867. Also *Owyhee Avalanche*, 27 Jan. 1866, 17 Feb. 1866; "Steamboat Down the Snake," 28; McIntosh, "Chico and Red Bluff Route," 19. In late 1866 a postal agent in California mailed eight letters to Boise—four on Mullan's route, and four on the Humboldt route. They were mailed several days apart, so each letter would go by a different dispatch. The Humboldt letters arrived within seven to ten days. One of Mullan's

letters took forty-nine days; the others never reached Boise. "The Chico route has been exceedingly irregular, imperfect, and indeed I may say worthless," reported the postal agent. Patera, "Chico Route to Idaho," 17-18.

43. Goodwin, "Beachey," 44-45. The quote is in Mcintosh, "Chico and Red Bluff Route," 12.

44. Larry E. Morris, *The Fate of the Corps: What Became of the Lewis and Clark Explorers After the Expedition* (New Haven: Yale University Press, 2004), 180; "John Baptiste Charbonneau," Idaho State Historical Society Reference Series No. 428, n.d.; *Owyhee Avalanche*, 2 June 1866. On this part of the line, Mullan utilized the Skinner toll road. See Stacy Peterson, "Silas Skinner's Owyhee Toll Road," *Idaho Yesterdays*, 10:1 (Spring 1966), 12-21.

CHAPTER 13

1. Rebecca Mullan, Reminiscences, Box 8, Fldr. 9, Mullan Papers, Georgetown. San Francisco *Daily Alta California*, 17 Dec. 1866.

2. For the wagon road, Mullan to Colonel Filton (?), 11 Oct. 1867, Box 3, Fldr. 214, William W. Miller Papers, WA-MSS S-1172, Yale. Mullan to Lincoln, 4 Mar. 1863, "Mullan, John" file, Applications and Recommendations for Public Office, 1861-69, General Records of the Department of State, RG 59, NA. For Mullan as a surveyor, Cullum, *Biographical Register*, 313.

3. Rebecca Mullan, Reminiscences.

4. *List of Lands in California Proclaimed for Sale by the President of the United States* (San Francisco: California Immigration Association, 1868), Bancroft. The booklet gave the association's address as N. 712 Montgomery Street, the address of Mullan's law office. *San Francisco Directories* from 1868 to 1876 track the moves of Mullan's business and residence addresses. He moved his law office to Jackson Street in 1875; the family moved from a home on Mission Street to Post Street in 1873. Rebecca's quote is in her Reminiscences. Also see San Francisco *Daily Alta California*, 11 July 1868 and 16 Aug. 1868, and *New York Times*, 10 Aug. 1868, for more on the Immigration Association.

5. Letterhead is in 7 Sept. 1876 letter, Mullan to San Francisco police chief Henry H. Ellis, Ellis Papers, MS 657, California Historical Society.

6. Gerald D. Nash, "The California State Land Office, 1858-1898," *Huntington Library Quarterly*, 27:4 (Aug. 1964), 347-56; Paul W. Gates, "Public Land Disposal in California," *Agricultural History*, 49:1 (Jan. 1975), 158-78.

7. Nash, "California State Land Office," 350-51; Gates, "Public Land Disposal," 167-68.

8. Nash, "California State Land Office," 351, 353; Paul W. Gates, "California's Agricultural Lands," *Pacific Historical Review*, 30:2 (1961), 102-22. The quote is from Edward Twitchell, a former employee in the surveyor general's office, Sacramento *Record-Union*, 8 Apr. 1893.

9. Nash, "California State Land Office," 351; Gates, "Public Land Disposal," 163, 166-67.

10. Gates, "California's Agricultural College Lands," 110-12; Gates, "Public Land Disposal," 170. Thomas LeDuc, "State Disposal of the Agricultural College Land Scrip," *Agricultural History*, 28 (1954), 99-107. For Mullan's clients and University of California lands, Mullan and Hyde, 1877 correspondence in University Archives, CU-1, Box 3, Bancroft. As late as the 1880s Mullan was acquiring University of California lands. See J. A. Bonte (?), Land Agent, University of California to Mullan, n.d., but referring to property purchased in 1883, Box 1, Fldr. 2, Mullan Papers, Georgetown.

11. The Dibblee quote is in Gordon Morris Bakken, *Practicing Law in Frontier California* (Lincoln: University of Nebraska Press, 1991), 79. Mullan also suffered squatters on some of his holdings. See Gates, "California's Agricultural College Lands," 118. For the necessity of hiring professionals for public land acquisition, Henry N. Copp, *The American Settler's Guide: A Popular Exposition of the Public Land System of the United States of America* (Washington: Henry Copp, 1894), esp. 12. Copp wrote at a later time, but the legal complexity was similar to the 1870s.

12. Rebecca Mullan, Reminiscences. Winfield J. Davis, *History of Political Conventions in California, 1849-1892* (Sacramento: California State Library, 1893), 361-62.

13. Davis, *History of Political Conventions*, 357, 360.

14. Mullan to Ellis, 7 Sept. 1876, Ellis Papers, Mss. 657, California Historical Society; San Francisco *Daily Alta California*, 18 Oct. 1876.

15. John Mullan, *Reports to Honorable George Stoneman, Governor of California, on Certain Claims of the State of California Against the United States, November 1, 1878-November 1, 1886* (Sacramento: State Office, 1886), 5-7, 55-56.

16. Ibid., quote, 6. The official appointment letter is on 55-56.

17. Ibid., 7.

18. *New York Times*, 9 Dec. 1908.

19. New York *Sun*, 23 June 1908.

20. Ibid. See *New York Times*, 13 Jan. 1904 and 18 Feb. 1904, and New York *Evening World*, 12 Jan. 1904 for the beginning of the long case.

21. One year later, Democratic President Woodrow Wilson reduced Hyde's sentence by a year; Klamath Falls *Oregon Evening Herald*, 24 Oct. 1913. For the Supreme Court ruling, Hickman, Kansas *Courier*, 13 June 1912. Also, New York *Sun*, 23 June 1908; Washington *Times*, 27 June 1908.

22. The quotes are from an interview with Edward Twitchell, who had personally witnessed the shenanigans. Sacramento *Record-Union*, 8 Apr. 1893.

CHAPTER 14

1. Squire to Mullan, 15 Apr. 1886, 15 Apr. 1886, Box 1, Fldr. 42, Mullan Papers, Georgetown.

2. Mullan, *Reports to Honorable George Stoneman*; William C. Fankhauser, *A Financial History of California: Public Revenues, Debts, and Expenditures*, University of Cal-

ifornia Publications in Economics, 3:2 (Berkeley: University of California Press, 1913), esp. 312-17. Mullan synopsized the cases he worked on behalf of Oregon—which were similar to those for his other clients—in a petition to Oregon seeking payment for his services. See *Petition of Captain John Mullan, Washington, D.C., December 20, 1906, to Honorable F.I. Dunbar, Secretary of State, the State of Oregon,* MHS.

3. The 5 percent payments to California totaled $1,015,141. Chief of Bookkeeping and Warrants, Treasury Department, to Mullan, 9 Dec. 1908, Box 1, Fldr. 41, Mullan Papers, Georgetown.

4. The lease terms for his office and home can be found in a receipt from Thomas Waggaman, Real Estate Broker, 22 Sept. 1880, Box 7, Fldr. 8, Mullan Papers, Georgetown. The Mullan Papers also contain examples of Mullan's letterhead at various times. Mullan also maintained a private practice, mainly with clients in the West.

5. "Inventory of the Household Effects of John Mullan, Washington, D.C.," Box 7, Fldr. 7, Mullan Papers, Georgetown. The inventory is not dated, but it would have been from a later period, though reflective of the household furnishings in the 1880s, as Mullan could not have afforded to add much after then period. The same Box, Fldr. 25 records the 1886 arrival of goods from Europe. The 1880 census for the District of Columbia notes the two servants, a man and a woman.

6. Jan Taylor, "Marketing the Northwest: The Northern Pacific Railroad's Last Spike Excursion," *Montana: The Magazine of Western History,* 60:4 (Winter 2010), 16-35; *New York Times,* 10 Sept. 1883.

7. The Northern Pacific had actually opened for business on Aug. 22, but 1,200 feet of the line had been taken up to reenact the connection.

8. The letter was initially published in the Missoula *Missoulian* in 1911 or 1912; republished in the Superior (Montana) *Mineral Independent,* 13 July 1933.

9. The letter was originally published in the *Eagle* in 1884. A copy is in "Mullan's Postscript," *Mineral County Pioneer,* 1884 File, MINCO.

10. Howard, *Northwest Trail Blazers,* 151. Rebecca Mullan, Reminiscences, stated that the interview appeared in the Tacoma *Ledger* in 1888, a mistake Howard and others have repeated. Mullan's remarks actually appeared in Apr. 1889.

11. Quoted in William S. McFeely, *Grant: A Biography* (New York: W.W. Norton & Co., 1981), 317.

12. Ibid., contains a synopsis of the Peace Policy, 309-17; quotes from this source.

13. *The Bureau of Catholic Indian Missions* (Washington, D.C.: Church News Publishing Co., 1895), 3.

14. Peter J. Rahill, *The Catholic Indian Missions and Grant's Peace Policy, 1870-1884* (Washington, D.C.: The Catholic University of America Press, 1953). "Bureau of Catholic Indian Missions," en.wikipedia.org/wiki/Bureau_of_Catholic_Indian_ Missions, retrieved 18 July 2011, provides a summary. Also helpful are two works by Francis Paul Prucha, *American Indian Policy in Crisis: Christian Reformers and the*

Indian, 1865-1900 (Norman: University of Oklahoma Press, 1976), and *The Churches and the Indian Schools* (Lincoln: University of Nebraska Press, 1979).

15. Kevin Abing, "Directors of the Bureau of Catholic Indian Missions: Reverend Jean Baptiste Abraham Brouillet, 1874-1884," www.marquette.edu/library/archives/ MSS/.../BCIM-SC1-directors1.pdf, retrieved 1 Sept. 2012.

16. Rahill, *Catholic Indian Missions*, esp. 64, 78-79.

17. *Bureau of Catholic Indian Missions*, 8; Rahill, *Catholic Indian Missions*, 322, 329.

18. Rahill, *Catholic Indian Missions*, 322.

19. For the Sherman quote, Rahill, *Catholic Indian Missions*, 332. For the other quote, *The Bureau of Catholic Indian Missions: The Work of the Decade Ending December 31, 1883* (Washington, D.C.: Bureau of Catholic Missions, 1883).

20. Brouillet to Mullan, 30 July 1883, Roll 7, Frame 958, BCIM, Marquette.

21. For examples of Mullan's legal work for the bureau, Mullan to Brouillet, 16 Aug. 1882, Roll 3, Frame 790, and Mullan to Ewing, 9 June 1883, Roll 3, Frame 802, ibid. Mullan's quote is in his *Miners and Travelers' Guide*, 46. For DeSmet, DeSmet to Mullan, 31 Mar. 1858, in Hiram M. Chittenden and Alfred T. Richardson, *Life, Letters and Travels of Father Pierre-Jean DeSmet, S.J., 1801-1873,* (New York: Francis P. Harper, 1895), 4:1500. Hoecken's quote is in "St Ignatius Mission Centennial Observance," supplement to the *St. Ignatius Post* and *The Ronan Pioneer*, 23 Sept. 1954.

22. For the quote, Mullan, *Miners and Travelers' Guide*, 44. It is possible Mullan met Brouillet as early as the 1850s, but the two for sure were well acquainted by the early 1860s, when Mullan lived in Walla Walla, where Brouillet was priest. Brouillet to Charles Lusk, Catholic Bureau, 11 Sept. 1882, Roll 7, Frame 963 for the formal request to appoint Mullan. Lusk to Brouillet, 19 Oct. 1883, Roll 7, Frame 967 for the announcement of the appointment. Both BCIM, Marquette.

23. Rahill, *Catholic Indian Missions*, 79-81, 334-36 for Brouillet's effectiveness, illness, and death; 339-40 for Stephan. Gibbons to Mullan, 14 May 1884, Roll 7, Frame 986, BCIM, Marquette, for Stephan's appointment. Stephan would serve until 1901.

24. For the growth in schools, students, and government allotments, *Bureau of Catholic Indian Missions: Work of the Decade*, 13-22, and *Bureau of Catholic Indian Missions*, 20. The quote is in the minutes of the bureau meeting of 28 June 1886. Meeting minutes for the years Mullan served record his frequent lobbying efforts on the bureau's behalf; for this period see Roll 14, BCIM, Marquette. Also see *Bureau of Catholic Missions for Support and Education of Indian People*, 48th Cong., 2nd Sess., House Ex. Doc. No 29, Serial Set No. 2296 for Mullan's 1884 appeal to the Secretary of the Interior for additional funding for the school on the Flathead Reservation.

25. For the 1885 budget, Bylaws of the Bureau of Indian Missions, Roll 12, Frame 933. Minutes of the bureau for 1885, same roll, note Mullan's fundraising efforts. For *The Catholic World* article, Mullan to Rev. Hacker, editor, 14 Jan. 1884, Roll 7, Frame 773. All BCIM, Marquette. The quote is in an 1885 fundraising appeal, St. Ignatius Mission Records, Box 2, Gonzaga. Mullan probably wrote the text for *Bureau of Catholic Indian Missions: The Work of the Decade*.

26. On the 1884 trip he stopped in St. Louis at the home of General William T. and Ellen Sherman. Ellen Ewing Sherman to Mullan, 16 July 1884, Roll 7, Frame 993. Mullan kept up an exhaustive schedule on his long jaunts, visiting as many schools as possible. Various letters from Mullan to the bureau in Roll 7 (Fall 1884), Roll 9 (Spring 1884), and Roll 14 (Fall 1886) record his travels. All BCIM, Marquette.

27. Kevin Abing, "Directors of the Bureau of Catholic Indian Missions: Reverend Joseph Stephan, 1884-1901," www.marquette.edu/library/archives/mss/.../ BCIM-SC1-directors2.pdf, retrieved 3 Sept. 2012.

28. Bureau Minutes, 28 Dec. 1884, Roll 7, BCIM, Marquette.

29. For the quotes, Stephan to the bureau, 4 Dec. 1886, Roll 14, Frame 242. The bureau rescinded the motion at its meeting on 20 Dec. 1886. Ibid.

30. Mullan to Gibbons, 23 Jan. 1887, Roll 15, Frame 385, ibid.

31. For the quote, Bureau Minutes, 28 Mar. 1887, Frame 437. Also see minutes, 4 July 1887, Frame 469; Jones to Marty, 5 July 1887, Frame 472. All Roll 15, ibid.

32. Perkins to Mullan, 11 May 1886, Box. 1, Fldr. 39. "Fat racket" from an undated clipping, Box 5, Fldr. 9. Both Mullan Papers, Georgetown.

33. Stoneman's quote, Sacramento *Daily Record-Union*, 5 Jan. 1885; the legislative resolution of 1883—similar to other resolutions concerning Mullan's work and compensation—appeared in the Woodland, California, *Democrat*, 20 May 1896.

34. Gardner's quote is in a Jan. 1888 clipping, Box 5, Fldr. 8, Mullan Papers, Georgetown. For Waterman's letter to Mullan, Sacramento *Daily Union-Record*, 6 Feb. 1888.

35. California State Lands Commission, "Robert Gardner, 1871-75," www.slc.ca.gov/ Misc_Pages/Historical/Surveyors_General/Gardner.html, retrieved 10 Sept. 2012. For Gardner's 1886 efforts to discredit Mullan, Woodland, California, *Democrat*, 20 May 1886.

36. Gardner's charges are summarized in the San Francisco *Call*, 31 Jan. 1888, and in an 1888 clipping, Box 5, Fldr. 8, Mullan Papers, Georgetown.

37. Mullan, *Reports to George Stoneman*, quotes on 5, 7.

38. San Francisco *Call*, 31 Jan. 1888.

39. The Mullan Papers, Georgetown, contain many clippings relating to Mullan's legal battle with California and other states regarding payment for services. Many do not include the newspaper's name or date of publication. The Gardner quote is from 6 Feb. 1888 and the Stanford quote from later in the spring of 1888. Both in Box 5, Fldr. 8.

40. The quotes are in clippings in Box 5, Fldrs. 8 and 9, ibid. Most of the clippings are undated, but the debate over Mullan's fees was particularly heated in the period from Jan. to Mar. 1888.

41. Hearst to Mullan, 28 Feb. 1889, Box 1, Fldr. 22, ibid.

42. Undated 1888-89 clipping, Box 5, Fldr. 8, ibid.

43. Sacramento *Daily Record-Union*, 23 Mar. 1889.

44. For a summary of the Civil War claims see Fankhauser, *Financial History of California,* 316-17.

45. San Francisco *Call,* 27 Oct. 1896.

46. The quote is in Johnson to J.W. Shanklin, 27 July 1896, Box 6, Fldr. 1. Additional letters attesting to Mullan's effectiveness are in Box 10, Fldr. 9. For a rebuttal to the 1899 governor's veto, which gives background to the political and legal case from Mullan's perspective, see Mullan, "Answer to the Veto Message of Governor [Henry] Gage," Box 7, Fldr. 11. All in Mullan Papers, Georgetown. For the 1897 and 1899 legislative bills see San Francisco *Call,* 19 Mar. 1897, 8 Feb. 1899, 17 Feb. 1899, 5 Mar. 1899, 6 Mar. 1899.

47. The quotes are in Mullan to "My Dear Children," 26 Jan. 1898 and 20 May 1898, both Box 2, Fldr. 2, Mullan Papers, Georgetown.

48. Reichert to Emma Mullan, 19 Jan. 1905, Box 6, Fldr. 3; Johnson to Mullan, 21 Dec. 1906, Box 1, Fldr. 25. Ibid.

49. San Francisco *Call,* 22 Sept. 1907.

50. For the Gardner quotes, San Francisco *Chronicle,* 30 Aug. 1906.

51. For the quote, Deputy Controller W.W. Douglas to Emma Mullan, 22 Mar. 1905, Box 6, Fldr. 3. The official compromise document, 22 Mar. 1905, is in Box 7, Fldr. 12. Both Mullan Papers, Georgetown.

52. George Lukens to H.F. Lange, 4 Apr. 1910, Box 6, Fldr. 8, Mullan Papers, Georgetown; Fankhauser, *Financial History of California,* 317.

53. Mullan to Emma, 6 Feb. 1907, and Mullan to California State Controller, 15 Mar. 1907, Box 2, Fldr. 7; Mullan to Lukens, 23 June 1906, Box 2, Fldr. 5. Chief of Bookkeeping and Warrants, U.S. Treasury to Mullan, 9 Dec. 1908, Box 1, Fldr. 41. All in Mullan Papers, Georgetown.

54. San Francisco *Call,* 9 Aug. 1894.

55. For Mullan's quote about Emma going to Oregon, Mullan to "My Dear Children Emma and May," 14 Nov. 1905, Box 2, Fldr. 3. For the final award of $9,465, F.W. Benson, Oregon Secretary of State to Mullan, 25 May 1907, Box 6, Fldr. 5. For "magnificent daughter," Benjamin Cohen to Mullan, 23 Feb. 1907, Box 6, Fldr 3. All Mullan Papers, Georgetown.

56. Mullan, *Reports to George Stoneman,* 51-52.

57. Moody to Sigmund Sizhel, State Senate, 1 Feb. 1907, Box 6, Fldr. 5, Mullan Papers, Georgetown.

CHAPTER 15

1. The story of the Mullans' laundry made its way to many papers. The quotes are from the Saint Paul *Globe,* 10 Jan. 1905, 19 Mar. 1905; Minneapolis *Journal,* 6 Jan. 1905; and San Francisco *Chronicle,* 8 Dec. 1904.

2. Emma to "Aunt Annie," n.d., Box 6, Fldr. 5, Mullan Papers, Georgetown.

3. The headline appeared in Minneapolis *Journal*, 6 Jan. 1905. Mullan wrote several letters to Emma and May expressing pleasure in the laundry's success, Box 8, Fldr. 11. Mullan's plea for $250 is in Mullan to King, 2 Oct. 1905, Box 2, Fldr. 14. The quote about possessing no property is from May in a statement about Mullan's funeral expenses, Box 7, Fldr. 23. All in Mullan Papers, Georgetown.

4. For "defender of the miner," Salt Lake City *Herald*, 3 Sept. 1891. For Mullan's work for missions, Box 1, Fldr. 2, St. Paul's Mission Papers, Gonzaga, and Mullan to Father Joseph Cataldo, 10 Sept. 1887, letterbook p. 355, Box 4, Fldr. 3, Mullan Papers, Georgetown. See Washington *Times*, 28 Dec. 1894 for Mandolin Club; 26 Nov. 1897 for Alibi Club; 8 Feb. 1897 for Goodwill Club; 6 Oct. 1901 for River and Harbor Congress. The 1880 census for the District of Columbia notes the two servants.

5. Rebecca Mullan, Reminiscences, Box 8, Fldr. 9. No record of John applying for or receiving a pension was uncovered. However, a 10 Oct. 1910 letter from King & King, Attorneys, to Emma details John's efforts with the War Department for additional pay. The case involved an ongoing dispute as to whether a cadet's time at West Point should be credited when computing pay. Box 6, Fldr. 8. Both Mullan Papers, Georgetown.

6. Summary of John's assistance to Virginia and Annie, 27 May 1908, Box 7, Fldr. 15, ibid.

7. Annie to John, 10 July 1907, Box 1, Fldr. 37; John to Annie, n.d., Box 2, Fldr. 8. Ibid.

8. Annie to May, 17 July 1907; Emma to Annie, n.d., Box 6 Fldr. 5, ibid.

9. Last Will and Testament of John Mullan, 12 June 1907, Box 7, Fldr. 3, ibid.

10. Washington *Evening Times*, 5 Sept. 1898. Bonnie Brae Cemetery has since been renamed New Cathedral Cemetery. Sixteen family members are interred in the Williamson family crypt, including John and Rebecca's children, Emma, May, and Frank—none of whom are buried with their spouses.

11. The quote is in Mullan to Wilbur Fisk Sanders, 25 Dec. 1898, Box 2, Fldr. 24, Sanders Papers, Mss. Coll. No. 53, MHS. For other letters detailing his ailments: Mullan to "Dear Children," 20 Jan. 1898, 20 May 1898, and 8 Feb. 1899, and to Emma, 8 Feb. 1899. All in Box 2, Fldr. 2, Mullan Papers, Georgetown.

12. John to Annie, 13 July 1907; "Cousin Joe" to Emma, 5 Mar. 1907. Both in Box 2, Fldr. 8, Mullan Papers, Georgetown.

13. Mullan to "Dear Children," 14 Nov. 1905 for ships; letter from Emma, 30 Jan. 1906 for suit. Both Box 2, fldr. 3. The "Captain" quote is in "Paul" to Emma, 21 Jan. 1905, Box 8, Fldr. 6. Ibid.

14. Frank to "Dear Father," 10 Aug. 1903, Box 1, Fldr. 37, ibid.

15. Frank to John, 10 Aug. 1903, Box 1, Fldr. 37, ibid.

16. Last Will and Testament of John Mullan, 2 June 1907, Box 7, Fldr. 3. For assigning potential states' commissions to Emma and May, Deed and Assignment, 3 July 1906 (California), 21 Dec. 1906 (Nevada), and 11 Sept. 1906 (Oregon), Box 5, Fldr. 6. Ibid.

17. Washington *Herald*, 2 May 1907; New York *Tribune*, 19 June 1907. For more on the engagement and Lukens's background, San Francisco *Call*, 19 Apr. 1907, 22 Sept. 1907.

18. Willey, "Building the M.R.," 638. As early as 19 Apr. 1889, the Sacramento *Daily Record-Union* had reported that "both his hair and whiskers are snow white."

19. Richmond *Times Dispatch*, 29 Dec. 1909; San Francisco *Call*, 29 Dec. 1909; the Washington newspaper obituary from search.ancestry.com, retrieved 23 Oct. 2011. The longest obituary ran in *Forty-first Annual Reunion of the Association of the Graduates of the United States Military Academy* (Saginaw, MI: Seeman & Peters, 1910), 140-42. Mullan's official cause of death was listed as "primary senility." John Mullan, Record of Interment, St. Mary's Parish, Annapolis, Microfilm Reel 2345, Maryland State Archives.

20. The funeral expense is noted in a petition by May, 28 Mar. 1911, Box 7, Fldr. 23, Mullan Papers, Georgetown. May's description is stapled to the back of Rebecca Mullan's Reminiscences.

CHAPTER 16

1. Mullan was quoted in Willey, "Building the M.R.," 640. Walla Walla *Washington Statesman*, 12 July 1862.

2. Audra Browman, "Early Land History of Missoula," typescript, Fldr. 7, and Browman research notes, Fldr. 17, both in Mss. 468, Box 1, Audra Browman Papers, University of Montana; Phillips, ed., *Forty Years on the Frontier*, 158, 189; Milner, *As Big as the West*, 100-01; Oviatt, "The Movement for a Northern Trail," 62-63, 79-81. Worden provided information of his time in the West up to that point in a letter to "Dear Uncle," 24 Dec. 1861, Mss. 21, Box 1, Fldr. 1, Francis Worden Papers, University of Montana. For the first wagon train, Verna Dolphin, typescript, "First Over the Mullan Trail," 1935, papers of the East Spokane Home Economics Club, Cage 4400, WSU.

3. For reports of wagons reaching Walla Walla and the first quote, McGregor, "Economic Impact of the Mullan Road," 7-8. For the second quote, Hewitt, *Across the Plains*, 362.

4. For a first-hand account, *Expedition From Fort Abercrombie to Fort Benton*, 37th Cong., 3rd Sess., House Ex. Doc. No. 80. Also see W.M. Underhill, "The Northern Overland Route to Montana," *Washington Historical Quarterly*, 23:3 (July 1932), 177-95; W. Turrentine Jackson, "The Fisk Expeditions to the Montana Gold Fields," *Pacific Northwest Quarterly*, 33:3 (July 1942), 265-82; and Hamilton, *From Wilderness to Statehood*, 148-65. Fisk hired Pierre Bottineau as guide. For Bottineau's role in the Stevens expedition, Richards, *Stevens*, 109-11.

5. A few miles out of Fort Benton, most of the emigrants abandoned Fisk's wagon train when they heard of recent nearby gold discoveries. Fisk guided the remnant into Walla Walla.

6. Kingston, "The Northern Route," 234-53, and David Hilger, "Overland Trail," *Contributions to the Historical Society of Montana* 7 (Helena: Montana Historical and Miscellaneous Library, 1910), 257-70. The quote from the Walla Walla *Washington Statesman* is in McGregor, "Economic Impact of the Mullan Road," 12.

7. The quote is in Trimble, *Mining Advance*, 10.

8. Kent Curtis, "Producing a Gold Rush: National Ambitions and the Northern Rocky Mountains, 1853-1863," *Western Historical Quarterly*, 40:3 (Autumn 2009), 275-97. Curtis pays particular attention to the significance of the Mullan Road.

9. Phillips, *Forty Years on the Frontier*, 211-17. For various routes taken to arrive at the Mullan Road, Trimble, *Mining Advance*, 80.

10. Trimble, *Mining Advance*, 56 for "beautiful gold." For cutting the journey by a day, McGregor, "Economic Impact of Mullan Road," 28. Mullan's road led Walla Wallans north to a connection with the Wild Horse Trail into Canada. Also see Watt, "Experiences of a Packer," 36. This was later published as *Journal of Mule Train Packing in Eastern Washington in the 1860's* (Fairfield, WA: Ye Galleon Press, 1978). "Uncle Dan" Drumheller also describes the route in *"Uncle Dan" Drumheller Tells Thrills*, 110-11.

11. Milos Conway Moore, "Life History of Miles C. Moore," R929/20973, Bonner County Historical Society, Sandpoint, Idaho; McGregor, "Economic Impact of Mullan Road," 28.

12. For the first quote, McGregor, "Economic Impact of Mullan Road," 40; for the second, Walla Walla *Washington Statesman*, 1 Sept. 1865. Also see Oviatt, "Movement for a Northern Trail," 139; and Madsen, *North to Montana*, 147.

13. Watt, *Journal of Mule Train Packing*, 41-46. For background on mule packing in this era, Oscar Osburn Winther, "Pack Animals for Transportation in the Pacific Northwest," *Pacific Northwest Quarterly* 34:2 (Apr. 1943), 131-46, and Nick Eggenhofer, *Wagons, Mules and Men* (New York: Hastings House Publishers, 1961), esp. 17-25.

14. For the quote, David Higler, "Camels in Montana," typescript, n.d., "Camels" Vertical File, MHS. In that same file also see Florence Johnson and Bernice DeHass, "Camels in Montana," typescript, n.d. And see William S. Lewis, "The Camel Pack Trains in the Mining Camps of the West," *Washington Historical Quarterly*, 19:3 (July 1928), 271-84; Oscar Osburn Winther, *The Old Oregon Country: A History of Frontier Trade, Transportation, and Travel* (Stanford: Stanford University Press, 1950), 198-200; Watt, *Journal of Mule Train Packing*, 31-32; McGregor, "Economic Impact of Mullan Road," 52-53.

15. Edwards, "Walla Walla," 29-43.

16. Oviatt, "Movement for a Northern Trail," 73-74, 140, 165, 175 for the impact of the Mullan Road on Helena's development. For the significance of the road generally in the development of Montana, Leland J. Hanchett Jr., *Montana's Benton Road* (Wolf Creek, MT: Pine Rim Publishing, 2008).

17. For the first quote by Hiram Upham, Paul C. Phillips, ed., *Upham Letters from the Upper Missouri, 1865*, Sources of Northwest History No. 19 (Missoula: State University of Montana, c. 1934), 8; for the second, Chittenden, *History of Early Steamboat Navigation*, 1:237-38.

18. Alton B. Oviatt, "Steamboat Traffic on the Upper Missouri River, 1859-1869," *Pacific Northwest Quarterly*, 40:2 (Apr. 1949), 93-105.

19. Ibid., 101; James H. Bradley, "Effects at Fort Benton of the Gold Excitement in Montana," *Contributions to the Historical Society of Montana* 8 (Boston: J.S. Conner and Co., 1966), 127-31; Lepley, *Birthplace of Montana*, 50-51; Oviatt, "Movement for a Northern Trail," 165-66; Madsen and Madsen, *North to Montana*, 152-53.

20. For the quote, Oviatt, "Movement for a Northern Trail," 180. For Fort Benton's seasonality, Oviatt, "Steamboat Traffic on the Upper Missouri," 97.

21. "Letter from Lt. Mullan," Walla Walla *Washington Statesman*, 16 July 1862.

22. Phillips, *Upham Letters*, 8; Oviatt, "Steamboat Traffic on the Upper Missouri," 101.

23. Madsen and Madsen, *North to Montana*.

24. Oviatt, "Movement for a Northern Trail," 147-52.

25. The quote is in Joe Baily, "The Rugged Bitterroots," Spokane *Spokesman-Review*, 27 Jan. 1957. Although the White Bluffs portion of the route proved a relative bust, the lake steamers continued to be used by packers who traveled north from The Dalles or Walla Walla via various routes—including the Mullan Road—and preferred to head east via the lake rather than over the mountains.

26. The Dalles *Daily Mountaineer*, 4 Nov. 1865 refers to the "Old Mullan Road."

27. For the first quote, Walla Walla *Washington Statesman*, 26 Oct. 1866; for the second, *Statesman*, 11 Sept. 1866. For a brief biographical sketch, Edwards, "Walla Walla," 39.

28. McGregor, "Economic Impact of Mullan Road," 10. Oviatt, "Movement for a Northern Trail," 131 describes the poor state of bridges.

29. The first quote is in McGregor, "Economic Impact of Mullan Road," 10; the second in Utah *Tri-Weekly Reader*, 4 Nov. 1869.

30. Goetzmann, *Army Exploration*, 350.

31. Walla Walla *Washington Statesman*, 8 Sept. 1865, 13 Oct. 1865, 27 Oct. 1865, 10 Nov. 1865, 2 Feb. 1866, 7 Sept. 1866; McGregor, "Economic Impact of Mullan Road," 43-44.

32. Walla Walla, *Washington Statesman*, 20 Apr. 1866; McGregor, "Economic Impact of Mullan Road," 44-45; Oviatt, "Movement for a Northern Trail," 144-47.

33. Virginia City *Montana Post*, 11 Nov. 1865.

34. The Dalles *Daily Mountaineer*, 16 Jan. 1866; Walla Walla *Washington Statesman*, 17 May 1867, 27 Mar. 1868.

35. The complete text of the memorial, passed in Dec. 1866, is in McGregor, "Economic Impact of Mullan Road," 103-09.

36. *Laws of the Territory of Montana Passed at the Third Session of the Legislature* (Virginia City: Jno. P. Bruce, 1866), 92-93; *Laws, Memorials and Resolutions of the Territory of Montana, 5th Session, 1868-69* (Helena: Montana Post Publishing Co., 1869), 115-16; *Laws, Resolutions and Memorials of the Territory of Montana, 11th Session, 1879*

(Helena: Herald Book and Job Office, 1879), 124-26. For Johnson's role in the 1866 petition, "Walter W. Johnson," undated typescript, MINCO.

37. Walla Walla *Washington Statesman*, 23 Nov. 1866; Jackson, *Wagon Roads West*, 278.

38. The quotes are in, respectively, Winther, *The Old Oregon Country*, 207; Jon Axline, *Montana's Historic Bridges, 1860-1956* (Helena: Montana Historical Society Press, 2005), 14; and Glen Adams's introduction to *Military Road 1863*, 9A.

39. McGregor, "Economic Impact of the Mullan Road," 90-92.

40. Mullan, *Miners and Travelers' Guide*, 67. In 1877, General William T. Sherman called Shaw "the most important fort in Montana." *Travel Accounts of General William T. Sherman*, 56. For the development of Fort Shaw and its role as "protector" of those traveling the Mullan Road, Hanchett, *Montana's Benton Road*, 77-91.

41. *Travel Accounts of Sherman*, 59.

42. Ibid., 64-65.

43. Ibid., 65-66.

44. Ibid., 128-31.

45. Ibid., 132; Paul Taylor, *Orlando M. Poe: Civil War General and Great Lakes Engineer* (Kent, OH: Kent State University Press, 2009).

46. *Travel Accounts of Sherman*, 69.

47. For the quotes, Boise *Idaho Statesman*, 21 Aug. 1879; *Weekly Missoulian*, 9 Jan. 1880. For road work in succeeding summers, *Weekly Missoulian*, 15 Oct. 1880; Nezperce, Idaho *News*, 22 Sept. 1881.

48. *Travel Accounts of Sherman*, 152 ff.

49. For the first quote, Oviatt, "Steamboat Traffic on the Upper Missouri," 103; for the second, Asa A. Wood, "Fort Benton's Part in the Development of the West," *Washington Historical Quarterly*, 20:3 (July 1919), 221.

50. Egbert to Adjutant, Fort Coeur d'Alene, 14 Apr. 1884, in Larry Jones Papers, ISHS. Wallace to Mullan, 24 Jan. 1887, Box 1, Fldr. 43, Mullan Papers, Georgetown.

51. For prospectors using the Mullan Road, Eugene V. Smalley, "The Great Coeur d'Alene Stampede of 1884," *Idaho Yesterdays*, 11:3 (Fall 1967), 4-5. For railroads entering the valley, John V. Wood, *Railroads Through the Coeur d'Alenes* (Caldwell, ID: The Caxton Printers, 1983).

52. The reminiscences of Ermal Steiner (Dunham) are from an exhibit panel, "Through Trip on the Mullan Road," MNI, 10 Mar. 2009. The other quote from A.P. Johnston in Mullan *Progress*, 31 May 1912.

53. *Missoulian*, 31 Aug. 1910; Thomas Flanagan, "The Fourth of July Tunnel," *Museum of North Idaho Newsletter*, 25:3 (Summer 2004), 1.

54. Earl Swift, *The Big Roads: The Untold Story of the Engineers, Visionaries, and Trailblazers Who Created the American Superhighways* (Boston: Houghton Mifflin Harcourt, 2011), 44-45, 98; Alice Ridge and John Ridge, *On the Yellowstone Trail* (Altoona, WI: Yellowstone Trail Publishers, 2003), iii.

55. Spokane *Spokesman-Review*, 10 Aug. 1913; Boise *Idaho Statesman*, 7 June 1914.

56. For the 21 June 1914 celebratory picnic, Flanagan, "Fourth of July Tunnel," 1. For the association's booklet, Ridge and Ridge, *On the Yellowstone Trail*, 5. The 1915 brochure is quoted in Spokane *Spokesman-Review*, 19 Oct. 1986. Telephone boxes had been placed at three-mile intervals along the route through the mountains in Idaho.

57. Spokane *Spokesman-Review*, 2 Nov. 1941. For the tunnel, Flanagan, "Fourth of July Tunnel." Also see "U.S. Route 10," en.wikipedia.org/wiki/U.S._Route_10, retrieved 8 Dec. 2012. During construction of Interstate 90 in 1958, the Fourth of July tunnel was buried and the road again went over the summit.

58. State of Idaho Department of Highways, *Coeur d'Alene—Junction of U.S. Highway 95A Route Study, 1964*, UISC. Swift, *Big Roads*, makes the case that Eisenhower gets too much credit for America's interstates, the system having been completely planned before he became president.

59. *Contributions to the Historical Society of Montana* 8, originally published in 1917, reprinted (Boston: J.S. Conner and Co., 1966). Quote, 169.

EPILOGUE

1. Caitlin Mullan Crain, emails to the author, 13 Apr. 2011; 21 Jan. 2013.

APPENDIX

1. For the quote, Hamilton, *Wilderness to Statehood*, 127. For Peter Mullan's obituary, St. Maries, Idaho, *Gazette Record*, 23 Mar. 1939; Spokane *Spokesman-Review*, 21 Mar. 1939. Laurant is also spelled in various sources as Laurient and Lauriente.

2. Mary Ann Finley's name is spelled in a variety of ways in the Catholic records, as Marianne and Marie Ann, and Finley is sometimes Fenley. For the marriage, St. Paul's Mission Marriage Records, St. Francis Regis Mission Collection, Box 3, Fldr. 7; for the baptism, Donald R. Johnson, "Natives and Newcomers of the Inland Northwest Frontier," typescript, 2006, citing records from St. Paul's. Both Gonzaga.

3. See "The Mystery of Peter Mullan," in Adams's reprint of Mullan, *Military Road 1863*, 25a–29a.

4. Louis C. Coleman and Leo Rieman, *Captain John Mullan: His Life Building the Mullan Road, As it is Today and Interesting Tales of Occurrences Along the Road* (Montreal: Payette Radio Limited, 1968), 54–66; quote, 63.

5. Shaun Miller, Davenport, Washington, shared family genealogical records with me. Letter to the author, 9 Feb. 2012; telephone conversation 23 Jan. 2012. I was unable to authenticate the relationship, but Cyprian Laurant was working at Fort Colville in the 1850s, and certainly could have been a relative to Rose. Johnson, "Natives and Newcomers," Gonzaga. The "Record Book of Burials" for St. Paul's Mission is difficult to decipher. Despite its title, the book records more than burials, although the actual event being recorded is not always clear. But for what appears to be the date 15 June 1855, the records note a Rose Tiputse (other variations of the spelling are possible, given the nature of the handwriting in the document). This is the only

Rose recorded during this period in the book. If this is a recording of a death, and the Catholic priests were attempting to interpret spelling for an Indian name, this could possibly be the Rose that the family claims died in childbirth, as the record corresponds with the birth date of Peter. This is speculation, but tantalizing speculation nonetheless. The Record Book is in St. Francis Regis Papers, Box 5, Fldr. 1, Gonzaga.

6. Christine Mullan Kitt's grave, with the marker noting the dates of her birth and death (1973), is in Highland Cemetery, Colville. For Peter on the reservation in 1894, Pullman, Washington, *Herald*, 10 Aug. 1894. For the 1909 and 1916 Mullan land claims, see "Native American Land Patents: Coeur d'Alene Land Patents," www.accessgenealogy.com/scripts/data/database.cgi, retrieved 8 Jan. 2012. Peter's donation of the pistol is noted in an article in Spokane *Daily Chronicle*, 24 Sept. 1917. The Eastern Washington State Historical Society, Spokane, assigned it the accession number 500.6, and the accession files contain a considerable amount of information regarding the pistol and its donation, including efforts in 1957 to attain additional information about the gun from Christine Mullan Kitt—who was unable to provide anything new. Investigation by the Historical Society shows that this particular type of Kerr Revolver was manufactured by the London Armoury Company between 1859 and 1866. Certainly, John Mullan could have acquired this pistol and had it with him during his road building from 1859 to 1862. Christine told Coleman and Rieman that John visited Peter when Peter was working at Lake Chatcolet, and she saw him another time when he visited the Mission School at DeSmet. Both could have occurred, for John was in the Northwest regularly in the 1880s in his position as commissioner of the Bureau of Catholic Indian Missions. John would have had ample opportunity in his many trips to the Northwest to have learned of the birth of a son.

7. Salem, Oregon *Daily Capital Journal*, 4 June 1907.

8. Last Will and Testament of Emma Mullan Lukens, 1 Mar. 1915, Box 8, Fldr. 7, ibid.

9. *New York Times*, 20 Feb. 1936; *Catalog of the Delta Kappa Epsilon Fraternity*, 1910, 1015, at books.google.com, retrieved 21 Feb. 2011; W. William Fogle Jr., ed., *Historical Register of the Delta Chi Chapter of Delta Kappa Epsilon at Cornell University* (Ithaca: The Delta Chi Association, 2011).

10. The quote is from a 2 June 2011 email to the author from Mariquita Mullan, then ninety-nine years old. She had married Hugh Mullan, grandson of John's brother Dennis.

11. Washington *Times*, 19 Jan. 1916.

12. Flather's career can be traced through notices that appeared in various newspapers: Washington *Herald*, 5 June 1912, 25 Dec. 1912, 3 Sept. 1913; Washington *Times*, 15 Mar. 1909, 7 Feb. 1910, 5 June 1911, 19 Mar. 1913; and New York *Tribune*, 22 Mar. 1918. Also see his obituary, Washington *Post*, 19 June 1946.

13. Washington *Times*, 28 Dec. 1916, 13 Apr. 1919, 24 Sept. 1919.

14. When Tulip Hill went up for sale it was the subject of a feature story in Washington *Post*, 27 Mar. 2010, which included the quote from architectural historian

Donna Ware. Also see "Tulip Hill," at en.wikipedia.org/wiki/Tulip_Hill, retrieved 13 Dec. 2010.

15. The first quote is from architectural historian Donna Ware, Washington *Post*, 27 Mar. 2010. The second, Mariquita Mullan email to the author, 2 June 2011.

16. Mariquita Mullan, email to the author, 2 June 2011. The White House invitations are in Box 8, Fldr. 1, Mullan Papers, Georgetown. Notices of May's appearances at various society events were recorded in Washington newspapers. See, for example, Washington *Times*, 13 Mar. 1917, 7 Dec. 1917, 8 Dec. 1917.

17. Washington *Post*, 19 June 1946; Mariquita Mullan, email to the author, 2 June 2011.

18. Box 8, Fldr. 1, Mullan Papers, Georgetown, details some of the gifts to the university, and includes the DeSmet quote. For details of the estate, Washington *Post*, 12 Feb. 1963; *Catholic Standard*, 17 Feb. 1963.

19. Mariquita Mullan, email to the author, 2 June 2011.

20. For the quote, May Flather to Howard, 12 Nov. 1926. Also see letters from May to Howard, 2 Feb. 1929 and 20 Feb. 1929. All Box 1, Fldr. 8, Helen Addison Howard Papers, Collection No. 188, University of Montana.

21. May to Howard, 3 Sept. 1934, Box 1, Fldr. 8, ibid. For Howard's works on Mullan, "Captain John Mullan," *Washington Historical Quarterly*, 25:3 (July 1934), 185-202; and "Captain John Mullan, the Road Builder," in *Northwest Trail Blazers*, 145-71. Howard's works provide a sketch of Mullan's road building exploits, briefly mention other aspects of his life, and rely too heavily on Rebecca's reminiscences, which are not always reliable. Rebecca's memoir is perhaps the only document in the large Mullan collection that May made accessible to Howard, and one can sense Howard's enthusiasm at having been granted access to this previously unknown source. While Howard's work has flaws, it has served as a foundation upon which other historians have built.

Bibliography

BIBLIOGRAPHICAL NOTE

The following is a partial bibliography of sources consulted. For more thorough documentation, readers are referred to the endnotes. In the endnotes, a full citation is provided in the initial reference. To assist readers seeking full citations, secondary sources that are cited in multiple chapters are listed below.

Ambrose, Stephen. *Nothing Like It in the World: The Men Who Built the Transcontinental Railroad, 1863-1869* (New York: Simon and Schuster, 2000).

Benjamin, Marcus. *John Bidwell, Pioneer: A Sketch of His Career* (Washington: 1907).

Burns, Robert Ignatius. *The Jesuits and the Indian Wars of the Northwest* (Moscow: University of Idaho Press, 1966).

Cannell, Lin Tull. *The Intermediary: William Craig among the Nez Perces* (Carlton, OR: Ridenbaugh Press, 2010).

Carriker, Robert C. *Father Peter John DeSmet: Jesuit in the West* (Norman: University of Oklahoma Press, 1995).

Cassidy, James G. *Ferdinand V. Hayden: Entrepreneur of Science* (Lincoln: University of Nebraska Press, 2000).

Chittenden, Hiram Martin. *History of Early Navigation on the Missouri River*, 2 vols. (New York: Francis P. Harper, 1903).

Clark, Pal, ed., "Journal from Fort Dalles O.T. to Fort Wallah Wallah W.T. July 1858, Lieut John Mullan U.S. Army," *Sources of Northwest History* 18 (Missoula: State University of Montana, c. 1932).

Cullum, George W. *Biographical Register of the Officers and Graduates of the U.S. Military Academy at West Point, New York, Since Its Establishment in 1802* (Cambridge: Riverside Press, 1901).

Drumheller, "Uncle Dan." *"Uncle Dan" Drumheller Tells Thrills of Western Trails in 1854* (Spokane: Inland-American Printing Co., 1925).

Ecelbarger, Gary L. *Frederick W. Lander: The Great Natural American Soldier* (Baton Rouge: Louisiana State University Press, 2000).

Edwards, G. Thomas. "Walla Walla, Gateway to the Pacific Northwest Interior," *Montana: The Magazine of Western History* 40:3 (Summer 1990), 29-43.

Evans, Lucylle H. *St. Mary's in the Rocky Mountains: A History of the Cradle of Montana's Culture* (Stevensville, MT: Montana Creative Consultants, 1976).

Gillis, Michael J., and Michael F. Magliari. *John Bidwell and California: The Life and Writings of a Pioneer, 1841-1900* (Spokane: Arthur H. Clark Co., 2004).

Goetzman, William H. *Army Exploration in the American West, 1803-1863* (Austin: Texas State Historical Association, 1991).

Hamilton, James McClellan. *From Wilderness to Statehood: A History of Montana, 1805-1900* (Portland: Binfords & Mort, 1957).

Hanson, Donna M., ed. *Frontier Duty: The Army in Northern Idaho, 1853-1876* (Moscow: University of Idaho Library, 2005).

Hardin, Martin D. "Up the Missouri and Over the Mullan Road," *The Westerners, New York Posse Brand Book* (1958).

Hemphill, John A., and Robert C. Cumbow. *West Pointers and Early Washington* (Seattle: The West Point Society of Puget Sound, 1992).

Hewitt, Randall H. *Across the Plains and Over the Divide: A Mule Trail Journey from East to West in 1862, and Incidents Connected Therewith* (New York: Broadway Publishing Co., 1906).

Howard, Helen Addison. *Northwest Trail Blazers* (Caldwell, ID: The Caxton Printers, 1963).

Hussey, Larry. *Fort Walla Walla: Then and Now* (Walla Walla: Privately Published, 1994).

Jackson, W. Turrentine. *Wagon Roads West: A Study of Federal Road Surveys and Construction in the Trans-Mississippi West, 1846-1869* (Berkeley: University of California Press, 1952).

Kemble, John Haskell. *The Panama Route, 1848-1869* (Berkeley: University of California Press, 1943).

Keyes, Erasmus D. *Fighting Indians in Washington Territory* (Fairfield, WA: Ye Galleon Press, 1988).

Killoren, John J. *"Come Blackrobe": DeSmet and the Indian Tragedy* (Norman: University of Oklahoma Press, 1994).

Kingston, C.S. "The Northern Route in 1867: Journal of Henry Lueg," *Pacific Northwest Quarterly* 41:3 (July 1950), 234-53.

Kip, Lawrence. *Army Life on the Pacific: A Journal of the Expedition against the Northern Indians* (New York: Redfield, 1859).

Kluger, Richard. *The Bitter Waters of Medicine Creek: A Tragic Clash between White and Native America* (New York: Alfred A. Knopf, 2011).

Lepley, John G. *Birthplace of Montana: A History of Fort Benton* (Missoula: Pictorial Histories Publishing Co., 1999).

Madsen, Betty M., and Brigham D. Madsen. *North to Montana! Jehus, Bullwhackers, and Mule Skinners on the Montana Trail* (Salt Lake City: University of Utah Press, 1980).

Manring, Benjamin Franklin. *Conquest of the Coeur d'Alenes, Spokanes & Palouses* (Fairfield, WA: Ye Galleon Press, 1975).

McDermott, Paul D. and Ronald E. Grim. *Gustavus Sohon's Cartographic and Artistic Works: An Annotated Bibliography* (Washington: Library of Congress, 2002), Philip Lee Phillips Society Occasional Paper Series No. 4.

_____. "The Mapmaker as Artist: Early Visuals of the American West," *Mercator's World* 1:1 (1996), 28-33.

McDermott, Paul D., Ronald E. Grim, and Philip Mobley. *Eye of the Explorer: Views of the Northern Pacific Railroad Survey, 1853-54* (Missoula, MT: Mountain Press, 2010).

McGregor, Alexander Campbell. "The Economic Impact of the Mullan Road on Walla Walla, 1860-1883," Honors thesis, Whitman College, 1971.

McWilliams, Jane Wilson. *Annapolis: City on the Severn, a History* (Baltimore: The Johns Hopkins University Press, 2011).

Milner, Clyde A., II, and Carol A. O'Connor. *As Big as the West: The Pioneer Life of Granville Stuart* (New York: Oxford University Press, 2009).

Morrison, James L., Jr. *"The Best School": West Point, 1833-1866* (Kent, OH: Kent State University Press, 1998).

Mullan, John. "From Walla Walla to San Francisco," *Oregon Historical Quarterly* 4:3 (Sept. 1903), 202-26.

_____. "Military Road from Fort Benton to Fort Walla Walla," *Letter from the Secretary of War, 1861*, 36th Cong., 2nd Sess., House Ex. Doc. No. 44. This is cited throughout the endnotes as Mullan, *Military Road 1861*. I have used the more accessible reprint of this document, *Military Road from Fort Benton to Fort Walla*, Michigan Historical Reprint Series (Ann Arbor: University of Michigan University Library, n.d.).

_____. "Remarks of John Mullan, 7 May 1863, on the Geography, Topography and Resources of the Northwestern Territories" in *Proceedings of the American Geographical & Statistical Society of New York*, 1864, Yale Collection of Western Americana, Yale University.

_____. *Report on the Construction of a Military Road from Fort Walla-Walla to Fort Benton* (Washington: Government Printing Office, 1863). This is cited throughout the endnotes as Mullan, *Military Road 1863*. I have used the more accessible reprint of this document, with the same title, which includes useful introductory materials (Fairfield, WA: Ye Galleon Press, 1998).

_____. "United States Military Road Expedition from Fort Walla Walla to Fort Benton, W.T.," *Report of the Secretary of War, 1861*, 37th Cong., 2nd Sess., Sen. Ex. Doc. No. 1, Serial Set No. 1118, Vol. II.

_____. *Miners and Travelers' Guide to Oregon, Washington, Idaho, Montana, Wyoming and Colorado* (Fairfield, WA: Ye Galleon Press, 1991).

_____. *Reports to Honorable George Stoneman, Governor of California, on Certain Claims of the State of California Against the United States, November 1, 1878-November 1, 1886* (Sacramento: State Office, 1886).

_____. *Topographical Memoir of Col. Wright's Campaign, 1859*, 35th Cong., 2nd Sess., Sen. Ex. Doc. No. 32, Serial Set No. 984.

Overmeyer, Philip Henry. "George B. McClellan and the Pacific Northwest," *Pacific Northwest Quarterly* 32:1 (Jan. 1941), 3-60.

Oviatt, Alton Byron. "The Movement for a Northern Trail: The Mullan Road, 1859-1869," Ph.D. diss., University of California, 1947.

Phillips, Paul C., ed. *Forty Years on the Frontier as Seen in the Journals of Granville Stuart* (Lincoln: University of Nebraska Press, 1977).

Richards, Kent D. *Isaac I. Stevens: Young Man in a Hurry* (Pullman: Washington State University Press, 1993).

Robison, Ken. "Mullan's Hardworking Wagonmaster John A. Creighton," *150th Anniversary Mullan Road Conference* (Fort Benton, MT: May 20-22, 2010).

Schafft, Charles. "Blazing the Mullan Road: Reminiscences," fortbenton.blogspot.com/2008/08/blazing-mullan-road-reminiscences.html, retrieved 24 Feb. 2009.

Scheuerman, Richard D., and Michael O. Finley. *Finding Chief Kamiakin: The Life and Legacy of a Northwest Patriot* (Pullman: Washington State University Press, 2008).

Schlicke, Carl P. *General George Wright: Guardian of the Pacific Coast* (Norman: University of Oklahoma Press, 1988).

Schmidt, Martin F. "From Missouri to Oregon in 1860: The Diary of August V. Kautz," *Pacific Northwest Quarterly* 37:3 (July 1946), 193-230.

Sherman, William T. *Travel Accounts of General William T. Sherman to Spokan Falls, Washington Territory, in the Summers of 1877 and 1883* (Fairfield, WA: Ye Galleon Press, 1985).

Stevens, Hazard. *The Life of Isaac Ingalls Stevens*, 2 vols. (Boston: Houghton, Mifflin and Co., 1900).

Stevensville Historical Society. *Montana Genesis: A History of the Stevensville Area of the Bitterroot Valley* (Missoula: Mountain Press Publishing Co., 1971).

Strachan, John. *Blazing the Mullan Trail Connecting the Headwaters of the Missouri and the Columbia Rivers and Locating the Great Overland Highway to the Pacific Northwest* (Rockford, IL: Edward Eberstadt & Sons, 1952).

Terrell, John Upton. *Black Robe: The Life of Pierre-Jean DeSmet: Missionary, Explorer, & Pioneer* (Garden City, NY: Doubleday & Co., 1964).

Tilghman, Tench Francis. *The Early History of St. John's College in Annapolis* (Annapolis: St. John's College Press, 1984).

Trimble, William J. *The Mining Advance into the Inland Empire* (Fairfield, WA: Ye Galleon Press, 1986).

Watt, James W. "Experiences of a Packer in Washington Territory Mining Camps During the Sixties," *Washington Historical Quarterly* 19 (Oct. 1928), 285-93.

Weisel, George F., ed. *Men and Trade on the Northwest Frontier as Shown by the Fort Owen Ledger* (Missoula: Montana State University, 1955).

Willey, Day Allen. "Building the M.R.," *Sunset* 24:6 (June 1910).

Williams, J. Gary, and Ronald W. Stark, eds. *The Pierce Chronicles: Personal Reminiscences of E.D. Pierce as Transcribed by Lou A. Larrick* (Moscow: Idaho Research Foundation, 1976).

Winther, Oscar Osburn. *The Old Oregon Country: A History of Frontier Trade, Transportation, and Travel* (Stanford: Stanford University Press, 1950).

Index